THE ENDANGERED ATMOSPHERE

THE ENDANGERED ATMOSPHERE

Preserving a Global Commons

Marvin S. Soroos

University of South Carolina Press

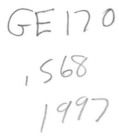
To my wife, Carol; my son, Joel; and my daughter, Valerie

© 1997 University of South Carolina

Published in Columbia, South Carolina, by the
University of South Carolina Press

Manufactured in the United States of America

01 00 99 98 97 5 4 3 2 1

Soroos, Marvin S.
    The endangered atmosphere : preserving a global commons /
Marvin S. Soroos.
        p. cm.
    Includes bibliographical references and index.
    ISBN 1-57003-160-6 (cloth). — ISBN 1–57003–203–3 (pbk.)
    1. Environmental policy. 2. Pollution—Environmental aspects.
3. Climatic changes—Environmental aspects. I. Title.
GE170.S68 1997
363.739'2—dc21   96–51243

CONTENTS

FIGURES

TABLES

Tables

PREFACE

My interest in international responses to global environmental problems goes back to the early years of my professional career, when I was drawn to the subject by the ferment provoked by the Club of Rome's influential and controversial book *The Limits to Growth* (1971) and by the landmark United Nations Conference on the Human Environment (1972). Reading Garrett Hardin's popular essays "The Tragedy of the Commons" and "Living on a Lifeboat," I became intrigued with the tendency for the resources of unregulated commons to be overused to their depletion and destruction. Many of my publications over the past two decades analyze the efforts of the international community to manage use of global commons, such as the oceans, fisheries, Antarctica, outer space, the geostationary orbit, and the electromagnetic spectrum.

The idea for a book on managing the atmosphere as a global commons grew out of my involvement with the Human Dimensions of Global Environmental Change Programme (HDGECP), sponsored by the International Social Science Council. In 1989 Harold Guetzkow, president of the International Studies Association, asked me to coordinate the association's participation in the HDGECP, which was to be a social scientific complement to the International Geosphere-Biosphere Programme being organized among natural scientists by the International Council of Scientific Unions. In this capacity I attended several international workshops of the HDGECP, which impressed upon me the depth of concern in the scientific community over human-induced changes in the basic Earth system and, in particular, critical alterations in the chemical composition of the atmosphere associated with depletion of the ozone layer and climate change. These experiences further convinced me of the importance of communication and collaboration among scientists and social scientists who share concern about disturbing trends in the global environment.

Preface

The book also draws upon my participation in a two-phase international research project directed by Oran Young and Gail Osherenko of Dartmouth College on the determinants of international regime creation and effectiveness. In the second phase I teamed with Marc A. Levy, Elena N. Nikitina (Russia), and Donald Munton (Canada) on a case study of the international regime addressing the problem of long-range transboundary air pollution (LRTAP), the subject of chapter 5 of this book. With funding from the Ford Foundation, the project provided support for a series of interviews with diplomats and scientists involved in the LRTAP regime, which I conducted in the Nordic countries in the spring of 1993.

Finally, my adoption of the concept and approach of "environmental security" grew out of my participation in conferences of the International Consortium for the Study of Environmental Security, founded by Paul Painchaud of Laval University in Quebec. While initially skeptical about the concept, over time I came to appreciate the possibilities of a security paradigm for analyzing environmental policies. The notion of environmental security continues to have its detractors, but I believe it stimulates new thinking in both the environmental studies and security studies communities. Moreover, it offers an especially appropriate approach for analyzing the problem of conserving the atmosphere, which provides all living species a thin, but fragile, protective buffer from the harsh conditions of space.

While other books have been written on the international politics of specific atmospheric problems, such as depletion of the ozone layer and global warming, *The Endangered Atmosphere* is unique for its holistic perspective on the atmosphere as a global commons. In this sense it seeks to make a significant contribution to the burgeoning literature of international environmental politics. As with my other work published by the University of South Carolina Press, *Beyond Sovereignty: The Challenge of Global Policy* (1986), I have written this book in a style I hope will appeal to a broad audience that transcends discipline and includes both professionals and students. Its message is too important to be directed exclusively at a small community of specialists in environmental regimes.

Writing this book has taken me into numerous subjects on which I had limited knowledge when I began the project. Thus, I have asked others with expertise on some of these subjects to read and critique earlier drafts of selected chapters; these include Christer Ågren, Daniel Bodansky, Roscoe R. Braham, Joseph Caddell, Geoffrey D. Dabelko, Jean-

Paul Hettelingh, Benedict Kingsbury, Philippe Le Prestre, Karen T. Litfin, Thomas F. Malone, Robert S. Norris, John T. Sigmon, Russel Van Wyk, and Jonathan B. Wiener. In addition, Vicki L. Golich and Barry B. Hughes read the entire manuscript for the press. I am deeply indebted to all of these reviewers for their insights and constructive suggestions, which have significantly improved the book. Whatever errors of fact or interpretation remain are exclusively my responsibility.

Lastly, I would like to acknowledge the assistance and inspiration of two distinguished scientists, Ellis B. Cowling and Thomas F. Malone, whom I am honored to refer to as faculty colleagues at North Carolina State University. Their contributions to international scientific cooperation in the atmospheric sciences are far too numerous to summarize here. I am appreciative of their willingness to lend encouragement to a social scientist delving into the scientific enterprises they have played key roles in shaping.

ABBREVIATIONS

ABM	antiballistic missile
AEC	Atomic Energy Commission (U.S.)
AOSIS	Alliance of Small Island States
ATCP	Antarctic Treaty Consultative Parties
BAPMoN	Background Air Pollution Monitoring Network
BIER	Scientific Committee on the Biological Effects of Ionizing Radiation
CCOL	Coordinating Committee on the Ozone Layer
CEGB	Central Energy Generating Board
CFC	chlorofluorocarbon
cm	centimeter
CO$_2$	carbon dioxide
COP	Committee of the Parties
COPOUS	Committee on the Peaceful Uses of Outer Space
EC	European Community
ECAFE	Economic Commission for Asia and the Far East
ECE	Economic Commission for Europe
EEZ	exclusive economic zone
EFTA	European Free Trade Organization
EMEP	Cooperative Program for Monitoring and Evaluation of the Long-Range Transmission of Air Pollution in Europe
ENDC	Eighteen Nation Disarmament Committee
ENSO	El Niño-Southern Oscillation

EU	European Union (post-1992 name of European Community)
FAA	Federal Aviation Agency (U.S.)
FAO	Food and Agriculture Organization
FCCC	Framework Convention on Climate Change
GARP	Global Atmospheric Research Programme
GATE	GARP Atlantic Tropic Experiment
GATT	General Agreement on Tariffs and Trade
GAW	Global Atmospheric Watch
GCM	general circulation model
GCOS	Global Climate Observing System
GDP	gross domestic product
GEF	Global Environment Facility
GEMS	Global Environmental Monitoring System
GEMS-Air	Global Environmental Monitoring System–Urban Air Quality Monitoring Project
GHG	greenhouse gas
GI	greenhouse index
GNP	gross national product
GRIT	graduated reciprocation in tension-reduction
GWE	Global Weather Experiment (GARP)
GWP	global warming potential
HCFC	Hydrochlorofluorocarbons
IAEA	International Atomic Energy Agency
IAMAP	International Association of Meteorology and Atmospheric Physics
ICAO	International Civil Aviation Organization
ICI	Imperial Chemical Industries
ICJ	International Court of Justice
ICSU	International Council of Scientific Unions

Abbreviations

IEA	International Energy Agency
IEER	Institute for Energy and Environmental Research
IGBP	International Geosphere-Biosphere Programme
IGOSS	Integrated Global Ocean Services System
IGY	International Geophysical Year
IIASA	International Institute for Advanced Systems Analysis
IJC	International Joint Commission
IMO	International Maritime Organization
INCO	International Nickel Company
IPC	International Cooperative Program (LRTAP)
IPCC	Intergovernmental Panel on Climate Change
IPPNW	International Physicians for the Prevention of Nuclear War
IR	infrared radiation
ITU	International Telecommunications Union
IUGG	International Union of Geodesy and Geophysics
LRTAP	long-range transboundary air pollution
MOI	Memorandum of Intent
mt	metric ton
NAPAP	National Acid Precipitation Assessment Program
NAS	National Academy of Sciences
NASA	National Aeronautics and Space Administration (U.S.)
NCAR	National Center for Atmospheric Research
nm	nanometer
NOAA	National Oceanographic and Atmospheric Administration (U.S.)
NO_x	nitrogen oxide
NOZE	National Ozone Expedition
NRDC	Natural Resources Defense Council

O	oxygen (atom)
O_2	oxygen (molecule)
O_3	ozone
ODP	Ozone depleting potential
OECD	Organization for Economic Cooperation and Development
PCB	polychlorinated biphenyl
ppb	parts per billion
ppm	parts per million
RAINS	Regional Acidification INformation Simulation
SANE	National Society for a SANE Nuclear Policy
SCOPE	Scientific Committee on Problems of the Environment
SO_2	sulfur dioxide
START	Global Change SysTem for Analysis, Research and Training
TOGA	Tropical Ocean-Global Atmosphere Programme
TOMA	Tropospheric Ozone Management Area
UNEP	United Nations Environment Programme
UNESCO	United Nations Environmental, Scientific and Cultural Organization
UNSCEAR	United Nations Scientific Committee on the Effects of Atomic Radiation
UV	ultraviolet radiation
VOC	volatile organic compound
WCP	World Climate Programme
WCRP	World Climate Research Program
WHO	World Health Organization
WIPO	World Intellectual Property Organization
WMO	World Meteorological Organization
WOCE	World Ocean Circulation Experiment
WWW	World Weather Watch

THE ENDANGERED ATMOSPHERE

Chapter 1

THE ATMOSPHERE AND GLOBAL PUBLIC POLICY

When photographed from a satellite in the shadow of the Earth, the atmosphere appears as a thin arc of intense blue and violet light that separates the darkened silhouette of the planet from the absolute blackness of outer space. Comprised of a mix of gases known as air, the atmosphere surrounds the Earth to a thickness that is less than 1 percent as great as the radius of the planet, or what has been compared to the skin on an apple.[1] The atmosphere is a source of oxygen essential to the respiration of animal life and carbon dioxide necessary for the photosynthesis of plants. It draws up water from the oceans and lakes, purifies it, and redistributes it to where it can become an essential ingredient of the tissues of living organisms. This thin gaseous veil also shields most life forms from the intense ultraviolet radiation released by the sun and maintains the radiative balance that moderates temperatures at the Earth's surface. The atmosphere vaporizes most of the millions of iron and stone meteoroids that plummet toward the planet each day from outer space.

Human beings have inhabited the planet Earth for millions of years without having any perceptible impact on the qualities of the atmosphere that account for the planet's uniquely habitable environment. The situation started to change several millennia ago when human communities began transforming the land cover over large areas in order to practice agriculture, which may have had perceptible impacts on regional climates. More substantial changes in the atmosphere have come about as a result of the greatly expanded human use of the atmosphere as a convenient sink for a myriad of gaseous and particulate wastes, especially since the advent of the industrial revolution in the eighteenth century, which led to great increases in the burning of fossil fuels. The human assault on the atmosphere has quickened even more since World War II due to a mushrooming world population, a spectacular rise in industrial activity, the spread of agriculture, and the massive clearing of forests.

Prior to the twentieth century significant air pollution was almost exclusively a localized problem in the vicinity of emission sources, in particular the large cities and industrial zones of Western Europe, the British Isles, and North America. London, more than any other great city of the era, was known for episodes of dark sooty smog that could bring life to a virtual standstill and caused death rates to rise. Urban air was further fouled in the twentieth century by the great growth in vehicular traffic, which contributed to the phenomenon of photochemical smog. Municipal and national regulations on industrial pollutants and automobile exhausts have substantially improved the quality of the air over the urban areas of the highly developed countries of the West. The worst air pollution now occurs mostly over the mushrooming cities of the Third World and in regions of eastern Europe and the former Soviet Union where mining, smelting, and heavy industry are concentrated.

The twentieth century has also seen the emergence of air pollution problems of international and global proportions. Tall smokestacks, which were mandated by laws designed to alleviate local air pollution problems, release waste substances such as sulfur and nitrogen oxides high enough in the sky to be picked up by wind currents that transport them over long distances and across international borders before they are deposited in an acidic form. The rapid buildup of other pollutants in the atmosphere, most notably greenhouse gases such as carbon dioxide, methane, nitrous oxides, chlorofluorocarbons, and halons, are contributing to basic changes in the flow of energy to and from the surface of the planet, which could have profound effects on the natural environment and human populations.

The atmosphere is often described as a global commons, along with the oceans, seabed, outer space, Antarctica, and the electromagnetic spectrum. In the absence of rules that regulate human use, commons are susceptible to being overused and misused, so that they become depleted, degraded, or congested. Excessive use of the atmosphere as a sink for pollutants has endangered human health, contaminated the natural environment, and now may even be altering some of the basic processes of the Earth system. Humanity faces the daunting challenge of constraining its release of air pollutants to preserve the essential qualities of not only the atmosphere but also of the larger Earth system. National laws have done much to limit the flow of some pollutants into the atmosphere with favorable regional results, but they are not adequate to address the transboundary and global atmospheric problems that have emerged and intensified during the twentieth century.

THE ATMOSPHERE AS AN INTERNATIONAL POLICY ISSUE

Atmospheric pollution first became an international legal issue early in the twentieth century when a conflict over transfrontier air pollution arose between Canada and the United States over emissions from a lead and zinc smelter that began operations in the town of Trail in southern British Columbia in 1896. The smelter emitted large quantities of sulfur and other pollutants, some of which drifted over the border into the state of Washington where they caused damage to orchards. The United States government took up the case in 1927 after two four-hundred-foot smokestacks were built at the smelter to allow for increased production, which raised the prospect of even more transfrontier air pollution. Failing to resolve their differences by negotiations, the United States and Canada agreed in 1935 to submit their dispute over the Trail Smelter pollution to a specially created arbitrational panel. In 1941 the tribunal rendered its final decision, which sided with the United States on grounds that "no state has the right to use or permit the use of its territory in such a manner as to cause injury by fumes in or to the territory of another or the properties or persons therein, when the case is of serious consequence and the injury is established by clear and convincing evidence."[2]

The Trail Smelter case was significant for applying certain principles of international customary law to damages caused by air pollutants that drift across international borders. More specifically it suggests that the sovereignty of states does not exempt them from the responsibility for ensuring that other states are not injured by acts committed by individuals or firms within their jurisdiction. Conversely, sovereign states have a right, although not an absolute one, to expect their territory to be free from outside intervention, including pollutants originating beyond their borders that cause significant damage to their national environments and threaten the health of their people. The Trail Smelter judgment and the principles of international customary law on which it is based have not proven to be as useful in addressing the broader range of international and global air pollution problems as might have been expected. In most cases of transboundary air pollution it is more difficult, if not impossible, to prove that pollutants from given sources in one country are the cause of specific damages in others. Nevertheless, the principle that sovereign states do not have the right to allow their territories to be used in ways that cause significant environmental harm beyond their borders underlies efforts to establish international regimes that address other pollution problems.[3]

Nuclear Explosions in the Atmosphere

The aboveground testing of nuclear explosives, which spewed large amounts of radioactive contaminants into the atmosphere, was the first major air pollution problem to provoke widespread concern in the world community and become the subject of an international regime. Five countries openly conducted nuclear tests in the atmosphere: the United States beginning in 1949, the Soviet Union in 1949, the United Kingdom in 1952, France in 1960, and China in 1964. Between 1945 and 1980 these countries conducted more than five hundred aboveground tests of nuclear bombs.

Atomic bombs were a revolutionary advancement in the technology of military explosives in view of their capacity to destroy cities and kill the inhabitants, as was demonstrated by the devastation reeked on Hiroshima and Nagasaki by single American bombs in 1945. Despite the destructiveness of these first atomic bombs, the radioactive pollutants they generated were deposited mostly in the vicinity of the explosion and thus did not arouse widespread concern. The situation changed in the early 1950s with the development of a new generation of weapons known as thermonuclear, or hydrogen, bombs, some of which were thousands of times more powerful than the first atomic weapons. The thermonuclear explosions also produced far greater amounts of radioactive debris, much of which was propelled by the force of the blast high into the atmosphere, where it remained long enough to be dispersed over thousands of kilometers and even globally.

The perils of nuclear testing for human health and the environment first became an international public issue in 1954 when the United States detonated a large thermonuclear explosive code-named BRAVO at a test site in the Marshall Islands in its Pacific trust territories. Radioactive pollutants rained down over a larger area than had been anticipated, exposing the residents of nearby islands and the crew of a Japanese fishing vessel to health-threatening doses of radiation and contaminating fisheries over a large area of the Pacific Ocean. As the pace of test explosions quickened in the mid 1950s, opposition grew among leaders and publics around the world, which prompted the superpowers to observe a moratorium on nuclear testing beginning in late 1958. Concern about the environmental and health effects of nuclear explosions rose again in the early 1960s after the Soviet Union broke the testing moratorium by conducting an intensive series of explosions in 1961–62 at its Arctic test site on the Novaya Zemlya archipelago, which included the largest nuclear devices ever detonated. The United States responded by hurriedly organizing an extensive series of tests of its own, first underground and then in the atmosphere.

The possibility of ending atmospheric nuclear tests during the 1950s was preempted first by international talks on grandiose proposals for a complete elimination of nuclear weapons, which had virtually no chance of being adopted in view of rising Cold War tensions. Later in the decade the subject of arms control talks in several international forums shifted to the less ambitious objective of a ban on all nuclear tests. These efforts floundered when the superpowers could not agree on the monitoring arrangements that could be used to detect underground explosions and distinguish them from seismic events. Finally, pressured to conclude a significant arms control agreement to ease East-West tensions in the aftermath of the Cuban Missile Crisis of 1962, the United States, the Soviet Union, and the United Kingdom resolved their remaining differences and compromised on the Nuclear Test Ban Treaty of 1963, which prohibited nuclear testing in the atmosphere, outer space, and the oceans, realms where tests could probably be detected without intrusive monitoring procedures.[4]

The Test Ban Treaty did little to stem the nuclear arms race between the superpowers, which simply shifted their nuclear testing programs to underground locations. The agreement is notable, however, for being the first multilateral treaty to address an air pollution problem and for becoming the cornerstone of a notably successful environmental regime. The frequency of atmospheric nuclear tests dropped sharply after the treaty was adopted, and within a few years there was a discernible reduction in the deposition of radioactive materials and residual radioactivity in the environment. Only two countries, both nonparties to the agreement, are known to have conducted nuclear tests in the atmosphere after the adoption of the treaty: France, which continued its aboveground testing program until 1974; and China, which set off the world's last known atmospheric test in 1980. More than one hundred additional countries have become parties to the treaty, thus waiving their rights to test nuclear explosives in the atmosphere. By virtue of the widespread acceptance of the treaty, the ban on testing of nuclear weapons in the atmosphere, outer space, and the oceans is now generally regarded a norm of international customary law, which means it is binding on all states, not just the ones that have formally ratified it.

Despite the existence of an almost universally accepted prohibition on the testing of nuclear bombs in the atmosphere, the nuclear powers showed no inclination to negotiate rules on the hostile use of nuclear weapons. A war in which large numbers of nuclear weapons were detonated would release huge quantities of radioactive materials into the atmosphere that could expose people throughout much of the world to heightened doses of radiation, including residents of countries having no involvement in the war. In the 1980s a group of prominent American scientists warned that dust and smoke injected into the atmosphere by the explosions and fires ignited in cities and forests as a result of the use of nuclear weapons would block out so much radiation from the sun that much of the planet would be plunged into an environmentally devastating "nuclear winter." Ironically, neither of these possibilities seemed to diminish the resolve of the nuclear powers to use their nuclear weapons arsenals if circumstances dictated.

Long-Range Transboundary Air Pollution

In the late 1960s the Swedish scientist Svante Odén advanced the revolutionary theory that the acid precipitation responsible for the disappearance of aquatic life in the lakes in his country was caused largely by pollutants transported by prevailing winds from the heavily industrialized regions of the British Isles and the European Continent. A study conducted by the Organization for Economic Cooperation and Development (OECD) between 1972 and 1974 bore out suspicions that the phenomenon, known as "long-range transboundary air pollution," or LRTAP, was a serious problem over much of the European Continent. By the end of the decade many of the lakes of eastern Canada displayed similar signs of acidification, which was believed to be caused largely by air pollutants from power plants and industries in the United States Midwest.

The Swedish government pushed its concerns about transboundary air pollution at the landmark United Nations Conference on the Human Environment, which it hosted in Stockholm in 1972. The agenda for the conference covered a broad spectrum of environmental issues, and thus the LRTAP problem received much less attention than the Scandinavian countries would have liked. However, the widely cited Article 21 of the declaration adopted at the conference reinforced the principle of state responsibility enunciated by the Trail Smelter decision of 1941. Article 21 declared that while states "have the sovereign right to exploit their resources in accordance with their environmental policies," they are also obliged to "insure that activities within their own jurisdiction or control do not cause damage to the environment of other states or areas beyond the limits of national jurisdiction."[5]

The first negotiations that focused exclusively on the LRTAP problem were a follow-up to the Helsinki Accord of 1975, which proposed air pollution as a potential subject of East-West cooperation that would contribute to a reduction of tensions between the two blocs.[6] Negotiations proposed by the Soviet Union and conducted under the auspices of the United Nations Economic Commission for Europe (ECE) led to the adoption of the Convention on Long Range Transboundary Air Pollution in Geneva in 1979.[7] The LRTAP Convention, being a typical framework treaty, did not require the parties to reduce their emissions of any types of air pollutants, but it did establish institutional mechanisms for further negotiations as circumstances warranted. The nascent regime also took over the air pollution monitoring network that had been coordinated by the OECD and developed it into a sophisticated international environmental monitoring program, which has provided a database that has been crucial to the negotiation of supplemental protocols.

Widespread damage to the forests of central Europe in the early 1980s gave impetus to negotiations on the 1985 Sulfur Protocol, which committed the parties to a 30 percent reduction in sulfur dioxide (SO_2) emissions from 1980 levels by 1993.[8] Additional protocols limiting emissions of nitrogen oxides (NO_x) and volatile organic compounds (VOCs) were concluded in 1988 and 1991, respectively.[9] Then in 1994 a revised sulfur protocol was adopted whose goals were couched in terms of "critical loads," the amount of acidic deposition that any given region could absorb without serious environmental consequences.[10] Unfortunately, full compliance with these protocols by the members of the LRTAP regime will do little more than stabilize levels of acidity on the European Continent. Deeper reductions are needed in emissions of sulfur and nitrogen oxides to mitigate the problems associated with acid rain and ground-level ozone, which include the disappearance of aquatic life in freshwater rivers and streams, widespread damage to forests, corrosion of exposed stone and metal surfaces, and threats to human health. The "countries in transition" of eastern Europe and the former Soviet Union will need substantial technological and economic assistance to address air pollution problems that are much more serious than the outside world had previously realized.

The LRTAP regime has proved to be an effective institutional mechanism for bringing the eastern and western European countries together, even during the resurgence of Cold War tensions during the early 1980s following the Soviet military intervention in Afghanistan. As members of the ECE, Canada and the United States have been participants in the LRTAP regime and are parties to the 1979 framework convention and several of the supplementary protocols, but they have been addressing the problem of transboundary air pollution in North America primarily through bilateral arrangements. Nor does the LRTAP regime offer anything more than a model for other regions of the world, such as the Far East, where there are growing problems of acidification, including a significant transboundary flow of pollutants from China and Korea to Japan.

The catastrophic nuclear accident at Chernobyl in the Soviet Ukraine in April 1986, which spewed large amounts of radioactive substances into the atmosphere that precipitated over much of Europe, was also an incident of transboundary pollution, but of a type not addressed by the LRTAP regime. The Soviet Union drew strong international criticism for lax safety procedures and flawed equipment at its nuclear installations and for not promptly informing other countries about the accident and the radioactive peril that it posed.[11] Questions were also raised, but not pushed, about whether the Soviet Union was liable for damages incurred by countries exposed to radiation from the Chernobyl plant. The International Atomic Energy Agency (IAEA) investigated the accident and sponsored negotiations on two treaties that were adopted later in 1986. The Convention on Early Notification of a Nuclear Accident spells out the responsibilities that states have to report accidents promptly to countries that might be adversely affected, but it does not address the issues of liability and compensation.[12] The Convention on Assistance in the Case of a Nuclear Accident or Radiological Emergency specifies obligations that the parties have to assist countries that are seriously affected by radiological disasters.[13]

Depletion of the Stratospheric Ozone Layer

At about the same time that Sweden began calling attention to the LRTAP problem in the late 1960s, several American scientists began speculating that human pollutants may be posing a threat to the sparse concentration of ozone in the stratosphere, which shields most species from harmful if not lethal doses of ultraviolet radiation. Early concern centered on the ozone-depleting potential of water vapor and nitrous oxides in the exhausts of a projected world fleet of more than five hundred supersonic aircraft. This threat receded when the American and Soviet SST programs were canceled and the British and French dramatically reduced the numbers of Concordes they would produce jointly. In 1974 Mario Molina and Sherwood Rowland of the University of California at Irvine offered the startling theory that CFCs, a family of synthetic chemical compounds used extensively in industry and consumer products, posed a much more serious threat to the ozone layer. This revelation quickly aroused a wave of public concern in the United States, which in 1977 banned nonessential uses of CFCs, in particular as a propellant in aerosol sprays, as did Canada, Norway, and Sweden. Since then, several other ozone threatening chemicals have been identified, including halons, carbon tetrachloride, methyl chloroform, and methyl bromide.

The United Nations Environment Programme (UNEP) quickly responded to the newly discovered threat to the ozone layer and in 1977 created the Coordinating Committee on the Ozone Layer to keep the world community abreast of scientific findings on the subject. However, the possibility that other chemicals in the atmosphere might counteract the effect of CFCs, along with less ominous forecasts of ozone loss, delayed serious efforts to negotiate an international treaty to respond to the problem. The Convention for the Protection of the Ozone Layer was finally adopted in Vienna in 1985.[14] As with other framework conventions, it failed to impose mandatory limits on the use of the chemicals linked to ozone depletion, it but did provide a forum for negotiating controls as circumstances warranted.

A second wave of concern about threats to the ozone layer soon arose due largely to two developments. Only months after the Vienna Convention was concluded, a team of British scientists reported the stunning discovery of an "ozone hole" over Antarctica. The following year the report of an international assessment sponsored by the World Me-

teorological Organization (WMO) and UNEP reemphasized the seriousness of the threat that human pollutants posed to the ozone layer, even
without taking into account the still-unexplained existence of the Antarctic ozone hole. These two reports set the stage for negotiations that
led to the Montreal Protocol on Substances that Deplete the Ozone Layer
of 1987, which obliged the parties to reduce their production and use of
CFCs by 20 percent by 1993 and by 50 percent by 1999.[15] Developing
countries having a low per capita use of CFCs were allowed ten additional years to accomplish these reductions.

The Montreal Protocol was hailed as a major diplomatic breakthrough, but soon it became apparent that the mandated reductions did
not go far enough. Scientists not only proved that anthropogenic pollutants were the cause of the Antarctic ozone hole, but they also observed a
substantial thinning of the ozone layer over the Northern Hemisphere
much sooner than anticipated by their models. Responding to the ever
more disturbing forecasts of ozone loss, representatives from more than
ninety countries met in London in 1990 and agreed on revisions to the
Montreal Protocol that would completely phase out CFCs, halons, and
carbon tetrachloride by the year 2000.[16] The protocol was amended again
in Copenhagen in 1992, this time to advance the phaseout dates for halons
to 1994 and for most of the other controlled substances to 1996.[17]

The ozone regime created by these agreements is arguably the most
remarkable achievement in international environmental diplomacy. If
the parties to the Montreal Protocol and its revisions fulfill their obligations to phase out CFCs and the other controlled substances, ozone concentrations can be expected to stabilize within a decade or two and begin
recovering to earlier levels. The regime demonstrates that sovereign states
may be willing to take decisive, anticipatory action when confronted by
compelling scientific evidence of a potentially serious problem, even
though it may be decades before the toll in human suffering and damage to the environment is readily observable. Richard Benedick, the chief
United States negotiator, suggested that the ozone negotiations were
indicative of a "new global diplomacy" that offers valuable lessons that
can be applied to negotiations aimed at addressing other international
environmental problems, such as global climate change.[18]

Weather Modification and Climate Change

Human societies have always been heavily dependent upon favorable weather conditions, to which they have adapted. Extreme forms of

weather such as hurricanes, cyclones, tornadoes, blizzards, and droughts can cause significant death, destruction, and hardship. Civilizations have gone into decline, and in some cases disappeared, when they could not adapt to long-term climate changes. Until the twentieth century it was presumed that weather was a force of nature that humans were powerless to affect, except perhaps by pleading for the intervention of gods who were believed to control the skies or by performing rituals in the superstitious belief that they would bring rain. Thinking about the potential for human impact on the weather has changed as science has resolved more of the mysteries of weather and atmospheric processes.

As early as the 1930s scientists began experimenting with the seeding of clouds to induce precipitation over a local area. In the coming decades several governmental and corporate projects were undertaken in the United States to explore the potential of a variety of weather modification techniques that would achieve such objectives as increasing precipitation, preventing frosts, dispersing fogs, and suppressing storms.[19] It was believed that weather modification held promise for important commercial and military applications, but by the 1960s it became apparent that weather was less susceptible to human influence than had been anticipated and that human tampering could have serious unintended results.

Initially there was little opposition to peaceful applications of environmental modification techniques within countries, as long as they did not have adverse consequences for other countries. In such events it has generally been presumed that international rules of liability would apply, as they had to transboundary air pollution in the Trail Smelter case.[20] Of greater concern was the possibility that much more potent techniques of weather modification might be developed to serve hostile purposes. The issue came to a head when the United States employed rainfall-enhancement techniques during the Indo-China war in an effort to impede the movement of supplies over jungle trails to the guerrilla forces it was fighting. Concerned that environmental alterations might become a more widely used tactic of war, the superpowers took the lead in negotiating the Convention on the Prohibition of Military or Any Other Hostile Use of Environmental Modification Techniques, known as the ENMOD Convention, which was adopted in the United Nations Conference of the Committee on Disarmament in 1977.[21] The ENMOD Convention prohibits manipulating the weather, but only if alterations have "widespread, long-lasting or severe effects." This latter clause, which was included at the insistence of the United States, significantly reduces the applicability of the convention. The agreement has been criticized for its narrow focus on deliberate environmental modifications that seek a military advantage and accordingly for its failure to regulate tactics of war that may have unintended but nevertheless serious environmental impacts.[22]

A century ago another Swedish scientist, Svante Arrhenius, was the first to speculate that humanity might inadvertently be altering the climate of the planet. He foresaw the possibility that burning large quantities of fossil fuels would emit carbon dioxide (CO_2) in large enough amounts to cause significant global warming. It was not until the late 1950s, however, that scientists began giving serious attention to the possibility raised by Arrhenius. A monitoring program begun in 1958 has shown a steady rise in CO_2 concentrations in the atmosphere. Air bubbles from ice cores extracted from deep in the polar glaciers reveal that current levels of CO_2 are substantially higher than at any time over the past 160,000 years. Scientists have also noted striking parallels between amounts of CO_2 in the atmosphere and average global temperatures revealed by the same ice cores and by other types of paleoclimatological data. This finding has fueled growing concern among scientists that CO_2 released by human activities will cause a catastrophic warming of the planet.

The First World Climate Conference, which was held under the auspices of WMO in 1979, heightened international awareness about the prospect for global warming and spurred an intensified worldwide research effort on climate change and the myriad of potential consequences. The 1980s saw a spate of the warmest years over the past century, along with other weather anomalies, such as unusually intense storms and persistent droughts. In the public mind these unusual climatic phenomena lent credibility to the warnings of the scientific community about the likelihood of human-induced global warming. By the end of the decade climate change was being discussed at summit meetings of world leaders, and several ministerial conferences were called to consider responses to the problem. The Second World Climate Conference, held in Geneva in 1990, set the stage for negotiations on the Framework Convention on Climate Change (FCCC), which was adopted at the Earth Summit in Rio de Janeiro in 1992.[23]

The FCCC acknowledged that the developed countries were largely responsible for the buildup of greenhouse gases (GHGs) in the atmosphere and called upon them to aim at bringing their GHG emissions back to 1990 levels by the turn of the century. However, at the insistence of the United States, the convention lacks the binding targets or deadlines for reducing CO_2 emissions that were favored by most developed countries and an outspoken group of small island states that believe themselves especially vulnerable to rising sea levels that would be caused by warmer temperatures. The first Conference of the Parties to the convention, which was held in Berlin in 1995, considered a proposal from the small island states for a 25 percent reduction in CO_2 emissions by 2005. In the end, however, the delegates could only agree on starting a new round of talks with the aim of having a draft protocol with binding limits on GHG emissions ready for adoption in 1997.

The climate change regime is at a much earlier stage of development than the regimes that address the problems of nuclear testing, transboundary air pollution, and depletion of the ozone layer. In view of the remarkable successes in negotiating the ozone layer regime, it is tempting to assume that the parties to the FCCC will soon conclude

Table 1.1. Major Treaties Pertaining to the Atmosphere and Air Pollution

Transboundary Air Pollution

LRTAP Convention (1979)

Sulfur Protocol (1985)

Nitrogen Protocol (1988)

VOC Protocol (1991)

Revised Sulfur Protocol (1994)

Nuclear Radiation

Partial Test Ban Treaty (1963)

IAEA Notification Convention (1986)

IAEA Assistance Convention (1986)

Ozone Layer

Convention for the Protection of the Ozone Layer (1985)

Montreal Protocol (1987)

London Amendments (1990)

Copenhagen Amendments (1992)

Climate Change

Environmental Modification Convention (1977)

Framework Convention on Climate Change (1992)

protocols that will stabilize concentrations of GHG in the atmosphere. However, climate change poses a much more complex and formidable challenge for the international community than does the threat of ozone depletion. To limit global warming to manageable levels will require drastic reductions in the use of fossil fuels, which can be accomplished only through fundamental changes in both the lifestyles of richer societies and the development strategies of Third World countries. Reaching agreement on strong international measures to combat climate change will be difficult because some countries view the problem with much less urgency than others, believing either that the effects of global warming will be minimal or even advantageous to them or that they have the capacity to adjust to whatever changes may occur. There is also the issue of how to divide equitably future rights to add GHGs to the atmosphere. What proportion should go to industrialized countries, which have already used up most of the atmosphere's capacity to absorb these pollutants? What is a fair share for countries with rapidly growing populations that have been planning to increase sharply their use of fossil fuels to fulfill aspirations for economic development?

The preceding overview suggests that the international community has been addressing atmospheric issues on a piecemeal basis. The regimes that have been established to address specific environmental problems were for the most part created independently of one another. No concerted effort has been made to negotiate an overarching treaty on the atmosphere that would be comparable to the Antarctic Treaty of 1959, the Outer Space Treaty of 1967, or the United Nations Convention on the Law of the Sea of 1982. It is by no means evident, however, that the lack of a law of the atmosphere has seriously hampered efforts to address the atmospheric problems that have arisen thus far, each of which has posed distinctive challenges for international negotiators.

INTERNATIONAL SCIENTIFIC COOPERATION

Science has played an important role in the creation and evolution of the atmospheric regimes described in the previous section. The problems that these regimes address—radioactivity, acid deposition, depletion of the ozone layer, and the buildup of GHGs—are discernible only by means of sensitive scientific instruments and extensive monitoring programs. Moreover, the potential impacts that these phenomena may have on human health and the natural environment can only be understood through a sophisticated scientific understanding of the complex dynamics of the atmosphere and its relationships to the sun, oceans, landmasses, and living species. Without the availability of the expertise of scientists from many disciplines, policy makers would have little appreciation of the urgency of the atmospheric problems that confront humanity and few clues about what is needed to address them effectively.

Scientific cooperation on an international scale is essential to an improved understanding of the atmosphere given its dynamic global circulation patterns. The directors of several national weather services first met in 1853 to discuss how to coordinate and standardize the collection and reporting of weather observations used in forecasting. Twenty years later they established the International Meteorological Organization (IMO) to institutionalize these activities. Over the next seventy-five years the IMO significantly improved not only the quantity and quality of weather data but also the communication networks through which they are compiled and disseminated. In 1950 the IMO was transformed into the intergovernmental WMO, which soon became a United Nations specialized agency and a key player in a profusion of international atmospheric projects undertaken over the past four decades.

The International Geophysical Year (IGY) of 1957–58 ushered in a remarkable era of international scientific cooperation, which has added enormously to knowledge on the Earth system including the dynamics of the atmosphere and which will continue into the twenty-first century. Organized by the nongovernmental International Council of Scientific Unions (ICSU), the IGY was the occasion for international teams of scientists to explore the remote realms of the Earth system, including outer space, the atmosphere, Antarctica, and the depths of the earth and seas. Programs to monitor changes in the atmosphere were begun that several decades later provided trend data that have illuminated the problems of ozone depletion and climate change.

Two major atmospheric programs were launched during the 1960s. One was WMO's greatly enhanced weather monitoring system called the World Weather Watch (WWW), which took advantage of major technological advances in satellites, telecommunications, and computing. The WWW has provided global coverage of weather conditions by means of a network of monitoring stations located on land, ships, buoys, and satellites. The second was the Global Atmospheric Research Programme (GARP), which is notable for the partnership that was struck between the governmental meteorologists of WMO and academic atmospheric scientists of ICSU. GARP featured two intensive data-gathering operations called "experiments" conducted during the 1970s, which contributed significantly to research on the atmosphere and the improvement of weather forecasting. In doing so GARP lay the groundwork for even more ambitious scientific endeavors undertaken in the 1980s on subjects such as human-induced climate change.

The 1970s also saw further development of international networks for monitoring the state of the atmosphere, in particular concentrations of air pollutants. Soon after its creation in 1973 UNEP began organizing the Global Environmental Monitoring System (GEMS) to coordinate the numerous monitoring programs of several United Nations agencies, one being WMO's WWW. Another component of GEMS is WMO's Background Air Pollution Monitoring Network (BAPMoN), which samples air in remote areas to provide reference points on the composition of relatively unpolluted air. BAPMoN is complemented by the Urban Air Monitoring Network (GEMS-Air) of the World Health Organization (WHO). GEMS-Air provides data on the air quality of the world's major cities, which are useful for studying the effects of air pollutants on human health. The modest network that the OECD assembled in 1972 for monitoring the transboundary flow of air pollutants in Europe was transferred to the ECE in 1977 and became known by the acronym EMEP. It soon became an integral part of the LRTAP regime and was expanded to nearly one hundred stations over the entire European region from Spain to Russia.

The World Climate Programme (WCP) and the International Geosphere-Biosphere Programme (IGBP) are two long-term scientific research programs begun during the 1980s that have been adding much to knowledge about the atmosphere. WMO, UNEP, and ICSU undertook the WCP shortly after the First World Climate Conference of 1979. The WCP is an ambitious, multifaceted data-gathering and research effort aimed at a better understanding of climatic changes and their impacts on the environment. The IGBP, which was inaugurated by ICSU in 1986, follows in the nongovernmental tradition of the IGY in its effort to mobilize the world's scientists to probe the relationships among atmospheric, marine, and terrestrial systems in order to understand better the basic changes taking place in the Earth system, in particular those that are attributable to human activities.

The burgeoning information on the atmosphere and the impact of human pollutants that has been generated by these international monitoring and research programs, and nationally based ones as well, is of little use to policy makers until it is assessed and summarized in reports that are both readily understandable and policy relevant. Numerous assessments are conducted for various purposes by nationally based groups, such as governmental agencies, scientific academies, and corporate trade groups. The objectivity of these assessments is often questioned in other countries, even when they are conducted by prestigious organizations such as the National Academy of Sciences of the United States. Thus, international assessment programs involving scientists from numerous countries have played a critical role in forging an international consensus on the nature and severity of atmospheric problems. The most prominent of these is the Intergovernmental Panel on Climate Change (IPCC), which was created in 1988 by WMO and UNEP to review and report on what scientists have learned about human-induced climate change and its likely consequences as well as to investigate options for addressing the problem.

The successes of these many international scientific programs can be attributed to several factors. WMO, which has been the central actor on atmospheric research, has long had a reputation for being a haven from international political conflicts, where rationality rather than ideology prevailed even during the height of the Cold War from the 1950s to the 1980s. WMO has also cultivated an image of objectivity by limiting its role largely to monitoring and scientific research while leaving policy questions to other institutions to address. Atmospheric research has also benefited from constructive partnerships between international organizations with complementary interests and expertise, including intergovernmental bodies such as WMO, UNEP, WHO, the Food and Agriculture Organization (FAO), United Nations Scientific, Educational and Cultural Organization (UNESCO), and the International Civil Aviation Organization (ICAO), as well as with ICSU and other nongovernmental organizations.

THE ATMOSPHERE AS A GLOBAL COMMONS

The atmosphere is often described as a global commons, but in what ways is it one? In this book a *commons* is construed to be a domain that encompasses resources used by multiple actors for their individual gain or profit. Moreover, the resources are limited in quantity and thus depletable, and once any specific resource unit is taken by a user, it is not available to others. A prototype of such a commons is the community pasture in Garrett Hardin's story of a mythical English village on which all of the villagers are permitted to graze privately owned cattle for their personal gain.[24] The pasture is the domain, and the clumps of grass are resource units that can be consumed by the cattle. Thus, what determines whether a resource domain is a commons is the pattern of its use, rather than whether it is owned collectively. Ownership does, however, have implications for who sets the rules about who is permitted to use the commons and under what terms.

The atmosphere is an unusual commons in several respects. First, it is an undifferentiated mass of gases, in contrast to most commons that are comprised of discrete resource units, such as clumps of grass on a community pasture or trees in a forest. Second, unlike other commons that have resources that can be harvested or extracted, such as fish from the oceans or mineral-rich nodules from the seabed, the atmosphere is a limited resource in the sense of what can be put into it, namely pollutants, without causing adverse consequences. Finally, in contrast to commons such as the seabed and outer space, which are demarcated by spatial boundaries, the atmosphere is identified not by where it is but by the aggregate of the gaseous substances comprising it, which are in constant motion. Thus, at any given time an ever changing portion of the gases resides in national air spaces and the remainder in airspaces above no country. In this respect the atmosphere is similar to stocks of migratory species of fish that swim through coastal waters of several states and spend part of their lives on the high seas.

Commons are susceptible to overuse that either depletes or degrades them or causes interference among the users, a tendency that Hardin refers to as a "tragedy of the commons." The "tragedy" occurs because the users seek to maximize the benefits derived from exploiting the resources, which accrue to them as individuals, while sharing the costs of its overuse with all the users. Even if the users are fully aware that a tragedy is unfolding, they may perpetuate their destructive behavior, concluding that any restraint they exercise in the interests of conserving the commons will be futile because others, who are less scrupulous, will persist in overusing the commons to the point of a tragedy. In Hardin's English village the tragedy occurs because the villagers added too many of their private cattle to the community pasture, causing it to become seriously degraded by overgrazing. The depletion of many of the ocean's once bountiful fisheries due to overharvesting is archetypical of contemporary tragedies of the commons.

The atmosphere is an example of an "open-access" commons, meaning that its oxygen is available to all people for respiration and combustion of fuels and as a medium for disposing of wastes. As a source of oxygen the atmosphere is a virtually infinite resource, but its capacity to absorb and disperse pollutants without highly undesirable consequences is limited. Concentrations of some types of pollutants, such as those responsible for acid rain, depletion of the ozone layer, and climate change, have already exceeded the capacity of the atmosphere as a sink for pollutants. This degradation of the atmosphere conforms to Hardin's tragedy of the commons in that the users individually derive all the benefits from the polluting activity and the low-cost disposal of wastes, while the harmful consequences of the pollution are transferred to downwind neighbors or shared with the world community as a whole.

A "tragedy" can be averted if rules are established and enforced that prohibit or limit certain uses of the commons. A substantial body of research on the use of common resources of local communities suggests that groups of users often succeed in developing social mechanisms that restrain exploitation of these resources to a level that can be sustained indefinitely.[25] Governments can pass laws that impose rules on the use of commons located within their territories, as many have done to regulate fishing in the two-hundred-mile exclusive economic zones (EEZs) off their coasts, over which they have jurisdiction under the 1982 Convention on the Law of the Sea. International or global commons are preserved by means of treaties negotiated among sovereign states willing to agree to limit their use of a commons in return for reciprocating commitments by others. Such agreements, along with the international institutions that oversee them, provide a form of governance known as international regimes.[26] Separate international regimes address the atmospheric problems of nuclear testing, transboundary pollution, depletion of the ozone layer, and climate change.

If the only objective of an international regime were to avoid an environmental tragedy, the simplest and most effective type of regulation would be a prohibition on the activities that are prone to excess, such as the ban on nuclear weapons tests in the atmosphere. However, the economic value of a commons usually dictates that a regulatory scheme should allow continuing use of its resources at a level the domain can sustain indefinitely, as is being done in the LRTAP regime through adoption of the concept of "critical loads" to define targets for reducing pollution. Increasingly, environmental regulations are guided by the goal of economic efficiency, which in the case of air pollution is furthered by rules in the form of limits, leaving it to states and industries to determine the most cost-effective way to cut their emissions. Equity can also be a critical issue since sovereign states are not obliged to accept and be bound by rules they consider unfair. Efforts to strengthen the climate change regime will continue to face the major challenge of devising an equitable way of distributing rights to emit CO_2 and other GHGs, in view of the vast inequalities in past and current emission levels between the developed and developing countries.

THE ATMOSPHERE AND GLOBAL ENVIRONMENTAL SECURITY

For decades the field of security studies has concentrated almost exclusively on the protection of nation-states from armed attack by hostile states or from the violent acts of nonstate actors such as guerrillas or terrorists. This narrow interpretation of security seemed germane to the era of the Cold War, when East and West threatened each other with nuclear annihilation, or what became known as the "balance of terror." As concern mounted about global environmental problems and rapid population growth, the suggestion was made in various circles that the most serious threats to human societies were not exclusively military in nature. Sentiment for redefining security to encompass a broader range of threats burgeoned as Cold War tensions dissipated in the late 1980s and anxieties rose about the potentially catastrophic consequences of depletion of the ozone layer and climate change. The term *environmental security* came increasingly into vogue among scholars and policy makers and even among leaders such as Mikhail Gorbachev and Eduard Shevardnadze of the former Soviet Union.

Qualms about the term environmental security have come from two quite different perspectives. Traditional security analysts warn that the concept *security* will lose its focus and meaning if recast more broadly to encompass environmental and other nonmilitary threats that pose fundamentally different challenges. Conversely, some environmentalists are leery of linking the environment to security on the grounds that this might foster nationalistic responses to ecological problems that are more appropriately addressed internationally. It is argued in this book, however, that environmental security is both an appropriate and a useful concept, albeit one that should be used prudently. It is appropriate because security is one of the most basic of human values, which can be defined as the realistic expectation of people that they will continue to enjoy the qualities of life that are important to them. The essential well-being of people is jeopardized in many ways other than armed attack from hostile forces, including changes in the natural environment that endanger their health or way of life. To take a rather extreme example, rising sea levels and increasingly frequent and intense storms, which are likely outcomes of greenhouse warming, would appear to be more serious threats to the basic welfare of the people of small island nations such as the Maldive Islands and Vanuatu than the unlikely prospect of military aggression.

The concept environmental security also challenges traditional patterns of thought that do not reflect contemporary realities. It encourages a reassessment of national security priorities and a recognition that the strategies that have been used to pursue military security have the effect of heightening environmental insecurities, as was the case with testing nuclear weapons in the atmosphere. Alternatively, looking at environmental problems from a security perspective affords them a greater sense of urgency in the minds of publics and policy makers, who will have a more realistic picture of relative threats. The security perspective is also useful for investigating alternative approaches for coming to grips with the major environmental problems that confront humanity.

Societies have two fundamental decisions to make as they seek to enhance their security. The first is between preventive versus defensive approaches. The preventive option strives to keep threatening circumstances from arising in the first place or to minimize them if they cannot be completely avoided. The defensive approach concentrates on enhancing society's ability to cope with whatever threatening circumstances actually materialize. The second decision is between whether to adopt a self-reliant approach to enhancing security or, alternatively, to deal with insecurities in a collective way by working with other similarly threatened societies. These two paired options define four strategies for pursuing security, two of which—self-defense and collective prevention—have been the dominant alternatives for seeking both military and environmental security.

In pursuing military security nations have usually opted for self-defense. Unfortunately, the armaments that countries acquire to defend themselves add to the insecurities of other countries, which respond by adding weapons to their arsenals. The result is an arms race that adds to the insecurity of all countries, who then face the prospect of a much more destructive war. Nations could enjoy a greater sense of military security were they to negotiate arms control agreements among themselves that limit if not prohibit the acquisition of weapons that are mutually threatening.

Similarly, in seeking environmental security, societies can decide to depend on their own adaptive capacities to cope with problems such as acid precipitation or climate change. The alternative is to reach agreements with other societies on regulating the activities that might cause environmental threats to arise in the first place. In most cases preventing or reducing environmental threats would appear to have significant advantages over defensively trying to cope with environmental disruptions when they occur. Will states be more inclined to cooperate among themselves to reduce threats in pursuing environmental security than they were in seeking military security? Or will they lapse back into the habit of working on their own to adapt to whatever environmental disruptions and emergencies might arise? The regimes created thus far to address atmospheric nuclear testing, LRTAP, and ozone depletion are indicative of a commitment to cooperative prevention in the pursuit of environmental security. It remains to be seen whether the international community will address the considerably more complex problem of climate change in a similar way.

OVERVIEW OF THE BOOK

This is a book about the atmosphere, how it is being altered and degraded by a rapidly growing human population, and what is being done to regulate its use by humans in order to preserve its essential qualities. The emphasis is on international efforts to limit the impact of human activities on the atmosphere through the development of international laws, policies, and institutions that comprise a form of governance known as international regimes. At this level nation-states are the pivotal actors as they engage in negotiations aimed at concluding international agreements on how to address regional and global atmospheric problems, which accommodate their conflicting perspectives and interests. International organizations, such as WMO, UNEP, and the European Union, often play influential roles, as do nongovernmental groups that provide scientific information or promote various causes. This focus on the international level is not intended to suggest that what happens within countries is unimportant. The bargaining positions that states bring to international negotiations are in most cases guided by complex domestic considerations. Moreover, international regimes will be successful in mitigating atmospheric problems only to the extent that national and local governments adopt laws and policies that bring their countries into compliance with international regulations.

The chapter that follows is a brief, nontechnical primer on the physical features of the atmosphere and the principal ways it is being polluted and altered that have international and global consequences. It is designed to provide the background information about the atmosphere that is needed to understand the major international policy issues that have arisen in recent decades. Chapter 3 traces the evolution of scientific knowledge about the atmosphere and air pollutants with emphasis on the roles played by international scientific programs and projects. The next four chapters are case studies of the principal international regimes that have been established to address atmospheric problems resulting from human pollutants, including the atmospheric testing of nuclear weapons (chapter 4), the long-range transboundary air pollution responsible for acid precipitation (chapter 5), the depletion of the ozone layer (chapter 6), and global climate change (chapter 7). The case studies delve into the unique challenges posed by each of these policy problems and trace the negotiations that led to creation of the international regimes. They also assess the impacts of regimes on national behaviors and how much promise they have for mitigating the problems they address.

The next two chapters analyze the larger problem of regulating use of the atmosphere from two theoretical perspectives. Chapter 8 looks at the atmosphere as a global commons that, as with other commons, is susceptible to overuse, which could lead to a Hardinian "tragedy." It also considers whether various strategies for avoiding such an outcome hold promise for preserving the atmosphere. Chapter 9 presents atmospheric changes as serious threats to the well-being of human societies and ponders whether these societies will seek environmental security in a preventive and collaborative way, rather than by a self-reliant and defensive strategy paralleling the ones that have been so costly and counterproductive in the pursuit of military security.

The concluding chapter (chapter 10) reviews the progress that has been made in recent decades in addressing atmospheric problems and looks to the even greater challenges that lie ahead as the world's population continues to grow and industrialize. It compares the ways in which the four regimes evolved, with an eye toward identifying factors that contribute to the successful creation and evolution of international environmental regimes. Chapter 10 then examines the prospects for strengthening the climate change regime, which as yet has no mandatory international controls on national emissions of greenhouse gases. The final chapter compares the development of international law pertaining to the atmosphere with that which governs use of other global commons and, finally, raises and briefly assesses the possibilities for creation of a comprehensive law of the atmosphere.

Chapter 2

A Primer on the Atmosphere and Pollution

Air is a rather simple but elusive gaseous substance comprised mostly of nitrogen and oxygen, which in a pure and stationary form is intangible to the human senses. The atmosphere, however, which includes the entire air mass surrounding the planet, is a highly complex component of the basic Earth system in view of its perpetual movement both horizontally and vertically, as well as its layering, temperature fluctuations, seasonal cycles, and the ways it is affected by solar radiation and interacts with the oceans, landmasses, and living species. International policy issues pertaining to the atmosphere cannot be adequately understood without some basic knowledge of the nature of the atmosphere and the forces that impact upon it. Thus, this chapter offers a brief nontechnical description of the atmosphere and some of the principal ways it is affected by human activities.

The Atmosphere

Scientists believe that the Earth has been surrounded by gaseous substances throughout all but the earliest portion of its estimated 4.6 billion years of existence. The mix of gases, however, has changed markedly over time, such that the current atmosphere, which has nourished an abundance of plant and animal life for several hundred million years, bears little resemblance chemically to the gaseous brew that surrounded the planet during its first billion years. The earliest atmosphere was probably comprised mostly of water vapor, carbon dioxide (CO_2), and nitrogen released from the earth by volcanic eruptions taking place over millions of years. Given the prevalence of CO_2, this primeval atmosphere may have become ten to twenty times as dense as the current atmosphere, with average global temperatures in the much warmer range of 85° to 110° C.[1]

Important changes began taking place about 3.8 billion years ago after the lifeless planet cooled and volcanic activity subsided. Much of the water vapor condensed and fell as rain, with the runoff collecting in rivers, lakes, and oceans. The rains washed most of the CO_2 from the atmosphere, which further contributed to its cooling. Then, about 3.5 billion years ago, primitive single-cell plants appeared in the oceans at a depth sufficient to avoid exposure to the intense ultraviolet (UV) radiation from the sun that bathed the planet. These first cells were critical to the evolution of the atmosphere because they were capable of photosynthesis, a process that absorbs CO_2 and releases oxygen. For billions of years these primitive photosynthesizers enriched the oceans and subsequently the atmosphere with growing quantities of oxygen, so that oxygen became the second most abundant gas in the atmosphere after nitrogen.[2]

Life was confined to the oceans until approximately 450 million years ago when enough oxygen had accumulated in the atmosphere to provide the chemical raw material for the formation of a sparse layer of ozone in the stratosphere. The ozone was important because it screened out certain wavelengths of intense UV radiation from the sun that are not absorbed by oxygen, making it possible for plant and animal species to emerge from the oceans and to colonize the landmasses. The photosynthesis of the flourishing plant life in the oceans and on land has not only raised oxygen concentrations in the atmosphere to their current levels but has also helped stabilize levels of CO_2, which keeps global average temperatures from rising beyond the ranges that most species can tolerate. Thus, the amount of oxygen in the atmosphere is at least a thousand times higher than it would have been without the profusion of plant life, while concentrations of CO_2 would be a hundred times greater. Paradoxically, plants generate the atmospheric gases upon which they and the earths fauna depend for their survival.[3]

Composition and Layers

The chemical composition of the atmosphere has been quite stable for the past 600 million years. Four gases comprise 99.99 percent of dry air: nitrogen (78.08 percent), oxygen (20.95 percent), argon (0.93 percent), and CO_2 (0.03 percent). The proportions of these gases are remarkably uniform up to an altitude of approximately 80 km.[4] The atmosphere also contains minute proportions of forty naturally occurring trace gases, such as neon, helium, ozone, hydrogen, krypton, and methane. Despite their extremely low concentrations, some of these trace gases play a critical role in atmospheric and biological processes. Another important component is water vapor, which is present in amounts varying from 0 to 4 percent of the volume of the atmosphere.[5] The lower levels of the atmosphere also contain varying amounts of minute liquid and solid particles known as aerosols, including such naturally occurring substances as soil dust, pollen, soot from forest fires, microorganisms, sea salt, and pollutants from human activities.[6]

The atmosphere is comprised of several layers that are defined by the vertical profile of temperatures displayed in Figure 2.1. The lowest level, known as the *troposphere,* is a region in which temperatures decline sharply with altitude. The upper boundary of the troposphere is the *tropopause,* the altitude at which temperatures level off at minus 75–80° C. before rising through the next layer, which is known as the *stratosphere.* The altitude of the tropopause ranges from an average of 10–12 km over the poles to 17 km over the equator and is generally highest during the summer and lowest in the winter. The upper boundary of the stratosphere is the *stratopause,* which is located at an altitude of approximately 50 km, where temperatures are a moderate -5° C. Temperatures decline through the next layer, called the *mesosphere,* reaching their lowest level of approximately -95° C at about 80 km, an altitude known as the *mesopause.* Beyond the mesopause is the *thermosphere,* which comprises only 0.0001 percent of the atmosphere's gases and extends upward to approximately 500 km. In the thermosphere temperatures again rise with altitude to as high as 1200° C due to heat released by the collision of highly energetic solar radiation with oxygen and nitrogen atoms and molecules. In the process electrically charged particles called ions are released, and thus much of the thermosphere is also known as the *ionosphere.* Beyond the thermosphere is the *exosphere,* which is comprised of thin interplanetary gases.[7]

The troposphere, which contains approximately 85 percent of the atmosphere's gases, is not only the densest layer of the atmosphere but also the region in which most of the atmospheric phenomena known as weather takes place. The dynamic weather conditions occur because the

Figure 2.1 . Layers and Temperatures of the Atmosphere

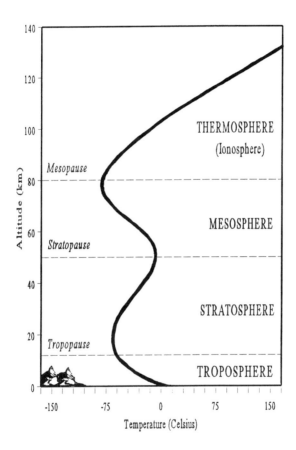

air of the troposphere is subject to vertical mixing through the process of convection, which has been compared to a boiling pot of water heated from below. The air adjacent to the Earth's surface is warmed by heat given off by rocks, soil, and the seas after they absorb solar radiation. As the surface air is warmed, it expands and becomes less dense, which causes it to rise to higher altitudes where it mixes with cooler air. As the rising air is cooled, the water vapor it contains condenses to form clouds and precipitation. As the warm air rises, its place is taken by descending cooler, denser air from the higher altitudes, thus completing the convection current. The temperature inversion created by the relatively warm stratosphere acts like a ceiling that prevents the further ascent of the turbulent air of the troposphere into the stratosphere. The resulting circulation patterns within the troposphere redistribute heat and moisture, which is essential for maintaining the climates that have been so conducive to life on the planet.[8] By contrast, the stratosphere is a region of relative calm and few clouds and is thus a preferable zone for jet traffic.

Solar Radiation and the Atmosphere

Fusion reactions within the sun's interior radiate enormous amounts of energy that move through space in the form of electromagnetic waves of various lengths, only about one billionth of which enters the Earth's atmosphere.[9] Because of the intense heat at its source, most of the solar radiation falls within a relatively energetic (short wavelength) portion of the electromagnetic spectrum, including the UV (9 percent), visible light (41 percent), and infrared (IR) (50 percent) regions.[10] Both UV and IR radiation are invisible to the human eye. UV radiation has wavelengths of less than 400 nanometers (nm) and is thus more energetic than visible light, which has wavelengths in the range of 400–700 nm. IR radiation, with wavelengths of more than 700 nm, is weaker than visible light. The most intense forms of ultraviolet radiation, UV-C (40–290 nm) and UV-B (290–320 nm), are highly damaging to most life forms. Less intense UV-A radiation (320–400 nm) is much less biologically harmful, and some exposure is even needed by humans to form vitamin D in their bodies.[11] Visible light and IR radiation are not strong enough to be harmful to most species but rather are essential to biological processes such as photosynthesis.

The aggregate of the solar energy approaching the outer reaches of the atmosphere is known as the *solar constant*, which is a misleading term given that the amount of radiation fluctuates considerably over time. As the incoming radiation continues toward the Earth, it encounters the gases and aerosols that comprise the atmosphere. Some of these substances reflect, scatter, or absorb radiation of certain wavelengths while not interfering with rays of other wavelengths. Reflection and scattering merely alter the direction of the radiation; absorption transforms the radiation into heat. Approximately 47 percent of the solar radiation that enters the atmosphere is diverted or intercepted in one of these ways, with the greatest reflector being the white tops of clouds, which reflect approximately 22 percent of incoming solar energy.[12]

Most of the higher energy UV radiation entering the atmosphere is absorbed in the upper levels of the stratosphere. Oxygen (O_2) is a plentiful and strong absorber of the more intense UV-C radiation in the wavelength range up to 210 nm. The collisions between UV-C radiation and O_2 not only stop the progress of the UV-C rays toward the Earth's surface but also break apart the O_2 molecules. The resulting two oxygen (O) atoms that are released combine with other O_2 molecules to form molecules of ozone (O_3). O_3 is an effective absorber of the slightly longer-wave UV-C and UV-B radiation in the range of 210–310 nm, which is weakly screened out by O_2.[13] In the process of absorbing UV rays, the relatively unstable O_3 molecules are broken into O_2 and O, which starts the process again. Thus, high-intensity frequencies of UV radiation play a role in creating O_3 in the stratosphere, which in turn absorbs the less energetic types of UV radiation. The combination of molecular ozone and oxygen in the atmosphere shields the planet from most, but not all, of the UV radiation that is intense enough to be highly damaging or fatal to life forms. The absorbing of UV radiation also warms the stratosphere, which accounts for the temperature inversion that confines the convection currents within the troposphere.[14]

Ozone is an important ingredient of the atmosphere even though it is present in minute proportions. If all the ozone were compressed at sea level, it would constitute a layer only 3 mm thick, while the entire atmosphere would be compressed to a thickness of 8 km.[15] Roughly 90 percent of atmospheric ozone is concentrated in a zone between 10 and 40 km above the Earth's surface, where it is known as the "ozone layer." This so-called layer is of very low density, accounting for only ten parts per million (ppm) where the ozone concentrations are greatest at 20 to 25 km in altitude.[16] Stratospheric concentrations of ozone vary considerably by geographical latitude and altitude. Over time there are naturally occurring fluctuations in the total amount of ozone in the stratosphere depending upon factors such as the seasons, solar cycles, and volcanic eruptions.[17]

Most of the 53 percent of the incoming solar energy that passes through the atmosphere to the Earth's surface is in the visible light and infrared wavelength regions. This radiation is absorbed by the seas, land, and vegetation except for a small proportion that is almost immediately reflected back into space after striking lighter colored surfaces such as snow and ice, which are said to have a high albedo, or reflectiveness. The Earth reradiates much of the absorbed energy, but in the form of longer-wave IR rays, in particular in the 8,000 to 20,000 nm range, because it is a much cooler source of radiation than the sun. The IR rays leaving the Earth would pass through the atmosphere to outer space without any warming effect were they not selectively absorbed by molecules of water vapor, CO_2, and the trace gases methane and ozone. In the process heat is given off, which warms the lower atmosphere and the Earth's surface.[18]

The substances that absorb the IR radiation coming from the Earth are known as "greenhouse gases" (GHGs) because of a somewhat misleading analogy that is commonly drawn with the way greenhouses keep the air within them relatively warm. Both the glass of greenhouses and GHGs in the atmosphere allow solar energy to penetrate, but whereas glass captures heat by stopping the upward flow of warmed air, the GHGs retard the escape of IR radiation. The naturally occurring concentrations of these GHG gases present in the atmosphere account for the hospitable climate of the planet Earth, with temperatures averaging 15° C, in contrast to the intense 400° C heat of Venus, which has five hundred times as much CO_2 in its atmosphere, and the frigid -60° C temperatures of Mars, which has less than 1 percent the concentration of GHGs.[19]

Other Biogeochemical Cycles

The formation and absorption of ozone comprise one of several critical biogeochemical cycles involving the atmosphere through which materials critical to life are distributed and recycled, two others of which will be briefly described here. The *hydrological cycle* redistributes water through a process that begins with the evaporation of large amounts of water from the oceans and lesser quantities from land into the atmosphere, where it resides as water vapor. Wind currents may carry the moisture-laden air considerable distances before it rises and cools, causing the water vapor to condense and fall back as precipitation over either the oceans or land areas. Most of the moisture that precipitates on land either evaporates directly back into the atmosphere or is carried by river systems to lakes or the seas to begin the cycle again. Some water percolates to subsurface rock formations to form groundwater. Plants absorb some of the moisture from soil and release it to the atmosphere as water vapor through the process of transpiration. Where there is heavy vegetation, as in tropical rain forests, transpiration may be a significant source of moisture for the rain in the area, with the water being recycled several times before it returns to the sea as runoff. Thus, the large-scale altering of ground cover can have a significant impact on rainfall patterns.[20]

The atmosphere is also a critical part of two *carbon cycles,* which distribute a chemical raw material required by all living organisms. In the shorter cycle carbon is fixed in green plants and in certain microorganisms, such as algae, through the process of photosynthesis. This process takes place when sunlight is absorbed by chlorophyll, which powers a process that breaks down CO_2 from the atmosphere to form organic molecules, such as glucose and amino acids, that accumulate in the biomass of the plants. Animals, which are not capable of photosynthesis, obtain the carbon they need to produce energy for maintaining their bodily processes by eating plants or other animals that are primary or secondary consumers of plants. Carbon is returned to the atmosphere in the form of CO_2 through the cellular respiration of living plants and animals and their decomposition upon death. The carbon in vegetation is also released to the atmosphere when it is burned, as in forest and range fires or slash-and-burn farming. The oceans absorb and release vast quantities of CO_2 and thus serve as a buffer that keeps the level of CO_2 in the atmosphere relatively stable.[21]

There is also a geological carbon cycle that takes place naturally on a much longer scale of time. The cycle begins when organic material from plants and animals slowly becomes locked into sedimentary deposits, where it may remain for hundreds of millions of years in the form of either carbonates containing the shells of marine organisms or organic fossils, such as coal, oil, and natural gas. Some of the carbon is eventually released when the geological formations in which it is locked are exposed to weathering and erosion. Human beings have greatly accelerated the release of this carbon by mining and drilling large quantities of fossil fuels and burning them to produce energy while in the process emitting CO_2.[22]

Weather and Climate

The variable states of the troposphere, the lowest level of the atmosphere, are what are known as weather and climate. *Weather* refers to the meteorological phenomena that occur at a given time and place. The principal components of weather are air temperature, humidity, wind, cloud cover, precipitation, storms, and barometric pressure. *Climate* refers to weather conditions that prevail over extended periods of time, including not only the average or typical weather but also the extremes that have occurred. Thus, while weather is a transitory set of atmospheric conditions that can fluctuate greatly by the hour, day, season, or even year, climate is the composite of weather conditions that occur in a given area over years, decades, and centuries.

Two of the principal shapers of weather and climate are the circulation patterns in the atmosphere and the oceans, which are driven largely by temperature differences and the rotation of the Earth. The tropics and lower latitudes are much warmer than higher and polar latitudes because they absorb significantly more solar energy per unit of area. In the equatorial regions, known as the doldrums, warm air rises and releases large amounts of rainfall as it cools. At high altitudes the equatorial air then flows poleward, either north or south, and at about 30° north or south latitude begins to sink. These so-called "horse latitudes" where the air is sinking are regions of few clouds and little rainfall, which accounts for the existence of many of the world's great deserts and steppes, such as the Sahara, Arabian, and Rajasthan to the north of the equator and the Kalahari and Australian to the south. Moving further poleward to the temperate 40–60° latitudes, the still relatively warm air from the equatorial regions encounters cold air flowing from the polar areas. The warmer and less dense equatorial air rises over the cooler polar air, resulting in storms that release moisture, which along with the moderate temperatures facilitates agriculture in areas such as the American East and Midwest. This boundary between equatorial and polar air masses, which is known as the polar front, moves toward the equator in the summer and poleward in the winter. Areas on the poleward side of the polar fronts receive sparse precipitation, but ice and snow cover nevertheless can build up because little evaporation takes place in the cold air.[23]

Weather and climate are also affected by physical features of the planet. Mountain ranges obstruct wind currents and force them upward, which accounts for heavy rainfall on the windward side of mountains and dry or desert conditions on the other side where the air descends. Vegetation is another factor influencing weather, especially in the tropics where vast forests absorb precipitation and then release it back into the atmosphere as water vapor, which may fall as rain locally or be transported by wind currents to other regions. Oceans and other large bodies of water have a moderating effect on the weather of adjacent land areas, keeping them cooler in summer and warmer in winter. Surface currents in the oceans move vast amounts of warm water from equatorial regions to the higher latitudes, an example being the combination of the Gulf Stream and North Atlantic Drift, which moderates the winters of western Europe, while deeper currents return colder, more dense water back to the tropics.

Climate includes not only the more typical, or "normal" weather conditions but also less frequent perturbations, such as hurricanes, typhoons, tornados, heat waves, droughts, and blizzards, which can be highly disruptive to human communities by causing substantial loss of life, destruction of property, and damage to agriculture. On a much larger scale, the El Niño Southern Oscillation (ENSO) is a major climatic anomaly that occurs over twelve- to eighteen-month periods at irregular intervals averaging four to five years.[24] First observed by Spanish colonists in the late fifteenth century, this puzzling phenomenon involves a complex interaction between the oceans and atmosphere across the equatorial regions of the Pacific Ocean. The more noticeable manifestations of an ENSO are the presence of unusually warm waters in the eastern Pacific, a weakening and reversing of the normally easterly (east-to-west) trade winds at the equator, and torrential rains over otherwise dry areas of northern Peru and Ecuador. Once thought to be solely a regional phenomenon of the eastern Pacific, the ENSO has been linked to extreme weather events in distant places, including heavy rains in the southern United States, Chile, and Argentina; the failure of monsoons in India; and severe droughts in eastern Brazil, eastern Australia, Indonesia, the Philippines, China, and regions of Africa.[25]

Major volcanic eruptions can also have a substantial effect on weather globally by spewing large quantities of aerosols into the atmosphere, causing a significant cooling over much of the planet for up to two years. Much of the Northern Hemisphere experienced a "year without summer" in 1816 following the eruption of the Tambora volcano in Indonesia the year before. Crop failures throughout the British Isles and Europe led to a severe famine that provoked widespread rioting and a rise in revolutionary fever among the dispossessed.[26] Large amounts of aerosols from the eruption of Mount Pinatubo in the Philippines in 1991, the greatest volcanic event of the twentieth century, are believed to have reduced global mean temperatures by 0.4° C for 1992–93, which temporarily off-set a pronounced warming trend that had prevailed for more than a decade.[27]

More basic shifts in climate take place over much longer sweeps of time, as is apparent from the geological evidence of periods of expanded glaciation known as ice ages, between which there have been warmer eras when the great ice sheets have retreated. The last major ice age peaked about eighteen thousand years ago, when average global temperatures were 4–6° C colder than the present. Historical accounts offer clues about more recent shorter-term climatic trends, including the Little Ice Age that occurred from 1400 to 1850, during which temperatures averaged about 1° C cooler than now. Earlier an unusually warm epoch in northern Europe during medieval times enabled adventurous Norsemen to navigate an ice-free north Atlantic and to establish viable colonies on Greenland beginning in A.D. 985. A cooling trend that began late in the twelfth century brought hard times to the colonies. Cut off from their homelands by pack ice, the colonies completely disappeared by 1500.[28] Scientists continue to debate theories about the causes of these long-term swings in climate, in particular whether they are attributable to fluctuations in radiation emitted from the sun, to changes in the orbit or tilt of the Earth, or to naturally occurring variations in the concentration of CO_2 in the atmosphere. There is also the question of whether human activities are causing climate changes by adding to atmospheric concentrations of GHGs, as will be discussed later in this chapter.

AIR POLLUTION

Pollution is a substance that is in the wrong place in the environment, in the wrong concentrations, or at the wrong time, such that it is damaging to living organisms or disrupts the normal functioning of the environment.[29] Pollution may be present in the atmosphere in the form of gases, liquid or solid aerosols, or larger particles such as dust. Some air pollutants originate in nature, such as ash from volcanic eruptions, dust and sand from wind storms, smoke from forest fires, salt from the sea, and pollen from blossoms.[30] Human beings are also responsible for large quantities of air pollutants, some of which are synthetic compounds that do not occur naturally and do not readily break down in the environment. Other anthropogenic pollutants, such as sulfur and CO_2, exist in nature, but human activities add to their concentrations or distribution in ways that are disruptive to the environment.

Air pollutants circulate through the atmosphere in many and complex ways. Larger particulates gravitate from the atmosphere quickly as fallout and thus are usually a local problem near the source of emission. Gases and aerosols may be suspended for extended periods during which they may be transported by wind currents over thousands of kilometers before returning to the Earth's surface, usually by being washed out with precipitation. Certain gaseous pollutants, such as CFCs, remain suspended for decades while rising slowly to higher levels of the atmosphere. Some pollutants are inert under normal atmospheric conditions and thus remain in their original chemical forms; less stable ones react with other chemicals or are broken apart by solar radiation and thus undergo a transformation, leading to the creation of what are called secondary pollutants.[31]

Historical Incidents of Pollution

Human beings have added pollutants to the atmosphere for as long as fire has been used for cooking, heating, and clearing land. Human-generated air pollution had few adverse effects until the growth of cities led to high concentrations of contaminants in localized areas. Classical writers of the first century A.D. mentioned the blackening of building surfaces in Rome and the unhealthy quality of the air. London began experiencing serious air pollution problems in the thirteenth century when the depletion of forests on the urban perimeter prompted residents to switch from wood to coal and charcoal as fuels for household uses.[32] In the seventeenth century John Evelyn wrote that London was enveloped "in such a cloud of sea-coal, as if there be a resemblance of hell upon earth, it is in this volcano in a boggy day: this pestilent smoak, which corrodes the very yron, and spoils all the moveables, leaving a soot on all things that it lights: and so fatally seizing on the lungs of the inhabitants, that cough and consumption spare no man."[33]

In succeeding centuries the industrial revolution added to the acrid, smokey brew of air pollutants over European cities, especially those of the British Isles. One author describes the bleak situation in Sheffield, England, in the 1930s as follows: "every square foot of exposed masonry was black and filthy. The sun rarely penetrated a vast umbrella of smoke and soot. Children were taken away from the city for the sake of their health. There were thousands upon thousands of back to back houses. Their occupants were as grim and grimy as the steelworks from which they drew their sustenance."[34]

It was London, however, that continued to have the most notorious air pollution problems with its smog episodes, otherwise known as "great stinking fogs" or "pea soupers," that plagued the city as early as the seventeenth century but peaked during the nineteenth and twentieth centuries. These smokey, sulfurous smogs could persist for days during temperature inversions, causing darkness at noon and bringing normal life to a virtual halt. Unusually high death rates from bronchitis, influenza, pneumonia, tuberculosis, and other respiratory illnesses were noted during smogs occurring in 1873, 1880, 1881, 1882, 1891, 1892, 1901, 1942, 1952, 1956, 1957, and 1962. The death toll from the "London killer smog" of December 5–8, 1952, was estimated at four thousand. Other deadly episodes of air pollution occurred in the Meuse Valley, Belgium (1930); Donora, Pennsylvania (1948); New York City (1953, 1962, 1963, 1966); and Osaka, Japan (1962).[35]

Contemporary Air Pollution

As recently as the 1960s air pollution was looked upon as primarily a localized phenomenon of smog over the major cities and industrial complexes of the industrial world. Over the past few decades, however, urban pollution has been substantially mitigated in most developed countries through the adoption of laws that either reduce emissions or disperse pollutants over a larger area. Concurrently, the nature and dimensions of air pollution problems have undergone several notable changes, as has scientific understanding of them.

First, localized air pollution has been becoming much more severe in other parts of the world. The burgeoning cities of the developing countries now hold most of the top positions in the World Health Organization's rankings of cities with the highest concentrations of sulfur dioxide and suspended particulates. Among the cities with the most polluted air are Mexico City, Santiago, Beijing, Shenyang, New Delhi, Rio de Janeiro, Sao Paulo, Jakarta, Manila, Cairo, and Teheran.[36] Recent years have also brought revelations of extremely high levels of air pollution generated by antiquated technologies in the heavily industrialized areas of the former Soviet Union and eastern Europe, which have caused serious health problems for local residents and shortened their life expectancies.[37]

Second, the world's rapidly growing and industrializing human population has been emitting many more chemical pollutants into the atmosphere. The increasing combustion of fossil fuels has released huge amounts of the greenhouse gas CO_2 into the atmosphere. Motorized vehicles powered by petroleum products emit large quantities of nitrogen oxides and hydrocarbons, which are the ingredients of the noxious photochemical smog that was first noticed in Los Angeles in the 1940s and now plagues numerous cities throughout the world. Industry has created many thousands of synthetic chemical compounds for a myriad of uses, PCBs and CFCs being two of the more notorious examples that become air pollutants. Substantial amounts of radioactive substances have entered the atmosphere from nuclear weapons testing and from the nuclear power industry and its accidents. Whereas the smokey, sulfuric pollution of the past assaulted the senses, many of the pollutants of contemporary concern can be detected only by scientific monitoring instruments.

Third, while air pollution was once primarily a problem for cities and industrial complexes, there are now air pollution problems that are clearly of international and even global scope. The industrial pollutants responsible for acid precipitation drift freely over national boundaries in North America and Europe; this occurs even more now that taller smokestacks have been mandated to alleviate localized pollution problems. It was generally assumed that air over the Arctic was pristine until the chance discovery in the 1970s that the region receives large quantities of pollutants during the winter and early spring that form what became known as "Arctic haze." Aerosols comprising the haze over the north shore of Alaska are carried by air currents as far as 6,000 km from the heavily industrialized mid-latitude regions of the Eurasian continent.[38] Depletion of the ozone layer and human-induced climate change are problems of truly global proportions.

Finally, there is a growing recognition of the diverse effects of air pollutants on human health and the environment. The sooty smogs of earlier eras blackened buildings and on occasion posed a deadly peril to people with respiratory illnesses. Human health is now endangered by a myriad of contaminants such as carbon monoxide, ozone, lead and other heavy metals, synthetic compounds, and ionizing radiation, which among other things may lead to cancer as well as neurological and genetic damage. Acidic precipitation has been linked to the disappearance of aquatic life in freshwater lakes and streams as well as to damage to forests, crops, and stone and metal surfaces. In recent decades scientists have become increasingly concerned that air pollutants are causing subtle changes in the chemical composition of the atmosphere, which could lead to significant alterations in the world's climate and expose fauna and flora to greater doses of damaging UV radiation from the sun.

Let us now briefly consider four major types of pollution problems having international and, in some cases, global dimensions: acid deposition, threats to the ozone layer, the enhanced greenhouse effect, and ionizing radiation.

Acid Deposition

The human-generated pollutants principally responsible for increasing the presence of acids in the environment are sulfur dioxide (SO_2) and nitrogen oxides (NO_x). SO_2 emissions come primarily from the combustion of coal and petroleum and various smelting and industrial processes. Power generating plants burning high sulfur coal have been especially heavy emitters of SO_2. NO_x, which accounts for a much smaller share of human-induced acid deposition, comes from many of the same sources as SO_2, but a far greater proportion is emitted from the tailpipes of automobiles and other motorized vehicles. Globally, sulfur and nitrogen emissions from human sources are on the same order of magnitude as those that occur naturally, although in certain regions the human component is much greater.[39]

There are two basic types of processes through which acidic substances are formed from industrial pollutants and contaminate the environment, as are portrayed in Figure 2.2. First, some of the oxides of sulfur and nitrogen fall out of the atmosphere in a dry form as gases or aerosols. They then combine with surface water to create acidic substances or are absorbed directly by plants to form acids. This dry type of deposition usually occurs within a few kilometers of where the pollutants are emitted. Second, much of the SO_2 and NO_x is transformed into sulfuric and nitric acids while in the atmosphere through a complex series of chemical reactions. The original pollutants are further oxidized in the presence of a photo-oxidant such as low-level ozone, which is created when pollutants such as hydrocarbons and NO_x are acted upon by sunlight. This process creates tiny droplets of sulfuric and nitric acid that dissolve in raindrops or clouds, resulting in acidic rain, snow, mist, or fog, or what is known as wet deposition. Wet deposition normally occurs farther from the pollution source than dry deposition because the process of oxidation occurs over an extended time during which the pollutants can be transported hundreds if not thousands of kilometers by wind currents. The extensive use of tall smokestacks at power plants,

smelters, and factories has significantly added to the problem by causing sulfur and nitrogen oxides to be released at altitudes where they
will remain in the atmosphere longer as they are carried by wind currents, increasing the likelihood that chemical reactions will take place
that transform them to acids.[40]

Figure 2.2.   The Process and Distribution of Acid Deposition

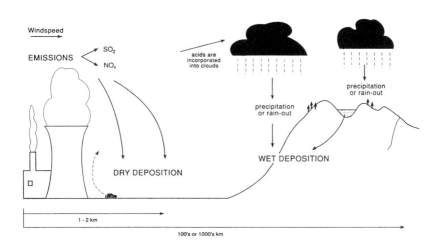

Reprinted with permission from Manion, Global Environmental Change, p. 162.

Rainwater is never as "pure" as distilled water, which has a pH
value of 7.0, indicating that it is neither acidic nor alkaline.[41] Even under pristine conditions, moisture in the atmosphere combines with naturally occurring chemicals, such as CO_2 or sulfur compounds, and thus
is slightly acidic when it falls as precipitation. This natural acidity of
precipitation has the effect of fertilizing plants and trees and therefore
is an essential part of the finely tuned chemical balance of the biosphere.
Determining the composition of pristine precipitation, and thus having

a baseline for human contributions to acidity, is complicated by naturally occurring variations in concentrations of acid-forming pollutants that occur over time and place. Studies of air and moisture in ice cores perhaps provide the best indication of pH levels prior to the industrial revolution. Thus, scientists have offered varying estimates of what the pH level of precipitation would be in the absence of human pollutants, with some suggesting that it could be as low as 5.0 and even 4.5 under certain circumstances. The most widely accepted standard for unpolluted precipitation is a pH of 5.6, which is twenty-five times the acidity of pure water.[42]

There is no single threshold value below which precipitation is considered to be "acid rain," although most scientists regard pH readings below 4.5 to be highly acidic, which is ten times more than the acid content of normal rain. Extensive areas of Europe and eastern North America are regularly exposed to precipitation with a pH of 4.0 or lower, forty times the acidity of normal rain. Precipitation from specific storms can have much lower pH levels. Rain falling over Pitlockry, Scotland, in 1974 had a pH of 2.4; while precipitation tested at Wheeling, West Virginia, in 1979 had a pH of 1.5, the latter being 12,500 times normal acidity.[43]

High levels of acid deposition can have severe consequences for the environment, especially for aquatic life and trees. Acidification first caused alarm when it was linked to the disappearance of fish in lakes and rivers in which the pH values of the water had dropped substantially. The problem was noticed early in the twentieth century in southern Norway and Sweden and later in eastern Canada, the northeastern United States, and the highland regions of the British Isles. The severity of the damage to aquatic life varies greatly from one place to another, even within the same region, depending upon the "buffering capacity" of the local soils and rocks. Areas rich in minerals that neutralize acids, such as those with limestone formations, display fewer manifestations of acid damage than those with other types of bedrock. The effects of acid deposition can be mitigated by spreading lime on the lakes and forest soils in affected regions, although this practice may have other undesirable effects.

Acid deposition also has significant impacts on many plant species. In relatively small doses it may have a fertilizing effect, thus stimulating the growth of agricultural crops. However, higher doses can have a harmful if not devastating impact on vegetation, especially forests. In the late 1970s scientists became concerned about unusual damage to Norwegian spruce trees in the forests of southern Germany, a condition that became known by the German term *waldsterben* (forest death) and later the more neutral term *neuartige waldschaeden* (new forest decline).[44] The phenomenon spread at an alarming rate through the forests of central Europe during the early 1980s. The proportion of German forests showing significant signs of disease grew from 8 percent in 1982 to 34 percent in 1983 and nearly 50 percent in 1984. By 1985 all major species of trees in central Europe were showing significant signs of disease.[45] A forest damage assessment conducted in 1991 revealed that 18.5 percent of Europe's broadleaf trees and 24.4 percent of its conifers had lost at least one-quarter of their foliage. In the United Kingdom 56.7 percent of trees were at least moderately defoliated, and in Poland 45 percent were.[46] Significant damage to forests, presumably linked to acid deposition, has also been noted in eastern North America and regions of Asia.

The processes through which these ecosystems are altered by acid deposition are complex and occur over extended periods. Species in aquatic environments can tolerate different levels of acidity. Numerous smaller species such as algae, zooplankton, phytoplankton, and aquatic insects cannot tolerate pH levels lower than 5.0 or even 5.5, which has serious implications because they are near the bottom of the food chain. As pH levels drop below 5.0, most fish and amphibian species disappear because of reproductive failures caused by the toxic effects of aluminum that the acids release into the water. Loss of fish reduces the food supplies of species such as birds that feed upon them.[47] The problem is most pronounced during "acid surges" that occur with spring runoffs or after droughts, when the pH values are especially low. Scientists have had greater difficulty isolating the causes of forest decline in acidified regions because other factors such as extreme temperatures, droughts, diseases, insects, and other pollutants such as ozone may also be damaging trees. Moreover, trees weakened by natural causes may be more vulnerable to increased acidity of their environments or, alternatively, trees affected by acid deposition may be more susceptible to other environmental threats. It has also been difficult to determine the extent to which acids damage trees by coming into contact with their foliage or bark as opposed to their effects on soils. In the latter case, acids not only leach nutrients such as calcium and magnesium from the soil but also free toxic chemicals such as aluminum that enter trees through their roots.[48]

These same pollutants can also adversely affect human health. Heavy concentrations of air pollutants such as SO_2, NO_x, particulates, and photochemical oxidants have been found to irritate the respiratory system, cause chronic lung disease, decrease pulmonary function, and increase heart stress, with the impact being the greatest among the young and elderly.[49] Human health may be jeopardized in an indirect way if toxic metals, such as mercury and lead, are released into drinking water.

Threats to the Ozone Layer

A distinction is often made between so-called "good" and "bad" ozone, which is based on where the ozone is located rather than on differences in its chemical composition. The naturally existing ozone comprising the stratospheric ozone layer has the highly beneficial effect of absorbing UV-B radiation from the sun that would otherwise reach the Earth's surface, where it would damage plant and animal life. The bad ozone, which is the product of anthropogenic pollutants, is found in the lower reaches of the troposphere, where it is an important component of the brownish photochemical smog that hangs over many large cities and a catalyst in the formation of acids in the atmosphere. A highly reactive chemical, ozone at elevated levels can cause eye irritation and respiratory distress in humans and damage to green vegetation.[50]

Good ozone is continually being created and destroyed in the stratosphere through the natural processes that were described above. Given their unstable chemical nature, ozone molecules are readily broken down by naturally existing trace gases that contain nitrogen, hydrogen, and chlorine. The ozone layer and its radiation-absorbing qualities remain intact as long as ozone molecules are being created and destroyed at roughly the same rate. Scientists have discovered, however, that certain human-produced chemicals accelerate the rate at which stratospheric ozone molecules are being destroyed, leading to a thinning of the ozone layer, which allows additional UV-C and UV-B radiation to reach the Earth's surface. The greatest threat to the ozone layer is posed by a family of synthetic chemicals known as chlorofluorocarbons (CFCs), which have been adapted to a variety of industrial and consumer uses, such as propellants in spray containers, solvents for cleaning electrical circuitry, foaming agents for polystyrene, and coolants in refrigerators and air conditioners. Other threats come from a similar family of bromine compounds known as halons, which are used as retardants in fire extinguishers; the industrial chemicals methyl chloride and carbon tetrachloride; methyl bromide, which is used primarily in agricultural fumigants; and nitric oxides from supersonic jets and nuclear explosions.[51]

CFCs had long been considered safe chemical compounds for numerous industrial uses because of their highly stable structure, which renders them nonflammable, noncorrosive, and nontoxic. Ironically, it is because of these desired nonreactive qualities that CFCs pose a threat to the ozone layer. In the atmosphere the highly stable CFC molecules neither react with other chemicals nor are they washed out by precipitation. Thus, they continue rising until they reach the stratosphere, where they eventually encounter solar radiation strong enough to break their chemical bonds. In the process the highly unstable chlorine atoms are released, and they engage ozone molecules in a catalytic reaction that transforms the ozone to oxygen while leaving the chlorine atom free to combine with another ozone molecule. Thus, a single chlorine atom from a CFC molecule can set off a chain reaction that may break apart many thousands of ozone molecules. Since it may take decades for CFCs to reach an altitude at which they encounter intense solar radiation, the ozone layer will be vulnerable to CFCs well into the next century even if their use is promptly phased out.[52]

The first significant loss of stratospheric ozone was observed over Antarctica in 1982. By the late 1980s ozone levels over certain Antarctic locations were down 60 percent from 1955 readings during the spring season. In some areas ozone was almost totally absent from the air column between the altitudes of 15 and 20 km. The horizontal size of the so-called Antarctic "ozone hole," a phenomenon of the spring season, became larger each year. By the early 1990s it was covering an area comparable to North America and extending outward to include parts of New Zealand, Australia, Argentina, and Chile. Scientists attribute this surprising and ominous phenomenon to anthropogenic pollutants, in particular CFCs and halons, which release highly reactive chlorine and bromine when they come into contact with ice particles that form in the frigid winter air over Antarctica. The spring sunshine then energizes the chemical reaction that destroys large quantities of ozone. The effect is concentrated by the polar vortex winds that prevail during the winter and spring seasons; these winds isolate the atmosphere over Antarctica from warmer air to the north. There is also evidence of a similar, but less pronounced, phenomenon occurring over the Arctic region.[53]

Ozone levels have also been diminishing at other latitudes, but to a far lesser extent. Between 1979 and 1994 ozone concentrations in the midlatitudes of the Northern Hemisphere declined at a rate of 6 percent per decade during the winter and spring and 3 percent during the summer and fall. The rate of ozone loss was only slightly less in the southern midlatitudes, while no significant change has been noted in the tropics. Ozone loss in 1992 and 1993 was significantly higher than had been projected from previous trends, a phenomenon that appears to be attributable to higher levels of sulfate aerosols in the atmosphere caused by the 1991 eruption of Mount Pinatubo.[54]

Is there evidence that the loss of ozone has been allowing greater amounts of UV-B radiation to pass through the atmosphere to the planet's surface, as scientists have theorized it would? Paradoxically, readings of UV-B radiation taken over the United States between 1974 and 1985 using broadband instruments indicated a slight decline in total radiation from all UV-B wavelengths (290–320 nm), which was attributed to the off-setting effects of a rise in UV-absorbing or reflecting pollutants, such as SO_2, NO_x, dust, and ground-level ozone. However, measurements made since 1989 using spectrometers geared to specific wavelengths document substantial increases in UV-B radiation in the more damaging wavelengths below 300 nm, both in the northern midlatitudes and the higher latitudes of the Southern Hemisphere.[55]

This increased exposure to UV radiation loss is likely to have serious implications for the planet's flora and fauna, which evolved in an environment in which they were not exposed to significant amounts of the more energetic UV-B radiation (below 300 nm). Scientific findings are still not conclusive about specific impacts of increased exposure, but the studies conducted thus far point to several significant reasons for concern. For humans there are indications that greater doses of UV-B radiation will trigger a greater incidence of skin cancers, including the more deadly but rare melanoma variety. UV-B radiation also poses a threat to the human immune system, which can lead to a greater incidence of diseases and reduce the effectiveness of vaccination programs.[56] The most vulnerable populations would be those that already have depressed immune systems or live in areas where infectious diseases are more prevalent, such as the tropics and subtropics. Greater doses of UV-B radiation, either directly from the sun or from reflections off light surfaces such as snow, can also trigger various eye disorders, including cataracts.[57]

Of perhaps greater concern are the effects that increased doses of UV-B radiation may have on other life forms and, more generally, on ecosystems. Unfortunately, research thus far has been limited to a small proportion of potentially vulnerable species. Laboratory studies of the effects of enhanced UV radiation on several hundred agricultural crop species have determined that roughly half of them exhibit symptoms such as leaf damage, lessened photosynthesis, mutations, and stunted growth. Among the more sensitive plants are peas, beans, squash, melons, cabbage, and soybeans.[58] Aquatic microorganisms, including phytoplankton and zooplankton, appear to be especially vulnerable to UV radiation, as is borne out by reductions in living organic mass in the Antarctic region under the ozone hole.[59] Any substantial decline in their numbers would jeopardize the species that feed on them, including fish and marine mammals. Thus far amphibians seem to display the most clear-cut evidence of the potential impact of increased UV-B exposure on larger fauna, as scientists have noted precipitous declines in populations of species of frogs, toads, and salamanders on every continent, phenomena that appear to be caused by damage to eggs.[60] The differential sensitivities of various species to UV radiation could have significant implications for ecosystems, which at this point are impossible to anticipate.

Enhanced Greenhouse Effect

The temperate climate over much of the Earth results from the way in which substances in the atmosphere moderate the incoming flow of intense short-wave energy coming from the sun and the outgoing flow of long-wave, infrared energy that is radiated out from the planet toward space. For several decades scientists have been warning that humanity may be disturbing this radiative balance by adding pollutants to the atmosphere that either block out additional amounts of the energy from the sun, which would have a cooling effect on surface temperatures, or retard the flow of heat from the Earth, which would have a warming effect. The dominant concern now is with the latter possibility, or what is known as the enhanced greenhouse effect.[61]

Much of the apprehension about the enhanced greenhouse effect has centered around the growing quantities of CO_2 in the atmosphere, but other gaseous pollutants also contribute to the phenomenon. Human beings have been adding to naturally occurring concentrations of

CO_2 since the advent of the industrial revolution, as they have burned fossil fuels, thereby releasing huge amounts of carbon that have been encased in rock formations for millions of years. The extensive clearing of forests has also added significantly to concentrations of CO_2 in the atmosphere, both from the release of carbon in the trees being destroyed and the reduction of green vegetation, which is a major sink for CO_2 from the atmosphere.

Atmospheric concentrations of CO_2 have risen from the preindustrial levels of 280 ppm to the current level of 360 ppm. If emissions remain at present levels, CO_2 concentrations will reach about 500 ppm by 2100.[62] The potential significance of this growing burden of greenhouse gases for climate change becomes more apparent when viewed on a timescale extending far into the past. Paleoclimatological research has revealed much about past climates through analyses of tree rings, pollen samples, and fossilized shells embedded in deep-sea sediments. Ice cores thousands of meters in length, which have been extracted from the glaciers of Antarctica and Greenland, provide a record of past states of the atmosphere. Scientists have plotted climate shifts over the past hundreds of thousands of years by calculating the ratio between certain oxygen isotopes in the ice cores. The air bubbles encased in the ice cores reveal that atmospheric CO_2 concentrations have ranged from 200 to 280 ppm over the same vast sweep of time. Data from the ice cores also show a striking parallel between CO_2 concentrations and average global temperatures. While it is not yet clear that changes in CO_2 levels caused the observed climate variations, the similarity in the trends gives compelling reason for concern about the implications of the contemporary, human-induced rise in CO_2 concentrations, which are already more than 20 percent higher than at any time over the 160,000 years preceding the industrial revolution.[63]

Several other human pollutants have been identified as greenhouse gases, including methane, ozone, nitrous oxide, CFCs, HCFCs, and halons. Concentrations of methane, a greenhouse gas that has twenty to thirty times the heat-retention capacity per molecule of CO_2, have doubled as a result of diverse human activities such as wet rice cultivation, livestock operations, forest clearing, the creation of landfills, coal mining, natural gas extraction, and use of leaky oil pipelines. It was thought that CFCs might contribute significantly to greenhouse warming because each molecule has as much as twenty thousand times the heat-retention capacity as a molecule of CO_2.[64] More recent calculations indicate, however, that the impact of CFCs on climate may be partly counteracted by the destruction of ozone molecules in the stratosphere, which also act as a GHG. Moreover, the flow of new CFCs into the atmosphere has slowed dramatically over the past decade as a result of international agreements, which will be discussed in chapter 6.[65]

Detailed analyses of meteorological records suggest that annual global average temperatures have already risen in the range of 0.3–0.6° C over the past century. Pronounced warming trends have been noted between 1910 and 1940 and after 1980, when the ten warmest years of the past century have occurred, provoking widespread concern about a possible acceleration of global warming.[66] Over most land areas average temperatures have risen more during the nights than the days. The warming tendency has not been uniform throughout the world. For example, in recent decades summers in the Northern Hemisphere have been the warmest since about A.D. 1200, while in certain smaller areas, such as the northwest Atlantic, cooling temperatures have been observed. It has not been definitively proven that these climatic anomalies are primarily the result of human activities as opposed to being naturally occurring fluctuations. However, there is now a virtual consensus among atmospheric scientists that it is unlikely that the long-term increases in global temperatures over the past century are being caused entirely by natural factors.[67] It is also possible that natural variations are obscuring an even larger human-induced impact on temperatures.[68]

It is difficult to forecast the amount of climate change that will occur due to human activities in view of the enormous complexity of atmospheric processes, the variations in climate that occur naturally, and uncertainties about policies that will affect emissions of GHGs. Large computerized general circulation models (GCMs) have been used to estimate the likely amount of future warming based on various assumptions. Recent projections suggest that by 2100 global mean surface temperatures will rise in the range of 1.0–3.5° C if the cooling effects of aerosol pollutants of human origin are factored in the calculations.[69] The amount of climate change will vary considerably by region, with the high-latitude areas expected to warm up three to four times as much as the global average increase, while only 50 to 75 percent of the global average warming is projected for the tropics.[70]

The magnitude and potential consequences of such climate changes can be appreciated by taking a long-term historical perspective. Recall that global average temperatures were only about 1° C cooler than current levels during the Little Ice Age that lasted from 1400 to 1850. A 2° C rise would take the planet beyond the temperature range that has prevailed at any time over the past ten thousand years; a 5° C rise would push temperatures beyond what has occurred over the last million years.[71] Moreover, the rate of human-induced global warming would be many times faster than naturally occurring climate changes and would thus have a much more drastic impact on environmental systems.

There are still substantial uncertainties about the timing, magnitude, and regional patterns of climate change. The potential impact of clouds on greenhouse warming is still not known; nor has it been possible to anticipate with confidence the capacity of the oceans to moderate temperatures or possible changes in the circulation patterns of ocean currents. Questions also remain about the extent to which warming tendencies might be counteracted by the cooling effects of sulfate aerosols from natural and anthropogenic sources, especially in the Northern Hemisphere, where the emissions are the greatest. The residence times of such aerosols in the atmosphere are very short relative to GHGs. Furthermore, efforts to combat acid rain can be expected to continue reducing the presence of sulfates in the atmosphere, which will presumably result in less of a cooling effect.[72]

Greater questions remain about the impacts that global warming will have on the natural environment and what the implications will be for human societies. A critical question in view of rapid world population growth is what the effects of an enhanced greenhouse effect will be on agriculture around the world. On the plus side, increased concentrations of atmospheric CO_2 have been shown under laboratory conditions to stimulate growth in certain types of crops. Moreover, farming in high-latitude countries such as Russia, Canada, and Scandinavia could benefit from warmer temperatures and longer growing seasons. However, soils, terrains, and precipitation in these regions may not permit more intensive agricultural use. Whatever gains there may be in these areas are likely to be more than offset by diminished production in key food growing areas in the temperate midlatitudes, such as the grain belts of North America, Australia, southern Africa, South America, northern India, and the southern regions of what was the Soviet Union, as a result of heat stress, diminishing rainfall, loss of soil moisture, a proliferation of pests, and less availability of irrigation water because of reduced stream flows.[73]

Warming climates will probably cause a rise in mean sea levels due to thermal expansion of ocean water and a more rapid melting of glaciers and terrestrial ice sheets. There is evidence that sea levels have already risen 10–25 cm over the past century. Looking to the future, if trends in global warming continue, sea levels are expected to rise an additional 10–120 cm by the year 2100.[74] The degree of rise will not be uniform throughout the world because in some areas, such as parts of Scandinavia and the Hudson Bay region of Canada, the land is rising as much as a meter a century due to isostatic rebound, which occurs following the retreat of large ice sheets from glacial periods. In other regions land is sinking due either to geological forces or human withdrawals of groundwater.[75] In other places, such as the cities of Shanghai and Bangkok, the land is subsiding due to the heavy pumping of groundwater.

Rising seas will inundate low-lying regions, some of which are critical food growing areas, such as the delta regions of Egypt and Bangladesh. Many of the world's large cities lie at sea level and thus would also be threatened, while salt water intrusions may jeopardize their underground water supplies. Warmer ocean waters could also spawn more frequent and intense tropical storms and accompanying storm surges that may be even more devastating for coastal regions and islands as sea levels rise. Higher sea levels could seriously disrupt coastal ecosystems such at wetlands and estuaries with serious implications for coastal fisheries.[76]

Global warming would also be highly disruptive to ecosystems, as climate zones shift toward higher latitudes, possibly as much as several hundred kilometers over the next fifty years. Some species, including disease vectors and pests that afflict humans, cattle, crops, and trees, will be more adaptable to these shifts than others. Less adaptable species will decline or disappear as the limits of their climatic tolerance are exceeded. Forests may prove to be especially susceptible to changing climates because of their slow rate of migration. Warmer and drier conditions might also trigger an increase in the number and intensity of forest and range fires.

Many other potential consequences of global warming could be cited, most of which would be undesirable, if not catastrophic. The inability of science to anticipate the vast number of relationships among the many environmental changes that would be taking place and the possibility of major "surprises" of the magnitude of the Antarctic ozone hole are reasons for vigilance about the threats posed by climate change. It is also possible that the initial environmental changes will trigger positive feedback loops that will further accelerate the process of climate change. For example, the albedo of large areas formerly covered by snow and ice would be altered such that they would absorb and radiate more heat; the melting of permafrost would release vast additional amounts of the GHG methane; and additional quantities of carbon would enter the atmosphere from decaying biomass from forests that die as climate zones migrate. Finally, there is the possibility of even more fundamental disruptions of the Earth system, such as changes in ocean currents that might occur if air temperature differentials between the equatorial and polar regions are significantly diminished.[77]

Ionizing Radiation

The term *ionizing radiation* refers to the transfer of intense forms of energy by media such as X rays, gamma rays, alpha and beta particles, electrons, protons, neutrons, or cosmic rays, which generate ions in the substances they penetrate. An ion is an atom that has a positive or negative charge, having either gained or lost one or more electrons. In living tissues these highly active atoms can initiate changes that eventually lead to cell death, cancers, and genetic mutations, which may take years or even decades to progress to the point where they can be detected.[78] Ultraviolet, visible, and infrared radiation are not intense enough to cause ionization.

For as long as they have populated the Earth, human beings have been exposed to ionizing radiation from two types of natural sources, cosmic and terrestrial. Most of the cosmic radiation, which comes from outer space either in the form of particles or electromagnetic waves, is intercepted by the atmosphere before it reaches the Earth's surface. Thus, it is only at high levels that cosmic radiation is a significant threat to humans, such as to the crews of high flying aircraft. Terrestrial radiation is emitted in varying amounts by rocks, soil, water, and air. The largest single source of terrestrial radiation is radon gas, which is formed from the decay of radioactive materials in soil and certain building materials. Exposure to natural radiation tends to be relatively stable over time at any given location, but the average levels can vary considerably from one geographic area to another.[79]

Human activities such as the atmospheric testing of nuclear weapons and the nuclear power industry have added to the amount of ionizing radiation in the environment, but in small amounts relative to naturally occurring radiation. Even when nuclear testing in the atmosphere reached its peak in the early 1960s, the total dosage from the explosions amounted to only 7 percent of the exposure the world's population was receiving from natural sources. Cumulatively, the radiation dosage from all of the atmospheric nuclear tests was equivalent to the exposure of the world's population to naturally occurring radiation over a four-year period.[80] However, when human-generated radiation is concentrated geographically for certain periods of time, as in the areas downwind from nuclear test sites or nuclear power facilities where accidents have occurred, the consequences for human health can be serious.

The radioactive materials generated by an aboveground nuclear test reaches the earth in the form of fallout at different times and distances from the detonation site. The types of fallout and the pattern of deposition are determined largely by the elevation and size of the blast. In the case of surface or low-altitude blasts, the convection forces created by the explosion draw up large quantities of soil or sand particles into the fireball, which upon cooling form the nuclei on which radioactive substances from the explosion condense. The relatively large particles generated in this way gravitate out of the atmosphere within hours, mostly within 100 km of the test site. This local fallout may account for as much as 50 percent of total deposition from surface blasts.[81]

With higher-altitude blasts a much larger proportion of the radioactive substances is dispersed in the form of smaller particles that reside in the atmosphere longer and are dispersed by wind currents over a large area before falling back to the Earth's surface. The radioactive particles from smaller nuclear bombs with yields of less than 100 kilotons stay within the troposphere, where they are transported by wind currents before being flushed out by storms or deposited in a dry form, mostly within two months, in a spotty pattern mostly over the same latitude range as the explosion. Explosions of the larger thermonuclear bombs project large amounts of radioactive materials high into the more stable stratosphere, where they may be present for a year or more and be carried around the planet and spread from pole to pole before descending to the troposphere and being washed to Earth's surface.[82]

Local "hot spots" of radiation far from the site of the explosion are possible when precipitation coincides with the passage of clouds of radioactive particles. Such was the case in the vicinity of Troy, New York, in April 1953, when a rainstorm doused the area with a higher dose of radiation than has been recorded anywhere in the United States, except in the region around the nuclear test site in Nevada.[83] Likewise, a combination of regional wind patterns and local precipitation after the Chernobyl accident caused certain regions of Europe, such as southern West Germany, southern and eastern Switzerland, and northern Italy, to receive more radiation than many areas closer to the disabled reactor.[84]

Radioactive substances, or what are known as radionuclides, have widely varying half-lives, the amount of time it takes for them to lose half of their radioactivity. Of the hundreds of types of radionuclides generated in nuclear explosions, most decay so quickly that they pose no threat to human populations, especially if they remain suspended in the atmosphere even for a few hours. Some radionuclides have considerably longer half-lives and thus can be sources of radiation exposure after they precipitate to the Earth's surface. The most important of these longer-lived substances are iodine-131, strontium-90, cesium-137, and carbon-14. Much of the radioactivity from iodine-131 dissipates during a few weeks, from strontium-90 and caesium-137 during a few decades, and from carbon-14 over thousands of years.[85] Thus, the radiation dosage from iodine-131 is normally concentrated in areas near test sites, whereas the long-lived radionuclides are still potent even after drifting in the atmosphere for a year or more and being distributed globally.

Radioactive pollutants become a threat to human health when skin is exposed to them or they are ingested into the body either through respiration or the consumption of contaminated substances, such as milk from cows that have eaten grass that has absorbed radioactive fallout. Iodine-131 is taken up selectively by the thyroid gland, where it may induce cancers. Strontium-90 reacts like calcium in the human body in that it is deposited in bone tissues, where it can cause bone cancer and leukemia. Ionizing radiation has been linked to a variety of other health effects including skin, lung, and breast cancers. It can be especially damaging to human fetuses by causing deformities and impairing growth and development. Mutations occurring in the chromosomes of reproductive cells exposed to ionizing radiation may be transferred to future generations and increase in incidence in succeeding generations.[86]

Direct exposure to large doses of radioactive fallout, as was experienced by residents of Hiroshima and Nagasaki in 1945, induces severe cases of radiation sickness that may be fatal within a few days or weeks. Those who survive the immediate effects are much more susceptible to radiation-related diseases later in life. The effects of lesser, so-called "global" doses of radiation are more difficult to track because the tumors they stimulate may not be detected for decades after the exposure, which raises uncertainties about whether they were caused by certain incidents of radiation exposure. Moreover, records are often not available on the specific amounts of exposure received by various groups, either because they were never kept or because they have been withheld by governments. Despite these complications, scientists have tried to ascertain whether there is a threshold level of radiation exposure beyond which delayed health effects are likely and whether repeated exposure to lower-level doses over an extended period of time has a cumulative effect. The preponderance of evidence now suggests that any level of exposure to ionizing radiation can be harmful and that the effects of repeated low-level doses of radiation are cumulative. The findings have led scientists to revise upward their estimates of the effects of low-level radiation, and some warn that no level of radiation is entirely safe.[87] By one estimate, the radioactive material from the atmospheric nuclear tests conducted between 1945 and 1980 that will be delivered to the world's population by 2000 will cause 430,000 cancer deaths, mostly in the Northern Hemisphere.[88]

Two Basic Types of Pollution Problems

The four major international and global pollution problems that have been described in this chapter—acid deposition, depletion of the ozone layer, the enhanced greenhouse effect, and ionizing radiation—are of two basic types. The first could be described as *transport and deposit* pollution, in which the atmosphere picks up pollutants emitted in one place and carries them laterally over the surface of the Earth until they gravitate out of the skies or are washed out of the air by precipitation. Most of these pollutants remain in the atmosphere for relatively short periods—normally a few hours, days, or weeks—during which they may be transported hundreds and even thousands of kilometers and in the process cross one or more national boundaries. While suspended in the atmosphere, some of the pollutants, such as the precursors of acid deposition, undergo chemical changes as they are exposed to solar energy and react with moisture and other chemicals.

Transport-and-deposit pollution is normally not a serious problem while suspended in the atmosphere, although it may reduce visibility and be aesthetically displeasing. It may also block solar radiation and thus have a slight cooling effect on the lower atmosphere, which may to some extent counter tendencies toward greenhouse warming caused by other pollutants. These types of pollutants do their damage when they leave the atmosphere as they are inhaled or ingested by human beings or other species or are deposited on soil, vegetation, bodies of water, or building surfaces. The atmosphere returns to its original composition once it is rid of the pollutants. However, the human and environmental toll from the deposited pollutants may be long-term if not irreversible, as in the case with genetic mutations caused by radioactive fallout or a freshwater ecosystem that is severely disrupted by acidic precipitation.

Air pollutants in a second group are troublesome because they trigger long-term *atmospheric changes,* in particular ones that alter the extent to which the atmosphere modulates the flow of energy moving to and from the Earth. These pollutants generally reside in the atmosphere for much longer periods, some for decades or even centuries. CFCs, halons, and other substances that deplete the ozone layer never do precipitate from the atmosphere but rather continue to rise until they are broken apart by intense solar radiation in the stratosphere. The principal greenhouse gases may eventually be absorbed by terrestrial or aquatic systems but without causing significant environmental damage. In fact, atmospheric carbon is an essential raw material for the growth of plants.

Because of the lengthy time polluting substances of this second type reside in the atmosphere, it may be decades before curbs on emissions have a significant effect on the problems they address. If the stream of new pollutants is interrupted, concentrations of greenhouse gases will eventually level off and begin to decline, and natural processes may begin restoring the atmosphere to its previous chemical balance, but over a period measured in decades if not longer. However, some of the effects of the atmospheric changes are likely to be irreversible. Marine food chains disrupted by the killing off phytoplankton by UV-B radiation may never recover. Significantly modified patterns of vegetation and ocean circulation patterns caused by global warming could drive long-term or permanent changes in the Earth system.

Conclusions

This primer has provided a brief introduction to the evolution of the atmosphere and its contemporary nature as well as to the impact of human activities, in particular those generating air pollutants. This overview suggests several general observations. First, the atmosphere has undergone and continues to undergo naturally occurring changes that range in timescale from hours and days to millions and even billions of years. Some of these changes are cyclical; others are evolutionary. Second, at any given time the state of the atmosphere is affected by many natural factors, the most important one being the flow of energy from the sun. It is also shaped by the terrestrial and marine components of the Earth system, including the living organisms residing in them, which in turn are affected by atmospheric conditions. Third, relatively small variations in the concentrations of certain trace gases can trigger major changes in atmospheric processes that can have immense environmental consequences. Finally, over the past century humanity has evolved to a point that the huge quantities of air pollutants it generates and its extensive alteration of land cover are having significant effects on the composition and dynamics of the atmosphere.

It is not possible in a single chapter to convey the immense complexity of the subject of the atmosphere and the ways in which it affects and is affected by the other major components of the Earth system, in particular the oceans, the landmasses, and the biosphere. Nor is it possible to delve into the scientific uncertainties and disagreements on many of the topics that were touched upon, such as the extent and severity of damage to forests caused by acidic precipitation, the risks that low doses of radiation pose to human health, and the amount of global warming that is likely if growth trends continue in the emission of greenhouse gases. More could also have been done to explore the numerous ways in which the atmospheric problems described in this chapter are interrelated, such as the impact that a substantial loss of phytoplankton due to ozone depletion may have on the amount of CO_2 absorbed by the oceans. It should also be borne in mind that our knowledge of the atmosphere and the impact of human activities on it are evolving rapidly. Within a decade or two scientists may have provided answers to many of the current outstanding issues, and new discoveries may have fundamentally altered our perceptions of the degree to which humanity is triggering significant changes in the atmosphere and ultimately to the larger Earth system.

Chapter 3

INTERNATIONAL SCIENTIFIC COOPERATION

Scientists have learned much about the complex nature of the atmosphere over the past 150 years, especially since the International Geophysical Year of 1957–58. They have solved many of the mysteries about how the atmosphere came into being billions of years ago and tracked how its chemical composition evolved to make the planet's environment so uniquely hospitable for a multitude of life forms. Systematic monitoring and research on atmospheric conditions have greatly improved the accuracy and temporal range of weather forecasts and identified many of the determinants of weather and climate, including global circulation patterns. Science has detected growing concentrations of anthropogenic pollutants and investigated their impact on human health and the environment and, more importantly, how human activities are irreversibly altering the basic chemistry of the atmosphere in ways that could have immense environmental consequences. Taking a holistic perspective on the Earth system and integrating information from numerous disciplines, scientists have explored how atmospheric phenomena are shaped by the oceans, the landmasses, the aggregate of living organisms, and, most importantly, solar energy.

The state of the atmosphere at any one time and location cannot be adequately explained without knowledge of the regional and global circulation patterns that govern local conditions. Thus, comprehending the complex nature of the atmosphere, which is without borders and in perpetual motion, is inherently an international and indeed a global challenge. This chapter traces the evolution of scientific knowledge about the atmosphere and climate and the human impacts on them. Emphasis is placed on the international dimensions of the scientific endeavors that generated this knowledge, in particular the data-gathering networks, research programs, and assessment projects that have been organized and implemented by international institutions and nongovernmental scientific unions.

The World Meteorological Organization (WMO) has taken the lead among United Nations agencies in studying the atmosphere, but numerous others have also played key roles. Among these are the World Health Organization (WHO), the United Nations Environment Programme (UNEP), the United Nations Economic Commission for Europe (ECE), the Food and Agricultural Organization (FAO), the United Nations Scientific Committee on the Effects of Atomic Radiation (UNSCEAR), the International Civil Aviation Organization (ICAO), and the United Nations Educational, Scientific and Cultural Organization (UNESCO).[1] These international organizations have often formed partnerships with national agencies, such as the National Aeronautics and Space Administration (NASA) and the National Oceanographic and Atmospheric Administration (NOAA) of the United States, and the national scientific academies of many countries. Nongovernmental organizations, such as the International Council of Scientific Unions (ICSU) and the International Institute for Applied Systems Analysis (IIASA), have also been important facilitators of research on atmospheric matters, often in partnership with international agencies such as WMO and UNEP. Especially noteworthy are the contributions that ICSU has made to global atmospheric research through its Scientific Committee on the Problems of the Environment (SCOPE) and several of its constituent unions, in particular the International Union of Geodesy and Geophysics (IUGG) and its subsidiary body the International Association of Meteorology and Atmospheric Physics (IAMAP).[2]

These international scientific endeavors have proceeded concurrently on several tracks. The original one, which dates back to the mid nineteenth century, has been directed toward improving weather forecasting both through systematic monitoring of weather conditions and research on the determinants of weather and climate. Another series of major international research projects, which goes back almost as far, has sought an enhanced scientific understanding of the composition and dynamics of the atmosphere in a more general way. In recent decades considerable attention has been given to the impact of air pollutants on the atmosphere, with largely independent series of international programs looking at the problems of the transboundary movement of pollutants that cause acidic deposition, the depletion of the ozone layer, human contributions to global climate change, and radioactive fallout and its health effects. Finally, over the past decade greater emphasis has been placed on studying the atmosphere as part of the larger Earth system as well as the fundamental changes in it being driven by human activities.

MONITORING WEATHER AND CLIMATE

For as long as they have inhabited the planet, humans have been fascinated by the vicissitudes of weather and climate, which until the modern era have been dominating forces in their lives. Records from early civilizations, such as those in Mesopotamia, Chaldea, China, India, and Egypt, contain numerous references to weather. Observers in these ancient societies undoubtedly noted patterns that made it possible for them to anticipate weather, such as a halo around the moon preceding precipitation. Lacking a scientific understanding of the relationships among such phenomena, traditional societies devised elaborate mythologies to anticipate and explain the occurrence of various weather phenomena.[3]

Meteorology, the scientific field devoted to the study and forecasting of weather and climate, can be traced to Aristotle's book *Meteorologica*, which disputes theories about the weather that were circulating in the fourth century B.C. Many of Aristotle's explanations of the weather prevailed through the Middle Ages until they were challenged during the Renaissance. Some of his hypotheses are consistent with modern explanations of certain weather phenomena.[4]

The evolution of meteorology was made possible by the systematic and standardized keeping of weather records. Data collected over time in one place, as it has been in some regions of China for five thousand years, is useful in describing the climate of a region and in anticipating seasonal cycles. Information on the means and extremes of temperature and precipitation is especially helpful to agriculture. Monitoring weather conditions simultaneously at geographically dispersed locations led to the realization that storms moved across the surface of the Earth with weather fronts, rather than being events that arose and died at the same location, as had been previously assumed.[5]

In 1653 King Ferdinand of Tuscany organized the first known weather reporting network, which included seven stations scattered around northern Italy and neighboring countries.[6] Concern about the dangers that the storms posed for seafarers led to the convening of the First International Meteorological Conference in Brussels in 1853, at which delegates from eight European countries and the United States agreed to uniform procedures for reporting weather conditions from ships plying the world's oceans. Twenty years later representatives from the national meteorological services of twenty countries, meeting at the First International Meteorological Congress in Vienna, established the International Meteorological Organization (IMO). The principal task of the IMO was to incorporate the weather stations operated by national meteorological and hydrological services into an international network that would collect data on weather and ocean conditions using uniform standards and procedures and then transmit this information via telegraph to a central location to be compiled and distributed. Over the next eighty years the IMO greatly facilitated weather forecasting as it expanded its network, refined its measuring techniques, and facilitated the timely dissemination of weather data.[7] Despite being an association of directors of national weather services, the IMO had operated as a nongovernmental organization, which limited its resources and the roles it could play in facilitating weather forecasting globally.

New challenges and opportunities for meteorology in the postwar era led the directors of IMO to dissolve what had been a highly effective organization and to transfer its functions to a new intergovernmental body, the World Meteorological Organization (WMO), which would assume the status of a specialized agency in the United Nations system.[8] The WMO has substantially expanded its mission since it was established in 1950, embarking on an array of major projects both on its own and jointly with other governmental and nongovernmental organizations as concern has grown about weather and climate and humanity's potential impact on them.

In 1961 the United Nations General Assembly adopted a resolution on international cooperation in the peaceful uses of outer space, which among other things challenged WMO to take advantage of recent technological breakthroughs in the fields of satellites, telecommunications, and computers in order to improve weather forecasting and advance the field of atmospheric science.[9] WMO responded by launching the World Weather Watch (WWW), which became an enhanced international

system for coordinating the weather reporting networks of the meteorological and hydrological services of the member states. This global
weather monitoring network, which became operational in 1969, has
been regarded as a highly successful project and a prototype for other
international monitoring programs.

The WWW became one of the original parts of the Global Environmental Monitoring System (GEMS), a program sponsored by UNEP that
now coordinates thirty international networks that track the state of atmospheric, terrestrial, and marine components of the Earth system.[10]
The WWW is comprised of three principal parts. The first is the Global
Observing System, a network of ninety-five hundred land stations that
is supplemented by a vast array of other platforms used to collect meteorological data on a global basis, including balloons, aircraft, ships,
satellites in polar and geostationary orbits, moored and drifting buoys,
and ice stations. The second component, the Global Data-processing
System, is comprised of three World Meteorological Centers, located in
Melbourne, Moscow, and Washington, D.C., along with a network of
eighteen Regional Centers. The system collects, compiles, and analyzes
the data generated by the monitoring system and issues forecasts that
are available to national weather services. The third part, the Global Telecommunications System, rapidly transmits data, reports, and forecasts
between weather stations and the various global, regional, and national
meteorological centers.[11]

An appreciation of the critical interrelationships between the atmosphere and oceans led WMO to collaborate with UNESCO's International Oceanographic Commission (IOC) in establishing the
Integrated Global Ocean Services System (IGOSS) to collect and dis-
seminate data on the oceans, such as surface and upper-layer temperatures, salinity, and currents at various depths. The program,
which parallels the WWW and uses many of the same automated
buoys as observation stations, as well as two hundred ships from
more than twenty countries, has been used to monitor the El Niño
phenomenon in the Pacific Ocean and will provide information for
forecasting and assessing the impact of global climate changes on
the oceans, including the rise of sea levels.[12]

WMO has undertaken several more specialized monitoring projects,
including one that focuses on tropical storms. Typhoons, cyclones, and
hurricanes, which originate in the tropical regions of the Pacific, Indian,
and Atlantic Oceans, respectively, have long been a bane of seafarers

and the cause of considerable loss of life and destruction on land due to storm surges, gale force winds, heavy rainfall, and floods when they reach land in any of fifty countries that are vulnerable to them. An unusually active typhoon/cyclone season in 1970, including a powerful cyclone that killed two hundred thousand in low-lying areas of Bangladesh, led WMO to work with the Economic and Social Commission for Asia and the Far East to create the Tropical Cyclone Project, which was later upgraded and renamed the Tropical Cyclone Programme. The program, which was initiated in 1971, provides timely warnings on the presence and course of these intense storms as well as the threat of related phenomena such as storm surges and flooding.[13]

EXPANDING KNOWLEDGE OF ATMOSPHERIC PROCESSES

While monitoring meteorological conditions over large geographical areas is an essential first step in enhancing weather forecasting, it has long been recognized that further improvements in the enterprise required a deeper scientific understanding of the geophysical processes that cause weather and climate. A series of international scientific research projects dating back to the nineteenth century have contributed much to a fuller understanding of atmospheric processes and how they are related to other parts of the Earth system, such as the oceans, land areas, the biosphere, and solar activity.

The First International Polar Year of 1882–83 was the earliest attempt to organize an intensive period of international scientific research on the natural systems of the planet. Twelve countries (Austria/Hungary, Denmark, Finland, France, Germany, the Netherlands, Norway, Russia, Sweden, the United Kingdom, Canada, and the United States) participated in the joint endeavor, which established fourteen research stations around the North Pole and sent two expeditions to Antarctica. The participants collected meteorological data and conducted research on geomagnetism, auroral phenomena, ocean currents, the structure and motion of ice, and the composition of air. Scientists from forty-four nations collected many types of data on a larger scale during the Second International Polar Year of 1932–33 and explored how meteorological information from the polar regions could improve the accuracy of weather forecasts in other parts of the world.[14]

The next major international scientific undertaking was the International Geophysical Year (IGY), which took place over an eighteen-month period in 1957–58 as Cold War tensions were deepening. Under the leadership of Lloyd Berkner, ICSU organized the IGY to provide the world scientific community with an extensive new body of data on the Earth's geophysical processes. The project was timed to coincide not only with the twenty-fifth anniversary of the Second International Polar Year but also with the first launchings of Earth-orbiting satellites by the Soviet Union and the United States and with what was anticipated to be an unusually intense period of solar activity.[15]

The IGY, which involved thirty thousand scientists and technicians from sixty-six countries, generated vast amounts of scientific information on previously unexplored realms of the planet, in particular the Antarctic continent, the depths of the oceans, the lower and upper reaches of the atmosphere, and outer space. Certain days were designated for intensive data collection to provide simultaneous observations of geophysical phenomena from locations scattered around the world. The ground rules of the project specified that the data gathered were to be made available to scientists and researchers throughout the world for further analysis. The project was hailed as a major success not only for what was learned about the geophysical processes of the planet and its atmosphere but also for demonstrating that international scientific cooperation could flourish in spite of superpower rivalries.[16]

In the aftermath of the IGY a group of leading American meteorologists called attention to the need for major research initiatives focusing on atmospheric processes if significant advancements in weather forecasting were to be achieved. Their efforts soon led to creation of the National Center for Atmospheric Research (NCAR) in Boulder, Colorado. The scientists went on to propose an international program of research on the global atmosphere. The General Assembly endorsed the idea in 1962 by adopting a resolution that invited ICSU, through its international unions and national academies, to plan an expanded program of atmospheric science research that would complement WMO's meteorological services and research programs.[17] ICSU took up the charge by joining WMO in sponsoring the Global Atmospheric Research Programme (GARP), which ran from 1968 to 1981.[18]

Immense amounts of data on atmospheric conditions were needed to develop quantitative models of the global atmosphere that would take advantage of revolutionary advancements in high-speed computer technologies. Thus, as was the case with several of the earlier international scientific undertakings, the principal components of GARP were intensive periods of data collection. The first was the Atlantic Tropic Experiment (GATE), in which seventy countries collaborated in collecting vast amounts of data from June to September 1974 that would enable scientists to gain new insights into the role the tropics play in global circulation patterns. GARP's second major data gathering effort was the Global Weather Experiment (GWE), which at the time was the most ambitious and complex international scientific undertaking in the field of meteorology. Conducted over a twelve-month period beginning in December 1978, GWE was a detailed study of the dynamics of the atmosphere as a whole, which enabled scientists to understand better the development of weather systems. The project yielded an immense amount of data on a wide range of variables that were collected by more than nine thousand land stations and seven thousand ships, along with numerous aircraft, ocean buoys, and a network of geostationary and polar orbiting satellites.[19]

GARP was a highly successful international scientific endeavor that achieved a quantum jump in knowledge of the complex circulation patterns of the global atmosphere. By furthering the development of quantitative models of atmospheric processes, it effectively transformed weather forecasting from an art to a science, thereby substantially enhancing the accuracy and range of weather forecasts. GARP also is notable for the way in which it combined the imagination and insight of the scientific community with the stability and resources of national governments through a partnership between ICSU and WMO. In these ways GARP laid the groundwork for even more extensive international projects begun during the 1980s on the phenomena of stratospheric ozone depletion and global warming.[20]

ASSESSING THE RADIATION THREAT

French physicist Henri Becquerel, while experimenting with the effects of sunlight on phosphorescent substances in 1896, unexpectedly discovered that uranium emitted rays that penetrated opaque surfaces.[21] Coincidentally, the discovery of naturally occurring ionizing radiation came only months after German physicist Wilhelm Conrad Roentgen noticed that he had created a new form of penetrating radiation, which became known simply as X rays, while experimenting with cathode rays. In the years that followed French scientists Marie and Pierre Curie identified other elements that gave off energy, including plutonium and radium, and used the term *radioactive* to describe this characteristic. For their work the Curies along with Berquerel received the 1903 Nobel Prize in physics. The Polish-born Marie Curie was also awarded the 1911 Nobel Prize in chemistry for her continuing research on radioactivity.[22]

Radioactive materials were used widely in consumer products in the early twentieth century until the perils they posed for human health became known. Radium compounds were painted on watch faces to make them shine in the dark. A belief that radioactive substances had medicinal and curative qualities led to their extensive use in health products such as facial creams, tonics, toothpastes, and mouthwashes as well as in treatments at health spas.[23] The implications of high doses of radiation to human health became apparent during World War I when extensive medical use of X rays led to the deaths of as many as one hundred radiologists.[24]

The International Society of Radiology convened the International Congress on Radiology in London in 1925, which created the International Commission of Radiation Units and Measures that was to standardize the definition of concepts and reporting practices in the field. A second Radiology Congress held in Stockholm in 1928 established the International Commission on Radiological Protection, whose members were elected on the basis of professional reputation rather than nationality, with the principal emphasis of the body being on worker safety.[25]

Growing international concern about the potential health effects of the atmospheric testing of nuclear bombs by the United States, the Soviet Union, and the United Kingdom led the United Nations General Assembly in 1955 to create the United Nations Scientific Committee on the Effects of Atomic Radiation (UNSCEAR). The committee's primary mission was to assess information provided by United Nations member states and specialized agencies that addressed two questions. First, what were the levels of ionizing radiation in the environment from both natural and human sources? Second, what effects was the radiation having on human health and the environment generally?[26] UNSCEAR's periodic reports to the General Assembly have been lauded as classics in international scientific cooperation.[27] While the committee works with the International Atomic Energy Agency (IAEA) on some matters, the latter's involvement with nuclear bombs has been limited primarily to preventing their proliferation to additional states.[28]

Research on the dispersion of radioactive substances from nuclear testing and accompanying health effects was hampered by the secrecy of the governments conducting the tests as well as by inadequate monitoring and record keeping on radioactive fallout and the doses received by specific people.[29] Nevertheless, UNSCEAR has been able to secure enough information to trace the movement of radioactive material through the atmosphere and to plot trends in deposition over time and space, which have given a fairly good indication of the relative exposure of human populations to ionizing radiation from natural and human sources. UNSCEAR has continued to monitor radiation levels, even though the peak exposures of the world's population occurred in the mid 1960s following the most intensive period of atmospheric testing.[30]

Miners working the eastern European mines of Schneeberg and Joachimsthahl in the late Middle Ages are the first known casualties of ionizing radiation. It was not known until the early twentieth century, however, that the high rates of fatal lung disease experienced by these miners were attributable to exposure to radioactive radon gas in the mines.[31] In recent decades UNSCEAR's assessments of the effects of ionizing radiation on human health and other living organisms have been based on numerous studies and reports of national governmental agencies and independent groups of scientists, a notable example of the former being the United States Academy of Science Committee on the Biological Effects of Ionizing Radiation (BEIR).

The most intensively studied groups of people exposed to ionizing radiation are the Japanese survivors of the Hiroshima and Nagasaki explosions, who have had higher rates of leukemia and other cancers than would normally be expected. Much has also been learned from epidemiology studies of the participants in various testing programs, including thousands of troops who were marched into highly radiated places immediately after explosions, as well as of people living immediately downwind from nuclear test sites in places such as the Pacific Islands, the American states of Nevada and Utah, and Kazakhstan in the former Soviet Union.[32] More will be learned in the coming decades from monitoring the health of people exposed to varying levels of radiation from the 1986 Chernobyl disaster.

MONITORING TRANSBOUNDARY AIR POLLUTION

Robert Angus Smith, an English alkali inspector—or pollution watchdog—is credited with being the first to study systematically the dispersal and impact of industrial age air pollutants. His 1852 report on the chemistry of rain water at locations in and around the industrial city of

Manchester noted substantially greater concentrations of sulfuric acid in the samples collected within the city, which he linked to the fading of color in textiles and the corrosion of metals. Smith's further research on air chemistry is summarized in his book *Air and Rain: The Beginnings of a Chemical Climatology* (1872), in which he coins the phrase "acid rain" and lays out some of the theories that underlie the contemporary understanding of the problem. Smith's pathbreaking work received little notice until the 1950s, when Canadian scientist Evil Gorham's studies of the chemistry of precipitation in the Lake District of northwestern England identified the combustion of fossil fuels at nearby smelters as the cause of the acid rain responsible for the deterioration of vegetation, soils, and the quality of lake water.[33]

Another early indication of the problem of acidification was the progressive decline of freshwater salmon fisheries in southern Norway as early as 1900, followed by the disappearance of brown trout in some lakes of the region by the 1920s, phenomena that were soon attributed to acidic deposition. In the coming decades the rivers and lakes of southern Norway and southeastern Sweden became increasingly acidic, but it was not until the postwar era that there was a serious and widespread deterioration of freshwater environments.[34]

Systematic monitoring of the chemical content of precipitation dates back to 1948, when soil scientist Hans Egnér set up a network of sampling buckets around Sweden. The network was first extended to Norway, Denmark, and Finland and later to most of western and central Europe. Poland and the Soviet Union were added to the network during the IGY, bringing the total number of sampling sites to more than one hundred. The project became known as the European Air Chemistry Network, and in 1956 the International Meteorological Institute in Stockholm assumed responsibility for its coordination.[35] Samples taken by the network over the next fifteen years revealed that the acidity of rainfall was rising and becoming more widespread geographically.[36]

The first clues that air pollutants drifted large distances were observations of dirty snow made more than a century ago in regions of Norway far from any known pollution source. At the time some Norwegians surmised that the cause of the phenomenon may be soot from the industrial regions of the British Isles. Little was known about the role that atmospheric processes played in the transport, dispersal, and chemical transformation of pollutants until the 1960s, when Swedish soil scientist Svante Odén used trajectory analyses of air masses to discover that the acidity of precipitation in Scandinavia was attributable to emissions of sulfur from the United Kingdom and western and central Europe.[37]

Odén's contention that an "insidious chemical war" was being waged among the nations of Europe was initially met with skepticism from other scientists but was confirmed by numerous later studies. The first of these was conducted by the Organization for Economic Cooperation and Development (OECD), which has investigated a number of environmental policy problems related to trade among its members. The OECD coordinated a network of seventy-six stations that monitored air pollution in eleven countries between 1972 and 1974, with the data being reported to the Norwegian Institute for Air Research. An OECD report released in 1977 noted that a substantial part of each country's sulfur emissions was transported by air currents beyond their borders. Moreover, over half of the deposition of sulfur pollutants in five of the countries was found to come from foreign sources.[38]

The United Nations Economic Commission for Europe (ECE), assisted by WMO and UNEP, then took over responsibility for coordinating the monitoring of air pollution in the larger European region by setting up the Cooperative Programme for Monitoring and Evaluating the Long-Range Transmission of Air Pollutants in Europe, usually known by the acronym EMEP. The EMEP network has grown to nearly one hundred nationally operated stations situated in rural areas of twenty-five countries, including the western parts of the former Soviet Union. Originally sulfur dioxide was the only air pollutant the stations monitored, but later data were also collected on nitrogen oxides and ozone. In addition the EMEP stations report on wind speed and direction as well as other meteorological conditions, information which is used to track the movement of the pollutants. These data on air pollution and meteorological conditions are compiled at centers in Lillestrøm, Norway, and Moscow and combined with figures supplied by states on emissions of certain air pollutants. This information is used to generate tables indicating how much each of the European countries contributes to the sulfur and nitrogen deposition in each of the other countries (see Table 5.3). These figures on the "export" and "import" of air pollutants, which are generally accepted as being valid by negotiators, have been critical to the development and enforcement of international rules on air pollution in the European region.[39]

Other clues about the great distances that the atmosphere transports air pollutants came with the surprising discovery that the air over distant reaches of the Arctic is quite heavily polluted during the winter and early spring. Glenn E. Shaw, an atmospheric scientist from the University of Alaska, first observed what became known as "Arctic haze" while taking samples of what he thought would be pristine air over Barrow on the northwest coast of Alaska in the spring of 1972. Since then, the phenomenon has been studied by a small community of scientists from the Arctic rim countries, who exchange their findings periodically at conferences of the Arctic Chemical Network that was formed in 1977. They investigated the source of the puzzling pollution by matching the distinctive "chemical signatures" (ratios of various chemicals) in the Arctic air samples to those of known pollution sources and by tracking distinct surges of air pollutants using meteorological data. This detective work revealed that most of the pollutants comprising Arctic haze originate in the heavily industrialized, mid-latitude areas of the Eurasian continent and are carried by seasonal wind currents on a journey thousands of miles northward and then clockwise around the Arctic basin. Scientists are still uncertain about the consequences of the haze, in particular the damage it may do to the fragile ecosystems of the region or the impact it may have on climate by altering the radiative balance of the atmosphere and land.[40]

Efforts have also been made within the long-range transboundary air pollution (LRTAP) regime to monitor and conduct research on the impacts of acid deposition. Several International Cooperative Programs (IPCs) were established during the mid 1980s to study the impacts of acidification on forests, bodies of fresh water, anthropogenic materials, and crops. In each case a country that was actively engaged in research on one of the types of impacts volunteered to undertake the development of a regional research program.[41] The IPC on forests that was organized by Germany has been especially active, having developed standardized criteria for forest damage that have been applied to more than 30 percent of Europe's forests.[42]

In North America, the other region where acid precipitation has long been a major transboundary issue, monitoring and research have been conducted on a national basis. In the United States heightened acidic precipitation was observed as early as 1963 at the geographically remote Hubbard Brook Experimental Forest in New Hampshire. It was not until 1978, however, that a national network was established for sampling and analyzing precipitation chemistry in the United States in the form of the privately operated National Atmospheric Deposition Program. In 1980 the United States government undertook the ten-year National Acid Precipitation Assessment Program (NAPAP), an ambitious $500 million project involving two thousand scientists that was to conduct a comprehensive assessment of scientific knowledge on the causes and consequences of acid precipitation. NAPAP reports issued in 1987 and 1990 were widely criticized for downplaying the effects of acid deposition for what some alleged were political reasons and for offering few policy-relevant conclusions.[43] Canada created a precipitation sampling network in 1976 and conducted an assessment of the effects of acid deposition from 1985 to 1990.

Pollution and atmospheric chemistry have also been monitored on a global basis through monitoring networks coordinated by UNEP's Global Environmental Monitoring System (GEMS). By the late 1950s WMO had become increasingly concerned about the changing composition of the atmosphere due to human-generated pollutants. Thus, the organization created the Background Air Pollution Monitoring Network (BAPMoN), which became operational in 1968 with twenty reporting stations. The network has grown to more than two hundred stations, many of which are also part of the EMEP network, that are located at varying distances from population centers and industrial regions. BAPMoN stations collect information on precipitation chemistry, aerosols and turbidity, and CO_2 but not necessarily on all of these variables at each station. By sampling air that is not heavily polluted from local sources and in some cases is virtually pristine, BAPMoN makes it possible to draw inferences about the extent to which the atmosphere as a whole is being contaminated after pollutants are mixed and distributed by air currents.[44]

WHO, with support from UNEP, established a complementary air pollution network known as the Urban Air Quality Monitoring Project, or GEMS/Air. The network, which became operational in 1973, is comprised of stations in more than eighty of the world's larger cities in fifty countries. Many of the cities have three stations—one each in commercial, industrial, and residential areas—that take measurements of SO_2 and suspended particulate matter. The principal purpose of the network is to monitor the impact of air pollution on human health and to identify cities with pollution levels that pose a serious threat to health.[45]

INVESTIGATING THREATS TO THE OZONE LAYER

While the existence of the ozone layer has been known since the nineteenth century, it was not until the 1930s that the first systematic observations were made by G. M. B. Dobson and a small number of meteorologists at scattered locations around the world, using an instrument Dobson developed known as the spectrophotometer. As one of its contributions to the IGY of 1957–58, WMO organized the first international network for standardized observations of the ozone layer. The Canadian government set up the World Ozone Data Center in Toronto in 1960 to collect and publish the data generated by the network. WMO upgraded its capacity to monitor the ozone concentrations at various altitudes by establishing the Global Ozone Observing System (GO_3OS) in 1969. The system has grown to 140 surface stations around the world, which are supplemented by satellites measuring ozone concentrations from space.[46]

Paul Crutzen, a meteorologist at the University of Stockholm, was the first to raise the possibility that human activities might pose a threat to the ozone layer. He surmised that nitrous oxides, because they are chemically inert, would rise to the stratosphere where they would be broken apart by UV radiation to form nitric oxide, which would destroy ozone molecules through a catalytic chain reaction.[47] Crutzen's theory soon prompted concern that nitrous oxides from the exhausts of the supersonic transport planes under development at the time might pose a threat to the ozone layer. By one estimate the operation of more than five hundred SSTs planned by the United States, the United Kingdom and France jointly, and the Soviet Union would cause an average global reduction of ozone in the range of 3–23 percent, with reductions as high as 50 percent in areas with heavy SST traffic.[48]

In 1971 the United States Department of Transportation undertook an extensive study called the Climatic Impact Assessment Program (CIAP), which was to investigate the potential environmental effects of the planes, including the alleged threat to the ozone layer from SSTs. The project, which involved scientists from ten countries, issued a report in 1974 that was misleadingly portrayed as debunking the theory that SSTs posed a threat to the ozone layer. The report actually concluded that it would take a world fleet of more than 125 SSTs to have a detectable effect on the ozone layer, while 500 aircraft would cause a 16 percent loss of ozone in the Northern Hemisphere and an 8 percent loss in the Southern Hemisphere. At the time a fleet of even 100 SSTs was considered unlikely due to the cancellation of the American and Soviet SST programs and a sharp reduction in plans for producing British/French Concordes. Thus, concern about the SST threat to the ozone layer quickly dissipated.[49]

While the CIAP assessment was in progress, two scientists at the University of Michigan, Richard Stolarski and Ralph Cicerone, speculated that chlorine present in the stratosphere could also destroy ozone.[50] One potential source of stratospheric chlorine was exhaust from the space shuttle being planned by the United States. This threat to the ozone layer was soon discounted because of the limited use the shuttle was expected to receive.

Attention then shifted to the possibility that chlorofluorocarbons (CFCs) might be a much larger source of ozone-depleting chlorine. In 1971 the British scientist James Lovelock was surprised to discover large quantities of CFC-11 and CFC-12 while experimenting with an instrument he invented to measure minute amounts of trace gases. Lovelock regarded this phenomenon as a curiosity, a potentially useful one that implied "no conceivable hazard."[51] Then in 1974 Mario Molina, a postdoctoral student working with Sherwood Rowland at the University of California—Irvine, theorized that CFC molecules released into the atmosphere would eventually rise to the stratosphere. There they would be broken apart by intense UV radiation, which would release highly reactive chlorine molecules that would break up large numbers of ozone molecules.[52] Two decades later Molina and Rowland along with Crutzen were awarded the Nobel Prize in chemistry for their pathbreaking work on threats to the ozone layer.

Numerous efforts were made during the following decade to test the Molina/Rowland hypothesis that CFCs posed a serious threat to the ozone layer. WMO responded in 1976 by initiating the Global Ozone Research and Monitoring Project to investigate the extent to which anthropogenic pollutants were responsible for ozone depletion. The United States began monitoring ozone concentrations from outer space in 1979, using an instrument called the Total Ozone Mapping Spectrometer (TOMS), which was on board the polar-orbiting Nimbus 7 weather satellite. Naturally occurring variations in ozone concentrations by time and latitude made it difficult to detect whether human-emitted pollutants were causing any loss of ozone.[53]

WMO and UNEP cosponsored a major assessment of scientific knowledge on the human impact on the ozone layer in partnership with NASA and NOAA, the West German Ministry for Research and Technology, and the Commission of the European Communities. The assessment involved 150 scientists from ten countries, who participated in thirty focused research workshops held in 1984–85. The group's 1986 report forecast that continued emissions of CFCs 11 and 12 at the 1980 rate could cause a 9 percent average global depletion of stratospheric ozone by the mid twenty-first century. It also identified several other compounds in the CFC and halon chemical families that also had ozone-depleting properties and thus should be included in predictive models of ozone loss.[54]

Just as the WMO/UNEP assessment was coming to a conclusion, the scientific community was jolted by the discovery of the "Antarctic ozone hole." The British Antarctic Survey, a little-known group of scientists led by Joseph Farman, had been taking readings of trace gases in the atmosphere using the Dobson spectrophotometer from Halley Bay on the Antarctic coast. The data collected was unremarkable until 1977, when ozone levels showed the first signs of slippage. By 1982 ozone concentrations during the Antarctic spring were 20 percent less than they had been during the 1960s. Concerned that this unexpected observation may be caused by the malfunctioning of equipment in the harsh climatic conditions of the Antarctic or by errors in their calculations, the British team did not report its findings until 1985. By that time they had observed a 40 percent decline in ozone concentrations in the spring of 1984, both over Halley Bay and 1500 km away at Argentine Island.[55]

The report of the British Antarctic Survey prompted NASA scientists at the Goddard Space Flight Center to reexamine the data on the ozone layer that it had collected using the Nimbus 7 satellite since 1979. It turned out that the satellite's instruments had detected a significant drop in ozone concentrations over the Antarctic during the spring seasons, but computers processing the data were programmed to disregard such low readings as anomalies attributable to equipment error. The satellite data showed that the area of unusually low ozone concentrations was approximately the size of the continental United States.[56]

Intense curiosity and anxiety over the Antarctic ozone hole prompted NASA, NOAA, and the National Science Foundation of the United States, with support from the Chemical Manufacturers Association, to organize hastily a project called the National Ozone Expedition (NOZE). A team of thirteen scientists led by NOAA atmospheric chemist Susan Solomon flew to McMurdo Sound, Antarctica, to make observations during the Arctic spring of 1986, which would hopefully determine the cause of the ozone hole. Using ground-based instruments and balloons, the team detected high levels of ozone-depleting compounds in the air over the station.[57] NASA sponsored a NOZE II expedition during the 1987 spring season, which included one hundred scientists, engineers, and technicians, including some drawn from industry. Research aircraft flying dangerous missions into the intensely cold Antarctic skies collected air samples that conclusively demonstrated that the ozone hole was caused by anthropogenic pollutants.[58]

The findings from the NOZE studies were fed into another major international major assessment effort being undertaken by a group called the Ozone Trends Panel, which was organized by NASA in October 1986 with support from WMO, UNEP, NOAA, and the Federal Aviation Agency (FAA). For sixteen months one hundred scientists from ten countries pored over data available from ground, aircraft, and satellite observations. The panel's disturbing report, issued in March 1988, concluded that ozone depletion was no longer just a theory but was a reality on a global basis. Ozone concentrations had dropped by 1.7 to 3.0 percent over populated areas of the Northern Hemisphere, which was much faster than had been anticipated by the scientific models of the day. Moreover, ozone levels over Antarctica were down 50 percent from normal levels during the spring of 1987, and the phenomena lasted longer and occurred over a larger area than in previous years. Finally, the report noted that the presence of pollutants of human origin in the skies over the Antarctic region provided definitive evidence that the ozone hole was not a naturally occurring phenomenon.[59]

Later in 1988 UNEP created four expert panels that continue to provide negotiators with timely assessments of scientific and technical information in the form of period synthesis reports that are relevant to negotiations addressing the ozone depletion problem. A science panel has been focusing on projections of ozone loss; a technology panel on the prospects for developing substitutes for ozone-depleting substances; an environmental effects panel on the consequences of ozone loss and increased exposures to UV radiation; and an economic panel on the costs entailed in phasing out ozone-depleting substances, shifting to substitutes and making this transition affordable in developing countries.[60] Monitoring of the state of the ozone layer has continued during the 1990s, with new data being reported periodically by agencies such as WMO, UNEP, NASA, and the United Kingdom's Stratospheric Ozone Review Group indicating additional thinning of the ozone layer both over Antarctica and the northern temperate regions, as well as signs that a hole may be developing over the north polar region.[61] Less scientific effort has been devoted thus far to monitoring and research on environmental impacts of ozone loss.

INVESTIGATING THE PROSPECTS FOR CLIMATE CHANGE

Several well-known European scientists of the nineteenth century laid the foundations for the contemporary understanding of climate change. In 1827 the French mathematician and physicist Jean-Baptiste-Joseph Fourier hypothesized that the atmosphere retains heat in much the same way as a greenhouse remains warm in winter on a sunny day. In the 1860s the English scientist John Tyndall measured the capacity of carbon dioxide (CO_2) and water vapor in the atmosphere to absorb infrared radiation and hypothesized that variations in the concentrations of these "greenhouse" gases could have an impact on the Earth's surface temperatures and that glacial periods may have been caused by unusually low levels of CO_2.[62]

Toward the end of the century Svante Arrhenius, a Swedish recipient of one of the first Nobel Prizes for chemistry, calculated that a doubling of concentrations of CO_2 in the atmosphere would cause a warming of the lower atmosphere of 4–6° C.[63] His calculations were only slightly higher than recent projections of warming that would result from a doubling of greenhouse gases (GHG). What Arrhenius did not anticipate, however, was the exponential growth in the burning of fossil fuels during the twentieth century, which would significantly advance the date when a doubling of CO_2 in the atmosphere was expected to occur. Several decades later the British scientist G. S. Callendar revisited the issue and analyzed weather data from two hundred sites that showed a warming trend since 1880, which he considered on balance to be a desirable development.[64] The prospect of significant human-induced warming received little further attention until the 1950s, when Roger Revelle and Hans Suess of the Scripps Institution of Oceanography warned that humans, by burning rapidly increasing amounts of fossil fuels, were "carrying out a large scale geophysical experiment of a kind that could not have happened in the past nor be reproduced in the future."[65]

Systematic monitoring of concentrations of CO_2 in the atmosphere was begun in 1958 in conjunction with the IGY. Charles Keeling, another Scripps scientist, set up CO_2 monitoring stations at the Mauna Loa Observatory in Hawaii and at the South Pole. These locations were chosen both for their distance from industrial pollution sources and for being places where the air was well mixed. The readings taken at these and several other stations reveal that, aside from seasonal variations, atmospheric concentrations of CO_2 have grown steadily from 313 ppm in 1958 to 360 ppm by 1995. More extensive data on CO_2 levels are now being gathered at twenty-three BAPMoN monitoring stations.[66]

Concern about climate change increased when a spate of unusual climatic phenomena occurred in different parts of the world during the late 1960s and the 1970s. Five years of widespread drought across the Sahel region of Africa prompted the United Nations Conference on the Human Environment in 1972 to call upon WMO to work with ICSU to undertake projects aimed at better understanding the causes of climatic changes.[67] Between 1972 and 1975 severe droughts also took place in the Soviet Union, seasonal monsoons were weak in India, unusually cold winters and short growing seasons plagued North American agriculture, and a strong El Niño phenomenon off the coast of Peru coincided with the collapse of the previously abundant anchovy harvest. These climatic aberrations, combined with the effects of new agricultural policies of the United States and Soviet Union and disruptions in energy supply resulting from OPEC's oil embargo in 1973–74, led to a period of global food scarcity that became known as the "world food crisis."

During the 1970s atmospheric scientists and climatologists were of two minds on whether the predominant climatic tendency was toward a general warming or cooling of the planet.[68] Some were of the belief that a slight global cooling trend that had prevailed for several decades would be reinforced by anthropogenic pollutants lingering in the atmosphere as aerosols, which would shield the Earth from enough solar radiation, causing temperatures to decline. Exceptionally cold winters occurring in the Northern Hemisphere during the late 1970s even prompted speculation that the world might be slipping into another ice age. The widespread uneasiness about the erratic weather of the decade was captured by the title of John Gribbin's book *What's Wrong with the Weather?*[69] Despite these signs of cooling and the climatic aberrations of the 1970s, a growing group of climatologists held to the belief that warming would become the dominant global climatic trend due to the rapid buildup of greenhouse gases in the atmosphere.[70]

The all too apparent vulnerability of human societies to variations in climate and the concern of a growing number of scientists that significant climate change could take place due to both natural and human factors prompted WMO to convene the First World Climate Conference in Geneva in February 1979.[71] The conference, which was attended by 350 scientists from fifty countries who represented a variety of climate-related disciplines, conducted what at the time was the most comprehensive review of scientific knowledge on climate and its relationship to other parts of the natural world; also under review were the impacts that climate changes have on human societies and in turn the effects that human activities are having on climate.[72] Agreeing on the critical need for more knowledge on the prospects for climate change as well as its causes and consequences, the conference participants proposed a major international effort to study climate to be known as the World Climate Programme (WCP).[73]

WMO, in partnership with UNEP and ICSU, inaugurated the WCP at its eighth World Meteorological Congress in 1979. The program is structured around four component projects: (1) the World Climate Data Programme, which seeks to compile all types of climatological and other data that may have a bearing on climate change; (2) the World Climate Applications Programme, which studies how climate data can be used in sectors such as food production, energy, and transport; (3) the World Climate Impact Study Programme on the consequences that climate change will have on natural systems and human communities; and (4) the World Climate Research Programme, which would build on the experience of GARP in assessing the extent to which climate can be predicted and the degree to which human activities influence the weather.[74] WMO has been responsible for the data and applications projects and shares responsibility with ICSU for the research programs, while UNEP oversees the impact studies. These programs have contributed much to knowledge of the highly complex subject of climate change, taking into account the influences of the oceans, ice masses, land surfaces, and the biosphere.

As part of the launching of the World Climate Programme, an international conference of climate specialists was convened in Villach, Austria, in 1980 to assess the role of CO_2 and other greenhouse gases in climate variations. The conference report concluded that the threat of human-induced climate change was an important international issue but that it was premature to give serious consideration to controlling CO_2 emissions in view of the state of scientific knowledge of the problem. Five years later WMO, UNEP, and ICSU invited scientists from twenty-nine countries to a second, and what turned out to be a landmark, assessment conference in Villach to consider new information on climate change, including the projections of global warming made by several large computerized general circulation models of the atmosphere. The resulting report suggested that a rise of 1.5–4.5° C in global mean temperatures was "highly probable" with a rise in atmospheric GHG concentrations equivalent to a doubling of CO_2, which would occur as early as the 2030s. Such a warming was in turn likely to cause sea levels to rise in the range of 20–140 cm. The report cautioned that major uncertainties remained but nevertheless argued that enough was now known to call upon policy makers to explore options for limiting emissions of greenhouse gases. It also recommended that more intensive research be undertaken on the probable impacts of global warming.[75] Two follow-up workshops were held in Bellagio, Italy, and Villach in 1987 to discuss the subject of developing policies for responding to climate change.

WMO and UNEP established the Intergovernmental Panel on Climate Change (IPCC) in 1988. The IPCC was to be a much more elaborate project to sift through and consolidate the rapidly growing body of knowledge that was developing on climate change. It was hoped that the IPCC would achieve an international scientific consensus on global warming that would inform negotiations on measures to curb climate change. Under the direction of Bert Bolin, who had brought Sweden's concerns about transboundary air pollution to the Stockholm conference of 1972, the initial phase of the IPCC involved upwards of a thousand scientists appointed by the governments of seventy countries. Among them were most of the scientists who had made significant contributions to the scientific literature on climate change and its impacts. Three working groups were created to carry out the work of the IPCC: one focusing on scientific evidence of global warming; a second on the impacts that climate change would have on agriculture, forestry, natural ecosystems, water resources, and human settlements; and a third on potential policy responses for limiting or adapting to global warming. The first report of the IPCC, which was released in Sundsval, Sweden, in August 1990, reaffirmed and expanded upon the principal conclusions of the 1985 Villach report, including the projections of temperature increases if atmospheric concentrations of CO_2 continued to increase.[76]

WMO and UNEP jointly sponsored the Second World Climate Conference held in Geneva from October 29 to November 7, 1990. The first part of the conference was a six-day technical meeting attended by 747 scientists, who met to review progress made during the first decade of the World Climate Programme and to consider its future directions in light of the recent report from the IPCC. The scientists issued a strongly worded statement expressing their general agreement with the IPCC's assessment of the seriousness of the threat of global warming. The statement went on to observe that a failure to limit GHG emissions would subject the world to climate change that "would place stresses on natural and social systems unprecedented in the past 10,000 years."[77] It further ventured the opinion that "technically feasible and cost-effective opportunities" were available to all countries to reduce CO_2 emissions and that industrial countries should be able to reduce their CO_2 emissions by 20 percent by 2005.[78] The ministers who attended the second part of the conference did not agree on such specific targets for reducing GHG emissions, as will be discussed in chapter 7.

The IPCC has continued its work during the 1990s in order to provide updated assessments of scientific knowledge on climate change that will inform ongoing international negotiations on further measures to address the problem. A supplementary report was issued in January 1992 in time for the final talks on the Framework Convention on Climate Change that was signed later in the year in Rio. It reaffirmed most of the conclusions drawn in the earlier report but revised slightly downward projections of the likely range of global warming and sea level rises. It also noted that aerosols from sulfur emissions may have had a cooling effect over the Northern Hemisphere.[79] The IPCC then undertook a second full assessment of the climate change phenomenon that took into account projections from a new generation of computer simulations studies. By allowing for the impact of sulfate aerosols of human origin, these simulation models had achieved a substantially closer fit between predicted and actual temperature patterns. This breakthrough was reflected in the draft summary of the results of the second IPCC assessment, released in September 1995, which suggested that the world's climate experts were now in agreement that human activities have been at least partly responsible for a 0.3°–0.6° C increase in average global temperatures observed over the past 100 years.[80]

INTEGRATED MONITORING AND RESEARCH PROGRAMS

As concerns about the state of the atmosphere came to the forefront of the global environmental agenda during the latter half of the 1980s, it was readily apparent that much about global atmospheric processes was still not adequately understood in spite of the growing array of monitoring and research programs initiated by WMO, UNEP, ICSU, and other international agencies. Intensified international scientific research efforts were needed to answer important questions about the nature of atmospheric changes and their consequences, the role of human activities in these changes, and the relationship of atmospheric processes to other components of the Earth system, in particular the oceans and landmasses. Only when these questions were more fully answered would it be possible for negotiators to agree upon international policy responses to mitigate these atmospheric changes.

Toward this end the Tropical Ocean-Global Atmosphere Programme, known as TOGA, was inaugurated in 1985 as part of the World Climate Research Program (WCRP). TOGA was a decade-long project aimed at more fully understanding how circulation patterns in the oceans are related to significant annual variations in climate, such as those associated with the El Niño and Southern Oscillation occurrences in the tropical and sub-tropical Pacific. An enhanced capacity to anticipate these powerful phenomena may be useful for mitigating the impacts of droughts, floods, and other extreme events that are often associated with them.[81] The WCRP's World Ocean Circulation Experiment (WOCE), which runs from 1990 to 1997, is a major international effort to collect data on ocean currents throughout the world that may have a bearing on climate variations. To follow up on the work of TOGA and the WOCE, the Joint Scientific Committee of the WCRP is undertaking a study of Climate Variability and Predictability, known as CLIVAR, which focuses on factors such as oceans, ice and snow masses, and land surfaces that are associated with relatively slow climate changes.[82]

A recommendation of the Second World Climate Conference led to the establishment of the Global Climate Observing System (GCOS), which will augment and link several monitoring systems providing data that is critical to models used in climate forecasting. GCOS, which is sponsored jointly by WMO, IOC, UNEP, and ICSU as part of the World Climate Programme, will build upon existing atmospheric monitoring systems, such as the World Weather Watch, but will also systematically collect information on phenomena such as clouds and aerosols, which have an inadequately understood impact on the atmosphere's radiative balance. Moreover, GCOS will be linked to other international networks that monitor certain aspects of the oceans, land surfaces, and hydrological cycles that influence weather and climate, one example being the IOC's Integrated Global Oceans Observing System (IGOOS). Once developed, it is hoped that GCOS will be as useful in anticipating climate changes as the World Weather Watch has been in forecasting short-term weather conditions.[83]

On another front the Executive Council of WMO decided in 1989 to create the Global Atmospheric Watch (GAW) to enhance and coordinate several of its monitoring programs, in particular BAPMoN and GO_3OS. This institutional umbrella was designed to improve the capacity to monitor changes in atmospheric concentrations of GHGs, the stratospheric ozone layer, levels of various pollutants, and the acidity of precipitation. The GAW is to serve as an early warning system for future changes in atmospheric chemistry and to provide a more adequate database for research on the atmosphere to inform policy making into the twenty-first century.[84]

These augmented monitoring programs will provide a broader database for efforts to understand a nexus of environmental developments that has become known by the rubric "global change." The international scientific community adopted this terminology to refer to changes taking place in the basic physical, chemical, and biological processes of the Earth system, including the atmosphere, which occur naturally or are attributable to human activities.[85] Global change became the subject of a major research initiative called the International Geosphere-Biosphere Programme (IGBP), launched by ICSU in 1986, which includes an extensive array of projects that will be carried out through the 1990s and beyond. The IGBP follows in the tradition of the International Polar Years of 1882–83 and 1932–33 and the IGY of 1957–58 but is much larger in the magnitude and duration of the scientific effort. With its headquarters at the Royal Academy of Sciences in Stockholm, the IGBP is linked to numerous other international and national research and monitoring programs. It complements the World Climate Research Program, one of the basic components of WMO's World Climate Programme, in a partnership that is informally known as the Global Change Research Program.[86]

Much of the emphasis of the IGBP is on the physical, chemical, and biological interactions that take place within and between the terrestrial, ocean, and atmospheric components of the Earth system in order to understand the changes in the Earth system that are taking place, including those that are influenced by human activities. The program is centered around six core projects that focus on the subjects of atmospheric chemistry, terrestrial ecosystems, the biological drivers of the water cycle, coastal land-ocean interactions, ocean circulation, and past global changes. A task force on Global Modeling and Analysis is exploring data needs and how large data sets can be integrated into models of the Earth system. A network of regional research centers known as the Global

Change SysTem for Analysis, Research, and Training (START) is being set up to involve more scientists from developing countries and to make scientific information on global change more readily available to policy makers.[87]

Soon after the IGBP was launched it became apparent that the social sciences should be drawn into global change research so that people could gain a better understanding of the dynamics and causes of the human behaviors that were altering the basic Earth system, the impact that global environmental change might have on human communities, and the types of policies that might lessen the human impact on natural processes.[88] Toward this end the International Social Science Council and UNESCO have sponsored the Human Dimensions of Global Environmental Change Programme (HDGECP) as a complement to ICSU's IGBP. Inaugurated in 1990 after several years of preparatory meetings, the program has a research agenda that is organized around six broad topics: demographic trends, industrial growth and resource use, land use patterns, human perceptions of environmental problems, the capacities of political institutions, and strategies for achieving environmental security and sustainable development.[89]

CONCLUSIONS

This chapter has plotted the long history of monitoring and research on weather, climate, the atmosphere, and pollution that preceded the extraordinary blossoming of atmospheric research over the past few decades, which was stimulated by international organizations such as WMO, UNEP, and ICSU. Important early breakthroughs in understanding these subjects were made by scientists such as Aristotle, Robert Angus Smith, Jean-Baptiste-Joseph Fourier, Jean Tyndall, Marie and Pierre Curie, Svante Arrhenius, Evil Gorham, Svante Odén, Paul Crutzen, Mario Molina, and Sherwood Rowland. The remarkable advancements of recent decades in knowledge of atmospheric processes and the effects of human pollutants would not have been possible without data from international monitoring networks, such as the European Air Chemistry Network, EMEP, the World Weather Watch, the Background Air Pollution Monitoring Network, the Urban Air Quality Monitoring Project, and the Global Ozone Observing System. Scientific assessments conducted by international groups, such as the United Nations Scientific Committee on the Effects of Atomic Radiation, the Ozone Trends Panel, and the Intergovernmental Panel on

Climate Change, have been an important foundation for negotiations on international atmospheric policies.

The success of international efforts to learn about the atmosphere can be attributed to many factors, not the least of which has been the availability and dissemination of new technologies in fields such as monitoring instruments, satellites, computers, and telecommunications. Meteorology and the atmospheric sciences have also benefitted from the close working relationships among international agencies, such as WMO, and independent scientific associations, in particular ICSU, on major international research endeavors such as the International Geophysical Year, the Global Atmospheric Research Programme, the World Climate Programme, and the International Geosphere-Biosphere Programme. It is also significant that international scientific cooperation on many aspects of the atmosphere was not significantly hindered by the political tensions of the Cold War era.

Chapter 4

THE NUCLEAR TESTING REGIME

The nuclear arms race, which had its origins in the Second World War and continued for the superpowers until the breakup of the Soviet Union in 1991, raised the specter of a cataclysmic war that could abruptly destroy modern civilization and drastically transform the global environment. The testing and production of the tens of thousands of nuclear bombs that could accomplish such an apocalypse contaminated the planet with quantities of radioactive substances that have posed a threat to the health of current and future generations of human beings.

Citing the imperatives of national security, the five nations that openly developed nuclear arsenals—the United States, the Soviet Union, the United Kingdom, France, and China—not only discounted but also painstakingly concealed the substantial environmental and health costs of their programs. These included the effects of thousands of tests of nuclear explosives conducted in the atmosphere, outer space, underwater, and underground; the huge quantities of perilously stored radioactive wastes from the production of nuclear warheads; and the intentional exposure of thousands of people to radioactivity in order to study its impact on the human body. The full extent of these problems is only now coming to public attention as the shroud of official secrecy over military-related nuclear activities is finally being lifted in the aftermath of the Cold War.

In keeping with the focus of the book on international efforts to preserve the atmosphere, this chapter examines the problems associated with radioactive contamination from the more than five hundred nuclear tests that were conducted in the atmosphere. Radioactive substances from these tests were dispersed liberally around the world, and thus there were problems of transboundary pollution and the contamination of a global commons by a few states in ways that posed threats to the welfare of the people of many others. This chapter does not dwell on the nuclear arms race generally or even the continuing efforts to achieve a comprehensive test ban that would also prohibit underground testing, which appears to be within reach in the mid 1990s.

Compared with the normally slow pace and inconclusiveness of efforts to deal with global problems, the case of atmospheric testing is an open-and-closed success story in the international regulation of an activity that was threatening to the environment and human health. The issue came to a head in the early 1960s when the superpowers conducted intensive series of tests in the atmosphere following a three-year hiatus. In 1963 the United States, Britain, and the Soviet Union, the three countries responsible for almost all of the early testing, reached agreement on a treaty that indefinitely bans nuclear testing in the atmosphere as well as in outer space or underwater. The agreement was also promptly embraced by most states that had not yet tested nuclear weapons. While France and China continued to conduct atmospheric tests until 1974 and 1980, respectively, the overall numbers of such explosions and the resulting radioactive fallout was down dramatically from the period before the treaty. No known atmospheric tests of nuclear explosives have taken place since October 1980.

THE HISTORY OF ATMOSPHERIC TESTING

The evolution of nuclear explosives can be traced to 1905 when Albert Einstein introduced his famous theory of relativity, which suggested that matter could be converted into energy. A second scientific breakthrough occurred during the 1920s with the discovery of subatomic particles, which led to speculation that large amounts of energy could be released by splitting atoms through the process of fission. In 1938 the German scientists Otto Hahn and Fritz Strassman became the first to induce a fission reaction by using neutrons to split the nuclei of uranium atoms, which released the energy locked in the atoms. Scientists working in the United States, including immigrants from Nazi Germany, soon discovered that the fissioning of a uranium atom set off a chain reaction in which neutrons emitted by successive fission reactions instantaneously split additional uranium atoms in a process that generated enormous amounts of energy.[1]

Reacting to warnings from scientists that the German government might take advantage of the discovery of fission to develop an atomic bomb so powerful as to be a militarily decisive weapon, the United States in 1941 embarked on the Manhattan Project, a multibillion-dollar crash program to ensure that America would be the first to develop such a bomb. The first sustained atomic chain reaction was set off at the University of Chicago in 1942, while the first test of an atomic explosive took place in the Alamogordo desert of New Mexico on July 16, 1945, two months after the surrender of Nazi Germany. The United States exploded atomic bombs over the Japanese cities of Hiroshima and Nagasaki in August 1945, bringing a quick conclusion to the Pacific theater of the Second World War. Ironically, Germany made a strategic decision during the war to concentrate on the development of rocketry and other experimental weapons rather than on the creation of a nuclear bomb.[2]

The United States continued to push ahead with its atomic weapons program after the war by setting off two highly publicized atomic explosives at Bikini Atoll in the Marshall Islands in 1946. Two years later a series of three tests was conducted under a veil of secrecy at nearby Eniwetak Atoll. The Soviet Union ended the American monopoly in nuclear bombs in 1949 by detonating its first atomic bomb in the steppes of its central Asian republic of Kazakhstan. Great Britain successfully tested an atomic bomb in 1952 near the Monte Bello Islands off the northwest coast of Australia. France joined the nuclear weapons club in 1960 with an explosion at a desert location in its colony of Algeria. China tested its first atomic bomb in its remote Xinjiang Province in 1964.

In 1952 the United States became the first country to test a new generation of nuclear weapons known as hydrogen, or thermonuclear, bombs, which it did at Eniwetak Atoll in the Marshall Islands. The Soviet Union detonated a similar bomb in 1953, as did Great Britain in 1957. The explosive yields of the hydrogen bombs, which were generated by a nuclear fusion process set off by a fission triggering device, could be more than a thousand times greater than those of the atomic bombs dropped on Hiroshima and Nagasaki. Compared to atomic bombs, the hydrogen bombs generated much more radioactive fallout and injected it far higher into the atmosphere, where it remained longer and became globally dispersed.

As is apparent from Figure 4.1, most of the testing of nuclear explosives prior to the adoption of the 1963 Test Ban Treaty was done in the atmosphere. The peak periods of atmospheric testing occurred in 1957–

58, which preceded a moratorium observed by the United States, the Soviet Union, and the United Kingdom, and in 1961–62 after the moratorium was abruptly ended by the Soviet Union. Comparable numbers of tests were conducted during the two periods, 154 and 162 respectively, but the yield was much larger during the latter. Tests conducted during a sixteen-month period from September 1961 to December 1962 accounted for more than half of the megatonage of all atmospheric tests, primarily due to a series of large explosions set off by the Soviet Union, including one of 57 megatons, the largest bomb ever tested.[3]

Figure 4.1. Atmospheric Tests by Year (1945-1995)

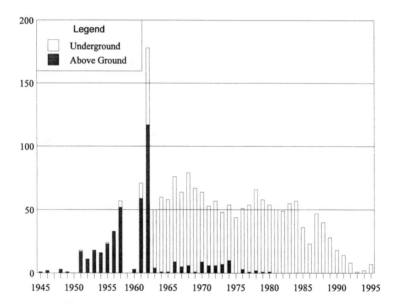

Source: Figures from Norris and Arkin, "Known Nuclear Tests Worldwide," p. 63.

The United States was the most active in conducting tests during the early stages of nuclear weapons development in the 1940s and 1950s. By the end of 1952 the United States had set off 31 nuclear test explosions, compared to only 3 by the Soviet Union and 1 by Great Britain.

When the initial moratorium on testing went into effect in 1958, 172 nuclear explosions had been set off by the United States, 84 by the Soviet Union, and 21 by Great Britain. By conducting 123 atmospheric tests in 1961–62, the Soviet Union nearly caught up with the United States in number of tests and far exceeded it in total megatonage of yield. During the same period the United States accounted for "only" 39 atmospheric tests. Great Britain conducted no tests after 1958, relying instead on an arrangement through which it received technical information from tests conducted by the United States. France and China accounted for all 69 of the atmospheric tests reported after the adoption of the Nuclear Test Ban Treaty in 1963.[4]

It is now known that at least 528 tests were conducted in the atmosphere between 1945 and 1980 (see Table 4.1). The United States conducted 215 of these atmospheric tests, compared to 219 by the Soviet Union, 21 by Great Britain, 50 by France, and 23 by China. The total yield of the atmospheric tests is believed to be approximately 428 megatons, the equivalent of twenty-nine thousand times the yield of the bomb dropped over Hiroshima in 1945.[5] Fifty-seven percent of the total explosive power from the atmospheric tests was released during a sixteen-month period from September 1961 to December 1962. The nuclear powers carried out their atmospheric tests in remote locations in order to minimize both the exposure of human populations to radioactive fallout and political opposition to the testing. The United States conducted 106 of its tests, including all of its hydrogen explosions, at Pacific locations. The earlier tests took place at the Bikini and Eniwetak Atolls in the Marshall Islands in the western Pacific, which were part of a non-self-governing trust territory assigned to the United States by the United Nations Trusteeship Council. In preparation for the test series, the native populations of Bikini and Eniwetak were relocated to other atolls in the island group. Later American tests were held at two locations south of Hawaii, Johnston Atoll and the British test site near Christmas Island. Roughly the same number of atmospheric tests were conducted at a sizable continental test site located in Nevada 140 kilometers northwest of Las Vegas, which was opened in 1951 to provide the United States with a more convenient and secure location for tests. While the bombs tested at the Nevada site were generally smaller ones being developed for tactical use, they nevertheless exposed Americans to health-threatening amounts of radioactive fallout, especially in downwind communities in Nevada and southern Utah.[6]

Table 4.1. Aboveground Nuclear Tests by Country

Country	# of Tests	Test sites	Years
United States	215	Marshall Islands Nevada	1945-1963
USSR	219	Kazakhstan Novaya Zemlya	1949-1963
United Kingdom	21	Australia Christmas Island	1952-1958
France	50	Algeria French Polynesia	1960-1974
China	23	Xingjiang Province	1964-1980

Source: Figures from Norris and Arkin, "Known Nuclear Tests Worldwide," p. 62.

The Soviet Union and China exploded all of their nuclear tests within their territorial boundaries. Most of the early Soviet tests were conducted in the Semipalatinsk region of northeastern Kazakhstan. Later the Soviet Union developed an alternative test site on Novaya Zemlya, a large archipelago in the Arctic Ocean east of the Barents Sea, which was used for testing large thermonuclear explosives from 1957 to 1963.[7] China did all of its atmospheric testing at a test site near Lop Nor in its northwestern Xinjiang Province, an autonomous region sparsely populated primarily by the Uygur people.[8]

Lacking remote, sparsely populated areas within their territorial boundaries, the British and French governments looked for test sites elsewhere. The British government persuaded an accommodative Australian prime minister to allow it to conduct twelve atmospheric tests between 1952 and 1957 at three sites in the vast western reaches of his country. Mounting public concerns in Australia about the large amount of fallout from these tests made it necessary for the United Kingdom to conduct its later tests elsewhere. Using a test site near Christmas Island south of the Hawaiian Islands, the British set off nine more nuclear devices in the atmosphere in 1957 and 1958, including seven hydrogen bombs.[9] France conducted its first four atmospheric tests in 1960–61 in a desert region of its colony Algeria. When Algeria declared its independence in 1962, France looked for new test sites, finally deciding upon Mururoa and Fangatuafa Atolls, located in French Polynesia in the South Pacific, approximately four thousand kilometers south of Hawaii. These sites were used for forty-six atmospheric tests between 1966 and 1974.[10]

THE PREEMINENCE OF SECURITY CONCERNS

From today's perspective, with its heightened environmental sensitivities, it is difficult to conceive how responsible national leaders could approve the detonating of hundreds of nuclear explosives in the atmosphere, thereby exposing their own people and the world's population to heightened amounts of radioactive fallout. The testing programs were initiated with little apparent concern about potential health effects from lesser doses of radiation in areas outside of the immediate vicinity of the explosions. Governmental officials publicly dismissed the potential health and environmental risks from atmospheric testing as being trivial compared to what they argued was the critical importance of developing nuclear weapons for national security. Furthermore, aside from purely strategic considerations, nuclear weapons were looked upon as an important ingredient of the stature and political influence of states in the world community, and a major source of national pride. Thus, the agencies charged with developing nuclear weaponry were permitted to carry out their missions with few rules to prevent contamination of the environment and protect human health.[11]

As the Cold War intensified during the 1950s the United States saw itself locked in a struggle with a diabolical enemy willing to pay any price to achieve world dominance and impose its alien political and economic systems. The overriding objective of the United States was to prevent the spread of communism, with one of the early tests being the Korean War of 1950–53. Believing that the Western alliance lacked the conventional forces needed to prevail against the massive land forces of the Soviet bloc, especially in the European arena, the United States regarded superiority in nuclear weaponry as a vital military equalizer that would deter aggression or blunt an attack if one did occur. The successful Soviet test of an atomic bomb in 1949, years earlier than had been expected, and a thermonuclear explosive in 1953 lent urgency to American efforts to maintain its superiority in nuclear weapons in order to make its deterrent threats credible.[12]

The astonishing destructiveness of the bombs dropped over Hiroshima and Nagasaki jarred the Soviet Union into the realization that it faced a fearsome new threat to its security. Thus, Soviet leaders concluded that their country would be in a vulnerable position vis-à-vis the United States until the Soviet Union ended the American monopoly in nuclear weaponry by developing a comparable nuclear capability. The Cold War tensions that arose between the former wartime allies in the late 1940s and 1950s gave greater urgency to catching up with the United States in nuclear weapons.[13] The Soviet sense of insecurity was further heightened by the establishment of a network of encircling military alliances that were organized by the United States, the rearmament of West Germany and its integration into the Western alliance, the emergence of the United Kingdom as a potentially hostile nuclear power, and the refusal of the United States to swear off the first use of nuclear weapons.[14]

Security and prestige were the overriding considerations for the other three countries that tested nuclear weapons. The British and French sought to develop nuclear arsenals for similar reasons. The McMahon Act adopted by the United States in 1946 ruled out an international partnership in the development of nuclear weapons, something that the British and Americans had actively considered during the Second World War. With the rapid development of Soviet nuclear capabilities during the 1950s, European strategists questioned whether the American nuclear umbrella was a credible deterrent to a Soviet attack on their countries. Europeans wondered whether the USSR was persuaded that the United States would use nuclear weapons in response to a massive Soviet conventional attack against Western Europe, knowing that the Soviet Union could retaliate by destroying American cities such as New York and Washington, D.C. Thus, the British and French governments thought it prudent to develop their own nuclear deterrents to ensure that their countries would not be subject to a Soviet attack.[15]

Possessing nuclear weapons was also a matter of prestige for both countries, whose long-held status as world powers had been diminished by World War II and the erosion of their colonial empires. Furthermore, being less reliant upon the nuclear shield of the United States for their security, they could chart a more independent course in international affairs. This was an especially salient consideration for the French government of Charles de Gaulle, which by the late 1950s was openly seeking ways to undermine the dominant role of the United States in the

Western alliance. Moreover, being regional rivals, neither Britain nor France was content for the other to be the only nuclear power in Europe.[16]

The early impetus for China's acquisition of a nuclear arsenal came from the possibility that the United States would use nuclear weapons to end the Korean War, as well as the more general concern that the United States would flaunt its nuclear advantage to force its will on the east Asian region. The United States had been more overt in its threats to China than the Soviet Union ever was to the American allies that developed nuclear weapons.[17] Moreover, the deep political and ideological rift that emerged between the Soviet Union and China during the late 1950s persuaded Chinese leaders that they should not depend on cooperation with the Soviets in nuclear matters. Having its own nuclear capability would enable China to play a stronger and more independent role in the communist world and be more aggressive than the Soviet Union in confronting the West and in supporting wars of national liberation in the Third World.[18]

POLITICAL REACTIONS TO NUCLEAR TESTING

The diplomatic efforts that led to the Nuclear Test Ban Treaty of 1963 were largely a response to growing uneasiness about nuclear bombs that arose in many parts of the world during the mid to late 1950s. There was concern not only about the uncertain environmental and health effects of radioactive fallout from nuclear tests, but also over the awesome destructive capacity of thermonuclear weapons and their civilization-ending potential if large numbers of them were to be detonated in an all-out nuclear war. Opposition came from national leaders, politicians, scientists, prominent people, public interest groups, and the publics of numerous countries.

International Opposition

An explosion code-named BRAVO, which was set off by the United States at Bikini Atoll on March 1, 1954, aroused the first wave of international concern and opposition to nuclear testing. With a yield of 15 megatons, considerably more than had been anticipated, the thermonuclear explosive was the largest nuclear device the United States ever tested. It left a crater nearly a kilometer in width and several hundred meters deep and thrust millions of tons of radioactive debris into the atmosphere. The blast deposited dangerously high amounts of fallout over an area of twenty-five thousand square kilometers. An unanticipated change in wind direction caused more than two hundred residents of the nearby islands of Rongerik, Rongelap, Ailinginae, and Utirik to be exposed to substantial doses of radiation from the ash that fluttered down on them hours later. The radioactive ash also rained down heavily on a small Japanese fishing boat, the *Fukuryu Maru* (Lucky Dragon), which was just outside a restricted zone declared by the United States. Within weeks ocean currents carried radioactive substances over a wide area of the Pacific, contaminating the catch of nearly seven hundred fishing boats in the eastern Pacific.[19]

The international reaction to the BRAVO test was strong and swift, especially in Japan. The *Fukuryu Maru* returned to its home port two weeks later with its twenty-three-member crew stricken with radiation sickness, two of whom later died. The incident immediately became front page news in Japan, where sensitivity to nuclear perils was high due to painful memories of the suffering caused by the Hiroshima and Nagasaki blasts.[20] The Japanese were especially concerned that American tests were contaminating fish being sold in their markets.[21] Japanese students took their outrage to the streets in violent anti-American demonstrations, while the Japanese government called upon the United States to conduct an official inquiry into the test. The BRAVO test also provoked a heated debate in the United Kingdom, where the opposition Labor Party introduced a parliamentary resolution calling for a summit meeting among the leaders of the nuclear powers to arrange for a cessation of all nuclear testing.[22]

Warning that the tests "showed that man is unleashing power which can ultimately get out of his control," Indian prime minister Jawaharlal Nehru called upon the United States and the Soviet Union to agree to a "stand still" agreement on testing until a comprehensive disarmament treaty could be reached in the United Nations. Nehru also questioned why dark-skinned Asian peoples should be the ones exposed to the effects of nuclear explosions. At a conference in Bandung, Indonesia, in 1955 Nehru joined with other leaders from the newly emergent Asian and African countries in expressing concern about exposure to nuclear fallout and requesting a cessation of nuclear testing.[23] The United Nations Trusteeship Council debated resolutions introduced by India and the Soviet

Union calling for an end to American tests in the Marshall Islands on grounds that they were inappropriate activities for a trust territory.[24]

A second wave of international opposition to nuclear testing gained momentum in 1957 in reaction to extensive new rounds of atmospheric testing by the United States and the Soviet Union as well as to the United Kingdom's announcement that it would test a thermonuclear bomb at its new Christmas Island test site. The strongest official protests came from Japan, which was receiving substantial doses of fallout from the large Soviet tests. The Japanese also feared that the British tests would further contaminate fisheries over a large area of the Pacific, thus endangering their fishing industry. The West German *Bundestag* passed a resolution asking the three nuclear powers to suspend nuclear testing pending negotiation of an arms control agreement. Nobel laureate Dr. Albert Schweitzer launched a campaign to arouse public opinion in opposition to further testing, and numerous scientists signed a petition calling for an end to nuclear testing. The argument against testing was increasingly being made on moral grounds, in particular that it was unethical for the nuclear powers knowingly to expose people throughout the world to growing amounts of radioactive fallout without their consent, or what was referred to as the injustice of "radiation without representation."[25]

The Debate in the United States

The BRAVO explosion provoked a lively public debate in the United States among scientists, politicians, and activists about whether radioactive fallout from the nuclear tests posed such a significant threat to human health that serious consideration should be given to discontinuing them. Prominent scientists such as Ralph Lapp and Linus Pauling were outspoken in warning that radioactive fallout posed a serious health threat to present and future generations. In rebuttal spokesmen for the Atomic Energy Commission (AEC), which was responsible for carrying out the United States testing programs, sought to reassure the American public by arguing that the radioactivity to which they were being exposed as a result of the tests was an insignificant addition to naturally occurring radioactivity and other sources such as medical X rays. Much of the scientific debate focused on the issue of whether there was a threshold level of radiation exposure below which there was no threat to human health or, alternatively, whether any radiation exposure could have adverse health effects.[26]

Nuclear testing became an issue during the 1956 presidential election campaign when the losing candidate, Democrat Adlai Stevenson, suggested that the United States declare a unilateral moratorium on testing as a first step to encourage the Soviet Union to do likewise.[27] Various associations and political action groups—the American Friends Service Committee, the Women's International League for Peace and Freedom, the National Society for a Sane Nuclear Policy (known as SANE), and the Council of the Federation of American Scientists, to mention a few—joined the chorus calling for a worldwide cessation of nuclear weapons tests.[28] In 1957 a subcommittee of the Joint Committee on Atomic Energy, chaired by Rep. Chet Holifield from California, conducted hearings on the threats posed by nuclear radiation and concluded (1) that low levels of radiation posed a more serious threat to human beings, especially as a cause of genetic mutations, than had previously been reported and (2) that the level of testing over the past five years could constitute a hazard to the world's population.[29] At that time there were opposing views within the Eisenhower administration on the desirability of a test ban, with the Department of Defense and the AEC arguing strongly against a ban, while the Department of State was more receptive to the possibility.[30]

Public opinion polls taken during the 1950s and early 1960s suggested that the American people were generally not concerned about nuclear fallout. The immense BRAVO explosion in April 1954 provoked some immediate public anxiety, but not as much to the radioactive fallout that was spewed into the atmosphere as to the fearsome power of the bomb, which AEC director Lewis Strauss suggested could destroy a city the size of New York City.[31] A Gallup poll conducted weeks after the BRAVO test found that 71 percent of those interviewed believed that the United States should go ahead with its planned hydrogen bomb tests in the Pacific.[32]

Public opposition to nuclear testing surged in 1957, as reflected in a Gallup survey that found that 63 percent of the respondents agreed that the United States should cease testing if other countries did likewise. This rise in public opposition to testing coincided with the rather intense public debate about the issue, including the congressional hearings. A year later, however, another Gallup survey found 60 percent of the respondents of the opinion that the United States should not stop testing. Concern about fallout declined during the 1958–61 moratorium, as indicated by a 1961 survey, which found 61 percent responding negatively to the question "Do you think there is enough fallout in the air right now to be a danger to people or not?" Four years earlier 52 percent believed that fallout from nuclear testing was dangerous. Sixty-six percent of respondents to a Gallup survey in March 1962 favored the resumption of atmospheric testing by the United States.[33]

Whatever anxieties Americans might have had about the health effects of radioactive fallout were effectively neutralized by an intensive public information campaign of the AEC, which sought to persuade the American public that there was nothing to fear from the atmospheric tests. The public also seemed persuaded that the potential risks associated with fallout from atmospheric tests were inconsequential compared to the threat that falling behind the Soviet Union in the nuclear arms race would pose to the survival of the Free World.[34]

THE PATH TO THE TEST BAN TREATY

The Test Ban Treaty adopted in 1963 was an outgrowth of negotiations that can be traced back to 1946 and which took place in a variety of forums both within and outside of the United Nations. The objectives of the negotiations shifted with time between general disarmament, disarmament limited to nuclear weapons, an end to all nuclear tests, and a stop to the spread of nuclear weapons to additional states. The negotiations specifically aimed at banning atmospheric nuclear tests were but a brief episode during the early 1960s in a larger process of international arms control efforts that continue to this day.

Negotiating Forums

While arms control was not explicitly a charter responsibility of the United Nations, it was soon recognized as being instrumental to the preservation of world peace. In its first resolution in 1946 the General Assembly established the United Nations Atomic Energy Commission, which was to make recommendations to the Security Council on how to eliminate nuclear weapons and ensure that atomic energy would be used only for peaceful purposes. In 1952 the commission was merged with a parallel body on conventional armaments to form the United Nations Disarmament Commission. Its membership, as with its predecessors, was limited to members of the Security Council plus Canada. The Disarmament Commission, which was enlarged to twenty-six members in 1957 and to include the entire membership of the United Nations in 1958, continues to be a general forum for discussing arms control issues.

By the late 1950s much of the negotiation on arms control generally, and more specifically on test bans, was taking place in smaller committees comprised of the major actors. The most significant of these was the Eighteen Nation Disarmament Committee (ENDC), which was created in 1961 at the initiative of the United States and the Soviet Union to report to the General Assembly and the Disarmament Commission. In 1969 ENDC was expanded to twenty-six members and became known as the Conference of the Committee on Disarmament. In 1979 the group was enlarged to forty members and became known as the Committee on Disarmament, which to the present has been the principal forum for discussion of a comprehensive test ban. At a more intimate level, the United States, the Soviet Union, the United Kingdom, France, and Canada began meeting privately in 1953 as a subcommittee of the Disarmament Commission in an effort to resolve their differences on disarmament priorities.[35]

Negotiations on the more specific subject of a nuclear test ban began in 1958 in Geneva in a forum limited to the United States, the Soviet Union, and the United Kingdom, known as the Conference on the Discontinuance of Nuclear Tests. When these talks were adjourned in January 1962, ENDC took up the test ban issue and encouraged the resumption of negotiations among the three original nuclear powers. The Test Ban Treaty was finally hammered out at an informal negotiating session among the three in Moscow in July 1963.[36] Table 4.2 presents a chronology of the events in the evolution of the test ban regime.

The Early Negotiations

For a brief period in 1946 it appeared that a nuclear arms race might be averted, making it unnecessary to test additional nuclear weapons in the atmosphere. The United States offered a proposal to the UN Atomic Energy Commission, labeled the "Baruch Plan" after its chairman, which would prohibit the manufacture of atomic weapons and destroy all existing weapons once an inspection system was in place. All nuclear materials would be transferred to an international authority that would have a monopoly over further nuclear activities undertaken for peaceful purposes. Violators would be subject to stiff penalties imposed by the Security Council that could not be vetoed. The Soviet Union rejected the proposal for a variety of reasons, including the intrusiveness of the

Table 4.2. Chronology of the Test Ban Regime

1945	(July)	First U.S. nuclear test
	(August)	Atomic bombs dropped over Hiroshima and Nagasaki
1946	(January)	Creation of UN Atomic Energy Commission
		Baruch Plan proposed
1949	(August)	First Soviet nuclear test
1952		UN Disarmament Commission (UNDC) established
	(October)	First British nuclear text
1954	(March)	U.S. BRAVO test at Bikini Atoll
1958	(March)	Soviet Union proposes a testing moratorium
	(October)	Informal testing moratorium begins
		Three-power talks begin
1960	(February)	First French nuclear test
	(May)	U-2 incident puts talks on hold
1961	(August)	USSR resumes nuclear testing
1962	(January)	Three-power talks adjourn
1962	(March)	Talks resume in Eighteen Nation Disarmament Commission
	(October)	Cuban Missile Crisis raises East-West tensions
1963	(July)	Test Ban Treaty Adopted in Moscow
1964	(October)	First Chinese nuclear test
1974	(September)	Last French above ground test
1980	(December)	Last Chinese above ground test

inspection procedures and the prospect that the United States would have a monopoly in nuclear weapons and know-how if the plan was not implemented to its conclusion.[37]

The Baruch Plan was one of several grandiose and unrealistic proposals offered during the first decade of the nuclear era that envisioned the possibility of a world free of nuclear weapons. The British and French jointly proposed an elaborate plan in 1954 that would require deep reductions in conventional forces followed by the elimination of nuclear weapons and the establishment of an inspection system. The next year the Soviet Union offered a plan that was largely compatible with the British/French proposal and appeared to be in the realm of what the United States had indicated it could accept. The prospects for such an agreement quickly dissolved, however, when it became apparent that it was not technically possible to detect concealed stocks of nuclear weapons with any measure of confidence. International discussions subsequently shifted away from the highly ambitious goal of disarmament to the more modest objective of banning the testing of nuclear weapons as a first step in slowing the nuclear arms race and discouraging the entry of other nations.[38]

The first negotiations on a test ban among the nuclear powers took place in London in 1957 at the last meeting of the subcommittee of the United Nations Disarmament Commission that included the three nuclear powers and Canada. The surge of international and domestic pressure for an end to nuclear testing at that time spurred the United States to suggest for the first time that it was willing to separate the test ban issue from the larger issue of disarmament. At the same meetings the Soviet Union indicated that it might accept a control system for monitoring an agreement prohibiting nuclear tests, after arguing for years that such a system was not necessary.[39]

The Moratorium

The Soviet Union put the United States in an awkward position by announcing on March 31, 1958, that it would discontinue all further tests of nuclear weapons if the other nuclear powers would do likewise. The announcement was condemned in the West as a Soviet propaganda ploy designed to mobilize world opinion to pressure the United States into calling off its HARDTACK series of tests planned for the Pacific during the summer, which had already evoked considerable controversy. To prevent the Soviets from gaining a technical advantage from the timing of a moratorium, the United States proceeded with the series, which became its most extensive program of thermonuclear explosions.[40]

To blunt international criticism of its HARDTACK series in the face of the Soviet proposal for a testing moratorium, the United States proposed that, as a first step toward a test ban agreement, scientists from both sides meet to determine whether it was technically possible to detect tests of nuclear explosives underground or in the atmosphere and outer space. A Conference of Experts with participants from eight countries, equally divided between East and West, convened in Geneva during the summer of 1958. The conference's report suggested that an international control system comprised of 160–170 manned control stations on land and ten on ships should be able to detect test explosions as small as five kilotons. Later another working group concluded that satellites could be used to detect explosions in space.[41]

Upon completing the HARDTACK series, the United States on August 22, 1958, offered to suspend its nuclear testing for one year beginning on October 31 provided the Soviet Union agree not to conduct additional tests during the period. Negotiations on a test ban agreement would be held during the moratorium. The American proposal mentioned the possibility of extending the moratorium to a second and third year if additional time were needed to complete negotiations on the test ban. The Soviet Union did not officially agree to the moratorium proposed by the United States but nevertheless did accept the invitation to negotiate a test ban. All three nuclear powers engaged in a round of testing in anticipation of the beginning of the moratorium. The United States series known as HARDTACK II, which was conducted in Nevada, demonstrated that nuclear testing could be done in underground locations, thereby greatly reducing the amount of radioactive fallout injected into the atmosphere. After conducting two tests early in November, the Soviet Union refrained from further testing until 1961. The only other nuclear tests conducted during the period of the moratorium were four explosions set off by France, which thus became the fourth nuclear power.[42]

Following up on the report of the Committee of Experts, the three original nuclear powers officially began negotiations on a test ban treaty at the Conference on the Discontinuance of Nuclear Tests, starting on October 31, 1958. Disagreements between East and West quickly surfaced on the issues of whether (1) the detection stations would be staffed by nationals or foreigners, (2) the three nuclear powers would have a veto in a Control Commission established to supervise a test ban, and (3) inspection teams would be organized on an ad hoc or permanent basis.[43] Negotiations bogged down further in 1959 when the United States introduced new technical information gleaned from its HARDTACK II tests suggesting that the monitoring system envisioned by the Conference of Experts in 1958 could not be relied upon to detect underground tests of explosives smaller than 20 kilotons, rather than 5 kilotons, as had been indicated originally. Another technical concern arose when a United States panel of seismologists reported that underground tests could be concealed from seismic detectors by conducting them in large underground cavities, a technique known as "decoupling."[44]

The United States argued that these revised technical findings made it necessary to augment the monitoring system and inspection procedures proposed by the Conference of Experts. Strong resistance from the Soviet Union to a more intrusive program for verifying a test ban agreement led the United States to alter its goals in the negotiations. Perceiving that the Soviet Union was intractably opposed to the type of verification system that would make it impossible to conceal nuclear tests but still sensitive to international pressure to achieve some type of agreement on testing, the United States in 1960 proposed a ban that would apply only to nuclear explosions that could be detected by the verification system proposed by the Conference of Experts. These would include all tests in the atmosphere, underwater, and in outer space at altitudes that could be monitored. Underground tests that generated a shock wave above 4.75 on the Richter scale would also be banned. The United States proposal also called for a joint U.S.-Soviet seismic research program to develop techniques to lower the threshold of permissible underground tests. The United States and the United Kingdom concurred that once agreement was reached on such a threshold treaty, they would be willing to observe a moratorium on underground tests below a 4.75 magnitude.[45]

A favorable Soviet response to the American proposal offered hope that remaining differences with respect to on-site inspections could be resolved through further negotiations, which would pave the way for agreement on a "threshold treaty" that would be a significant first step toward a comprehensive nuclear test ban. These hopes suddenly evaporated, however, when a crisis arose in Soviet-American relations after a high-altitude American U-2 reconnaissance plane was detected and shot down by the Soviet Union over Soviet territory on May 2, 1960. The Soviet Union canceled a planned summit meeting between Premier Nikita Khrushchev and President Dwight D. Eisenhower, and no further progress on a test ban treaty was made during the latter's administration, even though the three-power talks continued.[46] In 1961 the Kennedy administration revived the idea of a threshold treaty similar to the agreement that had seemed within reach prior to the U-2 incident, but the United States failed to reach a compromise with the Soviet Union on the issue of verification, in particular the number and procedures for on-site inspections and the nationalities of those who would staff monitoring stations.

The Final Steps to the Treaty

On August 30, 1961, what had become an undeclared moratorium abruptly ended when the Soviet Union surprised the international community by announcing that it would resume nuclear testing. Within days the USSR proceeded with the most intensive series of tests ever conducted, including numerous large thermonuclear explosions. Angered that the Soviet Union had violated the spirit of the moratorium by planning such a series of tests, the United States responded within weeks by commencing a series of underground tests of small explosives in Nevada. In 1962 the United States conducted operation DOMINIC in the Pacific, which included forty atmospheric tests over a six-month period.[47] While the American series was in progress the Soviet Union began yet another series of atmospheric tests, which included a 30 megaton explosion. These atmospheric explosions raised radiation levels in the environment well above previous peak levels. Fears over the fallout levels that could result from a continuation of unrestrained testing by the superpowers, as well as the prospects of additional countries following France's example, galvanized public opinion on the need for an international agreement to limit if not ban nuclear testing, especially in the atmosphere.

The sudden resumption of atmospheric testing by the superpowers in 1961 brought the initial phase of test ban negotiations to an end. The three-power talks begun in 1958 were adjourned indefinitely in January 1962. Strong international criticism of new rounds of tests led the superpowers to resume talks under the auspices of ENDC in the spring of 1962. The United States and the United Kingdom proposed two alternatives: a comprehensive test ban that would include all underground tests, or a prohibition on tests in or beyond the atmosphere or in the sea. The Soviets rejected the former because it required inspections and the latter because it permitted testing to continue underground.[48]

The ENDC negotiations assumed a greater urgency following the Cuban Missile Crisis in October 1962, which prompted the sobering realization by both leaders and their publics that a nuclear war had been narrowly avoided. Nevertheless, six more months of negotiations failed to resolve persistent disagreements between East and West on the terms of a comprehensive nuclear test ban. In an attempt to break the deadlock, President John F. Kennedy, at the urging of British prime minister Harold Macmillan, sent a mission headed by Ambassador Averell Harriman to Moscow for test ban talks, which began on July 15, 1963. Earlier in July the Soviet Union had broken the stalemate between the two sides by announcing that it would no longer oppose a partial test ban treaty. Within ten days the Moscow talks led to agreement on the Treaty Banning Nuclear Weapons in the Atmosphere, in Outer Space and Under Water.[49] This treaty is a relatively short document that, as its name suggests, bans the testing of nuclear weapons in the atmosphere, outer space, or the oceans. The parties to the treaty are not to conduct such tests themselves and must refrain from causing, encouraging, or participating in nuclear explosions conducted by other actors. Furthermore, the treaty prohibits the testing of nuclear explosives in any other environment that would cause radioactive debris to be deposited beyond the territorial limits of the country conducting the explosion, a provision that takes into account the possibility of radioactive substances being vented into the atmosphere or oceans from underground tests. The treaty can be amended by a majority vote of the parties if the three original parties concur. While the treaty is of unlimited duration, any party can withdraw with three months notice if the case can be made that "extraordinary events" related to the subject of the treaty have jeopardized that party's "supreme interests."

The first article of the Nuclear Test Ban Treaty proclaims that the accord was to be a first step toward "the speediest possible achievement of an agreement on general and complete disarmament" and "the discontinuance of all test explosions of nuclear weapons for all time." Ironically, what made the agreement acceptable to both the United States and the Soviet Union was its failure to prohibit underground tests. Leaving this option open placated hardliners on both sides who believed that further development of nuclear weapons was critical to national security. Thus, the Test Ban Treaty did little if anything to restrain the nuclear arms race between the superpowers, who went on to conduct large numbers of underground tests (see Figure 4.1). By 1992 the five nuclear powers had set off 1,506 known underground nuclear explosions, most of them since 1963.[50] The possibility of a comprehensive test ban has been a continuing fixture on the agendas of the various United Nations bodies that take up arms control issues, but there was little prospect of one being reached until the end of the Cold War in the 1990s. In fact the Test Ban Treaty may have significantly delayed a comprehensive nuclear test ban agreement by dampening concerns about the dangers posed by radioactive fallout, which previously had lent some urgency to test ban talks.[51]

COMPLIANCE WITH THE TEST BAN TREATY

The Test Ban Treaty promptly came into force on October 10, 1963, upon the filing of ratification papers by the three nuclear powers that negotiated it. The United States Senate approved the treaty by a vote of 80–19 after conducting sometimes contentious hearings. All other states were encouraged to become parties to the treaty, thereby committing themselves to abide by the restrictions on where nuclear tests could be conducted. By the end of 1965, 88 countries had ratified or acceded to the treaty, and by 1995 the treaty had 104 parties. These countries were not giving up a significant option, however, since none of them appear to have had aspirations to become members of the nuclear weapons club. Furthermore, if circumstances changed, any party could retract its commitment with only three months' notice.

None of the states that became parties to the Test Ban Treaty appears to have violated any of its provisions. While refraining from conducting atmospheric tests, the United States and the Soviet Union continued to develop their nuclear weapons through extensive underground testing. France and China were the only countries known to have conducted atmospheric tests after the treaty was adopted (India announced an underground explosion in 1974), but both had repeatedly declared their intentions not to be bound by the treaty. Having gotten off to a later start in testing weapons, France and China were determined to develop their own nuclear weapons and to conduct the number of tests, including atmospheric explosions, deemed necessary to achieve a viable nuclear weapons program, regardless of adverse international reaction. Thus, France proceeded to conduct forty-six nuclear explosions in the atmosphere in the decade after the test ban. China, which did not set off its first explosion until 1964, conducted twenty-three tests in the atmosphere. While the French and Chinese testing programs were not nearly as extensive as those of the United States and the Soviet Union prior to the ban, they did distribute substantial amounts of radioactive fallout throughout the world.

From the start France's atmospheric testing program conducted between 1966 and 1974 in its Polynesian territory drew criticism from countries of the South Pacific region, in particular New Zealand, Australia,
Chile, and Peru.[52] New Zealand monitored radiation levels at various of
the South Pacific locations, noting how they rose after test explosions,
and took up the cause of residents of islands that were the most directly
affected. Australians complained that the French tests were increasing
the exposure levels of their citizens to iodine-131, strontium-90, and ce-
sium-137. Opposition intensified in 1972 as vocal public protests took
place in New Zealand and Australia. The Australian Council of Trade
Unions disrupted the movement of French goods through the country's
ports and the flow of mail to and from France. South American countries to the east of the test site called for an end to the testing, and Peru
protested by breaking off diplomatic relations with France.[53] New
Zealand and Peru sponsored a resolution at the United Nations Conference on the Human Environment in Stockholm in 1972 calling upon
France to end its atmospheric testing program; a similar resolution was
adopted by the United Nations by a vote of 105–4.[54]

In 1973 the new Labor governments in New Zealand and Australia
launched a more aggressive campaign to pressure France into ending
its atmospheric tests. Both countries formally brought their complaints
about French testing to the International Court of Justice (ICJ), arguing
that the fallout from the tests reaching their territory violated their sovereignty. They further contended that pollution of the oceans and interference with ships and aircraft in the French-declared restricted zone
were infringements on the freedom of the high seas. France refused to
recognize the jurisdiction of the ICJ in the case and defended its position in a white paper that stressed that its tests were being conducted
with great care to minimize human exposure to fallout. In response to
the legal challenges, the document noted that the French tests were few
in number compared to those that had been conducted by other nuclear
powers. The white paper further questioned why New Zealand and
Australia had not earlier challenged the legality of tests conducted by
the United States and Britain in the Pacific region.[55]

In May 1973 the ICJ by a vote of 8–6 asked France to avoid further
nuclear tests that would cause the deposition of radioactive fallout on
Australian territory.[56] The French government defied the court's request
by continuing its atmospheric testing program into 1974 despite continued strong international opposition. Daring protests by operators of small
private boats, who sailed into restricted areas near the test sites, drama-

tized the issue and aroused adverse public opinion toward France in many countries.[57] After completing a series of seven atmospheric tests in 1974, the new government of Giscard d'Estaing announced that henceforth France would do all of its nuclear testing underground. The ICJ released an opinion that France now had a legally binding obligation not to conduct any further atmospheric tests in the South Pacific and declared the nuclear tests cases brought by New Zealand and France to be closed.[58]

France honored its pledge not to do any further nuclear testing in the atmosphere but continued with an extensive series of underground nuclear explosions at its Polynesian test sites. The underground tests also drew strong international opposition, which came to a head in 1985 when it became known that French intelligence officers were responsible for the sinking of the Greenpeace boat *Rainbow Warrior* in the Auckland harbor while it was being prepared for a protest voyage to the French test site.[59] France again became the target of strong international criticism in 1995 when it proceeded with a series of six underground tests at Mururoa Atoll, breaking a moratorium on underground tests that had been observed since 1992 by the nuclear powers, with the exception of China. The French government of Jacques Chirac defended the recent tests on grounds that they would make it possible for France to sign a comprehensive nuclear test ban treaty, which the five nuclear powers had pledged to conclude in 1996.[60]

Like France, China was not willing to forego development of its nuclear arsenal and thus refused to accept the Test Ban Treaty. Just a year after the treaty came into force, China exploded its first nuclear device. Since the mid 1950s China had adamantly opposed separating the test ban issue from the larger objective of a prohibition on nuclear weapons, a position that China had earlier shared with the Soviet Union. China vehemently condemned the Test Ban Treaty for being a thinly veiled strategy of the superpowers to preserve their virtual duopoly on the possession of nuclear weapons, which would serve their broader objective of perpetuating a global hegemony. China argued that its nuclear weapon capability served the interests of the nonaligned countries of the Third World by undermining superpower dominance of the world. Nevertheless, China's opposition to the treaty was criticized by many of the countries it hoped to influence in Asia, Africa, and Latin America, who were supporting the test ban and preferred that China abide by it also. In an effort to deflect criticism of its first nuclear test in 1964, China called for a summit conference of all countries to discuss the complete prohibition and destruction of nuclear weapons, contending that the Test Ban Treaty would not serve such an objective despite assurances by the United States and the Soviet Union that the agreement would be the first step toward nuclear disarmament. The disagreement between China and the Soviet Union over the test ban issue also deepened fissures in the international communist movement.[61]

China set off the last of its atmospheric tests in 1980, four years into the post-Mao era and six years after France shifted its testing underground. Not until 1986, however, did China announce that it would conduct no more atmospheric tests. After initially being criticized for joining the nuclear club and thereby openly flaunting an internationally popular test ban treaty, China's testing program received relatively little notice and attracted far less international protest than did the French nuclear testing program in Polynesia, even when the latter was conducted exclusively underground after 1974. The Chinese got off lighter in world public opinion presumably in part because their tests were fewer in number than the French tests, although they were comparable in total explosive yield. Furthermore, in contrast to the French tests, which were imposed on a colonial area that was relatively accessible to outsiders, the Chinese tests took place on Chinese territory in a remote region that allowed the program to continue in relative secrecy.

IMPACT OF THE NUCLEAR TESTING REGIME

The year 1963 was a significant turning point in the history of nuclear testing in the atmosphere. The three nuclear powers, which were responsible for all but 4 of the 356 known atmospheric tests prior to that date, complied with the ban on testing in the atmosphere, outer space, and the oceans. Radiation levels from fallout, which had peaked at approximately 7 percent of natural sources in 1963, declined to 2 percent by 1966 and 1 percent by the mid 1970s, despite continued atmospheric testing by France and China. Residual radiation in the environment has declined further since the end of aboveground atmospheric testing in 1980. By 1989 concentrations of radioactive strontium-90 and cesium-137 in pasteurized milk in the United States had declined to less than 5 and 3 percent of 1964 levels, respectively.[62] Thus, residual radiation from atmospheric tests no longer appears to pose a significant health threat, although people exposed to substantially higher doses in the past may continue to develop radiation-related cancers.

To what extent can the Test Ban Treaty be credited with bringing about an end to atmospheric testing? In the case of the superpowers, neither the United States nor the Soviet Union had set off any aboveground tests during the eight months of 1963 leading up to the agreement on the Test Ban Treaty and in its prompt coming into force. Without the treaty, however, it is likely that both countries would have resumed atmospheric tests. The hiatus in testing in early 1963 took place after both countries had done extensive tests and needed time to analyze the results before embarking on new rounds of tests that were already being planned.

The defense strategists of both superpowers believed there were compelling technical reasons for further tests in the atmosphere despite the option of using underground environments. The Soviet Union had relatively little experience with underground testing by 1963 and thus felt it would be at a disadvantage in the use of this environment. On the American side, in testimony at the hearings in the Senate on ratification of the treaty military analysts raised serious technical questions about the wisdom of forgoing the option of atmospheric tests. While underground sites were considered suitable for some types of tests, especially of smaller explosives, it was believed that aboveground tests were advantageous if not necessary for fulfilling other objectives. One concern was that the Soviet Union had gained a significant advantage in high-yield explosives from its extensive series of high-megaton tests in 1961–62. Explosives of this size could only be tested in the atmosphere. Atmospheric explosions would also be useful for determining the capacity of hardened missile silos to withstand a nuclear first strike, studying the communications and radar blackout problems following nuclear explosions, testing antiballistic systems, developing nuclear bombs that generate less fallout, and exploring certain peaceful uses of nuclear explosives.[63] Thus, were it not for the Test Ban Treaty and the overwhelming support it enjoyed internationally and domestically within the United States, it is likely that the United States and the Soviet Union would have resumed testing in the atmosphere in late 1963 and 1964.

The treaty clearly did not dissuade China and France from carrying out extensive nuclear testing programs in the atmosphere. How much of a factor it was in their later decisions to discontinue atmospheric tests is not clear. By that time the two countries had reached a point in their nuclear programs when atmospheric tests were less critical. The French decision in 1974 to end atmospheric tests does seem to have been swayed by the intense international protests that began to erupt in 1972. It is unclear, however, whether international opposition to the French tests would have been any less prevalent had there been no test ban treaty. Australia and New Zealand based their complaints against French testing in the nuclear test cases before the ICJ on general principles of customary international law, in particular that fallout from the tests constituted a violation of their national sovereignty.[64]

It can be argued that the Test Ban Treaty played an important role in introducing and establishing a principle of international customary law that testing nuclear weapons in the atmosphere is an inappropriate behavior for any state. Most states promptly took advantage of the opportunity the treaty offered them to go on record opposing further atmospheric tests, and thus quickly to establish the nearly universal acceptance of a principle that would otherwise have evolved more slowly and less decisively.[65] Any state defying the prohibition on atmospheric testing could expect to be branded an international outlaw, which could have serious consequences for how they were treated by other states in other realms of international activity. This prospect may have been a factor in the eventual French and Chinese decisions not to conduct additional atmospheric tests. Fifteen years after the last atmospheric test, the prohibition set forth in the 1963 Test Ban Treaty appears to be well established in international customary law.

CONCLUSIONS

In the atmospheric testing of nuclear weapons a few countries, albeit the dominant ones of the era, were engaged in activities that contaminated the global atmosphere and posed threats to the health of people throughout the world. The larger world community was uncomfortable with the activities and put increasing pressure on the nuclear powers to negotiate an agreement that would bring such testing to an end. These efforts led to the Test Ban Treaty of 1963, but only after potential dangers inherent in the Cold War and the nuclear arms race became dramatically apparent during the Cuban Missile Crisis of 1962. France and China initially refused to go along with the ban until they had conducted sufficient atmospheric tests to develop their own independent nuclear arsenals.

By the time the Test Ban Treaty was adopted, an extensive body of scientific knowledge had been accumulated on the harmful effects that exposure to radiation might have on present and future human generations. However, most of the evidence available at the time was confined to a small number of people who had received relatively heavy doses of radiation by virtue of their proximity to test sites. There was little concrete evidence then that low-level exposure to radiation resulting from global fallout from previous test explosions posed a significant threat to the health of the world's population. Nevertheless, there was widespread concern—some would say an ill-founded phobia—among the citizens of many countries about the long-term consequences of any additional exposure to radiation, no matter how slight. Thus, the Test Ban Treaty could be viewed as an early example of the so-called "precautionary principle" guiding an international response to a potential environmental and health problem about which there was still considerable scientific uncertainty.

The Test Ban Treaty seems to have been motivated more by political considerations than by scientific or technical concerns. The superpowers used the treaty to blunt international opposition not only to nuclear testing but also to the nuclear arms race generally and the dangers it posed for humanity. Domestic and world opinion seemed to demand that the superpowers reach some type of agreement in the arms control field that would move them away from the brink of nuclear war and begin a process that would lead to nuclear disarmament and a more peaceful world. The test ban issue was the only subject on which such an agreement appeared to be within reach in 1963. A treaty on nuclear testing was achieved only when there was agreement that underground tests could continue, enabling negotiators to sidestep the contentious issues of international monitoring and arrangements for inspections. Thus, the Test Ban Treaty was a product not only of concerns about radioactive fallout but also of the larger international political context in which nuclear warfare was feared to be a real possibility.

Chapter 5

THE TRANSBOUNDARY AIR POLLUTION REGIME

The international regime that addresses acid rain, otherwise known as the long-range transboundary air pollution (LRTAP) regime, is unique among the four atmospheric regimes for having been created and developed in response to environmental damage that had been readily apparent for several decades. The mysterious disappearance of fish from lakes in southern Scandinavia during the first half of the twentieth century prompted scientific investigations that attributed the phenomenon to abnormally high water acidity caused by anthropogenic air pollutants. Acid rain became an international issue in the late 1960s and 1970s when data from scattered monitoring stations confirmed suspicions that air pollutants were being transported hundreds, and even thousands, of kilometers and in the process were being chemically transformed into acidic substances. Nevertheless, serious negotiations on a timetable for reducing emissions of acid-forming pollutants took place only after reports of widespread damage to forests in western and central Europe evoked a strong public outcry in the early 1980s.

Acid rain is primarily a regional phenomenon because the pollutants that form acidic compounds do not rise high enough to become globally dispersed before precipitating out of the atmosphere. It has been an especially compelling international problem on the European Continent where many highly industrialized countries share a regional airshed. Transboundary pollution has also been a contentious issue in North America where pollutants drift across the borders of the United States with Canada and Mexico. In recent decades acidification has become a more widespread phenomenon in developing countries, such as China, India, Brazil, and South Africa, but for the most part the problem is greatest in those countries in which pollutants are emitted. One notable exception is Japan's acidic deposition, more than half of which comes from China and Korea, where increasingly large amounts of high-sulfur coal are being burned to produce energy.[1]

The problem of transboundary air pollution raises the issue of what responsibilities sovereign states have to restrict operations within their territories that have adverse environmental effects beyond their borders. Efforts to resolve this issue through negotiations have been complicated by imbalances in the directional flow of pollutants across countries. The most enthusiastic advocates of international measures that limit emissions of air pollutants have been the downwind states, in particular the Scandinavian countries and Canada, whose environments have been seriously damaged by air pollutants originating beyond their borders. Conversely, heavy net exporters of pollutants, such as the United States and United Kingdom, have strongly resisted international rules that would require them to invest in expensive pollution control technologies primarily for the benefit of other countries.

Despite these divergent interests, the United Nations Economic Commission for Europe (ECE) has established a remarkable regime to address the problem of acid rain in the larger European region, which includes a highly sophisticated air pollution monitoring network known as EMEP. International rules are in place that have required nations to reduce significantly their emissions of some acid-forming air pollutants and to cap the flow of others into the atmosphere. The reductions in pollution achieved thus far have not been sufficient to reverse the process of acidification in the region, but a new round of agreements being negotiated in the 1990s holds promise for reducing acid deposition to levels significantly closer to what the environment can absorb without serious damage.

THE EMISSION AND TRANSPORT OF POLLUTANTS

The contemporary problem of acid rain can be traced to the industrial revolution, which initially took hold in England in the mid 1700s and spread through the European Continent and North America in the nineteenth century. The industrial revolution was an era of major changes in the dominant mode of production from small numbers of goods being made by craftsmen working with hand tools in their homes in villages to much larger quantities of goods being manufactured using increasingly complex and powerful machines in factories located in rapidly growing cities. The industrial revolution also introduced new chemical processes for producing materials such as iron and steel, which entailed the smelting of great amounts of ores for the minerals that they contained. The new forms of production required large quantities of power, which in the first century of the industrial revolution came largely from the burning of coal, using technologies such as the steam engine. The much smaller demands for energy prior to the industrial revolution had been satisfied largely by animals, windmills, waterwheels, and wood.

Air pollution was an inevitable product of the industrial revolution and its dependence on fossil fuels. Large amounts of sulfur and nitrogen oxides were released into the atmosphere from the use of coal as the fuel for steam engines and later in power plants to produce electricity. The production of coal in Britain alone increased twentyfold during the nineteenth century. Smelting and other industrial processes were also major sources of acid-forming pollutants. SO_2 emissions rose steadily in the European region, reaching 5 mmt annually in 1880 and 20 mmt by 1940. After dipping during the Second World War, sulfur emissions rose sharply, peaking at nearly 60 mmt in the late 1970s (see Figure 5.1). Acid deposition was becoming a significant environmental problem by the late 1800s. A recent study suggests that the environmental critical load for acid deposition may have been exceeded before 1880 in areas of the British Isles, central Europe, and southern Scandinavia.[2] Over the past century the average pH of precipitation outside the heavily industrialized areas of these regions has declined from about 5.6 to 4.6, which is indicative of a tenfold increase in the acidity.[3]

Until well into the twentieth century environmental damage resulting from air pollution was largely localized around industries, power plants, and smelters, most of which were concentrated near major coalfields, such as the midlands of Great Britain, Belgium, the Ruhr Valley, northern Lorraine, and upper Silesia. Industrial operations were dispersed more widely in western Europe when petroleum, which is easier to transport, became widely used as an alternative source of energy.[4] Under central planning, however, the communist regimes of the Soviet Union and eastern Europe continued to cluster industries in enormous complexes, commonly near the principal mining and smelting operations in areas such as upper Silesia, the Donbass Basin, the Kola Penin-

Figure 5.1. Historical Emissions of SO_2 in Europe (1880-1994)

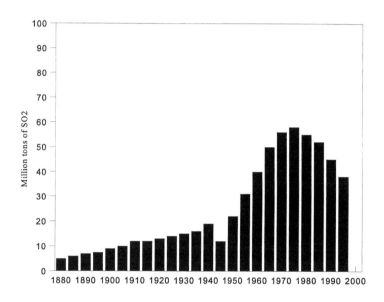

Source: Figures from Mylona, <u>Trends in Sulphur Dioxide Emissions...</u>, 22.

sula, the southern Urals, and the city of Norilsk in the Siberian Arctic. The result has been extraordinarily high levels of localized air pollution, while other large areas, especially in the vast territories of the Soviet Union, were left relatively unpolluted.[5]

Sulfur and Nitrogen Emissions

Sulfur emissions result largely from the burning of fossil fuels, in particular coal with high sulfur content. In recent decades coal-fired power plants have accounted for approximately two-thirds of total anthropogenic emissions of SO_2 in the United States and United Kingdom but have been a less dominant source in other industrialized countries, in particular those relying more heavily on nuclear energy for electrical power, such as France and Japan. More than half of Canadian sulfur emissions have come from smelters.[6]

The bulk of SO_2 pollution comes from large point sources. A recent study of Europe revealed that 42 percent of SO_2 emissions come from the region's one hundred worst polluters, ninety-five of which are power stations fired with fossil fuels. Among the other major sources are three smelters, one refinery, and one blast furnace.[7] In North America the copper and nickel smelting complex of the International Nickel Company (INCO) at Sudbury, Ontario, has long been the world's largest single source of SO_2 emissions.[8] INCO's operation emitted as much SO_2 in the early 1980s as the combined total for Sweden and Finland, even after an 80 percent reduction from 1969 levels.[9]

The greatest source of NO_X pollution in most countries has been motorized forms of transport, including cars, trucks, buses, and steamers. In the 1980s mobile sources accounted for 84 percent of NO_X emissions in Norway, 74 percent in Switzerland, and roughly 50 percent for western Europe as a whole.[10] In the United States 44 percent of NO_X emissions were attributable to motorized vehicles, while in Canada the figure was 61 percent. Most of the remaining NO_X pollution came from conventional power plants. In some countries, such as Sweden, sizable amounts of anthropogenic NO_X emissions originated in the agricultural and forestry sectors, which use nitrate-based fertilizers.[11]

Table 5.1 lists the sulfur emissions of many of the developed countries for 1980, which has been the benchmark year for negotiating future reductions in emissions. In that year the United States discharged 23.7 mmt of SO_2, which is slightly less than the approximately 25 mmt released in the Soviet Union. The United Kingdom was in a distant third place with nearly 5 mmt of SO_2 emissions. Other countries that emitted more than 3 mmt of sulfur included Canada, Spain, France, and Italy among the OECD countries, as well as East Germany, Poland, and Czechoslovakia of the former Soviet bloc.

The rankings of countries on SO_2 emissions change considerably when population is taken into account. The per capita emissions of the former East Germany and Czechoslovakia of 257 kg and 204 kg, respectively, were the highest in the world, roughly twice the United States figure of 107 kg/capita. The high figures of the eastern European coun-

Table 5.1. Sulfur Emissions by Country (1980)

	Total (thousands of tons)	Per Capita (kilograms)
OECD Countries		
United States	23,780	107
United Kingdom	4,897	88
Canada	4,643	196
Spain	3,377	91
France	3,348	63
Italy	3,211	58
Japan	1,263	12
Belgium	828	84
Finland	584	108
Netherlands	502	36
Sweden	489	59
Denmark	449	88
Austria	397	53
Norway	141	34
Switzerland	126	19
Former Soviet Bloc		
USSR	25,000	95
East Germany	4,323	257
Poland	4,100	119
Czechoslovakia	3,100	204
Hungary	1,633	168
Bulgaria	1,094	119

Sources: EMEP figures, printed in World Resources Institute, World Resources 1994-95, 367; USSR figure is a UNECE figure for 1982, quoted in McCormick, Acid Earth, 14.

tries are attributable to the burning of large quantities of high-sulfur coal, gross inefficiencies in industrial energy use, and little investment in pollution control technologies. With its extensive smelting operations, Canada's per capita SO_2 emissions of 196 kg were also among the highest in the world. The per capita emissions of the other European countries were considerably lower but still high compared to Japan's remarkably low figure of 12 kg/capita after the country reduced its SO_2 emissions by 75 percent during the 1970s.

The more limited data available on 1980 NO_x emissions, which are reported in Table 5.2, reveal that levels were highest for the North American countries, which depend heavily on automobiles for personal transportation. Thus, the NO_x emissions of the United States, which were comparable in volume to U.S. SO_2 emissions, were far greater than those of any other country, in spite of the fact that the United States has adopted some of the world's most stringent laws on automotive exhausts. The NO_x emissions of the United States were also the highest on a per capita basis at 107 kg, Canada placing second with 83 kg per capita. The western European countries, which have depended much more on public transportation, had per capita emission figures that ranged from about one-quater to one-half of the U.S. amount. The Soviet figure, which was for the European part of the country, was also relatively small because of a low rate of ownership of personal automobiles.

The Transboundary Movement of Pollutants

Air pollution would be exclusively a national problem if all pollutants were deposited within the countries in which they originated. That this was not the case initially became apparent from the research of Svante Odén in the 1960s, which documented the distant sources of acid pollution afflicting Sweden. Subsequent monitoring of air pollution and acid deposition by the OECD from 1972 to 1974 and by EMEP since the late 1970s has revealed more about the magnitude of the problem of long-range transport of air pollution. The tables of transboundary pollution flows that EMEP has published annually for SO_2 since 1980 and for NO_x since 1988 (see Table 5.3) have been important inputs for the continuing negotiations on limiting transboundary air pollution.

Several observations can be drawn from EMEP's SO_2 and NO_x tables that help explain the conflicting positions that ECE members have taken on limiting air pollution. First, more than half of the emissions of SO_2

Table 5.2. Nitrogen Emissions by Country (1980)

	Total (thousands of tons)	Per Capita (kilograms)
OECD Countries		
United States	23,560	107
West Germany	2,944	48
United Kingdom	2,365	42
Canada	1,959	83
France	1,646	31
Italy	1,585	28
Japan	1,400	12
Spain	946	26
Netherlands	571	41
Belgium	442	45
Sweden	424	51
Denmark	270	53
Finland	264	55
Austria	256	34
Switzerland	196	30
Norway	186	45
Former Soviet Bloc		
USSR (European)	3,167	
Czechoslovakia	1,204	79
East Germany	593	35
Hungary	273	26

Sources: EMEP figures, printed in World Resources Institute, World Resources 1994-95, 367.

and NO_x of the European countries were deposited beyond the borders of the countries of their origin, either on the territory of other countries or in regional bodies of water, such as the North Atlantic and the Baltic and Mediterranean Seas. The proportion of "exported" pollutants has

Table 5.3.   Estimated Sulfur Budget for Europe — 1992-93 Average (100 tons per year)

	AL	AT	BE	BG	DK	FI	FR	DE	GR	HU	IS	IE	IT	LU	NL	NO	PL	PT	RO	ES	SE	CH	TR	GB	BY	UA	MO	RU	EE	LV	LT	SI	HR	BA	YU	FYM	CS	SK	REM	BAS	NOS	ATL	MED	NAT	IND	SUM
AL	100	0	0	26	0	0	2	6	13	6	0	0	20	0	0	0	4	0	8	1	0	0	1	1	0	4	0	0	0	0	0	1	2	5	22	2	3	1	1	0	0	0	1	54		290
AT	0	92	12	6	2	0	73	215	1	57	0	1	218	2	4	0	68	0	22	12	0	14	0	34	1	6	0	0	0	0	0	56	12	6	16	0	118	23	1	0	3	1	0	1	196	1289
BE	0	0	306	0	1	0	114	98	0	3	0	2	3	3	24	0	7	0	2	10	0	0	0	92	0	2	0	0	0	0	0	0	0	1	0	15	1	0	0	12	2	0	2	44		746
BG	0	2	2	1257	1	0	6	54	16	65	0	0	18	0	1	0	44	0	274	2	0	0	6	6	5	60	7	8	0	0	1	2	6	10	140	2	30	14	1	0	1	0	0	2	196	2254
DK	0	0	6	0	137	0	10	96	0	3	0	2	1	0	5	1	38	0	2	2	4	0	0	82	2	2	0	2	0	0	0	0	0	0	20	2	0	6	8	1	0	4	44	481
FI	0	1	5	2	15	276	9	118	0	9	0	1	2	0	4	4	95	0	7	2	22	0	0	48	25	25	1	286	54	12	12	0	0	0	2	0	26	5	0	13	4	1	0	8	306	1400
FR	0	6	137	2	5	0	1988	384	1	22	0	10	298	10	33	0	55	14	10	368	1	22	0	316	1	4	0	0	0	0	1	12	7	5	11	0	67	9	8	1	42	30	0	27	652	4580
DE	0	17	196	6	44	0	472	7440	0	58	0	10	138	16	110	0	347	4	28	63	2	24	0	507	4	20	1	6	1	1	3	13	6	4	12	0	816	34	1	8	52	10	0	15	594	11038
GR	30	1	1	264	0	0	5	30	400	26	0	0	33	0	0	0	20	0	67	2	0	0	22	3	2	30	2	4	0	0	0	2	4	8	66	2	14	5	4	0	0	0	0	4	234	1296
HU	1	14	5	16	2	0	20	145	2	1126	0	0	52	0	2	0	125	0	114	5	0	2	0	15	3	22	2	2	0	0	1	20	33	20	84	0	108	103	1	0	2	0	0	1	144	2205
IS	0	0	0	0	0	0	0	3	0	0	4	0	0	0	0	0	0	0	0	1	0	0	0	0	0	0	0	7	0	0	0	0	0	0	0	0	0	0	0	0	0	1	0	10	30	62
IE	0	0	2	0	0	0	6	10	0	0	0	132	0	0	1	0	2	0	0	8	0	0	0	124	0	0	0	0	0	0	0	0	0	0	1	0	2	0	2	8	0	13	56		370
IT	4	11	6	28	2	0	121	122	12	60	0	1	2984	1	3	0	68	3	25	73	0	22	3	27	2	10	1	2	0	0	0	58	36	32	42	0	52	16	22	0	2	2	0	10	568	4440
LU	0	0	2	0	0	0	10	6	0	0	0	0	0	13	0	0	0	0	0	1	0	0	0	2	0	0	0	0	0	0	0	0	0	0	1	0	0	0	0	0	0	0	0	4	40
NL	0	0	76	0	2	0	62	200	0	4	0	2	2	1	138	0	16	0	2	6	0	0	0	226	0	2	0	0	0	0	0	0	0	0	31	2	0	0	20	2	0	3	53	799
NO	0	0	10	0	27	8	16	123	0	6	1	0	8	46	48	0	4	8	16	0	0	176	6	6	0	0	0	0	2	0	27	3	0	4	14	5	0	26	352	1056
PL	1	10	40	10	44	3	86	2263	2	155	0	4	37	2	24	2	4767	1	70	18	7	4	0	205	35	108	4	36	4	4	17	11	8	6	33	0	732	122	1	14	16	3	0	8	514	9416
PT	0	0	0	0	0	0	4	2	0	0	0	2	0	0	0	0	309	0	122	0	0	0	4	0	0	0	0	0	0	0	0	0	0	0	0	0	7	5	62	532
RO	6	6	6	134	2	0	22	192	10	313	0	0	46	0	4	0	206	0	2322	5	0	1	4	20	14	190	22	20	1	1	3	10	18	19	223	1	116	84	1	1	2	0	0	2	376	4418
ES	0	0	1	2	1	0	101	44	1	8	0	2	45	0	4	0	10	123	4	3206	0	2	0	45	0	0	0	0	0	0	0	3	2	2	4	0	5	1	20	0	4	32	2	17	413	4127
SE	0	1	18	1	100	37	30	302	0	14	0	4	2	0	13	18	160	0	13	5	136	0	0	183	17	18	1	70	14	8	11	1	1	6	0	62	10	0	24	17	4	0	20	426	1746
CH	0	2	4	1	1	0	78	44	0	4	0	1	208	0	2	0	8	0	2	18	0	82	0	18	0	0	0	0	0	0	4	2	2	3	0	9	1	1	0	2	1	0	1	108	612
TR	6	2	2	198	2	0	9	66	78	40	0	0	24	0	1	0	58	0	126	3	0	0	556	8	10	133	8	26	2	1	2	2	4	4	38	0	36	11	1	3	1	1	0	7	858	2324
GB	0	1	35	0	6	0	84	166	0	4	0	48	4	1	22	1	35	2	2	22	1	0	0	4983	1	3	0	2	0	0	0	0	0	0	40	3	0	1	49	24	0	34	216	5794
BY	0	2	6	12	14	6	16	208	1	46	0	1	14	0	4	1	366	0	55	6	4	1	2	50	850	155	6	97	12	17	46	4	3	3	14	0	78	20	0	6	4	1	0	2	334	2467
UA	3	6	16	102	14	6	38	529	10	236	0	2	44	1	10	1	832	0	408	8	4	2	16	80	196	4110	70	290	10	9	24	11	14	12	70	0	214	125	1	6	7	2	0	6	1022	8573
MO	0	0	1	11	0	0	2	32	0	19	0	0	4	0	0	0	44	0	82	0	0	0	0	3	5	78	88	0	0	1	1	1	1	8	0	14	4	2	2	0	0	0	0	0	56	471
RU	4	7	26	136	64	172	64	754	17	174	0	6	44	1	19	8	924	1	310	18	38	2	56	240	698	2172	39	10269	260	79	105	10	12	75	0	276	80	0	36	18	5	0	26	6714	23947
EE	0	0	1	0	4	11	2	35	0	2	0	0	0	0	0	0	27	0	2	0	2	0	0	10	8	6	0	17	127	8	5	0	0	0	0	0	6	1	0	0	1	0	0	1	49	338
LV	0	0	2	2	6	6	4	66	0	5	0	0	2	0	2	0	64	0	5	1	4	0	0	22	28	14	1	24	12	75	23	0	0	0	2	0	14	2	0	5	2	0	0	2	87	488
LT	0	0	4	2	6	3	7	100	0	10	0	1	2	0	2	0	138	0	10	2	3	0	0	28	26	20	1	26	4	13	162	0	0	0	3	0	22	4	0	4	2	0	0	2	102	724
SI	0	7	1	2	0	0	9	32	0	21	0	0	78	0	1	0	18	0	8	4	0	1	0	4	0	2	0	0	0	0	0	209	24	14	10	0	17	5	1	0	0	0	0	0	58	530
HR	2	6	2	8	1	0	12	58	2	68	0	0	104	0	1	0	41	0	16	6	0	1	0	6	1	6	0	0	0	0	0	20	182	60	40	0	36	13	2	0	1	0	0	1	110	810
BA	3	3	2	10	1	0	8	49	2	54	0	0	65	0	1	0	34	0	17	4	0	0	0	6	1	5	0	0	0	0	0	6	32	233	60	0	24	12	2	0	1	0	0	0	108	752
YU	20	4	2	78	1	0	10	82	10	130	0	0	62	0	2	0	46	0	87	4	0	1	2	9	2	16	2	2	0	0	0	7	21	54	1032	2	42	20	2	0	1	0	0	2	190	1954
FYM	14	0	0	42	0	0	1	8	8	20	0	0	8	0	0	0	5	0	15	0	0	0	1	0	4	1	0	0	0	0	1	2	4	39	10	3	1	0	0	0	0	0	42	224
CS	1	12	15	4	4	0	48	787	1	64	0	1	28	1	7	0	251	0	26	9	1	3	0	38	3	13	1	2	1	1	7	4	2	14	0	1876	44	0	4	1	0	1	140	3416
SK	1	8	3	7	1	0	13	142	2	198	0	0	19	0	2	0	178	0	48	3	0	1	1	13	3	23	1	2	0	0	1	6	6	4	24	0	139	412	0	0	1	0	0	1	87	1352
REM	2	0	3	0	0	0	34	22	14	8	0	0	95	0	2	0	9	4	6	98	0	2	4	12	0	4	0	3	3	8	0	5	1646	0	1	2	1	14	648	1672
BAS	0	2	32	4	266	113	60	809	0	32	0	6	8	1	24	8	584	1	26	12	86	1	0	288	42	46	2	194	110	50	46	2	2	2	12	0	150	23	0	120	26	4	0	27	493	3662
NOS	2	6	332	2	113	0	354	638	0	18	0	52	14	2	196	4	9	54	16	1	3685	8	15	0	14	4	2	2	4	0	179	12	0	12	306	38	0	147	683	7174
ATL	0	3	72	2	45	48	402	526	0	22	12	310	36	3	40	30	181	290	14	1806	22	4	1934	26	36	1	48	8	10	4	2	3	1	10	3	70	688	0	1476	4350	13490
MED	130	14	20	434	6	1	334	302	734	182	0	3	2304	2	9	0	190	22	214	942	1	13	166	84	12	115	10	20	1	1	3	48	90	106	232	3	134	47	382	2	8	11	2	140	2399	9886
BLS	4	3	6	417	4	2	16	168	30	84	0	0	24	0	3	0	182	0	344	4	2	1	150	20	34	579	34	108	3	2	6	4	8	8	64	0	82	30	1	2	2	0	0	18	836	3276

AL - Albania; AT - Austria; BY - Belarus; BE - Belgium; BA - Bosnia & Herzegovina;
BG - Bulgaria; HR - Croatia; CS - Czech Republic; DK - Denmark; EE - Estonia; FI - Finland;
FR - France; DE - Germany; GR - Greece; HU - Hungary; IS - Iceland; IE - Ireland; IT - Italy;
LV - Latvia; LT - Lithuania; LU - Luxembourg; FYM - Macedonia; MD - Moldova;
NL - Netherlands; NO - Norway; PL - Poland; PT - Portugal; RO - Romania; RU - Russia;
SK - Slovakia; SI - Slovenia; ES - Spain; SE - Sweden; CH - Switzerland; TR - Turkey;
UA - Ukraine; GB - United Kingdom; YU- Yugoslavia; REM - Rem. area (North Africa);
BAS - Int. trade, Baltic Sea; NOS - Int. trade, North Sea; ATL - Int. trade, rem. Atlantic;
MED - Int. trade, Mediter.; BLS - Int. trade, Black Sea; NAT - Biogenic sea emissions.

Rows indicate the origins of the sulfur deposited in each country listed along the left.

Columns indicate where the sulfur originating in each country listed across the top was deposited.

Source: EMEP figures reprinted in Acid News, December 1994, 15.

been especially great for the small, highly industrialized countries. Roughly 80 percent of the SO_2 emissions of Switzerland and the Netherlands drifted beyond their borders. More than 60 percent of sulfur pollution emitted in most of the other European countries was deposited outside their territories.

Second, the emissions of acid-forming pollutants of several countries significantly exceeded the amount that was deposited on their territories, which indicates that substantial amounts of the pollution they generated flowed beyond their borders. The sulfur emissions of the United Kingdom, former East Germany, Spain, and Italy have been approximately three times as great as the sulfur deposition within their borders.

Third, for some countries the amount of acid deposition has been considerably greater than the quantity of pollutants emitted within their borders, which means that significant amounts of the deposition in these countries came from foreign sources. Sulfur deposition in Norway was five times greater than the country's SO_2 emissions. The United Kingdom, Germany, Russia, and Poland each accounted for more of the sulfur deposition in Norway than did domestic sources. Austria, Switzerland, and Sweden received approximately 90 percent of their sulfuric deposition from foreign sources; the Netherlands, France, and West Germany received more than half. The United States has been the source of approximately half of the acidic deposition in Canada. In no other case has one country been responsible for such a large proportion of another country's deposition. Canada in turn has accounted for only about 20 percent of acid deposition in the United States.[12]

The countries that export a large proportion of their air pollution, while receiving relatively little pollution from other states, have had little stake in curbing the transboundary flow of air pollutants. They have often sought to delay the adoption of international rules of pollution emissions until further research could establish a more definitive link between their emissions and environmental damage in other countries. The heavy net recipients of pollutants, such as the Nordic countries, have consistently been in the forefront in calling for international action to stem the flow of transboundary pollution. States that are both significant exporters and importers of air pollutants, such Germany and its central European neighbors, have at times formed a critical swing bloc in negotiations.

ACID RAIN AS A PUBLIC ISSUE

For the most part governments have been willing to enter into serious negotiations on curbing transboundary air pollution only when acid rain has become a salient public issue within their countries. Acid rain first became a major subject of public concern in Sweden and Norway.

In the late 1960s the Swedish public reacted strongly to press reports of Odén's revelations about the distant origins of the acidic pollutants, which prodded the Swedish government to call for international cooperation on reducing transboundary air pollution. Since then Scandinavians have been generally well informed about subsequent scientific findings on the severity and origins of acid deposition. Accordingly they have been unified in their support both for international rules that would reduce acid precipitation and for domestic legislation designed to reduce SO_2 emissions in their countries by as much as 80 percent.

The problem of acid rain drew little attention in Continental Europe until the early 1980s when the startling spread of *waldsterben* provoked a strong response from an alarmed German public. The highly publicized revelations about forest damage fueled a rising tide of environmental activism and Green politics that spurred the West German government to take action on both the domestic and international fronts. Heightened public concern about the effects of acid rain was also growing in Switzerland, Austria, France, Denmark, and the Netherlands as *waldsterben* rapidly spread through the forests of these regions.[13]

Acid rain received relatively little attention in the United Kingdom until the mid 1980s. The British took pride in what their Clean Air Acts of the 1950s had accomplished to rid the air over cities of the more visible types of pollution, such as smoke and soot, and to avoid a reoccurrence of the deadly smogs. They were slow, however, to become attentive to the damage caused by invisible, acid-forming pollutants and to the growing evidence that the tall smokestacks, which had ameliorated local pollution problems, were inadvertently contributing to acid rain over more distant locations.[14] Through most of the 1980s the conservative government of Margaret Thatcher turned a deaf ear to a barrage of complaints from foreign governments and NGOs about Britain's refusal to agree to a 30 percent reduction in emissions of SO_2. British policy was shaped largely by the Central Energy Generating Board (CEGB), a government-owned utility that operated the nation's network of large power plants, which were Europe's greatest source of SO_2 emissions. Scientists from the CEGB took the lead in arguing that the evidence linking pollution from the United Kingdom to the acidification problems of foreign countries was not conclusive enough to warrant equipping its smokestacks with expensive pollution abatement technologies, such as flue-gas desulfurization equipment. This position especially incensed the Norwegian government, which in 1986 accused the British of a "provocation against international society."[15]

The thinking of the British public on the acid rain issue changed markedly during the later 1980s. This shift was due in part to embarrassment over the intensifying barrage of international criticism directed at the United Kingdom for its recalcitrance on making commitments to reduce SO_2 emissions, which had led to the country's being characterized as the "dirty man of Europe." Outside groups, such as the Swedish NGO Secretariat on Acid Rain, had orchestrated information campaigns designed to make the British more aware not only of the impact of their pollutants on other countries in the region but also of the extent to which their country had been a victim of its pollution. By the late 1970s the waters in some of the lakes of Scotland and northern England were as acidified as those of southern Norway and Sweden. By the early 1980s British forests displayed the same signs of disease that were so widespread in central Europe. Then in 1987 a report of an ECE Working Group on Effects bore the alarming news that the forests of the United Kingdom were among the most seriously damaged in all of Europe, with two-thirds of its conifers showing slight to severe damage.[16]

The first concrete indications of a shift in the British position on transboundary pollution came in 1986 when the CEGB conceded that its emissions were partly responsible for damage to the Norwegian environment and announced that it would invest in desulfurization equipment for three of its large coal-fired power plants. The conversion of the Thatcher government was not complete, however, until 1988 when it agreed to comply with a European Community directive pertaining to large combustion plants, which required a 60 percent reduction in SO_2 emissions by 2003 and a 30 percent reduction in NO_x pollution by 1998.[17]

The acid rain issue evolved in a strikingly parallel manner in North America. Canada, like the Scandinavian countries, has been a significant net recipient of acidic pollutants, although in Canada's case the pollutants received from abroad have come almost exclusively from one country, the United States. Moreover, as in Scandinavia, the lakes and forests of eastern Canada are highly susceptible to acidification because the Precambrian rock shield underlying the region is a poor neutralizer of acids. Fish and other aquatic life were disappearing from numerous lakes by the 1970s, and damage to forests was widespread by the 1980s. A series of articles appearing in leading Canadian newspapers in 1978 first brought the acid rain problem to the attention of the Canadian public. A survey conducted in 1983 reported that 77 percent of Canadians considered acid rain to be the country's most serious environmental problem.[18] Finally, in Canada, as in Scandinavia, the societal consensus on the need to address the problem was so strong that the two largest emitters of SO_2, INCO and the Ontario Hydro Electric Company, which operates large coal-fired power plants, put up little resistance to government directives to reduce significantly their emissions.[19]

As with the British, Americans took pride in the fact that the United States was a leader in adopting national laws to reduce air pollution, in particular the Clean Air Act of 1970 and its 1977 amendments. As in the United Kingdom, however, these early regulations were designed primarily to protect human health by cleaning up air in heavily polluted localities, with one of the means being the construction of tall smokestacks, which substantially increased the transboundary flow of pollutants to Canada. Thus, despite reports of the disappearance of fish in numerous acidified lakes in the Adirondack Mountains of New York as early as the 1970s, only 15 percent of Americans expressed awareness of the problem of acid rain in 1980. Later in the decade the problem was known to 50 percent of Americans, due in part to the sometimes controversial efforts of the Canadian government to educate the American public about the problem through printed materials and films, as well as to the vocal criticism Canadian prime ministers leveled at the United States for its failure to take action to reduce transboundary pollution.[20] Another factor was growing evidence of damaged forests in the United States, in particular in the higher elevations of the southern Appalachian Mountains.

Canada's claims on the United States would have been more persuasive but for that country's own slow pace in reducing domestic sources of air pollution. In the early 1980s per capita emissions of SO_2 were nearly twice as high in Canada as in the United States, which is largely explained by the former's failure to invest in abatement technologies, such as smokestack scrubbers at coal-fired power stations, and much laxer emission standards for automobile exhausts.[21] New Canadian prime minister Brian Mulroney suggested in 1985 that Canada needed to put its own house in order to strengthen its position on transboundary aid pollution vis-à-vis the United States. Toward this end he engineered an agreement between the federal and provincial governments that would reduce Canada's SO_2 emissions in half from 1980 levels by 1994.[22]

The Reagan administration handled the acid rain issue in much the same way as its conservative British counterpart by pointing to reductions that had already been achieved and would continue to occur as new technologies were phased in under existing laws. Moreover, the administration argued repeatedly that more stringent regulations should not be imposed until further scientific research demonstrated that they were needed and would be effective in mitigating the problem. The procrastination of the Reagan administration was condemned by domestic environmental groups, whose membership was burgeoning, and by the governments of northeastern states, several of which brought suit against the federal government to get relief from the flow of pollutants originating in the Midwest. Their efforts were often stymied, however, by opposition to stronger curbs on air pollution coming from powerful domestic lobbies, including midwestern electric utilities, which played a role similar in some respects to that of the British CEGB. Opposition also came from the companies that mined high-sulfur coal in the central Appalachians, whose interests were shielded by Senate majority leader Robert Byrd of West Virginia.[23]

The early involvement of the Soviet Union, and consequently the eastern European countries, in the LRTAP process was a response more to a diplomatic opportunity for East-West cooperation than to concern about acidification. Even in the early 1980s official ideology refused to recognize that pollution was a serious problem in communist societies, and the governments withheld information from their citizens about the magnitude of environmental degradation. Nor did the eastern European countries raise strong objections to the inflow of transboundary pollutants from western Europe.

Later in the decade, however, the population of the region did become aroused about pollution as the governments became more open about the condition of the environment and the occurrence of numerous environmental catastrophes, such as the 1986 Chernobyl disaster. Public outrage over the severity of environmental problems in their countries and what governments had done to conceal them became a significant factor in the overthrow of some of the communist regimes of the region. Environmental ills also became a focal point for the buildup of nationalistic resentments against the Soviet state, which soon led to its breakup in 1991.[24]

The specific problems of acid rain and transboundary air pollution have not been among the leading environmental concerns in the Soviet Union or its successor states, even though acidification has taken a toll in areas downwind from major sources of air pollution. For the most part, the soils and waters of the region are less susceptible to acidification than those of southern Scandinavia. The more immediate environmental priority has been to deal with the highly toxic brews of pollutants concentrated in the vicinity of huge mining, smelting, and industrial complexes, which have had devastating health effects for local populations. The experience with Chernobyl and revelations about other major nuclear accidents and the consequences of nuclear weapons testing have heightened sensitivities to radioactive pollution.

CREATION AND EVOLUTION OF THE LRTAP REGIME

The acid rain problem has been addressed in international institutions of the advanced industrial nations, which have been the first to experience the environmental ravages of acute acidification and to recognize its transboundary dimensions. The OECD, whose membership includes the economically advanced Western countries, took up the problem when it studied the flow of acid-forming pollutants in the early 1970s and issued an influential report on the large proportions that flowed across international boundaries.[25] Later in the 1970s the ECE became the primary locus for international policy making on acid rain because it offered a forum that would also engage the eastern European states, which shared the regional airshed and were both major emitters and recipients of air pollutants. Canada and the United States, being members of the ECE in spite of the organization's name, have participated in the development of the LRTAP regime but for the most part have addressed transboundary air pollution in North America through bilateral channels. The European Community (EC) has also been addressing the acid rain problem, as it seeks to harmonize national environmental regulations and standards in the interests of free and equitable trade among its members. Table 5.4 presents a chronology of the key events in the evolution of the LRTAP regime.

The Path to the Geneva Convention of 1979

Sweden brought its concerns about acid deposition and transboundary air pollution to the attention of the international community in a report presented to the United Nations Conference on the Human Environment in 1972.[26] While the conference did not adopt any measures that specifically addressed transboundary air pollution, the declaration that was adopted affirmed that the principle of state responsibility applies to damage to the environment of other states or nonnational areas.

Table 5.4. Chronology of the LRTAP Regime

1967	(October)	Swedish newspapers report Odén's findings on the sources of acid deposition in Scandinavia
1972	(June)	UN Conference on the Human Environment in Stockholm
1975	(August)	Conference on Security and Cooperation in Europe in Helsinki
1977	(July)	OECD report on transboundary air pollution
1979	(November)	LRTAP Convention Adopted in Geneva
1982	(June)	Acidification Conference in Stockholm
1984	(March)	Ministerial Conference on Acid Rain in Ottawa
	(June)	Ministerial Meeting in Munich
1985	(July)	Sulfur Protocol Adopted in Helsinki
1988	(November)	Nitrogen Protocol Adopted in Sofia
1991	(November)	VOC Protocol Adopted in Geneva
1994	(June)	Revised Sulphur Protocol Adoped in Oslo

The prospects for cooperation on transboundary air pollution were given an unexpected boost at the Conference on Security and Cooperation in Europe held in Helsinki in 1975. The conference, which was attended by thirty-five countries from the NATO and Warsaw blocs, was convened to develop ways of achieving peace and stability in Europe. The Final Act of the conference, which became known as the Helsinki Accord, included a section proposing cooperation in the fields of economics, science and technology, and the environment as part of a larger strategy for defusing tensions between East and West. Among the environmental possibilities for cooperation were "systems and methods of observation and control of air pollution and its effects, including the long-range transport of air pollutants."[27]

Soon after the accord was signed, Soviet general secretary Leonid Brezhnev proposed separate all-European ministerial meetings on the topics of energy, transport, and the environment. The West was initially cool to Brezhnev's proposal but in 1977 agreed to a ministerial meeting on the environment under the auspices of the ECE. Further talks narrowed the agenda to two topics, one being air pollution. Working groups were formed to draft concrete proposals for international cooperation on these topics. Following intensive negotiations the members of the ECE decided to convene the long-anticipated high-level meeting in November 1979 in Geneva, with air pollution being its topic.[28]

Serious differences arose among the Western countries during preparations for the high-level meeting in Geneva. Citing the 1977 OECD report on transboundary pollution, Norway and Sweden argued strongly for an international agreement containing legally binding provisions that would allow no further increases in SO_2 emissions and in the future require a 50 percent reduction. Canada supported the Swedish/Norwegian initiative out of growing concern about acid precipitation caused by pollution originating in the United States. Most of the other countries represented at Geneva declined to join Norway and Sweden in setting a schedule for limiting pollution. West Germany and the United Kingdom, which were the sources of much of the pollution afflicting Scandinavia, adamantly rejected any specific obligations to reduce emissions. The United States was also not ready to agree to binding limits on air pollution, although the Carter administration was less strident in its opposition than West Germany and the United Kingdom. The Soviet Union and the eastern European countries, being both heavy users of high-sulfur coal and recipients of significant amounts of pollution, did not participate actively in the debate, nor did the southern European countries.[29]

The Convention on Long-Range Transport of Air Pollutants (known as the LRTAP Convention), which was adopted at the high- level meeting in Geneva, was a compromise between the desires of the Scandinavian and European countries.[30] It recognized that airborne pollutants had become a major problem and reaffirmed that states have an obligation to ensure that activities taking place within their boundaries do not cause environmental damage in other countries. No specific limits were imposed on emissions of any air pollutants, but all parties were to "endeavor to limit and, as far as possible, gradually reduce and prevent air pollution, including long range trans-boundary pollution," using "the best available technology that is economically feasible." Finally, the agreement provided for scientific and technical cooperation, including the monitoring of emissions and the effects of air pollution. The LRTAP convention was signed by the thirty-four countries attending the Geneva meeting and entered into force in 1983 upon having been ratified by twenty-four of the signatories.[31]

The Sulfur Protocol of 1985

The LRTAP Convention is a typical framework treaty in acknowledging the seriousness of the problem of transboundary pollution, in declaring that the parties have a responsibility to take appropriate action to address the problem, and in providing an institutional framework for negotiating supplemental agreements, which could contain more specific obligations for reducing air pollutants, as circumstances dictated. Even before the LRTAP Convention came into force, Sweden used the tenth anniversary of the 1972 Stockholm Conference as an occasion for hosting a Ministerial Conference on Acidification of the Environment. The conference was comprised of two expert meetings attended by scientists, one on the subject of the ecological effects of acidification and the other on strategies and methods for controlling sulfur and nitrogen emissions. These were followed by a formal ministerial meeting attended by representatives from twenty-two of the signatories of the 1979 LRTAP Convention.[32] Despite Brezhnev's role in initiating the creation of the LRTAP regime, the eastern European countries were poorly represented, with East Germany being the only major polluting country from the region to attend.

The Nordic countries used the 1982 Acidification Conference to press their case for international commitments to reduce transboundary air pollution. Their position was buttressed by scientists attending the expert meetings, who concluded that enough was known about the nature and effects of acid rain to warrant remedial action using technologies that were available at an acceptable cost. The ministerial session was notable for the dramatic reversal of the position of West Germany from staunch opponent to active supporter of the international controls proposed by the Scandinavian countries. The German about-face was prompted by the strong public reaction to the growing evidence of *waldsterben* in the Black Forest of southern Germany. Switzerland reversed its position for similar reasons, while the Netherlands, Belgium, and Austria expressed stronger support than previously for international controls on air pollution.[33] By contrast the United Kingdom and United States distanced themselves from the growing sentiment among the European countries for international controls on air pollution, arguing that additional measures to limit emissions should not be adopted until the results of ongoing monitoring and research projects were known.[34]

The LRTAP regime's Executive Body, which is comprised of the ratifiers of the parties to the LRTAP Convention, met for the first time in

1983. A joint proposal from Sweden, Norway, and Finland that all parties make commitments to reduce their sulfur emissions by 30 percent between 1980 and 1993 drew support from Canada, Denmark, Austria, Switzerland, and West Germany. However, because of strong opposition from the United States, the United Kingdom, and France, the Executive Body did not adopt the Nordic proposal. The eastern European countries were also not ready to commit to a 30 percent reduction in their SO_2 emissions. The Soviets maintained that pollutants that were emitted and deposited within a country were an internal matter, but they indicated that they would be receptive to making a comparable percentage reduction in their exports of air pollutants, or what were referred to as "transboundary fluxes." This option of limiting transboundary fluxes as opposed to total emissions was important to the Soviet Union because only 1.5 percent of its SO_2 emissions drifted westward over European countries. Switzerland, Austria, and West Germany also proposed a reduction of NO_X emissions, which was supported by Canada and the Nordic countries, but this proposal was not adopted by the Executive Board.[35]

The Canadian government invited the ten nations supporting the Nordic proposal on SO_2 reductions to a two-day International Conference of Ministers on Acid Rain in Ottawa in March 1984. Norway called for a 50 percent reduction in SO_2 emissions by 1993, but the participating ministers could only agree on a communiqué calling for at least a 30 percent reduction of emissions of both SO_2 and NO_X by 1993, using 1980 as a baseline. The states participating in the Ottawa Conference thus became known as the 30 Percent Club. Several states made unilateral commitments to go further: Austria, Canada, West Germany, Norway, and France would cut back SO_2 emissions by 50 percent; Denmark and France by 40 percent.[36] West German chancellor Helmut Kohl invited the environmental ministers from the signatories of the 1979 LRTAP Convention to an International Conference on Environmental Protection in Munich in June 1984 in an effort to move the diplomatic process toward an agreement on reducing transboundary air pollution. At the Munich meeting Belgium, Luxembourg, and Liechtenstein announced that they would join the 30 Percent Club. The USSR (including the Ukraine and Belarus), East Germany, and Bulgaria also accepted the 30 percent goal, but only if they were given the option of cutting transboundary fluxes rather than national emissions. Thus, the 30 Percent Club had grown to eighteen countries, but several of the major emitters of SO_2 were still not members, including the United States, the United Kingdom, Italy, Spain, and Poland. The United States and the United Kingdom explained their reluctance to commit to a 30 percent reduction on grounds of continuing scientific uncertainties and the progress they had made since 1970 in reducing air pollution.[37]

The third meeting of the Executive Body of the LRTAP Convention was held in Helsinki in July 1985 to commemorate the tenth anniversary of the adoption of the Helsinki Accord. By then, three additional countries—Czechoslovakia, Italy, and Hungary—had joined the 30 Percent Club. The Executive Body adopted a protocol supplementing the LRTAP Convention, which would legally bind ratifying states to reduce either their total emissions or transboundary fluxes of SO_2 by 30 percent (from 1980 levels) as soon as possible and by 1993 at the latest.[38] Each country would devise its own strategy for achieving the 30 percent cutback. The twenty-one members of the 30 Percent Club signed the Sulfur Protocol, which came into force in September 1987 upon the sixteenth ratification.

Several of Europe's heaviest polluters—the United Kingdom, Poland, and Spain—as well as the United States, were among the countries not signing the Sulfur Protocol. The United States and the United Kingdom persisted in their contention that scientific evidence still did not warrant internationally mandated reductions of SO_2 emissions, which would require costly investments. Most of the other countries that refrained from signing the Sulfur Protocol cited their inability to bear the cost of complying with the protocol.[39] Poland, for one, had set ambitious goals for reducing air pollution but had conducted studies that revealed that the country could not afford the technology needed to reduce SO_2 emissions by 30 percent.[40]

At the time the Sulfur Protocol was adopted in 1985, eleven countries, principally the early members of the 30 Percent Club, declared their intention to achieve cutbacks that would go well beyond the 30 percent reductions mandated by the protocol. Each of the countries announced unilaterally a national goal for SO_2 emission reductions in the range of 50–70 percent (from 1980 levels) by dates ranging from 1990 to 1995. Most of these countries accomplished the additional reductions several years before their target dates.[41] Several countries later adopted even more ambitious schedules for emission reductions. For example, in 1988 the Swedish Parliament set a goal of an 80 percent reduction in SO_2 emissions (from 1980 levels) by 2000. By 1991 Sweden had already cut back its SO_2 emissions by 79 percent.[42] Norway and Finland set similar goals and promptly made substantial progress in achieving them.

The Nitrogen Protocol of 1988

Once the protocol on sulfur pollution was adopted, attention shifted to negotiating limits on NO_x emissions, which culminated in the adoption of a separate protocol in Sofia, Bulgaria, in November 1988. As the negotiations progressed, one group of parties to the LRTAP Convention, including Austria, the Netherlands, Sweden, Switzerland, and West Germany, pushed for a 30 percent reduction in NO_x emissions (from 1985 levels) by 1995, which would follow the precedent of the Sulfur Protocol. A second group of countries, including Denmark, Finland, France, Norway, Spain, and the United Kingdom, preferred only a freeze, while a third group comprised of the Soviet Union, the eastern European countries, and Italy favored an agreement that would allow some increases.[43]

Negotiations on the protocol were complicated by disagreements over rules designed to control automobile emissions, the principal source of NO_x pollution in the region. West Germany favored a requirement that cars be equipped with catalytic converters, which it was already encouraging domestically by means of tax incentives, while France, Italy, and the United Kingdom argued for "lean burn" engines that were more adaptable to their smaller, less expensive cars.[44] The Eastern bloc countries lacked the technical and economic means for significantly reducing automobile emissions in the short run. Moreover, reductions in their total level of NO_x emissions also seemed impossible in view of anticipated rapid increases in car ownership and use.

The protocol on nitrogen emissions adopted at Sofia, which was signed by twenty-seven countries including the United States and Canada, was a middle-of-the-road agreement in providing for a freeze on NO_x emissions.[45] More specifically, the protocol mandated that the parties would keep their NO_x emissions at or below their 1987 levels after 1994, which permitted short-term increases in NO_x pollution. The protocol also committed the parties to apply emission standards based on the "best available technologies which are economically feasible" and suggested in vague terms that there should be a transfer of technologies that could be used to reduce NO_x emissions. Finally, there was a clause providing that negotiations on reducing NO_x pollution would begin within six months after the protocol came into force. Twenty-seven countries promptly signed the protocol, which came into force in February 1991 upon the sixteenth ratification.

Disappointed that the Nitrogen Protocol did not go as far as they would have liked, the five countries that had favored a reduction in NO_x emissions drew up an agreement known as the Sophia Declaration, which committed them to cut NO_x emissions on the order of 30 percent by 1998, using the level of any year between 1980 and 1986 as the base. Seven countries (Belgium, Denmark, Norway, Finland, France, Italy, and Liechtenstein) added their signatures to the declaration after persuading the original group to push the target date back from 1995 to 1998.[46]

The VOC Protocol of 1991

After reaching agreement on the Nitrogen Protocol, the negotiators shifted their attention to the problem of volatile organic compounds (VOCs), also known as hydrocarbons. These chemicals react with nitrogen oxides and sunlight in the atmosphere to form photochemical oxidants, including ground-level ozone. Negotiations on limiting VOC emissions were complicated by the large number of chemical compounds in the hydrocarbon family, which have a myriad of uses in industrial societies. Moreover, most countries had not conducted a thorough inventory of their emissions of VOCs, and relatively little was known about the transboundary flow of VOCs and their environmental impacts.[47]

Nevertheless, the LRTAP parties succeeded in negotiating a protocol on VOC emissions that was signed by twenty-one countries meeting in Geneva in November 1991.[48] The protocol commits most parties to a 30 percent reduction in their emissions of VOCs by 1999. The suggested base year is 1988, but parties have the option of choosing any base year between 1984 and 1990. A party may elect to achieve a 30 percent reduction for the country as a whole or only for designated Tropospheric Ozone Management Areas (TOMAs), which are regions of the country that contribute significantly to ozone concentrations in other countries. Emissions from areas outside the TOMAs may increase as long as the total emissions of the country do not grow. Norway and Canada were the only two countries to elect the TOMA option, which other countries would have preferred not to include in the agreement. The protocol also permits countries that are light emitters of VOCs to freeze their annual emissions at 1988 levels by 1999. This provision applies to countries whose VOC emissions are less than 500,000 tons in total volume, 20 kg per capita, and 5 tons per square km. This provision applied to Bulgaria, Greece, and Hungary among the signatories.[49]

The VOC Protocol followed in the tradition of the other protocols appended to the 1979 LRTAP Convention in adopting an arbitrary across-the-board limit on emissions, although it offered parties more options and made special concessions to those with low levels of emissions. At the time the protocol was adopted, most states lacked regulations on VOCs and thus would have to take significant steps to fulfill their obligations to reduce emissions by 30 percent.[50]

Protocol on Further Reduction of Sulfur Emissions of 1994

Both the Nitrogen and VOC Protocols contain provisions suggesting they are only the first steps toward stronger controls that would be based on "critical loads" of pollution deposition. The concept of critical loads was first implemented in the Revised Sulfur Protocol adopted in Oslo in June 1994, which took the place of the expired 1985 protocol that mandated a 30 percent reduction in sulfur emissions or transboundary fluxes by 1993.[51] The practice of across-the-board reductions for all countries had fallen into disfavor on grounds of being arbitrary, inequitable, ineffective, and economically inefficient. The new protocol was designed to prevent environmental damage from acidification in the most cost-effective manner.

As defined in the Revised Sulfur Protocol, a critical load is "a quantitative estimate of an exposure to one or more pollutants below which significant harmful effects on specified sensitive elements of the environment do not occur according to present knowledge."[52] A grid comprised of square cells, 150 km to a side, was superimposed on the map of the European region. Prior to negotiations on the Revised Sulfur Protocol, scientists in each country calculated critical loads for sulfur deposition using as similar a methodology as possible in order to achieve compatibility of figures across Europe. Emphasis was on surface waters in northern Europe and on forest soils elsewhere. Within each grid cell, critical loads were calculated for numerous ecosystems. The critical load ultimately chosen for the cell as a whole would protect 95 percent of its ecosystems.[53]

Once critical loads were computed, it was possible to calculate the extent to which the actual sulfur deposition in each cell surpassed the critical load (see Figure 5.2). Early mappings for 1990 indicated that acidic deposition exceeded the threshold of environmentally harmful effects over about three-quarters of Europe, in some areas by as much as twenty times.[54] EMEP data in combination with an integrated assessment model (see below) made it possible to determine the principal sources of pollutants being deposited in each square.

Figure 5.2.   Extent to which Critical Loads for Sulfur Were Exceeded in 1990

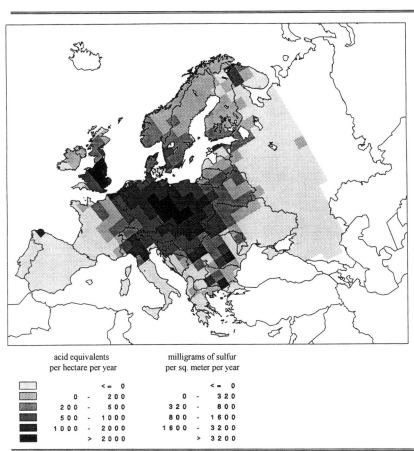

acid equivalents per hectare per year	milligrams of sulfur per sq. meter per year
< = 0	< = 0
0 - 200	0 - 320
200 - 500	320 - 800
500 - 1000	800 - 1600
1000 - 2000	1600 - 3200
> 2000	> 3200

Reprinted with permission from Hettelingh et al, "Maps of Critical Loads, Critical Loads....," 15.

Negotiations on the new sulfur protocol began in the summer of 1991 with the objective of reducing the extent to which the deposition of acidic pollution exceeded the critical loads in each of the EMEP grid cells by at least 60 percent from 1990 levels by the year 2000, which would leave 7 percent of Europe with excessive acid deposition. To achieve this "gap closure" each country was allocated its own sulfur-reduction target (from 1980 levels), which was to be achieved by 2000.[55] These targets were calculated using an integrated assessment model called RAINS (Regional Acidification INformation Simulation), which takes into account critical loads, data on emissions and deposition levels, and the projected cost of reducing emissions.[56] In most cases the reduction targets were greater than 50 percent, but they were in excess of 75 percent for ten countries in western Europe and Scandinavia, with Germany's being the highest at 90 percent (see Table 5.5). At the other extreme Greece was permitted a 49 percent increase. As the negotiations proceeded, it was up to each country to declare how much of a reduction it was prepared to make.[57]

The Protocol on Further Reductions of Sulfur Emissions was adopted after heated and sometimes acrimonious negotiations, during which the projected gap closure was reduced from 60 percent to 50 percent. The conflicting positions taken between the states advocating strong controls (namely Sweden, Norway, Germany, Finland, the Netherlands, Austria, and Switzerland) and those holding out for less ambitious reduction goals (the United Kingdom, Belgium, France, Ireland, and Spain) were reminiscent of coalitions that formed when the original sulfur protocol was negotiated.[58] In the end most of the European countries committed themselves to match, or at least come close, to the simulated reductions by the year 2000, although for some of them, most notably the United Kingdom, the effective date of their commitment was 2010. The protocol made allowances for the severe economic difficulties of the eastern European countries by allowing them five additional years to achieve their targets for SO_2 reductions. Despite their economic problems, the Czech and Slovak Republics, Poland, and Bulgaria indicated a willingness to cut their SO_2 emissions by nearly half or more by 2005. Moreover, with some assistance from the West, they thought they could fully achieve the reductions they had been allocated in order to achieve the 60 percent gap closure for the region by the turn of the century. If all of these commitments are fulfilled, SO_2 emissions in Europe would be down 42 percent (from 1980 levels) by the year 2000 and 51 percent by 2010.[59] For at least the time being the new protocol will not be applicable to North America because of the opposition of the United States, which has not accepted the critical-loads approach to limiting air pollution.[60]

Table 5.5.   Commitments to Reduce SO_2 Emissions under the 1994 Revised Sulfur Protocol (% from 1980 Levels)

	Previous Plan	RAINS Goal	2000 Goal	2010 Goal
Commitment for 2000 Matches RAINS Target				
Austria	80	80	80	
Finland	80	80	80	
Greece	−49	−49	−49	−45
Luxembourg	58	58	58	
Netherlands	77	77	77	
Norway	50	50	76	
Russian Fed.	38	38	38	40
Switzerland	52	52	52	
Commitment for 2000 Nearly Matches RAINS Target				
Belgium	48	77	70	74
Denmark	61	87	80	
France	67	80	74	78
Germany	90	90	83	
Sweden	81	83	80	
Commitment for 2010 Matches RAINS Target				
Czech Republic	30	72	50	72
Italy	48	73	65	73
Poland	37	66	37	66
Slovakia	30	72	60	72
United Kingdom	48	79	50	80
Commitment Significantly Short of RAINS Target				
Spain	35	55	35	
Ukraine	56	56	40	

Source: Figures from Acid News, October 1994, 10-11.

Having concluded the Revised Sulfur Protocol, the LRTAP negotiators have shifted their attention to the long-overdue task of revising
the 1988 NO_x protocol, which only froze NO_x emissions. As with the
new sulfur protocol, the next nitrogen protocol would be based on the
concept of critical loads. Such an agreement, which may also address
VOCs and tropospheric ozone, is not anticipated before 1998 because
the data and computer models that will inform the negotiations will not
be available until 1997.[61]

United States–Canadian Agreements

Being members of the ECE, the United States and Canada have been
participants in the negotiations on the LRTAP Convention of 1979 and
the series of subsequent protocols on specific types of acid-forming pollutants. As a major net importer of transboundary air pollutants, Canada
has allied itself with the Nordic countries in pushing for strong international regulations on emissions SO_2 and NO_x. The United States has been
in the company of the ECE's "laggard" states, in particular the United
Kingdom, in opposing specific international obligations to reduce
transboundary pollution through the LRTAP regime.

The United States and Canada have a long and extensive history of
using bilateral channels to address pollution problems that have arisen
between them. Transboundary air pollution first became an issue between the two countries during the extended litigation over the Trail
Smelter case that was concluded in 1941 (see chapter 1). The applicability of the case to the international dispute over acid rain in eastern North
America is limited, however, because it is difficult if not impossible to
link specific environmental damage in one country to a certain pollution source in another.

The long tradition of cooperation between the two countries on
water pollution has some bearing on air pollution. The 1909 Boundary Waters Treaty established the International Joint Commission
(IJC)to investigate disputes pertaining to transboundary pollution
that arose between the two countries.[62] The two countries signed the
Great Lakes Water Quality Agreements of 1972 and 1978 in response
to an increasing degradation of the lakes, including the dramatized
"death" of Lake Erie. The 1978 agreement recognized that air pollution deposited directly into the lakes or indirectly into the drainage ba-
sins of the tributary streams may be a significant source of contamination
of the lakes and called for consultations between the countries on remedial programs to address the problem.[63]

The United States and Canada began talks on the more specific problem of acid rain about the time the ECE took up transboundary air pollution in the late 1970s. The two countries created a Bilateral Research Consultation Group on the Long-Range Transport of Pollutants in 1978 to facilitate the exchange of scientific information on acid precipitation. The body concluded that the flow of SO_2 from the United States to Canada was two to four times as great as in the reverse direction, and for NO_x the flow from the United States was eleven times greater.[64] In 1980 the United States and Canada signed a nonbinding Memorandum of Intent (MOI) on the acid rain problem, which in some respects paralleled the 1979 LRTAP Convention in structure and content. The two countries agreed to take all possible action under existing domestic laws and policies to reduce transboundary air pollution in order to address the "already serious problem of acid rain." Negotiations were to begin the next year on a bilateral treaty that would formalize their cooperation on acid rain. Perhaps the most significant outcome of the MOI was the establishment of five bilateral working groups charged with providing the scientific and technical groundwork for future negotiations.

The budding cooperation between the United States and Canada on acid precipitation was abruptly interrupted in 1981 when the Reagan administration took office. Over the next years Canada continued to push the United States to agree to reduce the flow of air pollutants across its northern boundary with Canada. These Canadian entreaties were repeatedly rebuffed by the United States on grounds that additional research was necessary to determine the seriousness of the problem of acidification, the sources of the pollution causing the problem, and how the problem could be most effectively addressed.[65]

Little progress was made in resolving what had become a highly contentious issue between otherwise friendly neighbors until late in the decade, when the two countries separately adopted legislation designed to reduce air pollution significantly. Upon taking office in 1989, the Bush administration proposed amendments to the Clean Air Act, which were enacted by Congress in 1990. The United States legislation, which is notable for instituting a system of "marketable permits," was designed to reduce sulfur emissions by 50 percent by 2000. Meanwhile, the Canadian Environmental Protection Act of 1988 and the Canadian Green Plan announced in 1990 were to achieve comparable reductions in Canada's emissions of air pollutants. In 1991 President Bush and Prime Minister Mulroney signed the United States–Canada Agreement on Air Quality, an executive agreement that committed the two countries to cut SO_2

emissions in half by the year 2000 and to consult and cooperate with one another on matters related to transboundary air pollution. Disputes between the two countries pertaining to air pollution will be submitted to the IJC.[66]

COMPLIANCE WITH THE **LRTAP** PROTOCOLS

All thirty-four of the states that are members of the ECE, and the EC as a whole, have become parties to the 1979 LRTAP Convention. By August 1995 the Sulfur Protocol of 1985 had been ratified by twenty states and the Nitrogen Protocol of 1988 by twenty-five states. Among the nonratifiers of the Sulfur Protocol are the principal net exporters of air pollution—namely the United States, the United Kingdom, Iceland, Ireland, Spain, Portugal, Yugoslavia, and Greece—as well as Poland and Romania, which were reluctant to make a commitment to reduce pollutants that might be unrealistic given the state of their economies. The list of ratifiers of the Nitrogen Protocol is largely the same, although it does include the United States, the United Kingdom, and Spain but not Belgium and Denmark.

All of the countries that ratified the Sulfur Protocol achieved the required 30 percent reduction in SO_2 emissions (from 1980 levels) by the target date of 1993 (see Table 5.6), which was reflected in a 37 percent drop in emissions for the European region as a whole.[67] Several of the countries that in 1985 had unilaterally declared higher national goals for remission reductions were already largely in compliance with the protocol when it came into force in 1987. They went on to much greater reductions, led by Austria, Sweden, and Finland, which accomplished cutbacks of roughly 80 percent. Norway, France, the Netherlands, Denmark, and Belgium reduced their emissions by more than 60 percent. Among the nonratifiers Romania, Turkey, Poland, Spain, and the United Kingdom also achieved a reduction of at least 30 percent, while emissions rose in Portugal, Croatia, and Spain. The SO_2 emissions of the United States had fallen by only 16 percent by 1993.

Less can be concluded about compliance with the other protocols because of the later target dates: 1995 for a freeze in NO_x emissions, 1999 for a 30 percent reduction in VOCs, and 2000 for the new targeted reductions in SO_2 emissions. The most recent figures available on NO_x emissions are for 1993 (see Table 5.7). They show that emissions for most of the parties to the Nitrogen Protocol were already at or below those for the base year 1987, the primary exceptions being Ireland, Italy, and

Table 5.6.   Percent Changes in Sulfur Emissions (1980-1993)

Ratifiers of SO₂ Protocol		Non-ratifiers	
Austria	-82	Romania	-68
Sweden	-80	Turkey	-58
Finland	-79	UK	-35
Norway	-73	Poland	-34
Netherlands	-66	Spain	-30
France	-66	Ireland	-29
Belgium	-66	Slovinia	-23
Denmark	-65	USA	-16
Switzerland	-54	Iceland	0
Russian Fed	-52	Portugal	+9
Slovakia	-50	Croatia	+20
Hungary	-49	Greece	+28
Germany	-48		
Ukraine	-43		
Italy	-41		
Czech Rep	-37		
Bulgaria	-31		
Canada	-34		

Source: EMEP figures in Elvingson, Acid News, December 1995, 4.

Spain. Emissions had also increased in the nonratifying countries of Slovenia, Croatia, Romania, and Portugal. The three countries reporting reductions of 30 percent are former members of the defunct Soviet bloc, namely Bulgaria, Hungry, and the Czech Republic, which is largely an artifact of the severe decline in economic production of the region during the transition from communism.

Cutting NO$_x$ emissions by 30 percent by 1998 (using any year between 1980 and 1986 as a base year) has proven a more formidable challenge than had been anticipated for the twelve states that signed the supplemental declaration at Sofia. By 1993 only five of these countries—

Table 5.7.   Percent Changes in Nitrogen Emissions (1987-1993)

Signers of 30 % Declaration[a]		Ratifiers Only	
Switzerland	−25	Bulgaria	−43
Austria	−22	Hungary	−31
Germany	−15	Czech Rep	−30
Denmark	−12	Russian Fed	−14
Sweden	−8	United States	0
France	−7	Ireland	+6
Netherlands	−6	Italy	+8
Finland	−6	Canada	+9
Norway	−5	Spain	+4
Belgium	+9		
		Non-Ratifiers	
		Poland	−25
		Slovinia	+7
		Belgium	+9
		Croatia	+9
		Romania	+20
		Portugal	+111

[a] These countries also ratified the Nitrogen Protocol, with the exception of Belgium and Denmark, which only signed it.

Source: EMEP figures in Acid News , December 1995, 5.

Austria, Switzerland, the Netherlands, Germany, and Denmark—appeared to have a chance of achieving the 30 percent reduction. Norway has openly conceded that the goal is unrealistic. Sweden is projecting no more than a 27 percent reduction by 2000.[68]

When the Nitrogen Protocol and Declaration were adopted in Sofia in 1988, it was widely presumed that substantial reductions in NO_x emissions could be achieved by following the American lead in setting strict emissions standards on exhausts of new automobiles. NO_x emissions have not dropped as much as had been hoped in the countries, such as the Nordic ones, that had instituted new laws requiring catalytic converters on new automobiles. Vehicle traffic has increased more rapidly than anticipated, and old vehicles are being kept on the road longer than had been assumed. Disagreements between the countries producing large and small cars within the European Union (EU) delayed the adoption of stronger communitywide rules designed to reduce automobile emissions. Norway's difficulties in reducing NO_x emissions also stem in part from its substantial fleet of ships, which would be prohibitively expensive to retrofit and normally remain in service for about forty years.[69]

IMPACT OF THE ACID RAIN REGIME

Acid deposition in 1990 exceeded the scientifically calculated critical loads by approximately 28 percent over the European Continent and in some areas by as much as twenty times.[70] Thus far the steps taken to limit transboundary air pollution have only slowed the pace of acidification in Europe and North America. Emissions of SO_2 are down by more than one-third in Europe since 1980 but not enough to reverse the rising acidity of the region's waters and soils.[71] The Revised Sulfur Protocol of 1994 would add only about 12 percent to previous reductions in SO_2 emissions by the year 2000 and about 10 percent more by 2010, bringing the total reductions to little more than 50 percent over thirty years. By some estimates preventing further acidification will require cutting the total deposition of acids by 70 percent from 1990 levels; to reverse the trend will require even further reductions.[72]

To what extent has the LRTAP regime, and in particular its Sulfur and Nitrogen Protocols, affected trends in air pollution in the European region? Even though the reductions in SO_2 emissions of many European states coincide with the 30 percent cutback mandated by the Sulfur Protocol, these reductions may have taken place anyway. SO_2 emissions had been on a downward course in most of the western European countries since 1970, partly as a result of national laws enacted to address localized air pollution problems.[73] Furthermore, the sharp increases in oil prices instigated by OPEC in 1974 and 1979–80 induced most of the western European countries to revise their energy policies to reduce oil imports, either through conservation or increased use of other energy sources, such as hydroelectric and nuclear power. Thus, while motivated by economic considerations, these energy policies had the effect of reducing sulfur emissions beginning about 1980, the base year for the reductions spelled out in the Sulfur Protocol.

Most members of the 30 Percent Club did not need to enact additional measures to achieve the Sulfur Protocol's 30 percent reduction well in advance of the 1993 deadline. In fact many of them were willing to commit to much deeper cuts than were required by the protocol. These further reductions were in part a response to domestic political pressures to do whatever could be done to reduce air pollution. They also demonstrated to other countries, including those reluctant to commit to even a 30 percent reduction, that it was technologically and economically feasible to reduce SO_2 emissions by more than one-half. Furthermore, the countries heavily victimized by transboundary pollution, such as the Scandinavian ones, strengthened their case for international rules by showing a willingness to do all that they could on their own to reduce acidic deposition. Thus, the 1985 Sulfur Protocol and the prospects for negotiating a more stringent one within a decade were certainly part of the reason why some countries committed to deep reductions in SO_2 emissions.

The Soviet Union's 30 percent reduction in SO_2 emissions would probably also have occurred independently of any international commitments. Among the reasons for the decline were tighter laws on air pollution enacted during the early 1980s, the widespread substitution of natural gas for high-sulfur coal, and the movement of some highly polluting industries from the European part of the country to Siberia, which is outside of the region for which emissions figures are reported to EMEP. Moreover, strict enforcement of national laws during the last years of the Soviet Union forced numerous industrial plants to shut down. During the early 1990s air pollution declined further due to the economic turmoil in the country. Numerous firms equipped with antiquated, highly polluting technologies were closed because of their inability to compete in a market-oriented economy.[74] One apparent consequence of the LRTAP regime was a Soviet-Finnish agreement to reduce SO_2 emissions by 50 percent by 1995 on a reciprocal basis. Unfortunately, negotiations broke down on the transfer of pollution abatement technology from the Finnish corporation Outokumpu that would have drastically reduced emissions from huge Soviet smelters located on the Kola Peninsula near the Russian borders with Finland and Norway.[75]

Many of the countries that initially signed the Nitrogen Protocol did so in the belief that they could comply with the mandated freeze by 1994 with little additional effort. The protocol was adopted at a time when several countries were enacting laws with stringent emissions standards that could be met only by equipping new automobiles with catalytic converters. It was assumed that these laws on automobile exhausts, which were enacted prior to the adoption of the Nitrogen Protocol to take effect about 1990, would keep NO_x emissions from rising and hopefully make a significant reduction possible. When it became apparent that the auto emissions rules would not have the anticipated impact on NO_x emissions, most ratifiers of the protocol had to look for ways to curb NO_x emissions from power plants and other stationary sources in order to comply with the freeze mandated by the Nitrogen Protocol and, for some, the Sofia Declaration's goal of a 30 percent reduction.

The Revised Sulfur Protocol of 1994 was a disappointment to environmentalists for its failure to maintain the pace of SO_2 reductions of the 1980s. The commitments for reductions made by Austria, Finland, Luxembourg, the Netherlands, Russia, Sweden, Switzerland, Germany, and Spain were no higher than previous goals they had set. The United Kingdom's commitment to only a 50 percent reduction of SO_2 emissions by 2000, compared to its allocation of 79 percent, was especially discouraging, in particular to Norwegians, thousands of whom signed a petition protesting the devastation of the natural heritage of their country, which was presented to the British environmental minister at the signing of the protocol.[76]

The impact of the LRTAP regime may be less in the protocols that limit and reduce the release of acid-forming air pollutants than in the institutional processes it has set in motion. The reports issued by EMEP, based on its extensive air pollution monitoring network, have done much to raise consciousness among European governments and publics about the extent and severity of transboundary pollution and the related problem of acidification. EMEP has also provided negotiators with a consensual database that has been critical to concluding international agreements on reducing pollution and monitoring compliance. The meetings of the numerous committees and working groups of the LRTAP regime have been vehicles for scientists from countries with the most advanced knowledge on air chemistry and the effects of acidification to share their knowledge and techniques with their counterparts in countries where little was known about the problem, particularly those of southern and eastern Europe.[77] The regime also led to greater openness in the reporting of emissions data that had previously been kept secret, in particular by the eastern European countries, which has caused air pollution to become more of a public issue. For all these reasons it is unlikely that nearly as much would have been accomplished to address the acidification problem on the European Continent were it not for the LRTAP regime's smoothly operating institutions.

The LRTAP regime appears to have had little impact on how the issue of acid rain has been addressed in North America. As members of the ECE, Canada and the United States are parties to the 1979 LRTAP Convention and have been participants in the negotiations and, in some cases, ratifiers of the various protocols that target specific types of pollutants. The two countries have not, however, integrated their air pollution monitoring networks into EMEP, although a small but not inconsequential amount of the acid deposition in western Europe is believed to have originated in North America. Moreover, they have used bilateral channels for diplomatic discussions on the flow of air pollution across their border. The Canadian government had hoped that the LRTAP regime would become a mechanism for inducing the United States to reduce emissions of the pollutants responsible for acidic damage to Canada's lakes and forests. This possibility was not realized, however, as the United States refused to become a party to the 1985 Sulfur Protocol. Between 1988 and 1990 the United States and Canada adopted national laws aimed at significantly reducing air pollution, the goals of which were incorporated into their 1991 executive agreement on air quality. These national laws are hardly attributable to the involvement of the two countries in the LRTAP regime but rather were motivated primarily by political protests from downwind regions in both countries that were being victimized by the pollutants being transported from other domestic regions.

CONCLUSIONS

The LRTAP regime has in several ways been a striking achievement in regional cooperation to address a complex environmental problem. The regime pioneered several international strategies for reducing air pollution, including the flat percentage reduction for all countries, which was subsequently incorporated into global agreements designed to protect the ozone layer and may be the next step in efforts to limit global climate change. In recent years the regime has been an incubator of more sophisticated, cost-effective, and effects-based approaches for regulating air pollution, including the TOMA option in the VOC Protocol and the concept of critical loads upon which the Revised Sulfur Protocol is based.

The LRTAP regime is also noteworthy for the way it has thoroughly internationalized the monitoring of air pollution and scientific research on the effects of acidification in the European region. Thus, the data provided by EMEP on the transboundary movement of pollutants, in particular SO_2 and NO_x, are not only extensive and of a high quality but also have been accepted as being internationally unbiased by the membership of the regime, who have accepted them as the bases for negotiations. Without EMEP it is unlikely the negotiations on the protocols would have been nearly as successful.[78] By contrast, most of the information on air pollution and acidification in North America has been generated by national monitoring and research programs conducted by the United States and Canada, which has reinforced divergent assessments of the problem of transboundary pollution. The lack of a consensual base of knowledge on matters, such as the flow of air pollutants from specific sources to where they are deposited, is part of the explanation for why Canada and the United States have yet to negotiate a treaty to address their common acid rain problem, relying instead on vaguely worded executive agreements that do little more than reaffirm previously adopted national policies.[79]

An interesting aspect of the LRTAP regime has been the growing coalition of countries supporting international rules designed to reduce air pollution. When international discussions began in the 1970s on how to address the problem, Norway and Sweden stood almost alone in advocating international rules to curb transboundary air pollution, with little leverage over the recalcitrant upwind countries, in particular West Germany and the United Kingdom, which were responsible for much of the acidification plaguing their lakes and rivers. By the late 1980s the situation was reversed, with most of the European countries having joined forces with the Scandinavians in efforts to combat acidification, while members of the small group of persistent holdouts, led by the United Kingdom and the United States, were being relegated to the status of environmental pariahs. The key factors in the conversion of so many of the LRTAP states, including West Germany, Canada, and eventually the United Kingdom and the United States, were publics alarmed about the increasingly severe consequences of acidification in their countries.

Even with its accomplishments on the scientific and diplomatic fronts, the corner has still not been turned on the acid rain problem in Europe. Despite increasing serious effects of acidification for the region's lakes, forests, soils, and stone-surfaced buildings and monuments, public attention has been diverted to other compelling environmental problems, such as depletion of the ozone layer and climate change. The LRTAP regime has also had to contend with the emergence of new sovereign states from what was formerly the Soviet Union, Czechoslovakia, and Yugoslavia, which have been in the throes of a deep economic malaise since gaining independence. It is quite possible, however, that the institutional mechanisms that have been constructed over the past two decades, in particular EMEP, will sustain the momentum of the LRTAP regime as it seeks to reduce acid-forming pollutants to a level that can be tolerated by the environment.

Chapter 6

THE OZONE LAYER REGIME

Just over two decades ago, Mario Molina and Sherwood Rowland articulated their pathbreaking theory that chlorofluorocarbons (CFCs) might significantly diminish the stratospheric ozone layer and expose human beings and other life forms to harmful doses of ultraviolet (UV) radiation. A decade passed before observations of ozone losses began to bear out the Molina/Rowland theory, the most dramatic being the discovery of the Antarctic ozone hole. It was not until the 1990s, however, that significant evidence began to accumulate that increased amounts of UV radiation were passing through the atmosphere and harming some of the more sensitive organisms of the ecosystem.

Little progress was made on the diplomatic front in limiting CFCs and other pollutants contributing to the problem as long as the threat to the ozone layer was still only a theory, and forecasts of future ozone losses fluctuated widely. As scientific observations began to substantiate the principal components of the Molina/Rowland theory, it could no longer be plausibly denied that a potential environmental catastrophe was looming. Heeding the exhortations of Mostafa Tolba, the committed executive director of the United Nations Environment Programme (UNEP) from 1976 to 1993, diplomats from numerous nations acted decisively to preserve the ozone layer by negotiating the landmark 1987 Montreal Protocol and amending it in 1990, 1992, and 1995.

This series of international agreements imposed increasingly immediate target dates for the partial and then the complete phasing out of CFCs and most other chemicals believed to pose threats to the ozone layer. The agreements are remarkable for having been accepted not only by all of the industrial countries, which were producing most of the controlled substances, but also by many developing countries that have had plans for greatly expanding consumption of those chemicals as they modernized. The agreements are also of interest for the support received at critical stages from the chemical industry, which earlier had strenuously resisted national and international regulations on products that had been highly profitable. The regime defined by these agreements is perhaps most significant, however, for what it demonstrates about the potential for applying the precautionary principle in international environmental policy making in response to scientific warnings of problems that as yet have few evident harmful consequences.

PRODUCTION AND USE OF OZONE-DEPLETING SUBSTANCES

The origins of the ozone depletion problem can be traced to the creation of CFCs in 1928 by Thomas J. Midgley Jr., who had earlier invented antiknock ethyl gasoline. While employed by the Frigidaire Division of General Motors, Midgley was asked to work on developing a new coolant for refrigerators to replace the highly toxic chemicals that were being used in the rapidly growing industry. Midgley's CFCs were demonstrably nontoxic, noncorrosive, and nonflammable, as well as being efficient coolants. Within a few years E. I. du Pont de Nemours & Company began producing the chemical CFC-12 under the trade name Freon, and by 1935 the new product was being used in most of the eight million refrigerators produced in the United States. Freon was also the coolant used in the first home air conditioners, which came on the market in 1932.[1]

Several CFC compounds were adapted to an ever growing variety of uses during the next few decades. Beginning in the 1940s CFC-12s were used as a blowing agent for rigid foams, the best known being Dow Chemical's product Styrofoam, which became the preferred insulation in buildings and containers. During the Second World War CFC-11s and CFC-12s became the propellants in aerosol spray cans that dispersed insecticides to combat malaria. After the war CFC-11s and CFC-12s were adapted to numerous commercial spray products, such as perfumes, deodorants, hair sprays, and polishes. In the 1950s CFC-11s were employed in the production of flexible polyurethane foams used for cushioning material in furniture, bedding, and carpet padding. Rigid polyurethane foams made with CFC-11s and CFC-12s were used widely as insulating materials in commercial buildings, houses, and refrigerators.[2] In the 1970s a rapidly growing computer industry found CFC-113s to be ideal solvents for cleaning microchips and other sensitive electronic equipment. CFC-113s were also used as solvents in the dry cleaning industry.[3]

While CFCs have been the principal contributors to ozone depletion because of the large quantities that have been produced and their lengthy residence in the atmospheric, other chemicals have also been found to have significant ozone-depleting potential. Halons, which have been produced in much smaller quantities but are far more potent ozone depleters per molecule than CFCs, were initially developed by the United States Army Core of Engineers during the Second World War. Since then halons have been the primary retardants used in fire extinguishers because, like CFCs, they are nonreactive and thus do not stick to or damage objects onto which they are sprayed.[4] Methyl chloroform and carbon tetrachloride are two other chemicals that have been linked more recently to the chlorine levels in the atmosphere. The former is used primarily in solvents and adhesives, the latter as chemical feedstocks, solvents, fumigants, and pesticides.[5] Increasing attention has also been given in recent years to the ozone-depleting potential of methyl bromide, another chemical used as an agricultural fumigant. The chemical is also released in the exhaust of automobiles and from the burning of biomass.

The worldwide production of CFCs rose steadily in the decades following their discovery as they were adapted to a growing variety of products. Figure 6.1 plots how production of CFCs increased rapidly between 1960 and 1974, rising from 150,000 to 970,000 tons, largely due to their expanded use in aerosols and the dramatic growth of air conditioning in automobiles, homes, office buildings, and shopping centers. CFC production then leveled off and even declined slightly to 870,000 tons in 1982 due largely to the ban on their use in aerosol sprays in the United States. Production figures then began to rise again, peaking at 1,260,000 tons in 1988 as use of CFCs in nonaerosol applications continued to increase. The growth of CFC production was reflected in chlorine concentrations in the atmosphere, which had grown from natural background levels of .6 parts per billion (ppb) to 2.7 ppb by the mid 1980s.[6]

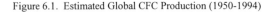

Figure 6.1. Estimated Global CFC Production (1950-1994)

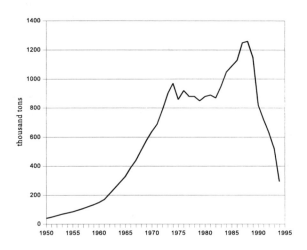

Source: Based on figures from Brown et al, <u>Vital Signs 1995</u>, 63.

Growth in the production and use of other ozone-depleting chemicals has been even more rapid. For example, demand for halons quadrupled between 1973 and 1984 and was growing by percent annually in the mid 1980s. Thus, bromine concentrations in the atmosphere rose at an even faster rate than CFCs and were projected to increase tenfold over the next century.[7]

While the ozone depletion problem is of global scope and consequences, most production and consumption of CFCs has taken place in the industrial countries. The United States accounted for approximately half of the production and consumption of CFCs until the 1970s, but its share of the world total diminished considerably after 1978 when it banned nonessential uses of CFCs.[8] During the same period European production of CFCs increased considerably, in the case of Britain almost doubling between 1974 and 1986.[9] Thus, by 1986 U.S. production of CFCs had dropped to 28 percent of the world's total, while the share of other OECD countries had risen to 57 percent. At the time the Soviet bloc was responsible for 11 percent of world production and the developing countries for only 4 percent. The regional shares of world consumption of CFCs were similar for most regions, except that Europe exported substantial amounts of its production to the developing countries. China and India, with more than one-third of the world's population, combined for only 2 percent of CFC consumption, but their share was beginning to grow rapidly as they modernized and sharply increased their use of refrigeration.[10] In the absence of international regulations, China was expected to increase its annual consumption of ozone-depleting substances by 12 percent, India by 15 percent.[11]

Aerosols accounted for more than half of world CFC use in 1974 but dropped to 25 percent by 1985, due largely to the United States ban, while growth continued in other uses. Air conditioning and refrigerants consumed 20 percent of world CFC production in 1985, while solvents and rigid foam insulation each accounted for 19 percent. The pattern of use of CFCs among the industrialized countries varied considerably in 1985, with the European countries still using them extensively in aerosol sprays, while the United States employed them most heavily in refrigeration and air conditioners, and Japan used them as solvents in its electronics industries.[12]

In the mid 1980s CFCs were produced by only twenty-one companies in sixteen countries.[13] Du Pont was the leader among the five companies manufacturing CFCs in the United States, with its principal overseas competition coming from Imperial Chemical Industries (ICI) of the United Kingdom, Farbwerke Hoechst of Germany, and Elf-Aquitaine of France. The total sales of CFCs by U.S. producers amounted to only about $750 million in 1987, but there were as many as ten thousand companies that used CFCs in producing $28 billion worth of goods and services, while installed equipment that used CFCs had an estimated value of $135 billion.[14]

OZONE DEPLETION AS A PUBLIC ISSUE

The warning of Molina and Sherwood about the potential effects of CFCs on the ozone layer received extensive media coverage in the United States, which evoked a strong public response that spurred governmental action. Initially attention focused on the use of CFCs in aerosol sprays. Environmentally concerned consumers quickly cut back their purchases of aerosol products with CFC propellants, reducing the market for such sprays by two-thirds in the United States and prompting some firms voluntarily to phase out use of CFCs.[15] Congressional hearings begun in 1975 sifted through scientific evidence on the seriousness of the ozone-depletion problem and then considered bans on nonessential uses of CFCs, in particular their use in aerosol sprays. The same year several state legislatures debated bills that would restrict the use of CFCs, with Oregon being the first to ban CFCs in aerosols. New York passed a law requiring manufacturers of aerosol spray cans with CFCs to place labels on containers warning that their use could be harmful to the environment.[16]

The United States Congress acted quickly to establish the legislative basis for restricting use of CFCs at the national level. The Environmental Protection Agency (EPA) was given broad authority to regulate CFCs under terms of the 1976 Toxic Substance Control Act. EPA's mandate was augmented by the 1977 amendments to the Clean Air Act, which required the EPA administrator to regulate any substance that in his/her judgment may reasonably be expected to affect the stratosphere, especially its ozone layer, thereby endangering the public's health or welfare. As the first step in carrying out its responsibility, the EPA imposed a ban on the nonessential use of CFCs in aerosols, which took effect at the end of 1978. These regulations led to a 95 percent reduction in CFC use in aerosols in the United States, as affordable substitutes soon came on the market.[17]

The United States was not alone in taking action to regulate nonessential uses of CFCs during the late 1970s. Norway and Sweden, neither of which was a producer of CFCs, followed the lead of the United States in prohibiting the use of CFCs in aerosols. Canada, a minor producer of CFCs, banned their use in several of the principal types of aerosol products. The Netherlands, a significant manufacturer of CFCs, required warning labels on aerosol spray cans. West Germany, another major producing country, set a goal of a one-third reduction of CFC use in aerosols. These restrictions on nonessential applications of CFCs were adopted in the belief that the benefits of their use paled in comparison with their potential environmental consequences.[18]

Reacting to pressure from the United States and growing public concern about ozone depletion, the European Community (EC) in 1980 enacted a 30 percent reduction in CFC use in aerosols by 1991 (from 1976 levels) and a freeze on CFC production capacity.[19] The EC directive had virtually no practical impact, however, because CFC use in aerosols had already been reduced by 28 percent, due largely to German cutbacks, and no further legislation would be necessary to achieve the 30 percent goal. Moreover, the EC countries had a substantial excess capacity for producing CFCs and thus could significantly increase production from current levels without expanding their productive capacity.[20]

The sense of urgency about the ozone layer was much less pronounced in most of Europe and in Japan, where the prevalent view was that regulations on CFCs could await definitive evidence that these highly useful chemicals were actually causing ozone loss that would have adverse human and environmental consequences. There were suspicions in the other CFC-producing countries that proposals by the United States for international limits on CFCs were a veiled strategy to enable its chemical companies to take advantage of their lead in the development of chemical substitutes. The skepticism of France and the United Kingdom was also partly a reaction to an earlier decision of the United States to drastically limit landing rights of their Concorde aircraft at American airports, citing what the European nations believed were exaggerated environmental concerns, including the threat to the ozone layer.[21] It was not until evidence of the ozone depletion threat became incontrovertible in the late 1980s that most other developed countries went so far as to ban the use of CFCs in aerosols.

The EPA viewed the aerosol ban as only a first step toward fulfilling its legislative mandate to take action to protect the ozone layer. The agency then turned its attention to the possibility of regulating other uses of CFCs and in October 1980 proposed limiting CFC production to current levels, which would be followed by a gradual schedule of reductions. These regulations did not come into effect, as the Reagan administration that took office the next year was not persuaded that further controls were justified in view of continuing uncertainties about the threat of ozone depletion. Other uses of CFCs, such as in refrigeration, were viewed as being more "essential" than in aerosols, in part because no viable substitutes had been developed for these applications. This point was emphasized by the industries that produced and used CFCs, which in 1980 established a trade group called the Alliance for Responsible CFC Policy, which became a potent lobbying force against further regulations on the use of CFCs. There was also a reluctance in the United States to proceed further on its own if other major consuming countries of CFCs were not even willing to ban nonessential uses.[22]

By the early 1980s the American public was becoming complacent about threats to the ozone layer, perceiving that the ban already enacted on nonessential uses of CFCs in the United States would significantly slow ozone loss. The public was also confused by what appeared to be conflicting scientific estimates of the seriousness of the problem. A flurry of studies had been undertaken in previous years to investigate the validity of the Molina/Rowland theory and project future ozone losses, by groups ranging from the prestigious United States Academy of Sciences to the major chemical companies that had a stake in continued production of CFCs. Additional chemicals were incorporated into increasingly complex atmospheric models, including several, such as halons, that it was believed would accelerate ozone loss, while others, such as chlorine nitrate, carbon dioxide, methane, and nitrous oxide, might offset the impact of CFCs, either by absorbing chlorine molecules or by increasing ozone production.[23]

As different assumptions were built into the atmospheric models and new data became available, projections of the amount of ozone loss that would occur by the mid twenty-first century fluctuated widely, as reflected in a series of reports of the National Academy of Sciences (NAS). The first NAS report, issued in 1976, projected an ozone loss of between 2 and 20 percent, with 7 percent being the most likely, which was in line with the initial estimates of Molina and Rowland two years earlier.[24] A 1979 NAS report estimated a 16.5 percent depletion, while a 1982 report reduced the projected ozone loss to 5–9 percent.[25] A 1984 NAS report lowered the prediction for ozone loss further to 2–4 percent, while even suggesting that a 1 percent increase in stratospheric ozone was possible over the next decade.[26] Part of the reason for the lower forecasts of ozone loss of the early 1980s was the substantial decline in the use of CFCs in aerosol sprays in the several countries that had banned this application in the late 1970s.

Even during the lull in interest and concern about the ozone depletion problem during the early 1980s, some scientists—most prominently Sherwood Rowland—continued to make the case for precautionary steps that would reduce emissions of the implicated ozone-depleting substances, at least until there was definitive evidence refuting the Molina/Rowland theory. Others, including representatives of the industries that produced and used CFCs, cited the varying projections in arguing against any further restrictions on the implicated chemicals until the scientific confusion abated and there was actual evidence of declining stratospheric ozone levels.

Anxiety about the ozone layer began to rise again in the mid 1980s as worldwide production of CFCs began to climb again. A group of Harvard scientists warned in 1984 that the impact of chlorine on the ozone layer may increase dramatically once a critical threshold was surpassed, resulting in a "chlorine catastrophe" that might cause an ozone loss of more than 15 percent.[27] At about that time the first reports of actual reductions in concentrations of stratospheric ozone lent greater credibility to the Molina/Rowland theory. Then the startling announcement of the Antarctic ozone hole in 1985 and the media coverage it received quickly brought the ozone depletion issue back to a prominent place on the public agenda, even though the cause of the hole was still in doubt. The reemerging concerns were reinforced the next year by the authoritative report on the scientific assessment coordinated by the World Meteorological Organization (WMO) and UNEP, which projected a 9 percent loss of stratospheric ozone by late in the next century if 1980 levels of CFC emissions continued.[28]

CREATION AND EVOLUTION OF THE OZONE LAYER REGIME

UNEP was quick to assume the lead in organizing an international response to the ozone depletion problem, even though the Organization for Economic Cooperation and Development (OECD) was perhaps better suited to the task, given that all the major CFC producer countries at the time were members and the organization had considerable experience in harmonizing environmental policies. In a long-term planning document known as the Montevideo Programme of 1982, the UNEP Governing Council listed ozone depletion along with land-based sources of marine pollution and the handling and disposal of toxic wastes as the three problems to be given priority in the development of international environmental law.[29] Throughout its involvement with the ozone depletion problem, UNEP has worked with other specialized agencies, in particular WMO, which has coordinated international scientific efforts to monitor and better understand the problem, and to a lesser extent the World Health Organization (WHO), which was concerned with the potential health effects of increased human exposure to ultraviolet radiation. Table 6.1 is a chronology of the evolution of the ozone layer.

Table 6.1. Chronology of the Ozone Layer Regime

1974	(June)	Molina/Rowland theory about impact of CFCs on the ozone layer
1977	(April)	World Plan of Action on the Ozone Layer adopted in Washington, DC
	(November)	Coordinating Committee on the Ozone Layer (CCOL) created
1978	(October)	United States adopts ban on nonessential uses of CFCs
1982	(January)	First Meeting of Working Group of Legal and Technical Experts
1984	(September)	Meeting of Toronto Group
1985	(March)	Convention on the Ozone Layer adopted in Vienna
	(May)	Farman's revelation about the Antarctic "ozone hole"
1986	(January)	WMO/UNEP/NASA report on the status of the ozone layer
	(May)	Economic Workshop in Rome
	(September)	Economic Workshop in Leesburg, Virginia
1987	(June)	Adoption of Montreal Protocol
1988	(March)	Report of the Ozone Trends Panel
1989	(March)	Conference on Saving the Ozone Depletion in London
	(May)	Declaration adopted at first conference of the parties to the Montreal Protocol in Helsinki
1990	(June)	Amendments to the Montreal Protocol adopted in London
1992	(November)	Amendments to the Montreal Protocol adopted in Copenhagen

The Path to the Vienna Convention of 1985

The first international forum to take up the Molina/Rowland theory was a scientific meeting convened by WMO in 1975 at the request of UNEP, which issued a statement of concern about the problem. UNEP organized the first intergovernmental conference on the ozone depletion problem in Washington, D.C., in March 1977, which was attended by experts from thirty-three countries and several IGOs and NGOs. The conference agreed upon a World Plan of Action on the Ozone Layer that called for international cooperation in monitoring and researching threats to ozone depletion, but it suggested no controls on the production of CFCs. Later that year the UNEP Governing Council created the Coordinating Committee on the Ozone Layer (CCOL) to implement the plan of action. In the years that followed the CCOL brought together scientists from government, industry, universities, and international agencies to discuss the risks of ozone depletion and to keep policy makers informed of the latest scientific thinking on the subject.[30]

The United States hosted an international conference in April 1977, also in Washington, D.C., to broach the possibility of negotiating an international agreement designed to curb the flow of CFCs into the stratosphere. At the time, however, it was not even possible to engineer a consensus on voluntary measures to limit nonessential uses of CFCs. For the remainder of the decade the countries that had already adopted unilateral regulations on nonessential uses of CFC pushed for talks on international controls, but they were frustrated by persistent opposition from other states that questioned the immediacy and severity of the alleged perils to the ozone layer.

In 1980 the UNEP Governing Council adopted a nonbinding resolution that encouraged a reduction of CFC use but set no specific targets. Two years later, acting on a Swedish proposal, the Governing Council established the Working Group of Legal and Technical Experts for the Preparation of a Global Framework Convention for the Protection of the Ozone Layer, to which the CCOL would serve as a technical and scientific advisory body. The Working Group, which was made up of experts and observers from fifty states and eleven international organizations, met seven times between 1982 and 1985 and eventually drafted a framework convention that was adopted in Vienna in March 1985.[31]

The negotiations that began in 1982 on an initial ozone layer treaty quickly became polarized between two blocs of industrialized countries. On one side were the states strongly committed to an anticipatory response to the threat of ozone depletion. Early in the talks Sweden and Austria offered a draft protocol, known as the Nordic Annex, which would ban CFCs in aerosols and limit their use in other applications. In 1983 Sweden, Norway, Finland, Canada, Austria, and Switzerland formed an informal coalition, which became known as the Toronto Group after they met in the Canadian city in September 1984 to agree on a negotiating strategy. While not an original member of the coalition, the

United States aligned with the Toronto Group when William Ruckelshaus, who was appointed EPA administrator in 1983, reoriented American policy back toward advocacy of international protection for the ozone layer, after a hiatus during the first years of the Reagan administration.[32]

The Toronto Group offered a series of proposals for substantially reducing use of CFCs, which would bring other industrial countries into line with the restrictions that some of them had adopted unilaterally in the 1970s on nonessential uses. These proposals were resisted by a second bloc of countries that included most members of the EC, Japan, and the USSR, where there was lingering skepticism about the threat to the ozone layer and a strong stake in a lucrative export market for CFCs. Furthermore, the impact of banning nonessential uses would have a greater impact on the European countries, where aerosols had always comprised a much larger proportion of CFC use than in the United States.[33] Concern was also expressed that the proposals of the Toronto Group did not adequately provide for what were considered to be "essential" uses of CFCs, such as in refrigeration. The EC's bargaining position was little more than the weak response it had adopted in 1980, which had provided for a 30 percent reduction (from 1976 levels) in aerosol use of CFCs and a limit on capacities for producing CFCs. The Toronto Group considered the proposal to be seriously inadequate but was unable to overcome the EC's intransigence on mandating a schedule for cutting back on the manufacture and consumption of ozone-depleting substances.[34]

The initial phase of negotiations led to the adoption of the Convention for the Protection of the Ozone Layer at a UNEP sponsored conference in Vienna in March 1985, which was attended by representatives from forty-three states, only twenty of which signed the convention at the conclusion of the meetings.[35] The Vienna Convention was typical of framework treaties for its failure to set a timetable for specific reductions of pollutants. The parties did, however, accept the general obligation to adopt "appropriate legislative or administrative measures . . . to control, limit, reduce, or prevent human activities under their jurisdiction or control should it be found that these activities have or are likely to have adverse effects resulting from modification or likely modification of the ozone layer."[36] The convention also calls for international cooperation in monitoring, research, and scientific assessments and the exchange of information on the impacts of human activities on the ozone layer, and in turn the consequences of ozone changes on human health and the environment. As with other framework agreements, the Vienna Convention provided for a conference of the parties that would meet periodically to review further scientific information on the ozone layer and to consider and adopt supplementary protocols or amendments to either the framework convention or protocols.

The Vienna Convention was criticized for doing little more than re-affirming the international plan of action adopted in 1977. It was significant, however, for declaring that the ozone depletion problem should be addressed in an anticipatory way and for establishing a process for adopting stronger measures.

The Montreal Protocol of 1987

The grounds for skepticism about the seriousness of threats to the ozone layer were soon undermined by the British Antarctic Survey's report on the Antarctic ozone hole in 1985 and the authoritative report of WMO/UNEP in 1986. Discussions on strengthening the international response to the ozone depletion problem began even before the Vienna Convention came into force in 1988. UNEP sponsored two economic workshops in Rome and Leesburg, Virginia, in May and September 1986, respectively. While the first proved to be quite divisive, the second broke down the polarization between the Toronto Group and the EC and forged a general consensus on the need for controlling CFC production and use. Between the two workshops UNEP and the United States EPA convened an International Conference on the Health and Environmental Effects of Ozone Modification and Climate Change. These meetings set the stage for three negotiating sessions held in Geneva and Vienna between December 1986 and April 1987 to prepare a draft protocol for consideration at a ministerial meeting set for Montreal in September 1987. The negotiating sessions gradually drew larger numbers of participants, with sixty nations taking part in the Montreal meetings, half of which were from developing countries. For the first time in the ozone talks there were numerous observers from environmental organizations, industrial firms, and the media.[37]

Several developments lent momentum to the talks, which culminated in the adoption of the Montreal Protocol. The first was the discovery and announcement of the Antarctic ozone hole. The negotiators involved in the new round of talks agreed to ignore the ozone hole until its cause had been determined. Nevertheless, the shock of its revelation contributed to a general mood of urgency that seemed to spur agreement on cutting back production of CFCs, more so than would have occurred solely on the basis of the WMO/UNEP assessment report issued the next year. The discovery of the ozone hole also had the effect of framing the ongoing debate in a way that led to greater support for anticipatory action. While such a response might later prove to be an overreaction, it was widely thought to be more prudent than underreacting to an increasingly ominous threat.[38]

A second factor was the leadership of the United States, which called for emissions of ozone-depleting substances to be frozen in the short term and cut back by 95 percent within ten to fourteen years. The position had the backing of a Senate resolution passed by an 80–2 vote. The State Department used its worldwide network of embassies to distribute updated scientific information designed to persuade foreign governments and publics of the need for international controls.[39] At the time the American EPA was under some domestic pressure from a lawsuit filed by the National Resources Defense Council (NRDC) insisting that it fulfill its obligation under the Clean Air Act Amendments of 1977 to regulate any substance that could reasonably be expected to affect the stratosphere. The suit lent greater credibility to an American threat to adopt stiff unilateral controls on CFCs and to impose trade sanctions on countries that did not reciprocate, in the event the negotiations failed to produce a strong enough protocol. The NRDC suit was apparently not the only driver of the American proposal on ozone-depleting substances, given that it went well beyond what the NRDC expected or was apparently required by the 1977 law.[40]

The third development was a critical shift in the position of the American chemical industry, which previously had maintained a strong and unified voice against further controls on CFCs. Du Pont, which accounted for approximately 50 percent of CFC production in the United States and 25 percent globally, had begun research on substitutes for CFCs in the 1970s. These efforts were put on hold during the early 1980s when the prospects of further national or international controls receded. In 1986 Du Pont announced that if a regulatory environment were created that ensured a market for substitutes for CFCs, the company was willing to resume research efforts and was confident that alternative products for most uses could be developed within six to eight years.[41] Later in the year the Alliance for Responsible CFC Policy supported international controls on the rate of CFC growth, which signaled that the American chemical industry was now resigned to international regulations on CFCs and foresaw a large enough market to make the development of substitutes profitable.[42]

Finally, the bargaining stance of the EC shifted substantially as cracks appeared in the unified resistance of its members to internationally mandated controls on CFC production and use due partly to mounting public concern about the ozone depletion problem. Belgium, West Germany, Denmark, and the Netherlands openly criticized the two most intractable holdouts, the United Kingdom and France, which were homes to Europe's largest CFC producers. After considerable internal political maneuvering, the EC relented on its refusal to go beyond the weak measures adopted in 1980 and agreed to as much as a 50 percent reduction in the production and consumption of CFCs by the end of the century.[43] The EC continued to complicate negotiations, however, by insisting that it be treated as a single unit in reporting data on CFC production and use, which would allow some member countries to avoid cutbacks if the reductions of other countries exceeded the mandated percentages. A compromise was reached in which production figures would be reported for each country but consumption only for the EC as a whole.[44]

The Montreal Protocol adopted in September 1987 provides for specific limits on ozone-deleting substances.[45] Annual production and use of CFCs were not to exceed 1986 levels by the year beginning seven months after the protocol came into force. A 20 percent reduction (from 1986 levels) was to be achieved by the year ending June 30, 1993, and a 50 percent reduction by the year ending June 30, 1999. Production and consumption of the principal halons were not to exceed 1986 levels by the fourth year after the protocol came into effect, which turned out to be 1993. The calculation of CFCs would be the aggregate of five types of CFCs—11, 12, 113, 114, and 115—with the figures for each being weighted according to its ozone-depleting potential (ODP) relative to CFC-11. Putting CFCs into one "basket," as opposed to setting target reductions for each type individually, allowed producing and consuming countries greater flexibility in achieving the mandated cutbacks, which was critical for gaining widespread acceptance of the protocol. For example, Japan, which would have been reluctant to commit to drastic reductions in its use of CFC-113, upon which it depended for solvents for its electronics industries, had the option of complying with the protocol by making deeper cuts in less essential uses of other types of CFCs.[46]

Several potentially contentious issues pertaining to trade in controlled substances also had to be resolved if the protocol was to have its desired effect. National production limits could cause countries to favor domestic over foreign consumers as supplies of controlled substances declined. If this occurred, frustrated importing countries may find it necessary to reject the protocol and satisfy their needs by building up their own productive capacity both for domestic consumption and for export to other countries cut off from foreign suppliers. To address this concern the concept of "adjusted production" was adopted, which is calculated by subtracting exports and adding imports to national production of CFCs. Allowing producers to subtract exports from their calculations would offer some protection for importers.[47] It was also agreed that the parties would cease imports of bulk amounts of the controlled substances from nonparty states within one year of the protocol's entry into force and suspend all exports to nonparties by January 1, 1993. Furthermore, the import of products containing controlled substances from nonparties would cease within three years of the protocol's entry into force, and procedures would be developed to extend the ban to products produced with, but not containing, the controlled substances.

To encourage developing countries to become parties to the protocol, those that annually consumed less than 0.3 kg per capita of controlled substances were given ten additional years to comply with the scheduled reductions. During that period they would be allowed to increase their consumption to the 0.3 kg level in order to meet their domestic needs. The 0.3 kg level amounted to approximately 25–30 percent of the average consumption of residents of the industrialized countries in 1987 and 50–60 percent of what they would be permitted to consume when the reductions mandated in the protocol were achieved.[48] The agreement also included provisions for economic and technical assistance for adopting alternative substances and new technologies, but their lack of specificity raised concern about whether they would have much impact.

The Montreal Protocol was to come into force when it had been ratified by at least eleven countries that accounted for more than two-thirds of the consumption of the controlled substances, which it was hoped would take place by January 1, 1989. This goal was met as twenty-nine states, accounting for 83 percent of the consumption of CFCs, as well as the EC, ratified the protocol by the target date.[49] Among the early ratifiers were most of the industrial countries, including the members of the Toronto Group and the EC, as well as Japan and the Soviet Union. The American Senate ratified the protocol in March 1988 by an 83–0 vote, even though complying with the scheduled reductions posed a more formidable challenge for the United States and the other countries that had earlier banned aerosol uses of CFCs. They would have to reduce use of controlled substances in applications for which alternative products had not yet been developed, whereas the other industrial countries could achieve much of the required cutbacks by doing what the United States had done ten years earlier to eliminate nonessential uses.[50]

The protocol was embraced by some developing countries, including Mexico, Venezuela, Egypt, Indonesia, Kenya, and Thailand, but many others—most prominently India and China—did not accept it because they were less persuaded of the seriousness of the problem and anticipated a continuing need to increase consumption of the controlled substances as they modernized.[51] To the extent that preservation of the ozone layer was viewed as a global problem, they regarded it as one for the rich countries to solve. Questions were raised about whether it was fair to allow industrialized countries a significantly higher per capita consumption of the controlled substances, even though they were largely responsible for the existing concentrations of ozone-depleting chemicals in the atmosphere.

The London Amendments of 1990

Upon its adoption in September 1987 the Montreal Protocol was widely applauded for being a bold international response to the threat of ozone depletion. The adequacy of the agreement came into question in early 1988 when the Ozone Trends Panel issued its report, which both implicated anthropogenic pollutants as the cause of the Antarctic ozone hole and noted that the ozone layer was thinning elsewhere more rapidly than had been anticipated.[52] Thus, the scientific presumptions that underlay the negotiations on the Montreal Protocol were suddenly superseded by the alarming new evidence that the ozone depletion problem was much more serious and immediate than previously realized.

The conclusions of the Ozone Trends Panel stimulated efforts to move to stronger measures to protect the ozone layer. By the end of 1988 the industrial countries were united on the need for a total phaseout of substances threatening the ozone layer by the end of the century if not sooner. Two years earlier most of these countries had rejected a similar goal as being too radical, when it was proposed by the United States in the negotiations on the Montreal Protocol. Public concern about depletion of the ozone layer and the state of the environment rose to high levels throughout much of Europe, which was reflected in the electoral successes of Green parties in some countries.[53] Responding to a groundswell of public opinion and a report of British scientists affirming the conclusions of the Ozone Trends Panel, British prime minister Margaret Thatcher, in a speech to the Royal Society in September 1988, abruptly reversed her position from opponent to proponent of strong international action to conserve the ozone layer. Thatcher cosponsored a meeting with UNEP in London in March 1989, which was attended by representatives of 123 countries, in order to encourage more countries to ratify the Montreal Protocol as well as to build political support for substantially stronger controls.[54]

The chemical industry also offered support for phasing out ozone-depleting substances, even though only months earlier it had argued that the state of scientific evidence did not even warrant the reductions mandated in the original Montreal Protocol. Reacting to the report of the Ozone Trends Panel, Du Pont announced in March 1988 that it would stop producing CFCs and halons by 1999. Later in the year, after an industry-sponsored review confirmed the conclusions of the Ozone Trends Panel, the Alliance for Responsible CFC Policy also endorsed a phaseout of the chemicals causing ozone depletion.[55] Yielding to consumer pressures, the British Association of Aerosol Manufacturers announced that its members would cease using CFCs in most aerosol products. ICI, which accounted for approximately 80 percent of the British production of CFCs, announced that it would follow Du Pont's lead in phasing out the production of CFCs and in accelerating the development of substitutes.[56]

The Montreal Protocol was revised through a review process carried out by the four expert panels UNEP set up to explore the topics of science, technology, environmental effects, and economics. Their reports were combined into a *Synthesis Report,* which informed discussions on revising the protocol that took place in seven sessions of a negotiating body called the Open-Ended Working Group held during late 1988 and early 1989.[57] The negotiations took advantage of a broad international political consensus that was forged both at Prime Minister Thatcher's Conference on Saving the Ozone Layer in London in March 1989 and at the first meeting of the parties to the Montreal Protocol, which was held in Helsinki in May 1989. The latter meeting, at which eighty nations were represented—many at the ministerial level—adopted the Helsinki Declaration on the Protection of the Ozone Layer, a strongly worded but nonbinding document calling for a phaseout of CFCs "as soon as possible but not later than the year 2000" and halons as soon as feasible. Considerable attention was also given to the funding needed to enable developing countries to comply with phaseouts of ozone-depleting substances.[58]

The Montreal Protocol was updated at the second conference of the parties, which was held in London in June 1990 with more than ninety countries represented, including forty-two that were not yet parties to the protocol. The resulting agreement, which became known as the London Amendments, was substantially longer and more complicated than the original Montreal Protocol.[59] Fifteen types of CFCs would be totally phased out by the year 2000, with achievement of a 50 percent reduction (from 1986 levels) by the year 1995 and an 85 percent reduction by 1997. Previously controlled halons were also to be completely phased out by the year 2000, with a 50 percent reduction by 1995; however, the parties had until 1992 to make cases for exemptions for uses for which no substitutes were available. Other halons would be studied further before a phaseout schedule would be established. The London Amendments also expanded the list of chemicals that were controlled. Carbon tetrachloride and methyl chloroform, each of which has been found to be contributing 16–17 percent of chlorine concentrations in the atmosphere, were to be completely phased out by 2000 and 2010, respectively. Finally, use of hydrochlorofluorocarbons (HCFCs), leading substitutes for CFCs that are significant but less potent depleters of stratospheric ozone, was to end by 2040 if not substantially sooner.[60]

The schedule for reductions and phaseouts of ozone-depleting substances was designed to bring the concentration of chlorine in the atmosphere back down to 2 ppb by the late twenty-first century, which was about their level in the late 1970s when the Antarctic ozone hole first appeared. The chlorine loading stood at 2.7 ppb in 1985 and was rapidly rising. Even with the cutbacks in CFCs mandated by the original Montreal Protocol, the chlorine loading had been projected to rise to 11 ppb, which would be nearly twenty times the natural level.[61]

The most contentious issues taken up in the negotiations on the London Amendments involved concessions to developing countries to induce them to become parties to the agreement. As in the original Montreal Protocol, developing countries were given a ten-year grace period to meet the schedule of reductions of ozone-depleting substances. The developing countries were more concerned, however, about whether the industrial countries would provide additional funding and make technologies available to facilitate their use of substitutes for the controlled substances. The London Amendments provided for a Multilateral Fund to be administered by the World Bank with the assistance of the UNEP and the United Nations Development Programme. The fund would have an initial three-year budget of $160–240 million, with the higher figure being contingent on China and India becoming parties. Loans and grants would be made to finance a defined list of "incremental costs" encountered by developing countries in implementing their programs for phasing out ozone-depleting substances. The developed countries would contribute to the fund on the basis of the United Nations scale of assessments. A fourteen-member Executive Committee comprised of equal numbers of industrialized and developing countries was established as a policy-making body for the fund. A clause was inserted at the insistence of the United States that the fund should not be regarded as a precedent for establishing similar arrangements to address other environmental problems.[62]

Negotiators had more difficulty resolving the issue of technology transfer. Seeking to ensure access to new technologies on terms that they could afford, the developing countries pushed for language suggesting the appropriate technologies would be provided on a "preferential and non-commercial basis." This wording was troublesome to the technologically advanced countries, which argued that mandating artificially low prices for technology transfers would discourage corporate investment in research on substitutes for ozone-depleting substances. Furthermore, the governments of these countries had a responsibility to respect the proprietary rights of the private patent holders of the technologies, which were protected by national laws and the rules of the World Intellectual Property Organization (WIPO). In the end the developing countries agreed to the transfer of environmentally safe substitutes and related technologies "under fair and most favorable conditions," with the additional acknowledgment that their capacity to fulfill obligations spelled out in the agreement depended upon the effective implementation of financial assistance and technology transfer.[63]

The Copenhagen Amendments of 1992

The fourth meeting of the parties to the Montreal Protocol drew representatives from eighty-seven countries to Copenhagen in November 1992, three months after the London Amendments came into effect. New scientific reports indicated that ozone depletion was proceeding substantially faster than had been projected just years earlier, especially over the heavily populated latitudes of the Northern Hemisphere. This information added even more urgency to the task of phasing out the chemicals responsible for the problem. Agreement was reached on further revisions to the Montreal Protocol in the form of a document known as the Copenhagen Amendments, which entered into force in June 1994 upon being ratified by twenty of the parties to the Montreal Protocol. The Copenhagen Amendments advanced the date for phasing out CFCs, carbon tetrachloride, and methyl chloroform to January 1, 1996, and halons even earlier to January 1, 1994. HCFCs are to be limited to 1989 levels by 1996 and reduced 35 percent by 2004, 65 percent by 2010, and 90 percent by 2020, and they are to be totally phased out by 2030.[64]

No agreement was reached in Copenhagen on phasing out methyl bromide. Some developing countries objected to restrictions on methyl bromide on grounds that there were still scientific uncertainties about the impact of the chemical on the ozone layer and that it was critical to their economic and agricultural development. Thus, the only agreement that could be reached on methyl bromide was that developed countries would freeze production of the chemical at 1991 levels by 1996. Further consideration of restrictions on the chemical would await a scientific assessment report.[65]

The status of the Multilateral Fund was taken up again in Copenhagen. The industrial countries agreed to increase the level of funding to between $350 and $500 million for the period 1994–96. A British and Dutch proposal would have shifted responsibility for funding the adaptation of developing countries to the Global Environment Facility (GEF), which had been established by the World Bank, UNEP, and UNDP to finance environmental projects in the developing countries. Third World countries strongly objected to the proposal on grounds that the World Bank was dominated by the industrial states and thus not responsive to their special needs.

The Vienna Amendments of 1995

Representatives from 149 countries met in Vienna in December 1995 for the seventh meeting of the parties to the Montreal Protocol. These talks led to the agreement among 110 countries on a third major set of amendments to the Montreal Protocol, which will establish a tighter schedule for the reduction and phasing out of the remaining chemicals that threaten the ozone layer. The industrialized countries agreed to cut back on methyl bromide by 25 percent by 2001 and by 50 percent by 2005 and to phase out the chemical completely by 2010, with exemptions for certain trade-related applications and undefined "critical agricultural uses." The latter exemption was included at the insistence of a small number of countries led by the United States. Agricultural interests in Florida and California had strongly lobbied the Clinton administration on this issue, warning of large losses of agricultural exports if they are prohibited from using methyl bromide as a soil fumigant.[66] The regime's Technical and Economic Advisory Panel is to propose a definition for determining critical agricultural uses, presumably a rather narrow one, for consideration at the meeting of the parties in 1997. The developing countries agreed for the first time to limit their use of methyl bromide, specifically a freeze on consumption that would come into effect in 2002 based on their average consumption for the 1995–1998 period. A phase-out schedule for developing countries will be discussed at the 1997 meetings. Trade in methyl bromide will be banned with any country that is not a party to the 1992 Copenhagen Amendments.

The Vienna Amendments also advance the phase-out date for HCFCs for the industrialized countries from 2030 to 2020, except for a small amount of production that could continue until 2030 for servicing previously existing equipment, or what is known as the "service tail." Developing countries agreed to freeze HCFC use in 2016 at 2015 levels despite a recommendation from the regime's Technology Assessment Panel for a freeze that would take effect in 2006. The issue of assistance was also brought up, as China and India warned that their willingness and ability to follow through on their commitments to limit ozone-depleting substances was contingent on the industrialized countries providing greater amounts of economic and technical assistance. Thus far the industrialized countries have provided $438 million to the Multilateral Fund that was created in 1991.[67]

COMPLIANCE WITH THE OZONE ACCORDS

The ozone layer regime is remarkable not only for the series of agreements limiting and phasing out the production and use of ozone-depleting substances but also for the broad acceptance of them and apparent high rate of compliance with the controls. While the ratifications were not registered as promptly as would have been desirable in view of the urgency of the ozone depletion problem, the pace has nevertheless been considerably faster than that of numerous other international treaties. The 1985 Vienna Convention did not receive the twenty ratifications needed to come into force until 1988, the year after the Montreal Protocol was signed. However, the Montreal Protocol and its two major amendments all came into effect within eighteen to twenty-six months of their adoption. By December 1995, 150 countries were parties to the original Montreal Protocol, 100 to the London Amendments, and 37 to the Copenhagen Amendments.[68]

The parties to the Montreal Protocol have the obligation to report on the amounts of the controlled substances that they produced, exported, and imported in 1986, the base year for calculating percentage reductions, and to provide updated figures in subsequent years. This information, which some countries and companies had previously been unwilling to divulge for commercial reasons, is essential for monitoring the compliance of the parties with the various mandated reductions. Implementing a reporting system, however, has not been without its complications. While it is fairly easy to quantify production and international movements of bulk quantities of CFCs and other restricted substances, difficulties have arisen in devising a system for calculating the amounts of these chemicals that are present in manufactured products.[69] Thus far, few countries have been submitting their reports on time, and even by 1994 more than forty parties had not yet provided baseline data for 1986. Many of the latter were developing countries that lacked the technical capacity to make the reports and thus were in need of international assistance. The European Union (EU) has only been reporting export and import data for the community as a whole while internally monitoring data for individual countries.[70]

Despite this lack of diligence in reporting, it appears that most countries have been fulfilling, and in many cases exceeding, their obligations to freeze, reduce, and finally to phase out CFCs and other ozone-depleting substances under terms of the Montreal Protocol and its amendments. Figure 6.1 portrays the sharp downward trend in global CFC production since 1987. Production of CFCs by the reporting countries declined 40 percent between 1986 and 1991 even though the Montreal Protocol required only a 20 percent reduction by mid 1993.[71] Almost all of the OECD countries were quick to adopt programs that would enable them to achieve the mandate of the London Amendments for a total phaseout of most ozone-depleting substances by 2000. In most cases they projected a phaseout sooner than the document required. For example, even before the Copenhagen conference of the parties in 1992, Germany had adopted legislation that would eliminate CFCs by 1993 and halons by 1996; President Bush announced that the United States would end production of CFCs by the end of 1995.[72]

The OECD countries and the EU were equally prompt in passing implementing legislation to effect phaseouts by the dates specified in the Copenhagen Amendments. The United States allocated tradeable production and import allowances for ozone-depleting substances to firms on the bases of their previous production and imports, and taxed consumption at rates that increased steeply with the approach of the phaseout dates. Use of methyl bromide is to be discontinued in the United States by 2001 in accordance with provisions of the 1990 Amendment to the Clean Air Act, which appear to be at odds with the exemption for critical agricultural uses that the United States had included in the Vienna Amendments of 1995. The members of the EU decided to phase out CFCs one year in advance of the date specified by the Copenhagen Amendments but were only able to agree on a 25 percent reduction in methyl bromide consumption by 1998.[73] The EU will need to adopt additional measures in order to comply with the phase out of methyl bromide by 2010 that was agreed to by the industrial countries in Vienna in 1995.

Rapid progress toward the phaseout of ozone-depleting substances in the developed countries has been made possible by the prompt and decisive action taken by the chemical industry in North America and Europe to end the production and use of the controlled chemicals. By 1994 CFCs had virtually disappeared in flexible polyurethane foams and aerosols in the United States and western Europe, and the market for CFCs as solvents has collapsed and was expected to vanish by 1996.

Production of all CFCs in the industrial countries ended in 1995.[74] Ironically, Du Pont's announcement that it would cease production of CFCs by the end of 1994 prompted the United States EPA to request the firm to delay this action for one year to ease the transition to substitutes in some applications, in particular automobile air conditioners.[75] There are, however, reasons for concern about compliance. Domestic and international black markets for CFCs are developing, which if uncontrolled will detract from the effectiveness of the international agreements.[76] Moreover, the potential of a political backlash to strict regulations to protect the ozone layer was apparent in Arizona's adoption of a law in 1994 that would have permitted the manufacture and use of CFCs in the state.[77]

The prospects for phasing out ozone-depleting substances is not as promising in other regions. In the countries of the former Soviet bloc production of the controlled substances dropped by about half between 1988 and 1994, but largely because of the severe economic decline in the region. The Russian Federation failed to comply with the January 1, 1994, deadline for phasing out halons set by the Copenhagen Amendments. Furthermore, the federation has announced that it will not be able to comply with the January 1, 1996, deadline for ending production of CFCs and requested a four-year extension.[78] In view of their economic problems, if the former communist countries are to achieve the internationally mandated phaseouts of ozone-depleting substances, they will need technological and economic assistance that will enable them to use substitutes and to recover and recycle controlled substances. Most of these countries do not qualify for grants from the Montreal Protocol's Multilateral Fund for this purpose because their annual consumption of CFCs exceeded the cutoff of 0.3 kg per capita. They have, however, received some assistance from the GEF for reducing use of ozone-depleting substances.[79]

Little progress has been made toward controlling, much less eliminating, use of ozone-depleting substances in the developing countries. Thus far most of them are not in violation of any treaty commitments since, as low-volume users, they qualify for the ten-year grace periods that were written into the agreements. One promising sign is that several of the major developing countries—including China, Mexico, and Thailand—have announced their intentions to achieve reductions sooner than required.[80] One reason for concern, however, is that the commitments of developing countries, as spelled out in the London and Copenhagen Amendments, were made contingent on the support they received for adopting substitutes for the controlled substances. As with most other international funds, contributions to the Multilateral Fund from donor countries have lagged behind the amounts that had been promised.[81] Furthermore, few awards have been made from the Multilateral Fund thus far because of disagreements that have arisen in attempts to establish criteria for making them. Complications have also arisen in establishing terms for the transfer of technologies needed to phase out ozone-depleting substances.[82]

IMPACT OF THE OZONE DEPLETION REGIME

With the rapid phasing out of CFCs and halons, the prognosis for the ozone layer has already improved considerably. By some calculations, loss of stratospheric ozone may peak as early as 1998, after which the layer could begin a gradual recovery to earlier concentrations.[83] To what extent can this remarkable development be attributed to the international ozone layer regime embodied in the Vienna Convention, the Montreal Protocol, and the London and Copenhagen Amendments? In the absence of such a regime, how likely was it that the major producing and consuming states would act on their own to mitigate the looming threat to the ozone layer?

There have been a few examples over the past two decades of unilateral actions being taken to lessen the ozone depletion problem. In the mid 1970s strong public concerns aroused by publication of the Molina/Rowland theory prompted several American state governments and then the federal government to impose regulations on the use of CFCs in aerosols. Several other countries, which were primarily consumers of CFCs, followed the lead by adopting similar bans. At that time, however, the citizenry in many of the other industrialized countries, including the other major producers of CFCs, did not seem to share the depth of concern that Americans had about a thinning of the ozone layer. Accordingly, their governments delayed taking the relatively painless first step of banning CFCs in aerosols for nearly a decade.

The limitations of unilateralism to effect a solution to the ozone depletion problem became quickly apparent during the early 1980s. While consumers in the United States had been willing to give up CFCs in aerosol products, reducing or phasing out other uses such as in refrigeration and air conditioning would require greater sacrifices that were less politically palatable. Thus, the United States was loath to go to a second level of unilateral controls, which would inconvenience consumers and might jeopardize the competitiveness of industries, until other countries—in particular the members of the European Community, Japan, and the Soviet Union—took at least the first step of eliminating CFCs in aerosols. Ironically, the substantial reduction in aerosol use between 1974 and 1984 resulting from the unilaterally enacted bans lowered projections of future ozone loss, which diminished the sense of urgency about the problem in the United States and reinforced skepticism in other countries about the seriousness of the problem. Thus, no other significant unilateral cutbacks on ozone-depleting substances were imposed until after the adoption of the Montreal Protocol of 1987, which mandated that all parties would reduce production and consumption of commonly used CFCs and halons by across-the-board percentages by specified years.

The situation changed markedly in 1988 when incontrovertible evidence arose suggesting that the ozone layer was already being depleted, and at a rate that was much more rapid than previously projected. Several industrialized countries that had steadfastly opposed international controls several years earlier, most notably the United Kingdom, declared their intentions to phase out the implicated substances more rapidly than was required by the Montreal Protocol and then the London Amendments. It is unlikely, however, that these unilateral pronouncements would have been made were it not anticipated that they would add momentum for stricter international regulations on ending production and use of the principal ozone-depleting chemicals. The evolution of the ozone layer regime had a marked impact on the decisions of the chemical industry, which in turn were significant factors in agreements on more stringent international policies. Chemical producers and their trade groups, such as the Alliance for Responsible CFC Policy, strongly resisted national controls on CFCs, which would fragment the market for their products and put them at a disadvantage relative to producers in other countries that were not subject to similar rules. Furthermore, they were reluctant to invest heavily in substitutes for CFCs and ozone-depleting chemicals until the regulatory situation ensured a sizable market for the new products. Once persuaded that international regulations would soon be adopted requiring a phaseout of the previously used substances, the chemical industry quickly fell into line and within a few years had developed viable substitutes for most of the controlled substances. The process was reciprocal in that the chemical producers hastened the adoption of international regulations on ozone-depleting substances by expressing confidence in their capacity to create and market these substitutes in a timely manner. Without such assurances, it is unlikely the industrialized states would have agreed to push up the dates for phasing out the previously used chemicals, as they did in adopting the London and Copenhagen Amendments.

The restrictions on trade with nonparties that were imposed by the Montreal Protocol and subsequent amendments have been a significant factor in bringing a large number of countries into the regime. States refusing to ratify these documents have had to contemplate the consequences of having the party states abruptly stop exporting the controlled substances to them. Some of the nonparties could perhaps develop the capacity to produce sufficient quantities of the chemicals to satisfy their own needs or import them from other nonparties. However, within a few years any of their products that contained the controlled substances or that were produced with them could not be exported to the parties. Thus, as the roster of parties to the Montreal Protocol grew rapidly during the late 1980s and included all of the industrial countries, other countries recognized that there were significant disadvantages to staying out of the fold.

These considerations pertaining to trade weighed heavily on developing states. While by no means inattentive to the dangers that ozone depletion posed for their citizenry, they were also reluctant to give up the option of using the controlled substances, which for the foreseeable future would be considerably less expensive for applications critical to their modernization than the substitutes. The Multilateral Fund and the commitment of the industrialized countries to facilitate the transfer of technologies needed to produce and use substitute substances offered them an opportunity to become players in the rapidly growing market for a new generation of chemicals more benign to the ozone layer, which would not be available to them as nonparties.[84]

CONCLUSIONS

The story of the ozone layer regime illustrates how science can be a critical factor driving international public policy. It was through science that the invisible ozone layer was discovered, as was the role the layer plays in shielding the planet from ultraviolet radiation. Scientists also uncovered the threat that CFCs and several other synthetic chemical compounds posed to the ozone layer and sounded the alarm about the ominous ozone hole that began appearing over Antarctica during spring seasons since the late 1970s. These latter two revelations were fortuitous given the serendipitous path of the Molina / Rowland inquiry into what happened to CFCs in the atmosphere and the propitious presence of the British Antarctic Survey on the inhospitable continent of Antarctica. Without them knowledge of the anthropogenic threats to ozone depletion and the subsequent international response may have been delayed considerably.

Science alone did not drive the evolution of the international ozone layer regime. When covered extensively in the media, the reported dangers associated with ozone depletion aroused strong public concern, which spurred governments and the chemical industry to act to address the problem. The North American and Nordic publics became alarmed about the problem during the 1970s, prompting their governments to impose unilateral bans on the use of CFCs in aerosols. It was not until the late 1980s, however, that the intensity of concern among European publics spurred their governments to work for a total phaseout of ozone-depleting chemicals.

The regime demonstrates the potential of a flexible approach for addressing international environmental problems in which a framework convention is supplemented by protocols as circumstances dictate. As scientific evidence became increasingly conclusive and public concern grew, organizational mechanisms were available to the parties for reconvening and considering stronger measures to address the problem. The regime also illustrates how rules on trade can induce the participation of states that might otherwise perceive it advantageous to remain nonparties and in effect be free riders benefiting from a public good, in this case the ozone layer, which is being preserved by the sacrifices of the parties. Finally, the regime provides a model for addressing the different needs and interests of developing countries, as well as their concerns about the inequity inherent in being asked to comply with rules that were established to deal with a problem that they played only a small role in creating.

The ozone layer regime is an adaptation to the unique features of the environmental threat that it addresses. It does not necessarily provide a model for international environmental cooperation that can be readily transferred to other problems, such as climate change. It does, however, offer a significantly expanded vision of what can be accomplished in the form of an international anticipatory response to a complex global environmental problem.

Chapter 7

THE CLIMATE CHANGE REGIME

A century has passed since Swedish scientist Svante Arrhenius first raised the possibility that humans may unwittingly be warming the planet's climate by adding large quantities of carbon dioxide (CO_2) to the atmosphere as they burn ever greater quantities of fossil fuels. It is only in the last two decades, however, that rigorous modeling and other investigatory tools have been used to investigate the human impact on the global climate and the consequences that such changes may have for human societies and the natural environment. Paradoxically, some of the most important clues about the potential future impact of human activities on the global climate have come from increasing knowledge of naturally occurring climate changes over the past hundreds of thousands of years, which paleoclimatologists have gleaned from such sources as ocean sediments, polar ice cores, and tree rings.

Climate change was the last of the four major atmospheric problems to be the subject of international talks aimed at the creation of a regime. The official negotiations that began in 1991 succeeded in drafting the Framework Convention on Climate Change (FCCC), which was signed the next year at the Earth Summit in Rio. The convention goes further than the framework agreements that address the LRTAP and ozone depletion problems, in particular in setting a goal for the developed countries of returning their net emissions of greenhouse gases (GHGs) to 1990 levels by the turn of the century and requiring them to report on what they are doing to fulfill that goal. Due primarily to the opposition of the United States, the agreement does not impose the binding targets and timetables for limiting GHG emissions that most of the other OECD countries favored, as did a vocal coalition of small developing island nations fearful of rising sea levels.

The FCCC is only a first step toward an effective international response to address the problem of climate change. The parties will need to negotiate supplementary agreements with deep cutbacks in GHG emissions if concentrations of these gases in the atmosphere are to be stabilized. The swift evolution of the ozone depletion regime from 1985 to 1992 suggests that such agreements are possible, even as an anticipatory response to a problem that does not yet have readily demonstrable manifestations or impacts, as is also the case with climate change. Furthermore, the lessons learned from negotiating the agreements that first reduced and then banned the substances responsible for ozone depletion may have some applicability to future negotiations on strengthening the climate change regime.

In some respects, however, global warming poses a much more formidable challenge for international negotiators than did ozone depletion. The science of climate change is considerably more complex, and significant scientific uncertainties remain about the phenomenon, which have been cited by some as reasons for postponing the adoption of strong international rules. Moreover, while numerous countries are highly vulnerable to climate change and thus committed to preventing it, others appear to be much less concerned about global warming and are thus more inclined to try to adapt to it. A substantial reduction in emissions of GHGs will require fundamental changes in the energy, industrial, transportation, agriculture, and forest sectors of most nations. Developed countries will be asked to make changes in their modern energy-intensive lifestyles, and developing countries will be asked to reformulate their basic development strategies to limit use of fossil fuels and forest clearing. In certain key countries, such as the United States, strong opposition will be mounted by the politically powerful industrial and consumer groups that would be affected by such fundamental policy changes. Thus, the climate change problem will prove to be a compelling test of the resolve and capacity of the international community to respond to what could be the most important environmental threat humanity has faced.

THE BUILDUP OF GREENHOUSE GASES IN THE ATMOSPHERE

As with the problem of acidification in Europe and North America, the origins of human-induced climate change can be traced to the industrial revolution that began in the eighteenth century and stimulated a rapid growth in the burning of fossil fuels to satisfy rapidly growing demands for energy. Large amounts of first coal and later petroleum and natural gas were burned to power machines that were adapted to an ever expanding range of human uses, including manufacturing and motorized transport. In the twentieth century fossil fuels became the principal sources of electrical power that was critical to modern lifestyles. The burning of fossil fuels releases the carbon locked in them, which is the principal human contributor to the enhanced greenhouse effect.

Human beings are also contributing to the greenhouse warming through land-use practices, in particular the widespread clearing of forests, which has accelerated markedly in recent decades, and the expansion of agriculture. When trees burn or decay, the carbon contained in them escapes into the atmosphere, and the forests that are removed no longer exist to absorb CO_2 from the atmosphere. Agricultural operations such as wet rice cultivation and animal husbandry as well as leakage from natural gas pipelines and oil wells are the primary causes of the human- induced doubling of methane concentrations in the atmosphere since preindustrial times.[1]

Global population growth has been and will continue to be an important underlying factor in human contributions to potential climate change, especially with the mushrooming of population in much of the Third World. The widespread conversion of forested land to agriculture in developing countries has been triggered in large part by the needs of rapidly growing populations for food and income, although the problem is exacerbated by acute inequalities in the distribution of income and land. Population growth has also contributed to the increase in industrial emissions of CO_2 over the past two centuries, although there has also been a significant rise in per capita emissions up until the past two decades. The full impact of the past rapid population growth in developing countries on global industrial carbon emissions will be felt only as these countries undergo industrialization in the coming decades.[2]

Global Trends

The burning of fossil fuels has accounted for approximately three-quarters of carbon emissions from human activities since 1860. Consumption of fossil fuels grew fivefold between 1860 and 1900 and then more than doubled again by 1929 before leveling off during the Great Depression of the 1930s and World War II.[3] Use of fossil fuels accelerated rap-

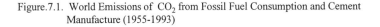

Figure.7.1. World Emissions of CO_2 from Fossil Fuel Consumption and Cement
Manufacture (1955-1993)

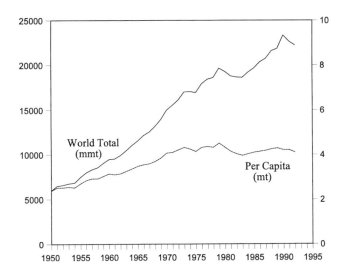

Figures from World Resources Institute, World Resources 1996-1997, 330.

idly following the Second World War, with a 3.5-fold increase taking
place between 1945 and 1973. Annual per capita emissions of CO_2 from
fossil fuel burning and cement production (a small proportion) rose
from 2.4 metric tons (mt) in 1950 to 4.3 mt in 1973.[4] See Figure 7.1 for an
overview of these trends during the postwar period.

The global growth in use of fossil fuels has slowed over the past
two decades, largely because of the sharp rises in oil prices engineered
by OPEC in 1973–74 in conjunction with the Arab-Israeli war and in
1979–80 due to the Islamic revolution in Iran and the beginning of the
Iran-Iraq war. This slowing down was also sustained in part by a shift
away from energy-intensive forms of industrial production in the ma-
ture economies of the highly developed countries.[5] Thus, industrial emissions of CO_2 rose by only about 28 percent from 1973 to 1989, or an

average annual rise of about 1.6 percent, compared to 4.6 percent between 1950 and 1973. Global per capita emissions of CO_2 peaked at 4.5 mt in 1979 and in 1992 stood at 4.1 mt.[6]

By the mid 1980s scientists had become increasingly concerned about the contributions that human emissions of other GHGs, such as methane, CFCs, and nitrous oxides, were making to global climate change. Methane and CFCs were of particular concern, not only because emissions of them were growing at 1 percent and 4 percent annually, respectively, but also because each molecule of them traps many times as much heat as a CO_2 molecule. The Intergovernmental Panel on Climate Change (IPCC) has calculated the relative contribution of the various GHGs to global climate change by multiplying the volume of emissions of each by an index called the Global Warming Potential (GWP), which takes into account the molecular heat retention capacity of each GHG and the length of time it normally resides in the atmosphere. Apart from CFCs, whose net impact as GHGs is now being downplayed (as explained in chapter 2), CO_2 is responsible for about 70 percent of the enhanced greenhouse effect, methane for about 23 percent, and nitrous oxide for about 7 percent.[7]

There were some indications in the early 1990s that global GHG emissions were stabilizing and perhaps even declining. World industrial emissions of CO_2 grew by less than 2 percent between 1989 and 1991, even including the pollution from the five hundred oil wells in Kuwait that were set on fire by the defeated Iraqi army, which accounted for 2 percent of industrial emissions of CO_2 in 1991. During the same period CO_2 emissions from land clearing declined by 47 percent due primarily to a slower rate of tropical deforestation. Emissions of methane were down 7.4 percent, while those of CFCs were 16.7 percent lower.[8]

This slowing down in the growth of GHG emissions in recent years is likely to be a temporary phenomenon unless significant policy changes are enacted to reduce energy use around the world and meet needs through sources other than fossil fuels. The leveling off of industrial emissions of CO_2 was due largely to the political turmoil and economic disarray in the former Soviet Union and eastern Europe, which caused a sharp decline in energy consumption, as well as to widespread economic stagnation elsewhere. Economic recovery in the former communist countries and a robust growth in the world economy generally could stimulate substantial increases in global energy use and an accompanying rise in CO_2 emissions.

Even a permanent leveling off of global GHG emissions, however, would not be reason for complacency about climate change. Atmospheric concentrations of GHGs will continue to rise substantially because of the long time that some of them will reside in the atmosphere, in particular CO_2 and nitrous oxides. The IPCC calculated that stabilizing concentrations of GHGs in the atmosphere at 1990 levels would require an immediate reduction of at least 60 percent in emissions of CO_2, of 70–80 percent in emissions of nitrous oxides, and of 15–20 percent in emissions of relatively short-lived methane.[9]

Regional and National Comparisons

The industrialized countries, including the former Soviet Union, were responsible for approximately 86 percent of the cumulative energy-related emissions of CO_2 between 1860 and 1986.[10] In recent decades their share has declined gradually, but in 1985 they still accounted for nearly three-quarters of global emissions, with approximately one-half coming from the members of the Organization for Economic Cooperation and Development (OECD) and one-quarter from the Soviet bloc. Most of the remaining one-quarter originated in the developing countries (see Table 7.1). If business-as-usual trends continue until 2025, the IPCC predicts that the OECD's share will drop to about one-third of the world total, which is projected to be twice as large as the 1985 figure. The share of the countries of the former Soviet bloc is expected to decline to about 20 percent.[11]

With a continuation of current trends, the developing countries' proportion of worldwide industrial emissions of CO_2 is projected to rise from 26 percent in 1985 to 44 percent in 2025 due to their much higher population growth rates and rises in per capita energy use as they proceed through the early stages of industrialization.[12] Energy use in the developing countries has doubled since 1970 and is projected to double again by 2010. If by 2025 their per capita energy demands rise from one-eighth to one-fourth of current levels in the industrial countries, global energy consumption would increase by 60 percent, and CO_2 emissions accordingly, unless there is a significant shift away from fossil fuels as an energy source.[13]

The regional distributions of nonindustrial sources of CO_2 and the other GHGs are quite different. By one calculation the countries of Central and South America were responsible for nearly half of global emis-

Table 7.1. CO_2 Emissions by Region (1985)

	Total (bmt)	%	per capita (mt)
OECD Countries	**9.16**	**48**	**12.1**
North America	4.91	26	18.6
Western Europe	3.11	16	7.8
Pacific	1.14	6	7.8
Soviet Bloc	**4.87**	**26**	**11.7**
Developing Countries	**4.87**	**26**	**1.3**
Africa	.62	3	1.1
Cent. Planned Asia	1.98	11	1.7
South and East Asia	.98	5	.7
Latin America	.81	4	2.0
Middle East	.48	3	4.4
Global Totals	**18.9**	**100**	**3.7**

Figures from IPCC, Climate Change: The IPCC Response Strategies (1991), xxxiii.

sions of CO_2 from land-use changes in 1991, with Brazil alone accounting for 30 percent of the world total, primarily due to the deforestation taking place in the Amazon region. Asia contributed an additional quarter of land-use-related emissions of CO_2, with Indonesia being responsible for approximately 10 percent of the world total. Africa's share was 19 percent, while North America and Europe combined for less than 2 percent. Turning to methane, Asia accounted for nearly half of global emissions, with China and India alone combining for 30 percent of the world total. Other sources of methane were North America (13 percent), Europe (12 percent), the USSR (11 percent), Central and South America (9 percent), and Africa (6 percent).[14]

Several indexes have been used to compare the overall contributions that individual countries are making to atmospheric burdens of GHGs.[15] One that is frequently cited is the Greenhouse Index

(GI) published by the World Resources Institute, which aggregates the emissions of all the major greenhouse gases after weighting each gas by its Global Warming Potential. The United States has had by far the largest GI of any country, 19.1 percent of the world total in 1991, which was slightly less than its 21.7 percent of industrial CO_2 emissions (see Table 7.2). These contributions are much greater than its 4.7 percent of the world's population but roughly equivalent to its share of world's gross domestic product. The next greatest contributors to the enhanced greenhouse effect were the former Soviet Union (13.6 percent), China (9.9 percent), Japan (5.1 percent), and Brazil (5.3 percent). These five countries alone accounted for 52 percent of the human contributions to atmospheric concentrations of GHGs.

When calculated on a per capita basis, the four highest ranking countries on the GI index were the small oil-rich states of Qatar, Gabon, the United Arab Emirates, and Brunei. The United States ranked seventh with a per capita figure that was almost nine times the world average. Australia ranked ninth and Canada eleventh. The former Soviet Union ranked eighteenth with per capita emissions that were nearly six times the global average. These high rankings of the developed countries are largely attributable to the level of fossil fuel consumption in industrial processes. The average American added 19.4 mt of CO_2 to the atmosphere from industrial sources in 1991, compared to a world average of only 4.2 mt per capita. In India per capita CO_2 emissions were only 0.8 mt, and in Bangladesh they were an even lower 0.15 mt.[16]

The vast differences in levels of GHG emissions have been a significant factor shaping international negotiations because the onus falls on the countries most responsible for the problem, namely the industrial nations, to make the greatest sacrifices to address it. In some instances the statistics have been a bone of contention among countries seeking to minimize the proportion of the problem attributable to them. Some developing countries have argued, for example, that the World Resources Institute's GI index overestimates the effects of agriculture and land-use changes.[17]

EMERGENCE OF CLIMATE CHANGE AS A GLOBAL ISSUE

The general state of the planet's weather became a major international concern during the 1970s when the period of uncommonly "normal" weather that had prevailed for much of the postwar era was

Table 7.2.   Energy-Related Greenhouse Index Rankings (1991)

	% of Global Emissions			Per Capita Emissions	
Rank	Country	%		Country	× World Average
1	United States	19.1		Qatar	18.6
2	USSR (former)	13.6		Gabon	17.0
3	China	9.9		United Arab Emirates	16.2
4	Japan	5.1		Brunei	11.5
5	Brazil	4.3		Luxembourg	11.4
6	Germany	3.8		Iraq	10.8
7	India	3.7		United States	9.0
8	United Kingdom	2.4		Bahrain	8.4
9	Indonesia	1.9		Australia	7.7
10	Italy	1.7		Bolivia	7.7
11	Iraq	1.7		Canada	7.1
12	France	1.6		Bulgaria	6.7
13	Canada	1.6		Surinam	6.6
14	Mexico	1.4		Trinidad & Tobago	6.5
15	Poland	1.2		Singapore	6.3

Source: Figures from World Resources Institute, World Resources 1994-95, 201-2.

interrupted by a spate of aberrant climatic events (described in chapter 3). At the time, however, there were widely discrepant views on what was happening to the planet's weather and why it was occurring. The abnormal climatic conditions that triggered the "world food crisis" in the early 1970s appeared primarily to be naturally occurring perturbations, some of which could be linked to an El Niño episode in the Pacific. Moreover, there was speculation that the severe winters in the Northern Hemisphere in the late 1970s may be the advent of an overdue cycle of glaciation. While humans were seen as powerless to alter such potent natural tendencies, it was hoped that further scientific research would unlock their causes, thereby making it possible to anticipate them and adopt timely adaptive measures.

Concurrently, there was a growing awareness that humans may unwittingly be altering the planet's climate. Research on the severe droughts that had plagued the African Sahel suggested that population, overgrazing, and deforestation could be having greater impacts on climate of the region than had been previously realized. Moreover, the continuing buildup of CO_2 in the atmosphere led other scientists to believe that it was only a matter of time before greenhouse warming became the dominant trend and to begin speculating about its social implications.[18] There was not, however, enough of a consensus during the 1970s to spur any national or international action to address climate change other than an expansion of research efforts to determine the impact of human activities on the environment.

The subject of climate and its implications for human societies came up repeatedly at the spate of major international conferences on environmental problems held during the 1970s, in particular the United Nations Conference on the Human Environment (1972), the World Food Conference (1974), the United Nations Water Conference (1977), and the United Nations Conference on Desertification (1977). Later the cumulative concerns about the abnormal weather conditions of the 1970s and the potential for human-caused global warming prompted the World Meteorological Organization (WMO) to convene the First World Climate Conference, which was held in Geneva in February 1979. The report of the conference emphasized that climate is a vital natural resource and urged governments to anticipate and prevent undesirable human-induced climate changes, in particular the warming that might be caused by increased concentrations of CO_2 in the atmosphere resulting from the burning of fossil fuels, clearing of forests, and other land-use changes. The report also highlighted the need for a major international program of research on climate change, including its causes and potential consequences.[19]

In the early 1980s public anxieties about an ice age were dispelled by a sequence of abnormally warm years that continued through the decade. An emergent consensus among scientists that global warming was the predominant climatological trend did not yet provoke widespread public apprehension because of uncertainties about the amount of change that would occur as well as conflicting assessments of whether the consequences would be largely desirable or undesirable. At the time more public attention was given to warnings of another type of potential climatic cataclysm that could result from a nuclear war between the superpowers. A group of prominent American scientists warned in 1983 that a war in which large numbers of nuclear explosives were detonated over the Northern Hemisphere would not only inject vast amounts of dust high into the atmosphere but also ignite enormous fires in cities and forests that would generate huge quantities of smoke and soot that would darken the skies for months. These pollutants would screen out much of the solar radiation that warms the Earth, causing temperatures over much of the hemisphere to plunge by as much as 25° C below normal ranges for several months and major changes in air circulation patterns, with potentially devastating consequences for human survivors of the initial blasts and many other species.[20]

The prospect of global warming began receiving substantial public attention following the release of the report of the international meeting of scientists in Villach in 1985, which warned that mean annual global temperature was likely to rise in the range of 1.5–4.5° C. as early as the 2030s if prevailing trends in CO_2 emissions continued.[21] The Villach report on global warming was issued about the same time that the stunning revelations of the Antarctic ozone hole were provoking renewed concern about the problem of ozone depletion. The juxtaposition of these two developments in 1985 drew considerable media attention to the fragile state of the atmosphere and the extent to which humans were responsible for the alarming changes taking place. While the public in the industrialized countries tended not to distinguish between the threats of ozone depletion and climate change, there was a growing sense of urgency about the need for governments to take action to preserve the atmosphere in a more general way.[22]

Global warming suddenly became a major public issue in many countries in 1988, as the stretch of abnormally warm years continued throughout much of the world. Northern Europe experienced an unusually mild winter followed by an exceptionally warm and dry summer. In the United States anxieties about climate change mushroomed when a long siege of abnormally hot and dry summer weather over much of the country caused crops to wither and set the stage for huge forest fires that roared through much of Yellowstone Park. The year saw a tenfold increase in the number of articles in the popular press on the greenhouse effect.[23] In the fall the American presidential candidates expressed concern about ozone depletion and global warming.[24]

In widely publicized testimony to a Senate committee, James E. Hansen, director of NASA's Goddard Institute for Space Studies, observed that the weather of the 1980s was warmer than at any time in the history of measured observations, which he attributed with "a high degree of confidence" to the greenhouse effect rather than chance fluctuations in temperatures. While Hansen conceded that specific heat waves and droughts could not necessarily be imputed to the increased presence of GHGs in the atmosphere, he did warn that the warming trend increased the likelihood of such events.[25] The public was more inclined than climatologists to draw a connection between the hot summer of 1988 and an enhanced greenhouse effect caused by humans. A public opinion poll taken in late 1988 found that 60 percent of Americans had heard about the greenhouse effect; a year later the proportion had risen to 80 percent.[26] In 1989 the United States Congress responded to public concerns by holding hearings in nine committees on thirty-two bills on the subject of the greenhouse effect.[27] The Toronto City Council set a goal of reducing the city's net CO_2 emissions by 20 percent from 1988 levels by 2005.[28]

By the end of the decade many of the world's leaders were discussing the problem of climate change. It was prominent on the agenda of the annual economic meeting of heads of state of the Group of Seven leading industrialized nations in Paris in July 1989, prompting the meeting to be called the "environmental summit." The leaders' communique declared that a framework or umbrella convention on climate change was "urgently required." Later in the year the climate change problem was brought up at the United States–Soviet Union summit meeting in Malta as well as the summits of the nonaligned countries in Belgrade, Yugoslavia, and the Commonwealth countries in Langkawi, Malaysia.[29]

The ominous report of the IPCC on the threat of global warming, the Second World Climate Conference, and the continuation of unusually hot summers and mild, largely snowless, winters in much of North America and Europe kept the climate change issue in the news through the end of 1990. In the years that followed, however, the issue lost some of its urgency in the public's mind. While 1991 turned out to be the second warmest year globally over the past century, temperatures declined slightly over the next two years presumably because of the cooling effects of aerosols from the volcanic eruption of Mount Pinatubo in 1991. The American Midwest, which was ravaged by heat and summer droughts in the late 1980s, was plagued by excessive rainfall and flooding in 1993, and snowfall was especially heavy in eastern North America during the winter of 1993–94. The IPCC issued reports in 1992 and 1995 that only slightly modified its earlier projections of global warming, but skepticism was being expressed in some quarters about the long-term projections of global temperatures based on general circulation models, which are taken into account in the assessments of the IPCC.[30]

On the diplomatic front fewer newsworthy intergovernmental conferences were convened once formal negotiations on a climate change treaty began in the Intergovernmental Negotiating Committee in 1991. The Earth Summit in Rio briefly drew public attention to the issue in 1992, largely due to controversy surrounding the refusal of the United States to yield to pressure from many other countries to include specific targets and deadlines in the Framework Convention on Climate Change that was up for signature at the meeting.[31] The follow-up talks on implementation of the convention have received relatively little attention from the media.

PRELUDE TO NEGOTIATIONS ON CLIMATE CHANGE

The WMO and the United Nations Environment Programme (UNEP) bore the primary responsibility for addressing climate change within the United Nations system through 1990. WMO's concern with weather and climate dates back to the creation of its predecessor, the nongovernmental International Meteorological Organization (IMO), in 1873. Even after it assumed its current status as an intergovernmental organization and a specialized agency in the UN family, WMO was inclined to limit its role to generating and disseminating meteorological information and scientific knowledge that informs public policy on climatological and atmospheric matters. To maintain its reputation for scientific impartiality, WMO has resisted the temptation to become involved in the formulation of international rules designed to address atmospheric problems, including ozone depletion and climate change. In this respect the organization has played a more limited role than have some other United Nations specialized agencies, such as the International Maritime Organization (IMO) and the International Telecommunications Union (ITU), which have assumed substantial rule-making and implementing functions.[32] Thus, it is understandable that the WMO entered into a partnership with UNEP, the latter being better equipped to play the political roles of exploring policy alternatives and facilitating international talks on how to address environmental problems. The two organizations collaborated in sponsoring the World Climate Programme, begun in 1980; the Villach meeting of scientists in 1985; the IPCC, established in 1988; and the Second World Climate Conference in 1990. Table 7.3 presents a chronology of the evolution of the climate change regime.

Early Intergovernmental Conferences

The report of the scientific gathering in Villach in 1985 strongly encouraged policy makers to begin the complicated task of forging international agreements on limiting the flow of greenhouse gases into the atmosphere. However, it was not until global warming began to receive substantial public attention in 1988 that serious talks were held on how the threat of global warming should be addressed. The next two years saw a spate of international conferences that set the stage for the beginning of formal negotiations on a framework convention on climate change in 1991. These meetings, which were held while the IPCC was deliberating on new scientific evidence and policy options, aired many of the conflicting positions of states that later frustrated the formal negotiations on the framework convention.

The nongovernmental Conference on the Changing Atmosphere, hosted by Canada in Toronto in June 1988, was the first major meeting to take up international policy responses to global warming. Attended by more than 340 people from forty-six countries, including scientists and governmental officials as well as representatives from international agencies, nongovernmental organizations, and industry, the conference examined the full range of threats to the atmosphere resulting from human activities. The conference statement called for a comprehensive framework convention to protect the atmosphere that could be supplemented later by protocols addressing specific problems. The conference also proposed creation of a World Atmosphere Fund, financed by a tax on fossil fuel consumption in the developed countries, to facilitate the transfer of technologies to developing countries. On the subject of global warming, the conference statement called upon the industrial countries to take the lead in reducing emissions of CO_2 by 20 percent (from 1988 levels) by 2005, as an initial step toward stabilizing GHGs in the atmosphere.[33]

Table 7.3. Chronology of the Climate Change Regime

1979	(February)	First World Climate Conference in Geneva
1980	(November)	Scientific Conference in Villach, Austria
1985	(October)	Scientific Conference in Villach, Austria
1988	(June)	Changing Atmosphere Conference in Toronto
1989	(February)	Regional Climate Change Conference in New Delhi
	(March)	Summit on Protecting the Atmosphere in the Hague
	(November)	Noordwijk Ministerial Conference on Air Pollution and Climate Change
		Small State Conference on Sea Level Rise in Malé, Maldive Islands
1990	(April)	White House Conference on Climate Change
	(May)	Action for a Common Future Conference in Bergen, Norway
		Conference on Global Warming and Climate Change in Nairobi
	(August)	First Report of the Intergovernmental Panel on Climate Change
	(November)	Second World Climate Conference in Geneva
1991	(February)	Negotiations begin in Intergovernmental Negotiating Committee
	(June)	Conference of Developing Countries in Beijing
1992	(June)	Framework Convention on Climate Change Signed in Rio
1995	(March)	First Conference of the Parties in Berlin
	(December)	Second Report of the Intergovernmental Panel on Climate Change

Several noteworthy international conferences on climate change were held in early 1989. As a follow-up to the Toronto Conference, the Canadian government hosted the International Meeting of Legal and Policy Experts on the Protection of the Atmosphere in Ottawa in February, at which preliminary discussions were held on developing a law of the atmosphere. In March the Netherlands, Norway, and France jointly sponsored a conference in The Hague, attended by representatives from twenty-four countries, including seventeen heads of state.[34] The impact of the meeting was limited by the absence of the United States and the Soviet Union, which were not invited, and the United Kingdom, which elected not to attend. The declaration adopted at The Hague proposed creation of a "new institutional authority" with nonunanimous decision-making rules to protect the atmosphere and combat global warming.[35]

The Netherlands hosted another major meeting in November 1989, this time a two-day Ministerial Conference on Atmospheric Pollution and Climate Change in Noordwijk, at which seventy countries were represented. The conference was the first to make a concerted effort to reach a multilateral agreement setting specific goals and target dates for countries to limit their GHG emissions. Most of the participating countries favored a provision that all countries make a commitment to freeze their emissions of CO_2 at 1988 levels by 2005. However, four of the major CO_2-emitting states—the United States, the Soviet Union, the United Kingdom, and Japan—opposed such an explicit timetable. In the interest of reaching a consensus, the conference declaration simply called upon the industrialized nations to take action to stabilize their GHG emissions at levels to be set by the IPCC in its preliminary report to the Second World Climate Conference.[36] The conference also set a goal of reversing deforestation trends by early in the next century, thereby retaining, if not enhancing, the capacity of the world's forests to absorb CO_2.[37]

The pace of international conferences discussing climate change, either exclusively or as part of larger agendas, picked up during the first six months of 1990. The Soviet Union hosted the Global Forum on Environment and Development in Moscow in January, at which President Gorbachev proposed that the United Nations Conference on Environment and Development scheduled for Rio de Janeiro in 1992 be designated a summit meeting to encourage attendance by heads of states. In May global warming was one of the principal issues taken up at the Action for a Common Future Conference held in Bergen, Norway, which was attended by ministers from the thirty-four European and North American member states of the Economic Commission for Europe (ECE). Most of the industrialized states represented agreed informally to stabilize emissions of CO_2 and other important GHGs at 1990 levels by the year 2000 and asked the IPCC to investigate the feasibility of a 20 percent reduction in GHG emissions by 2005.[38]

The American White House convened a two-day meeting for representatives from eighteen countries on the subject of global warming in April 1990. The Bush administration used the conference as a forum to explain U.S. unwillingness to join most other industrialized countries in making specific commitments to curb emissions of CO_2. The United States hoped to win other countries to its position by educating the participants on the substantial scientific uncertainties that remained regarding global warming and on the magnitude of the economic costs that would be entailed in limiting CO_2 emissions. The outcome was hardly what the White House had hoped for, as the American "go-slow" approach on global warming was sharply criticized by outspoken representatives of several of the European countries, in particular the Netherlands, West Germany, and Norway, which maintained that scientific uncertainties should not be used as an excuse for further delays in taking action to reduce CO_2 emissions.[39]

The prenegotiation stage of international discussions on the global warming issue came to a climax at the Second World Climate Conference in November 1990. Ministers from 144 countries converged on Geneva for the last two days of the conference, which followed six days of technical meetings (described in chapter 3). Efforts to reach an agreement among the industrialized nations that would set a timetable for freezing or cutting back on CO_2 emissions, which was now supported by the United Kingdom and Japan, were thwarted by the continuing opposition of the United States, the Soviet Union, and Saudi Arabia. Recognizing that any agreement on climate change would be ineffective without the concurrence of the superpowers, who were by far the leading emitters of CO_2, the majority relented on the demands for a specific timetable for limits on CO_2 emissions.[40] Thus, the declaration adopted at the conference simply urged nations to "now take steps toward reducing sources and increasing sinks of greenhouse gases through national and regional actions, and negotiation of a global convention on climate change and related legal instruments."[41]

National and Regional Responses to Climate Change

By the time of the Second World Climate Conference, a growing number of the OECD countries had acted on their concerns about global warming by unilaterally establishing national policy goals or targets for limiting emissions of CO_2 and other GHGs. These national commitments on GHG emissions took a variety of forms. Finland, Norway, and Switzerland set a goal of stabilizing CO_2 emissions at 1990 levels by the year 2000, the United Kingdom by 2005. Canada adopted a similar goal but included other GHGs not controlled by the Montreal Protocol. France and Japan would also stabilize GHG emissions but on a per capita basis, which would permit total emissions to rise with population growth. Several other countries went a step further in specifying reductions in CO_2 emissions that they hoped to achieve by 2005. Australia, Austria, Denmark, Italy, Luxembourg, and New Zealand would aim at 20 percent reductions; Germany planned an even more ambitious 25 percent cutback. The Netherlands indicated it would achieve a reduction of 3–5 percent in CO_2 emissions (or 20–25 percent for all GHGs including CFCs) by the year 2000.[42]

Two regional organizations also took up the issue of limiting GHG emissions. In October 1990 the European Community (EC) established a goal of stabilizing emissions at 1990 levels by the end of the decade. These freezes would be accomplished on a community-wide basis, which left open the possibility that some members, in particular the less highly developed ones—namely Spain, Greece, and Portugal—would be allowed to continue increasing their CO_2 emissions if compensated by the reductions of others. Spain, for example set a goal of holding its increase in GHG emissions to 25 percent, compared to a 45 percent growth that would otherwise have been anticipated. The five members of the European Free Trade Association (EFTA) adopted the same target as the EC in November 1990.[43]

Most of these countries announced strategies for how they would accomplish their targets on GHG emissions. Since carbon emissions are an inevitable by-product of the combustion of fossil fuels, these plans included policy mechanisms that would bring about a reduction in the consumption of energy and fossil fuels. In 1990 Finland became the first country to adopt a tax on the carbon content of fuels to discourage the burning of fossil fuels contributing to greenhouse warming. Within the next two years Denmark, the Netherlands, Norway, and Sweden followed suit. The carbon tax imposed in Sweden in 1991 added approximately eighteen dollars to the cost of a barrel of oil.[44] Carbon taxes were being considered by other countries and by the European Union, but in the latter some members were unwilling to agree to such a tax unless other OECD countries, including the United States, adopted similar taxes.[45]

The United States was conspicuous for not making a specific commitment to stabilize or reduce its GHG emissions, although several of its state governments, including Oregon, Vermont, and New York, set goals to reduce GHG emissions.[46] The reluctance of the United

States can in part be explained by its extensive reserves of fossil fuels, in particular coal, which have favored an energy-intensive lifestyle that the American people have come to expect. By contrast, with the exception of Australia, Norway, and the United Kingdom, the OECD countries making commitments to limit CO_2 emissions rely heavily on foreign sources for fossil fuels and thus have had a tradition of heavily taxing energy consumption to encourage conservation as a way of limiting imports.[47]

The Climate Change Issue in the Developing Countries

The rising concern about global warming among leaders and publics during the late 1980s was concentrated in the highly developed countries of the North, where virtually all of the research on climate change was being conducted. The developed world realized, however, that mitigating the greenhouse threat would require the cooperation of the developing countries of the South, which were responsible for a significant and growing proportion of the annual worldwide additions of GHGs into the atmosphere. Moreover, without such a partnership the South's GHG emissions could be expected to rise substantially in the coming decades both because of its relatively rapid population growth and its continuing industrialization using fossil fuels as the primary source of energy.

Thus, the North became anxious when the South initially displayed little concern about climate change. Relatively few of the developing countries sent representatives to the early international meetings convened to take up the question of how to address the problem, including the sessions of the IPCC held between 1988 and 1990. This apparent disinterest or ambivalence of the developing countries was partly attributable to their paucity of experts who could interpret the mounting scientific evidence of climate change and inform leaders and publics about the potentially serious implications it could have for their countries. Limited diplomatic and scientific personnel also made it impossible for many developing countries to be represented at numerous international meetings, and if they were, by knowledgeable delegates who could meaningfully participate in discussions of complex technical matters.[48] The IPCC sought to remedy the situation by forming a Special Committee on the Participation of Developing Countries and holding meetings in Third World locations to heighten awareness of climate change among their scientists, leaders, and publics.[49]

Climate change soon became a more salient issue in the Third World. The first international conference on climate change to be held in a developing country took place in New Delhi in February 1989, which was attended by 150 scientists and policy makers, mostly from the Indian subcontinent.[50] Representatives from the African nations met in Nairobi in May 1989 to discuss their perspectives on the global warming problem.[51] A similar meeting for the Latin American region was held in Sao Paulo in June 1990, and one for the Asian nations took place in Bangkok in June 1991.[52] Climate change was one of the issues pertaining to environment and development that was discussed at a ministerial meeting held in Beijing, also in June 1991, which was attended by representatives from forty-one developing countries. Having had these opportunities to discuss the climate change issue from the perspective of developing countries, the South was better prepared to play an active role in the talks taking place at the Second World Climate Conference in 1990 and the Intergovernmental Negotiating Committee in 1991–92.[53]

Southern thinking about greenhouse warming coalesced around three general themes. First, the highly developed countries were primarily to blame for the past buildup of concentrations of GHGs in the atmosphere; therefore they should absorb most of the burden for remedying the problem. Second, even though they bear little responsibility for the problem, developing countries were coming to realize that they might be affected disproportionately by climate changes. Some were especially vulnerable because of geographical factors, such as the susceptibility of key low-lying areas to rising sea levels. Furthermore, the economies of many of the developing countries are generally more dependent on the agricultural sector, which could be heavily impacted by warmer and drier conditions and have far fewer national resources for adapting to climate-induced changes. Finally, developing countries were resolute that international policies on climate change must not detract from their economic development, especially in view of their frustrations with an international economic order they considered to be inequitable and unresponsive to their needs.[54]

The early disinterest and skepticism of most of the South about global warming was not shared by a sizable group of small—indeed tiny—island and coastal states, most of which were less developed economically. Many of them were especially vulnerable both to a general rise in sea levels and to a greater incidence of tropical storms likely to result from global warming. Warning that global warming threatened to erase at least seven island nations from the map, President Maumoon Abdul Gayoom of the Maldive Islands, a small island nation in the Indian Ocean, hosted a meeting attended by ministers of fifteen such countries in November 1989. These countries became the core of a caucusing group known as the Alliance of Small Island States (AOSIS), which was formed at the Second World Climate Conference to press their case for prompt international action designed to minimize greenhouse warming. By working together, the thirty-six member states of AOSIS, which comprise roughly 20 percent of the voting members of the United Nations, have had a much stronger voice on the climate change issue than they would have had as mini- or microstates acting on their own.[55]

NEGOTIATING THE FRAMEWORK CONVENTION ON CLIMATE CHANGE

Within a month after the Second World Climate Conference, the United Nations General Assembly adopted a resolution establishing the Intergovernmental Negotiating Committee on a Framework Convention on Climate Change (known as the INC) under its auspices to be the venue for negotiations on a binding agreement.[56] The alternative would have been for UNEP and WMO to sponsor the negotiations as an extension of their collaboration on the IPCC, especially in view of UNEP's success in shepherding the negotiations on ozone depletion. The decision to create the INC reflected the preference of developing countries for a political arena that would be more sensitive to their aspirations for economic development, as opposed to one organized by specialized agencies more narrowly committed to environmental and technical issues.[57]

At the invitation of the United States, the INC began work in Chantilly, Virginia, in February 1991, with 135 countries participating. Its charge was to draft a framework agreement on climate change to present to the United Nations Conference on Environment and Development (UNCED) in Rio in 1992. This deadline put considerable time pressure on the negotiators, given the large number of countries participating in the talks and the complexity of the issues. Over the next fifteen months the INC held five negotiating sessions, with the last one being divided into two parts, all of which were on a separate track from the other preparatory meetings for the Earth Summit. The often contentious negotiations that took place inside and outside the formal INC sessions finally led to agreement on a draft convention, which was signed by more than 150 states at Rio.

Conflicting Positions

The multiple lines of conflict that emerged during the series of ministerial meetings on the climate change problem between 1988 and 1990 carried over to the negotiations in the INC. The members of the EC and EFTA supported to varying degrees a treaty that would include not only the features of a framework convention but also specific targets and timetables for reducing CO_2 emissions of the type normally included in protocols negotiated later. Germany, the Netherlands, Denmark, France, and Italy were the leading advocates of such an ambitious convention, while the United Kingdom and the southern, less affluent members of the EC were more cautious about making such commitments. The AOSIS countries called for the most immediate stabilization of GHGs emissions, with 1995 being the target year. The so-called CANZ coalition of Canada, Australia, and New Zealand, along with Finland, were more inclined to limit all GHGs not controlled by the Montreal Protocol. Japan suggested the softer and more ambiguous alternative of a "pledge and review" arrangement whereby countries would be expected to announce commitments to reduce GHG emissions, which would then be reviewed and evaluated by an international body of experts.[58]

The proposals of the European countries for including targets and timetables in the climate change convention for the most part mirrored the various unilateral commitments they had made to limit or reduce emissions of CO_2 or GHGs generally. In pushing their position they noted that the IPCC had already done extensive preparatory work, both in assessing available scientific evidence of greenhouse warming and its probable effects and in exploring various policy options. They regarded the problem to be sufficiently immediate and threatening to justify precautionary steps to minimize it, even while there were still some potentially significant scientific uncertainties. From their perspective, delaying strong international action until there was more definitive evidence of climate change and its negative impacts would allow GHGs to continue accumulating in the atmosphere and lose whatever opportunity remained for keeping climate change within a manageable level.[59]

The United States persisted in its opposition to binding targets and timetables in the initial international agreement on climate change, despite a continuing barrage of criticism from other OECD members and environmental NGOs. The American preference was for a process-oriented framework convention calling for an ambitious scientific research effort, information exchanges, and education but lacking firm national commitments on stabilizing emissions in the short run. In defending its position the United States continued to call attention to lingering scientific uncertainties about the extent of global warming that was likely to take place and what it contended would be the burdensome economic costs of substantially reducing CO_2 emissions.[60]

The United States also stuck to a position it had first taken in 1989 that efforts to mitigate global warming should be based on a "comprehensive approach" that took into account all sources and sinks of GHGs. Such an approach would allow the United States and other countries to include substantial reductions in the production of CFCs, as mandated by the Montreal Protocol and London Amendments, in calculations of the progress they had made toward stabilizing GHG emissions. This position was consistent with American support for taking "no regrets" steps to limit GHG emissions. Such actions serve other beneficial purposes, in this case preserving the ozone layer, and thus can be beneficial on balance even if later proved to be unnecessary to mitigate global warming.[61]

Developing countries were well represented throughout the INC negotiations, in contrast to the talks on the ozone depletion problem, which up through the adoption of the Montreal Protocol were conducted primarily among the developed countries. The Third World countries attempted to forge a common front at the negotiating sessions by meeting as the Group of 77—the caucusing coalition they had formed in other United Nations bodies and meetings since the 1960s. As the negotiations proceeded it became apparent that there were some basic differences of interest among the Group of 77 that could not be readily reconciled.[62]

A major obstacle to the unity of the South was the urgent stake that the small developing island countries comprising AOSIS felt they had in immediate and substantial reductions in global GHG emissions. To countries such as Vanuatu, whose very existence was threatened by rising sea levels, it makes little difference whether additional atmospheric GHGs originated in the highly industrialized North or in developing countries. Yet China and India were unwilling to agree to any international constraints on using their large coal reserves to power national economic development. The major petroleum producing countries, led by Saudi Arabia, opposed any international rules designed to reduce CO_2 emissions from the burning of fossil fuels in the developed world, fearing they would jeopardize the oil exports critical to their economies.

States with large areas of tropical forests, such as Indonesia and Malaysia, were leery of agreements aimed at protecting carbon sinks that might infringe on what they considered to be their sovereign prerogative to determine natural resource policies.[63]

Despite these differences many of the countries of the South aggressively pursued their interests and confronted the North on numerous issues. They insisted that any internationally mandated limits on GHG emissions should apply only to the industrial countries, which had previously helped themselves to most of the atmosphere's capacity to absorb greenhouse gases. Moreover, the reductions of the developed countries should be deep enough to allow developing countries to increase their emissions of CO_2 as needed to achieve their development objectives. Southern countries raised the question of what would be equitable criteria for allocating permissible levels of GHG emissions among countries. India, for example, suggested that there should be a convergence of emissions toward a common per capita level, which would require substantial reductions by the United States and other industrialized countries.[64] The developed countries conceded that they should take the lead in addressing the climate change problem, but they were not willing to go as far toward equalizing emissions as India proposed.

Issues pertaining to funding were also major sources of conflict between North and South. The developing countries maintained that the North should compensate them for all the incremental costs they would incur in complying with any of the convention's provisions. While most of the developed countries accepted the need to provide assistance to gain the cooperation of the developing countries, they resisted making any specific guarantees on the amount or agreeing to any mechanisms that would automatically generate funds. The developed countries preferred to have the funds dispensed through the Global Environment Facility (GEF), which the developing countries opposed on grounds that it was subject to the granting procedures of the World Bank, which were controlled by the donor countries. Underlying this disagreement was the deeper question of the basic rationale for the assistance. The developing countries argued that funds should be provided them with few strings attached on grounds that historically the industrial countries were primarily responsible for the greenhouse problem that affected all countries, including those that had made no significant contributions to the problem and had little capacity to adapt to the changes. The developed countries, in particular the United States, were more inclined to explain their willingness to provide assistance on grounds of their much greater economic and technical capacities.[65]

Numerous compromises on the language of the climate change convention were struck during and between the two parts of the fifth session of the INC held in February and May 1992. The most important was the deal between European countries and the United States that was brokered by the United Kingdom outside of the formal negotiations. To gain the support of the United States for the convention, the European countries reluctantly relented on their insistence for a binding timetable and target for emission limitations by agreeing to a somewhat vague statement of goals that would apply not only to CO_2 but also to other GHGs not controlled by the Montreal Protocol.

Provisions of the Convention

The rather lengthy United Nations Framework Convention on Climate Change (FCCC) signed at the 1992 Earth Summit has the typical attributes of framework conventions. It acknowledges the importance of protecting the climate system for present and future generations. It sets a long-term goal of the "stabilization of greenhouse gas concentrations in the atmosphere at a level that would prevent dangerous anthropogenic interference with the climate system" but is conspicuously vague on what is implied by the term "dangerous" or on how this goal is to be achieved. The parties are expected to cooperate in numerous ways, such as conducting and exchanging scientific and technical research, adapting to the consequences of climate change, conserving and enhancing sinks and reservoirs for GHGs, and sharing technologies that can reduce GHG emissions. Finally, the convention provides for an institutional mechanism in the form of a conference of parties to implement the agreement and provide a venue for further negotiations on strengthening the regime.

The FCCC is notable for acknowledging that the largest share of historical and current GHG emissions has originated in the developed countries. It further observes that the per capita emissions of the developing countries are still relatively low and can be expected to increase as they meet the social and developmental needs of their people. Thus, the convention assigns the principal responsibility for reducing GHG emissions and preserving carbon sinks to the developed countries, which are listed in annex 1 of the convention. The initial list includes all of the

OECD countries, as well as the eastern European and Baltic states, the Russian Federation, the Ukraine, and Belarus.

The developed countries listed in annex 1 are obliged to adopt national policies that will mitigate climate change by limiting anthropocentric emissions of GHGs and preserving GHG sinks and reservoirs. The treaty establishes no binding targets or timetables, but it does suggest that the developed countries, acting either individually or jointly, should "aim" at returning their GHG emissions to 1990 levels by the end of the decade. The annex 1 countries are further obliged to provide detailed information on the measures they have adopted to limit GHG emissions, with the first report to be made within six months after the convention comes into force, so as to be reviewed at the first COP. What is expected of these countries after the year 2000, such as a continued stabilization of GHG emissions or reductions of them, is not spelled out.

The convention offers the developed countries the option of "joint implementation" as a way of fulfilling their obligations to stabilize GHG emissions. This provision, initially proposed by Norway, offers the developed countries the option of fulfilling their expected reductions by helping other countries cut back on their GHG emissions, rather than achieving them domestically. This alternative would be cost efficient for the developed countries because it permits them to take advantage of lower costs of achieving GHG reductions in developing countries, recognizing that emission reductions or enhancements of carbon sinks ultimately have the same effect on climate regardless of where they take place since GHGs mix globally in the atmosphere. Joint implementation would also stimulate a flow of resources and technology to developing countries. While such an arrangement has had broad support for being cost-effective strategy, it has been criticized by the South and some environmental groups for allowing the rich countries a convenient way of being allowed to continue their extravagant use of energy.[66]

All parties to the FCCC, including the developing states, assume a variety of other responsibilities, such as to provide inventories of anthropogenic GHG emissions and the removal of sinks of GHGs; to report on national and regional programs to mitigate climate change that pertain to sources and sinks of GHGs; to promote sustainable development; and to take climate change into account to the extent feasible in social, economic, and environmental policies. Developing countries are given three years to make their first reports, and only then if sufficient financial resources have been provided them to fulfill these responsibilities.

A smaller group of the highly developed countries, listed in the document's annex 2—principally members of the OECD—is "to provide new and additional financial resources to meet the agreed full costs" that the developing countries encounter in fulfilling these responsibilities, the most immediate one being to prepare inventories of GHG emissions. While the original framework convention does not obligate the developed countries to provide financial assistance to developing countries to undertake abatement measures, it does commit them to promote, facilitate, and finance the transfer of environmentally sound technologies. Consideration is to be given to providing funds, insurance, and technology to the developing countries that would be most adversely affected by climate change, such as small island countries and those that have low-lying coastal areas and fragile mountain ecosystems or are prone to natural disasters, drought, and desertification. Another group of developing countries whose special needs are to be taken into account consists of those that would be impacted by steps taken to implement the convention, such as the states that are highly dependent on income from the production, processing, or export of fossil fuels and energy-intensive products.

FOLLOW-UP TO THE CLIMATE CHANGE CONVENTION

The FCCC was signed by 154 countries and the EC at the Earth Summit in 1992, and in the following months the number rose to 166. The original signatories included all of the OECD countries, except for Turkey, which protested the fairness of its inclusion in the annex 1 and 2 lists of developed countries. The convention came into force on March 21, 1994, three months after the required fiftieth ratification was filed by Portugal. The United States was the fourth country to ratify the convention and the first among the industrialized ones. The number of ratifiers had risen to 127 by the time of the first meeting of the Conference of the Parties (COP I), which took place in Berlin in March 1995, in accordance with the provision of the convention that it be held within a year of the coming into force. In the meantime the INC met five times to provide a continuing forum for international talks on implementing the convention following the Rio summit.

A potentially significant development was the shift in the U.S. position under the Clinton administration, which declared its intentions to return American emissions of all GHGs to 1990 levels by the year 2000. The American pledge differed from those made previously by many of the industrial countries in referring to net emissions, which take into account changes in CO_2 sinks and reservoirs that counteract GHG emissions. Moreover, rather than addressing each GHG separately, the stated goal of the United States was to stabilize the aggregate of GHG emissions, making allowances for the global-warming potential of each gas.[67] Couching its GHG stabilization goals in this way would allow for a 3 percent increase in CO_2 emissions during the 1990s.[68] Environmental NGOs soon questioned whether the Clinton administration had a realistic plan for stabilizing GHG emissions, especially in view of the refusal of Congress to enact key parts of its Climate Action Plan, including a modest energy tax. Furthermore, much of the anticipated reduction in GHG emissions was to come from voluntary public and private partnerships that would promote energy efficiency, commercialize renewable energy, and encourage tree planting.[69]

Early efforts to implement the FCCC were devoted primarily to building an information base as the parties begin to fulfill their responsibilities to inventory their GHG emissions and report on the policies and measures they had adopted to stem the flow of GHGs into the atmosphere. The IPCC and the OECD, which had considerable experience in developing procedures for country environmental reports, did much of the initial technical work on standardizing the national emission inventories, but this task is now being assumed by COP's Subsidiary Body for Scientific and Technological Advice. The IPCC has worked on revising the formulas for aggregating the emissions of the various GHGs into a single global-warming potential index, taking into account new scientific findings on the enhanced greenhouse effect. The International Energy Agency (IEA) and OECD took the lead in reviewing and synthesizing the first round of country reports, but after COP I this function was assumed by the new Subsidiary Body on Implementation. Continuing efforts will be made to develop a common format for the reports to make them more informative and comparable.[70]

At the COP I in Berlin in 1995, many of the industrialized countries continued to argue for binding targets and timetables for stabilizing or reducing GHG emissions. It was the AOSIS group, however, that took the strongest stance in pushing aggressively for a protocol that would require the industrial countries to reduce their emissions of CO_2 by at least 20 percent (from 1990 levels) by 2005. The AOSIS proposal was too ambitious to have a chance of being accepted. The document adopted at the meeting, which became known as the Berlin Mandate, did acknowledge, however, that the commitments contained in the FCCC, most notably the goal of returning GHG emissions to 1990 levels by the year 2000, were not adequate to address the threat of climate change. It was further agreed that negotiations should begin on a protocol or other legal instrument to be ready for adoption by the COP III in 1997, which would set "limitation and reduction objectives" for GHGs that would take effect in the years 2000, 2005, and 2010. Whatever limits were negotiated would still apply only to the developed countries, despite suggestions by the United States and Australia that at least the newly industrialized countries should be subject to them.[71]

What are the prospects that the developed countries listed in annex 1 of the FCCC will achieve the goal of reducing GHG emissions to 1990 levels by the end of the decade? Industrial emissions of CO_2 rose by 3 percent in western Europe between 1990 and 1994, and in North America by 5 percent.[72] By the turn of the century CO_2 emissions of the United States are expected to be 10 percent higher than in 1990.[73] Most developed countries have shown little inclination to reformulate energy policies in ways that would significantly reduce fossil fuel use and thus CO_2 emissions. By the COP I in 1995, only seventeen of the thirty-five countries listed in annex 1 had submitted reports on the national measures taken to limit GHG emissions. Three years of talks in the European Union failed to produce a community-wide carbon tax, leading its commission to project a 5–8 percent increase in CO_2 emissions between 1990 and 2000.[74]

The prospects of meeting the goals of the FCCC are more promising in some countries. CO_2 emissions in the United Kingdom, Italy, and Japan had remained close to 1990 levels through 1994 and in Germany had dropped by 10 percent. The German reductions were made possible by closing numerous inefficient and heavily polluting factories and shifting away from the use of brown coal in the former East Germany. Substantial reductions in CO_2 emissions had also been achieved between 1990 and 1994 in several countries of the former Soviet bloc, including Poland (4.5 percent), the Russian Federation (24 percent), and the Ukraine (43 percent), due primarily to economic restructuring and a decline in their energy-intensive industries.[75] Turning to future goals, eight countries—Australia, Austria, Canada, Denmark, Germany, Luxembourg, the Slovak Republic, and New Zealand—have incorporated the so-called Toronto target of a 20 percent reduction of CO_2 emissions by 2005 (from the 1988 Changing Atmosphere Conference) into their national plans.[76]

Most developing countries signed the FCCC in Rio, and many have subsequently ratified it, but the significance of their acceptance is diminished by the fact that so little is expected of them. Moreover, the developed countries are to provide incremental assistance for the relatively minor obligations that they do incur, such as developing inventories of their GHG emissions. In its current form the treaty does nothing to constrain the 5 percent annual increase in industrial CO_2 emissions in the developing countries, which is in part made possible by loans from international development banks for fossil-fuel-based energy systems.[77] Between 1990 and 1994 CO_2 emissions increased by 13 percent in China, 16 percent in Brazil, 23 percent in India, and 44 percent in South Korea.[78]

Representatives of several of the developing countries made it clear at the COP I that they would consider limiting their GHG emissions only after the industrialized world had fulfilled the goal of stabilizing its emissions.[79] The cooperation of the developing countries would also most certainly be conditional on the commitment of much larger amounts of economic and technical assistance from the developed countries, which will be difficult to negotiate.

CONCLUSIONS

Climate change quite suddenly became a major international issue in the late 1980s and reached a peak of public attention at the time of the Second World Climate Conference in 1990. This wave of official and public concern was triggered by two developments. The first was a convergence of international scientific opinion that an increase in the range of 1.5–4.5° C of average global temperatures was likely within the next century if current trends in GHG emissions continued. Uneasiness about the condition of the atmosphere was compounded by the concurrent discovery of the Antarctic ozone hole and reports linking it to human pollutants. The second development heightening concern about climate change was a run of unusually warm years between 1980 and 1991, which gave the climate issue a greater sense of urgency in the public mind, even though most climatologists were cautious about attributing the recent weather to the buildup of GHGs in the atmosphere.

These anxieties over climate change gave impetus to the negotiations that began in the INC in 1991 and resulted in the signing of the FCCC at the Earth Summit the next year. The convention lacked the binding targets and timetables that had been advocated by many of the developed countries, primarily due to the persistent opposition of the

United States. It did, however, establish a goal for the developed countries of bringing their GHG emissions back down to 1990 levels by the end of the decade and instituted procedures for the continuing development of the climate change regime. A report and review procedure may prod the developed countries to formulate and strengthen plans for stabilizing GHG emissions, but some of the developed parties have been slow to submit the required reports.

It remains to be seen whether the climate change regime will follow the course of the acid rain and ozone depletion regimes, in which framework conventions were supplemented by protocols that specify binding targets and timetables for reducing the pollutants. The first COP of the FCCC parties, held in Berlin in 1995, failed to adopt such commitments, even though there was general agreement that stronger measures were needed to mitigate the problem of global warming. Reaching an agreement on controlling GHG emissions is complicated by the stark differences among countries in their historical and current contributions of GHGs to the atmosphere, which inevitably lead to contentious issues regarding what is a fair international division of future responsibilities for addressing the problem. The willingness of countries to accept limits on GHG emissions also depends in large part upon how they meet their energy needs, in particular the extent to which they depend upon domestically available fossil fuels. Finally, the sense of urgency among countries varies considerably as some, such as the small island nations and others with key low-lying regions, are highly vulnerable to the effects of climate change, whereas others, including some that are major sources of GHGs, seem less concerned about the changes and are more confident of their capacity to adapt to them.

The developing countries were drawn into the negotiations on climate change at a relatively early stage, and most have accepted the FCCC. Nevertheless, the FCCC postpones the day of reckoning between North and South on dividing up future rights to add GHG emissions to the atmosphere. If greenhouse warming is to be mitigated, the North will soon have to insist that the South curb its rapidly growing GHG emissions. When this happens the South will be asking whether the North has done enough to stabilize its GHG emissions, as provided in the FCCC. The South can also be expected to raise again the troublesome question of what is a fair allocation of the privilege of adding to the atmospheric burden of GHGs. Then there is the whole nexus of development issues that are carryovers from the North-South dialogue of recent decades, including most recently the Brundtland Commission and the Earth Summit. The great potential of the South for increasing GHG emissions could give it considerable leverage in striking a bargain with the North on the future of the climate change regime and development issues generally. The developing countries may, however, be cautious about pressing their demands, realizing that if they obstruct the evolution of an effective climate change regime, many of them may be seriously victimized by the additional global warming that takes place.[80]

As of the mid 1990s the possibilities for significantly strengthening the climate change regime do not appear favorable. The sense of urgency about global warming dissipated somewhat in the 1990s as global temperatures moderated for several years following the eruption of Mount Pinatubo. Concern may begin to rise again in prominence, however, as global mean temperatures have resumed their gradual rise in 1994 and 1995 and a new report of IPCC issued in 1995 suggests an even stronger consensus among the world's climate experts that the warming was at least partly induced by human pollutants. However, it may take a climatic surprise or shock on the order of the Antarctic ozone hole to rekindle public concern about global warming and invigorate negotiations on strengthening the climate change regime. Each year that passes without substantial progress on constraining GHG gases relegates humanity to the need for increasingly severe measures if future global warming is to be held within manageable levels.

Chapter 8

THE ATMOSPHERE
AS A GLOBAL COMMONS

The tendency for shared resources, or what have become known as commons, to be degraded by overuse and misuse is a timeless problem of human societies that has been noted by scholars as early as Aristotle, who opined that "what is common to the greatest number has the least care bestowed upon it. Everybody thinks chiefly of his own, hardly at all of the common interest."[1] While Aristotle did not have the atmosphere in mind—it had not been discovered by his time—his observation is now as applicable to the atmosphere as to any other planetary resource. Humanity has long used the atmosphere as a sink for many of its wastes with little awareness and concern for the ways it is being altered and degraded. Once believed to be vast enough to accommodate all human assaults, only in recent decades has it become apparent how limited the capacity of the atmosphere is for absorbing, dispersing, and disposing of anthropogenic pollutants without undergoing fundamental changes that will severely impact the Earth system, in particular the biosphere.

The problem of commons overuse is often associated with the writings of biologist Garrett Hardin, especially his seminal article "The Tragedy of the Commons." Hardin explains the all too frequent fate of commons by drawing upon a parable, told in the nineteenth century by a little-known Oxford professor named William Forster Lloyd, in which the residents of a mythical old English village overuse a common pasture to its destruction by adding privately owned cattle to increase their personal profit, even to the point that their aggregate herd exceeds significantly the number of cattle the pasture can sustain and nourish.[2] The grass is consumed or trampled so that eventually the pasture can no longer support even a much smaller herd. Unfortunately, the realization that the pasture is being severely degraded does not dissuade the villagers from continuing to add cattle, as they anticipate that whatever restraint they exercise individually for the good of the community will be more than compensated for by the excesses of the less scrupulous among them.

Numerous examples could be cited of commons that have been degraded or destroyed by a syndrome of overuse paralleling Hardin's story of the village pasture. The collapse of many of the once bountiful ocean fisheries due to overharvesting, such as cod in the northwest Atlantic and Alaska pollack in the Bering Sea, has the elements of Hardin's story.[3] Fishers have sought to maximize their short-term catch of a limited resource in the belief that whatever fish did not end up in their own nets would be caught by somebody else. Hardin sees human population growth as an unfolding "tragedy" that is depleting the planet's natural resources and damaging the environment in much the same way that populations of other species multiply and die back when their numbers exceed the carrying capacity of their habitats.[4] A "tragedy of the atmosphere" has also been unfolding as the cumulative burden of pollutants emitted into it by human activities causes critical changes in its chemical composition, such as the thinning of the stratospheric ozone layer and increases in greenhouse gases far beyond naturally occurring concentrations.

Such "tragedies" are not inevitable, even when the resource being used is limited, as Hardin acknowledges in entitling a later article "The Tragedy of the *Unmanaged* Commons." The challenge for a community having a commons is to devise a management scheme that restrains use of its resource to a level that does not exceed its natural carrying capacity. While limits on the exploitation of a resource may be imposed upon users by the governments having jurisdiction over a commons, it is also not unusual for a community of users to take collective action among themselves to preserve the resource upon which they depend.[5] Such arrangements, however, are most common and effective in relatively small, cohesive communities in which strong social pressure can discourage environmentally irresponsible behavior. There are, however, instances of the successful management of international commons, an example of which is the regulatory scheme for the electromagnetic spectrum that has been established and revised at the World Administrative Radio Conferences of the International Telecommunications Union, which is designed to minimize interference between competing users from different countries.[6] Managing use of the atmosphere as a global commons poses much more complicated challenges for the international community.

WHAT IS A COMMONS?

A *commons* has three defining characteristics. First, it is a domain or collectivity of resources, which in the mythical English village is the pasture. Second, the resource domain is available to multiple actors who use it for their individual benefit. In the English village a number of households derive personal benefits from having their privately owned cattle eat grass from the pasture. Third, the resources of the commons are both subtractive, meaning that what is taken by one actor is not available to others, and finite, implying that they are limited in quantity and thus depletable. Accordingly, a clump of grass eaten by one household's cow is not available to the cattle of others, and there is only so much grass available for the combined herd of the villagers.

This conception of a commons distinguishes between a *resource domain,* or what Elinor Ostrom refers to as "resource system," and the *resource units* that comprise the domain.[7] A commons is the more encompassing resource domain that can be defined in spatial terms, such as a tract of forestland, or an aggregate of resources, such as a fish stock. The users help themselves to a portion of the pool or stream of resource units for their individual gain, such as the grass their cows eat in the pasture, the trees they cut down from a forest, or the fish they catch from an ocean fishery.[8] A landfill is a resource domain, locations of which are the resource units. Similarly, the geosynchronous orbital arc thirty-six thousand kilometers above the equator is a resource domain, whereas specific locations in the arc where satellites might be positioned are the resource units.

Resources of the Commons

In a generic sense a resource is something that is useful to humans. It may either be present in nature or be produced by humans. Natural resources contained in commons are of many types, which have implications for how they may be used or managed. Resources are usually thought of as being physical substances that under normal conditions are in the form of solids, such as coal or minerals; liquids, such as petroleum or water; or gases, such as helium or natural gas. Resources may be stationary, such as coal and forests, or mobile and thus fugitive, such as whales. Some resources are living, such as fish, grass, and trees, while others are inanimate, such as hard rock minerals.

It is often assumed that the use of natural resources invariably involves taking something out of the environment. Coal is extracted from the ground, trees are removed from a forest, fish are harvested from the oceans, and water is diverted from rivers. Alternatively, a resource may be something into which humans put things. A municipal landfill is a resource into which people put their garbage. Likewise, the rivers and oceans are used as mediums for disposing of a wide variety of waste substances, commonly referred to as pollutants. The geosynchronous orbit is an important resource in outer space that is highly useful as a set of "parking places" for communication and weather satellites.

The common pasture of the mythical English village was used exclusively for grazing cattle. Some commons, however, have a variety of types of resource units. Exploiters of one type of resource may come into conflict with those who are making other uses of the commons, which complicates the task of managing the domain. A publicly owned forest plot may be a source of wood for the lumber industry, a provider of nuts and berries for indigenous peoples, a repository of genetic material for biotechnology firms, and a sink for carbon dioxide for the world community. The oceans have been used as a medium for navigation, a source of fish, and a sink for many types of pollutants. Cutting a forest precludes other uses of it; marine pollution contaminates ocean fisheries, rendering the catch from them unfit for human consumption.

The Users of a Commons

A commons is a resource domain that has multiple users who appropriate its resource units for individual profit. The community of users for resources can be large or small, which has implications both for the likelihood of a tragedy occurring from overuse and how such an outcome can be avoided. Use of a *limited-access* commons is restricted to a specified group of actors, while all others are excluded. For example, in the English village it might be assumed that the privilege of grazing cattle on the common pasture would be limited to the permanent residents, with outsiders being prevented from adding their cattle. Other commons are *open-access* in the sense of being available to any actor who desires to make use of them, which has traditionally been the case with fishing on the high seas beyond the territorial jurisdiction of coastal states. Commons may be left as open-access because they are vast in relation to the use of them or because it is not technically feasible or is economically too costly to exclude other determined users.[9] Resource domains having one of these latter qualities in addition to being finite have been referred to as *common pool resources*.[10]

Subtractiveness and Finiteness

Multiple actors may make use of a commons, but the resource units are *subtractive* in the sense that those that are appropriated by one actor are not available to the others. For example, a fish that is harvested by one fisher can no longer be caught by others. The attribute of being subtractive distinguishes the resources of commons from "public goods," as conceived by Mancur Olson.[11] Public goods can sustain "joint use," which means that consumption by one actor is not subtracted from, or does not diminish, what is available to other potential users. A second condition of a public good is the impossibility of excluding users, which may or may not be the case with commons.[12] A television news program going out over the airwaves is a public good in that one individual watching it does not diminish its value to other viewers and it is impossible to keep people with television sets from receiving the signal.

Resource domains are also generally not considered commons unless they are *finite* in that there is an ultimate limit to the amount of use they can sustain without their resources being significantly depleted or altered. In some cases the cumulative effect of the consumption of resource units may eventually diminish the capacity of the domain to produce new resource units, as when overfishing reduces the stock that is available for reproduction.[13] The number of cattle that could be nourished sustainably on the pasture is limited, as is the amount of fish that can be harvested without reducing the capacity of a fish stock to regenerate itself. If no such natural limits exist, subtractiveness and the ultimate depletion of the resource never become reasons for concern and there will be no need to conserve the resource. All actors can help themselves to resource units as they like without lessening in any significant way the amount that others can consume, even though any specific resource unit cannot be consumed by more than one of them. Certain resources, such as the ocean's fisheries, once seemed boundless in comparison to the amount of fish being taken, but use increases with time and eventually reaches and exceeds the amount of consumption that can be sustained. As this point approaches, subtractiveness becomes an important consideration for the users who find themselves competing for the increasingly scarce resource units.

THE ATMOSPHERE AS A COMMONS

The atmosphere is a natural resource domain that is not simply useful but is essential to human life and the existence of most other species. The atmosphere is not a spatial domain but an aggregate of the physical substance known as air. The air comprising the atmosphere moves over the surface of the earth in ever changing directions and velocities and thus could be considered a fugitive resource. A specific volume of air that is not used at one time and place drifts away, while its place is immediately taken by another volume of air. Because air is a fluid, undifferentiated mass, its resource units are not discrete objects, such as a tree in a forest or a fish in the ocean. In this respect air is more similar to the waters of the oceans. Thus, resource units of air are of no naturally occurring size, nor can they be distinguished from one another.

Human beings use air and the atmosphere in many ways. Some uses extract gases from the air, such as oxygen in the acts of breathing or burning fossil fuels. Human consumption of atmospheric gases is minuscule compared to the available supply, so there is no danger of the resource being depleted. Other uses entail putting substances into the atmosphere to dispose of them, or, in other words, the emitting of pollutants. Human communities also make use of the atmosphere by taking advantage of its climate, for example in agriculture. This is normally done passively with no impact on climate. However, experiments have been conducted with techniques that could be used to alter weather intentionally in ways that serve agricultural or military purposes.

The atmosphere has generally been treated as an open-access resource. To deny people the use of the atmosphere for respiration, assuming it was possible, would be tantamount to refusing them the right to live. Traditionally all people have also been free to use the atmosphere as a convenient medium for disposing of many of their waste substances. In recent decades, however, the right to pollute has been significantly circumscribed by domestic and international laws and policies that restrict emissions of certain pollutants in order to enhance air quality in the common interest.

For certain uses the atmosphere is an infinite natural resource that permits joint exploitation; for others it is finite and subtractive. All human beings can take advantage of the UV-B shielding qualities of the stratospheric ozone layer without depleting it or diminishing its value to others. Likewise, there is no limit to the number of people who can take advantage of the climatic conditions maintained by the atmosphere without interfering with the use of climate by others. Nor is it possible to deny people access to the benefits of the atmosphere and climate. Thus, in these respects the atmosphere provides what are called "pure" public goods.

Subtractiveness comes into play for other uses of the atmosphere, although not in as apparent a way as with Hardin's pasture or an ocean fishery. Units of oxygen consumed in the processes of respiration or combustion are not available to other users, and thus are subtracted from the totality of the resource. However, even with billions of people the proportion of oxygen that is extracted in these ways is so infinitesimal that the atmosphere resembles a public good that is infinite in its supply of life-sustaining gases. Even looking into the distant future, there is no reason for concern that human consumptive uses of atmospheric gases would deplete them in any meaningful way because other environmental constraints would limit population growth well before this point would be reached.

Is the atmosphere a subtractive resource as a sink for pollutants? In one sense there appears to be no physical limit to the amount of pollutants such as SO_2 and CFCs that can be suspended in the atmosphere, which would suggest that it can be subjected to unlimited joint use and thus be considered a public good. The emissions of one actor do not prevent others from adding their wastes to the same volume of air, although the mix of pollutants will become increasingly noxious. Thus, the atmosphere would be similar to rivers or large bodies of water for absorbing pollutants but differs from a landfill that has a finite amount of space that can accommodate no more garbage once it is filled.

The picture changes, however, when it is recognized that there are limits to the capacity of the atmosphere to absorb certain pollutants without serious consequences for human health or the environment, such as respiratory diseases, acidification, depletion of the ozone layer, or global warming. Thus, the pollutants put into the atmosphere by one actor have the effect of subtracting from the amount that others can emit without bringing the total burden of pollutants to levels that have adverse impacts. The subtractiveness of the atmosphere as a sink for pollutants is not apparent from the perspective of individual sources, such as operators of motorized vehicles, because the discharge of pollutants from each is inconsequential compared to total human emissions and to the vast capacity of the atmosphere to disperse pollutants. The subtractive characteristic becomes more apparent when emissions are aggregated at the national or global level. For example, a relatively small number of highly developed countries have already preempted a large part of the capacity of the atmosphere to absorb CO_2 without triggering significant global climate change.

The limits of the atmosphere as a sink for pollutants without serious consequences are not as easy to determine as the number of cattle that can be nourished by a village pasture. Many types of pollutants are released into the atmosphere, where they mingle and undergo complex chemical changes. Furthermore, each type of pollutant is but one of many factors that contribute to a myriad of consequences for human health and the environment, such as human cancers, disappearances of aquatic life, and *waldsterben*, making it difficult to establish cause-and-effect relationships. Causal links are further blurred by the lengthy time lags between when a pollutant enters the atmosphere and when it has an observable impact, which in the cases of radioactive fallout and ozone-depleting chemicals may be decades. Finally, the contributions that pollutants are making to environmental problems are more difficult to anticipate when there are few if any observable impacts until a critical threshold is exceeded, after which the damaging consequences mount quickly.

OWNERSHIP, JURISDICTION, AND LEGAL STATUS

As defined in this book, a resource domain is considered a commons by virtue of a combination of physical qualities and who uses it and for what purposes, *not* on the basis of who owns it or has legal jurisdiction over it. Ownership or legal jurisdiction over a commons does, however, have implications for who has the right to make the rules regarding its use.

It is often presumed that a commons is owned by the group of actors who use it; for example, the pasture in the English village would be owned by the residents who graze their cattle on it. This is a possibility but not the only one.[14] If a commons is considered the property of a community, it falls under the category of *common property* and is subject to the control of the community's membership or governing institution, if it has one. Such common property may have been given to the community or purchased by it, or it may have been created by the members merging their individually owned parts to create a larger and more useful resource. Alternatively, a domain may simply be considered common property by tradition or have been declared as such. If the members of the community decide to allow individuals to use the commons for their own gain, it becomes a commons. They can make it a limited-access commons by excluding outsiders, if that is possible, or open it up to all who desire to use it for their individual gain.[15] They could also establish rules that are inconsistent with the concept of a commons, such as by prohibiting all use of the domain or by allowing it to be used only in ways that benefit the community as a whole rather than individuals; for example, only community-owned cattle might be permitted on the village pasture.

A second possibility is that a resource domain belongs to a certain party who permits others to use it as a commons. The pasture in Hardin's village could, for example, be the property of a wealthy absentee landowner, the state, or the king, who has no immediate use for it and is benevolent or disinterested enough to allow the villagers to graze their cattle on it. Similarly, some countries permit fishing vessels from foreign countries to operate within the confines of their two-hundred-mile exclusive economic zones, in particular when their own fishing industry has not been able to take full advantage of the calculated "total allowable catch." At some point the owner may decide to exclude those who have been using a domain as a commons.

Finally, a resource domain may have no recognized owner and thus be open to use by any parties who wish to exploit it. Unowned domains are normally not considered commons unless it is understood that they may not be claimed in part or in whole by individual actors for their exclusive use. In the international sphere such nonappropriable domains have traditionally been referred to by the Roman law concept of *res communis*.[16] Alternatively, domains or resources that may legally be appropriated, as was the case with new lands discovered by explorers, have been designated *res nullius*. It should be noted that while a commons, such as a forest tract, may be an unowned *res communis* domain, the unowned resource units contained in the common that may be appropriated for private use, such as trees, berries, or mushrooms, would be considered *res nullius*.[17]

There has been considerable ambiguity about the ownership of resource domains that have been treated as international commons. For centuries the high seas, which include all ocean areas beyond a narrow band of territorial waters belonging to coastal states, were considered to be nonappropriable and thus *res communis*. Under the doctrine of "freedom of the seas" all states could make use of the high seas for activities such as navigation and fishing so long as they did not interfere with the rights of others to do likewise. While areas of the high seas could not be claimed under the customary law of the seas, the fish found in them became the possessions of whoever caught them. Thus, individual fish were considered *res nullius* resources.

The 1960s saw the concept *common heritage of mankind* enter the lexicon of international law as an alternative legal designation for certain domains beyond the territorial jurisdiction of sovereign states. The common heritage doctrine was proposed in the United Nations by Arvid Pardo of the small Mediterranean island nation of Malta to counteract national claims being made to parts of the deep seabed. Pardo's concern was that deep-sea mining companies from a few of the technologically advanced states would help themselves to the huge quantities of mineral-rich nodules lying on the ocean floor, which he contended belonged to all nations.[18] A 1970 General Assembly resolution declared the seabed beyond the territorial jurisdictions of coastal states to be "common heritage of mankind," as did the Convention on the Law of the Sea of 1982.[19] The "common heritage" language has also been applied to the moon and other celestial bodies but not explicitly to other realms beyond national jurisdictions, such as the oceans, Antarctica, or outer space.[20]

Rather than being unowned and available to all to exploit freely, common heritage areas are considered to belong to all states and thus are international common property. If such domains are owned collectively by the international community, then presumably all states are entitled to share in the benefits derived from exploitation of these domains and to participate in making rules about how they will be used. The community of states may decide to treat the domain as a commons that all can make use of for their own profit, but conditions could be imposed on users to ensure that all owners share in the benefits even if they lack the technological means to exploit the domain on their own.[21] Alternatively, a common heritage domain could be set aside for the exclusive exploitation of its resources by an international public enterprise, with the proceeds being distributed among all states. Such a position was initially taken at the United Nations Conference on the Law of the Sea during the 1970s by developing countries on the mining of mineral nodules on the seabed.[22] Under the latter arrangement the domain would not be a commons, nor would the resource units be considered *res nullius*, because they could not be appropriated by individual or national actors.

In approaching the question of who owns and has jurisdiction over the atmosphere it is important to distinguish the atmosphere, and the air that comprises it, from airspace. *Airspace* is the three-dimensional region located above a certain geographical area. The legal status of airspace above states did not become an international issue until the invention of aircraft early in the twentieth century. Two diametrically opposed positions on legal rights to use airspace were espoused at the first international conference on air navigation, which was held in Paris in 1910. France and Germany advocated a "freedom of flight" doctrine, modeled after the long-standing tenet of the "freedom of the seas," which would permit planes from one state to fly freely above other state. Anticipating the military potential of aircraft, other states argued for a restrictive doctrine that would recognize the right of states to exercise sovereignty over the airspace above them, including the prerogative of excluding aircraft from other countries.[23]

The latter doctrine of sovereignty over airspaces soon won out as Great Britain in 1911 claimed the right to control the entry of foreign aircraft to its airspace, and to prohibit them completely from certain zones. Numerous other states claimed sovereignty over their airspaces by the early stages of the First World War. The first article of the 1919 Paris Convention on Aerial Navigation declared that each state was entitled to "complete and exclusive sovereignty over the airspace above its territory," including colonial areas and territorial waters.[24] The principle of sovereignty over airspace was further defined and reinforced in a series of international agreements, most notably the 1944 Chicago Convention on International Civil Aviation. Airspaces over other areas, such as the high seas and Antarctica, remain in the international domain and have been treated as *res communis* realms.

The advent of artificial orbiting satellites in the late 1950s raised the issue of the upper boundary of airspace. Although the subject has been discussed extensively, no agreement has been reached on a specific upper boundary of airspace.[25] It is generally assumed under international law that airspace extends to the highest altitudes at which aircraft fly, approximately 30 kilometers, while outer space, which is subject to a different body of international law that treats it as a *res communis* area, begins at the lowest levels that satellites orbit the earth, or approximately 160 kilometers. Thus, the proposed boundaries between airspace and outer space are typically about 100 kilometers, which would mean that the airspace of states would extend upward through the troposphere, the stratosphere, the mesosphere, and even part of the thermosphere. Accordingly, virtually all of the air above the territory of a state would reside within its airspace.

Having legal jurisdiction over airspace, however, does not confer upon states absolute sovereignty regarding its use. The international customary law of state responsibility, which is increasingly being applied to environmental matters, obliges nations to ensure that activities taking place in areas over which they have jurisdiction do not cause damage to other states.[26] This doctrine is the corollary of the basic principle of state sovereignty, which recognizes the right of each state to maintain its territory free of outside interference and to protect the lives, property, and interests of its people. Pollution that a state permits to be emitted into its airspace, which subsequently drifts into the airspace of another state where it causes significant damage, is generally considered an infringement on the latter's sovereignty. Attempts to manipulate weather that have undesirable consequences in other states would also appear to violate the doctrine of state responsibility.[27] The 1963 ban on atmospheric testing of nuclear weapons is also a constraint on the way nations are permitted to use their airspaces.[28]

By contrast, the atmosphere does not have a well-defined legal status.[29] There is a long-standing principle of international customary law that nations may exercise sovereign rights over the resources located within their territories. This right, which has been reaffirmed in numerous international declarations and treaties, is generally unambiguous when applied to stationary resources found within their borders, such as forests and minerals. The situation becomes more complicated, however, for resources that are mobile and thus pass through the spatial jurisdictions of two or more states, such as river waters or migratory stocks of fish. Such resources are sometimes referred to as "shared resources." An extensive body of international customary and treaty law has been applied to the use of some of these shared resources based on the principles of limited sovereignty and equitable use. On the subject of shared river systems, the widely acknowledged Helsinki Rules, which were drawn up by the nongovernmental International Law Association in 1966, suggest that "Each basin State is entitled, within its territory, to a reasonable and equitable share in the beneficial uses of the waters of an international drainage system.[30]

The atmosphere as a whole is not a pure example of a shared resource because more than 70 percent of it is not occupying national airspaces at any given time but is above the oceans and Antarctica, where it is under the jurisdiction of no country. Nor could the atmosphere be considered a pure example of a common resource because more than one-quarter of it resides in national airspaces at any given time. Thus, the atmosphere could hardly fall under the designation common heritage of mankind, thus implying that it is owned by all states.[31]

The ambiguous legal status of the atmosphere has received little attention in talks on establishing international atmospheric regimes. States have not been inclined to assert sovereign rights over the air in their airspaces, presumably because it is impossible to divide and take possession of substantial units of air in the way that river water can be dammed up and used for irrigation, nor would there seem to be any benefit from doing so, assuming it was technically feasible. Moreover, states have not been making cases for a "right to pollute" that is linked to their sovereign right to make use of the air in their airspaces, presumably because of its transient nature. Conversely, however, states have shown no inclination to relinquish claims to sovereignty over the air in their airspaces in order that the atmosphere in its entirety be designated the common property or common heritage of mankind.

Existing treaties that address atmospheric problems do little to resolve questions pertaining to the legal status of the atmosphere. The Vienna Convention and Montreal Protocol simply refer to the ozone layer as a "global unity" that is located "above the planetary boundary layer." The issue has also been sidestepped in talks on climate change. When Malta proposed to the General Assembly in 1988 that the global climate be conserved as part of the "common heritage of mankind"—as it had successfully done for the seabed two decades earlier—a compromise was reached on referring to global climate change as a "common concern of mankind." The term *common concern* also appears in the Declaration of the 1989 Noordwijk Conference on Atmospheric Pollution and Climate Change and the 1992 Framework Convention on Climate Change

(FCCC). As a relatively new concept in international law, it is not clear whether common concern implies anything more than the idea that climate change is a legitimate object of international attention, thus overriding assertions that it be dealt with by individual states as a matter that lies solely within their domestic jurisdictions.[32] It should be noted that the concept is applied to a potential problem rather than to the atmosphere as a domain and thus does not suggest any changes in jurisdiction over the atmosphere or airspace.

TRAGEDIES OF THE ATMOSPHERE

William Forster Lloyd and Garrett Hardin are but two of many writers who have warned of the tendency of commons users to overexploit the resource domain to the point of overcrowding, depletion, or destruction. Some commons are so vast that they can sustain unrestrained human use for long periods without becoming significantly degraded, as was the case until the twentieth century with ocean fish stocks that had endured millennia of human harvesting without becoming noticeably depleted. The situation may change, however, if the number of users increases and they apply new technologies that magnify their impact. The carrying capacity of what once seemed a boundless resource domain may be approached and overshot, sometimes much more suddenly than had been anticipated. In recent decades humanity has rapidly approached and exceeded the capacity of the global atmosphere to absorb and disperse pollutants without serious environmental effects.

Ironically, the users of a commons may persist in overexploiting its resources even when they are fully aware of an impending tragedy. Such behavior is the outgrowth of a rational assessment of self-interested actors who calculate that all the proceeds from using the commons will go exclusively to themselves as individual actors, while the environmental costs associated with overgrazing will be shared with the entire community. A herder in the English village may decide to add more cows to the common pasture, believing that the profits from his cattle will be substantially greater than his share of the additional costs of overgrazing, which are shared by all the villagers.

The behavior patterns that have contaminated and altered the atmosphere parallel those of Hardin's villagers, but the calculations of the polluters are more varied and complex. Those who pollute the air derive two types of benefits: the proceeds from the activity that generates the pollutants and the savings from venting gaseous and particulate wastes, which would be more costly to dispose of in other ways. These benefits go exclusively to the polluter. As wind currents disperse the pollutants, the resulting environmental damages are spread over a larger area. Thus, from the polluter's perspective, his share of the costs resulting from his own emissions may pale in significance when compared with the benefits he derives from the polluting activity.

The incentive for using the atmosphere to dispose of pollutants is all the more compelling in the case of the transport-and-deposition types of pollution, such as those that cause acid rain, especially when tall smokestacks significantly reduce the amount of pollution deposited near the emission source. The generator of the waste substances in effect transfers, or externalizes, most if not all of the costs associated with disposing of waste substances to the residents of downwind areas, who typically receive none of the benefits from the polluting activities. The downwind victims often protest the injustice of this situation but to little effect, as the Scandinavian countries and Canada have done in complaining about the large quantities of acid-forming pollutants they receive from the United Kingdom and the United States, respectively. Similarly, numerous Pacific countries denounced the nuclear testing programs of the United States, Britain, and France in their region for exposing their populations to potentially dangerous levels of radioactive fallout. Meanwhile, the people of the distant states conducting the tests, who were the beneficiaries of the knowledge gleaned from the testing programs, received much smaller doses of "global radiation," which posed only a minor threat to their health.

The situation is somewhat different with pollutants, such as CFCs and CO_2, that trigger basic atmospheric changes on a global scale. The polluter again enjoys the benefits of the polluting activity but is less able to avoid sharing the environmental costs, which are dispersed globally rather than primarily in downwind areas. No country can escape increased exposure to ultraviolet radiation due to a thinning of the ozone layer, although the effects will vary across geographical regions. Similarly, all countries can expect to experience climate changes, but here again the types of changes and their severity are likely to vary considerably from one region to another. Nevertheless, the polluters may conclude that the benefits they derive from their polluting activities significantly outweigh their share of the costs of atmospheric change caused by their own emissions. The consequences of atmospheric change will become much more troublesome, however, if other countries are guided by the same logic and add significantly to the global burden of pollutants, thereby accelerating the change process.

TRAGEDY-AVERTING STRATEGIES

Human communities can adopt a variety of strategies to avoid overexploitation and degradation of a common resource domain. None of them, however, is a sure bet for averting an environmental tragedy. How successful they are depends upon the circumstances in which they are applied and how they are implemented. One potential solution to the tragedy is to try to persuade the users to act responsibly by exercising *voluntary restraint* in exploiting their common resource domains, so that their combined use will remain within its carrying capacity. As part of the strategy, information may be provided to the users to impress upon them the undesirable consequences of continuing to exploit the common resource in an unrestrained fashion. A second strategy would establish a *regulatory regime* that includes mechanisms such as bans, quotas, technological specifications, and user fees designed to limit the amounts or types of use that are made of the resource domain.

Two other solutions to the tragedy would discontinue the commons system for utilizing a resource and replace it with alternative arrangements. Thus, a third course of action would be to *partition* the resource domain into sections, which are assigned or transferred to individual members of the community for their exclusive use. Under this so-called "privatization" solution, a user will presumably have a greater stake in conserving the resources of his section because he will absorb all of the costs from its overuse. The last option, which could be described as the "socialist" approach, would have the resource domain utilized exclusively by a *public enterprise*, which would distribute what it produced or earned among the members of the community. Not being driven to maximize personal profit, the public managers of such an enterprise could, at least in theory, balance the goals of production and conservation of the resource.[33]

Each of these approaches can be readily envisioned in the case of the mythical English village. The residents could exhort each other to act responsibly by not adding more cattle to an already heavily grazed common pasture in the interests of preserving it. If voluntary measures were not enough, the village government could impose a limit on the number of cattle each household would be allowed to graze, with any surplus cattle being confiscated. Alternatively, the herders may be assessed grazing fees on each head of their cattle, which if set high enough would discourage excessive use of the pasture; or the pasture could be divided into fenced sections assigned to individual villagers for exclusive grazing by each one's cattle. Finally, grazing could be limited to animals belonging to the community as a whole, with the products and profits being distributed among all of the villagers.

A more limited range of approaches can be used to limit pollution of the atmosphere. Given the dynamic movement of air, it would be physically impossible to divide up the atmosphere into enclosed sections for exclusive use by individual actors. It is also inconceivable that an international public enterprise could be created that would have exclusive rights to pollute the atmosphere. Thus, the remaining possibilities for averting tragedies of the atmosphere are voluntary restraint and various regulatory mechanisms.

Voluntary Restraint

Hardin places little stock in voluntary restraint as an approach for averting a tragedy of the commons. An individual thinking about acting in an ecologically responsible manner may anticipate absorbing all of the opportunity costs of curbing his use of a commons, while the benefits of his restraint will be shared with all users regardless of whether they also exercise restraint. Thus, the responsible actor is creating a public good in the form of less polluted air that will be shared by all.

Few actors can be expected to be so altruistic on a continuing basis, especially if others fail to reciprocate. The resource units the environmentally responsible actor passes up for the good of the community may be taken by less scrupulous actors, known as "free riders," who persist in trying to maximize what they derive from the commons. The more responsible members of a community may soon realize that not only is the environmental tragedy continuing to unfold, but they are receiving a smaller share of the resource units. Moreover, they may even be disadvantaged in their competition with the free riders, whose industries will have lower costs of production due to laxer environmental standards. Frustrated with the situation, the environmentally concerned actors may yield to the temptation to exploit the resource of a commons as rapidly as possible to secure a fair share of what it has to offer. Thus, the herders in Hardin's mythical English village could be expected to

continue adding cattle to an overburdened pasture, and fishing opera-
tives would invest in more and more boats despite signs that the fisheries they are planning to harvest are already declining.

It is therefore paradoxical that a number of states have taken unilateral steps to reduce emissions of air pollutants that have transboundary
or global effects. In the late 1970s the United States, Norway, Sweden,
and Canada enacted bans on nonessential uses of CFCs, including aerosol sprays, long before the establishment of international rules on the
manufacture and consumption of ozone-depleting substances. During
the 1980s twelve European countries committed themselves to reducing SO_2 emissions that went well beyond the 30 percent cutbacks mandated by the 1985 Sulfur Protocol. Similarly, most industrialized countries
unilaterally declared their intentions to freeze or reduce their emissions
of CO_2 by the turn of the century, in advance of the negotiations on the
FCCC that began in 1991.

These unilateral actions appear to defy Hardin's logic in that the
countries taking them will endure all of the costs entailed in reducing
air pollutants to create a benefit that will be shared by the larger community of states, including the free riders that are doing nothing to curb
their emissions. Unilateral reductions by large states that are responsible for a sizable proportion of global emissions, such as the United
States in the case of CFCs, are more understandable because their restraint can make a significant contribution toward addressing an environmental problem. Steps by smaller states, such as the Nordic countries,
Denmark, Austria, and Switzerland, to reduce their much lower vol-
umes of emissions will have little favorable effect on those countries or
the overall problem. Yet in the case of the pollutants that are the precursors of acid rain, it was the smaller states that were in the forefront in
making unilateral commitments to reduce emissions of SO_2 and NO_x.

How can these unilateral commitments of states to reduce pollutants be explained? They may simply be responses to domestic political
pressures from aroused citizenry, and nongovernmental organizations
as well, for their governments to do whatever can be done within their
jurisdictions to address environmental problems of growing concern.
Such was the case with the American ban on nonessential uses of CFCs
that was adopted in 1978. In such cases domestic publics may not even
seem to be concerned about whether other countries are taking reciprocal steps nor dwell on the small extent to which their sacrifices will mitigate the larger problem.

Alternatively, unilateral pronouncements may be part of a strategy for influencing other states to make similar commitments to reduce pollutants, which seems to have been a major factor in the decision of the Nordic countries to move far ahead of other European countries in reducing emissions of SO_2. As countries whose acidification problems were caused largely by air pollution originating beyond their borders, their task was to persuade the upwind states to take corrective action. By unilaterally setting ambitious goals for reducing air pollution and then achieving them, the victimized states could undermine the rationales that offending states frequently cite for their failure to curb their emissions: first, that the complaining state was not concerned enough about the pollution problem to do what it could on its own to mitigate it; and second, that substantial reductions are technically impossible or too costly. Thus, the declarations may be part of a strategy by concerned advocate states to lend momentum to the process of negotiations on international conventions and protocols that would commit all parties to reduce emissions of pollutants. This also appears to have been the primary motivation behind the unilateral goals set by numerous developed countries in the late 1980s on stabilizing or reducing CO_2 emissions. Without the prospect of negotiating such an agreement, substantially fewer states may have been inclined to set these goals.

These unilateral cutbacks have been only a small part of what is needed to address the problems of acid rain, ozone depletion, and climate change. It will be necessary for many more countries to make similar, if not more ambitious, commitments if these problems are to be kept from intensifying. Nor can it be assumed that the countries making unilateral reductions will continue to sacrifice for the welfare of the larger community unless other key states reciprocate. In 1980 the United States backed away from taking further steps to reduce its production and consumption of CFCs, as long as other major countries were profiting from playing the role of free rider by failing to phase out their nonessential uses of CFCs. Likewise, some countries have warned that their announced goals of reducing or stabilizing CO_2 emissions were contingent on other states making similar commitments.

Regulatory Regimes

Since states are unlikely to take strong enough action on their own to avert major global problems such as acidification, ozone depletion, and climate change, international regulations appear to offer the best hope for preserving the critical qualities of the atmosphere. Applicable rules may be found in international customary law, such as the responsibility of states to prevent damage to other states or to areas outside any jurisdiction. These principles of customary law have generally proven to be too vague, however, to define limits on polluting activities, especially where specific sources of pollution cannot be definitively linked to specific damages. Thus, it has been necessary to create international regulatory regimes based on negotiated treaties containing specific rules that are binding on ratifying states. Such regulations may take a variety of forms and be used in combination with one another in international regimes.

The simplest and most decisive form of regulation is a *prohibition* on activities that cause environmental damage. A temporary ban may be enacted to allow a resource to recover from overuse, an example being the moratorium on commercial harvesting of whales that was put in place by the International Whaling Commission in 1986. Permanent bans may be imposed on uses that are considered to be intrinsically harmful to human health or the environment, such as testing nuclear weapons in the atmosphere. Similarly, the 1992 Copenhagen Amendments to the Montreal Protocol provide for a permanent end to the production and use of CFCs and certain other chemicals that pose threats to the ozone layer. Bans are practical when the activity generating the pollution can be discontinued without prohibitive costs or serious disruptions. The superpowers agreed to stop nuclear tests in the atmosphere after underground testing became a viable option. Ozone-depleting substances were phased out only after the leading chemical companies expressed confidence that affordable chemical substitutes could be produced in a timely way.

A second type of regulation merely sets a *limit* on the use of a commons at a level that can be sustained without serious damage to the resource. The limit may be on the aggregate use of the commons by all parties, with users helping themselves to its resources on a first-come, first-served basis until the limit is reached. Alternatively, each of the individual users could be allocated a share of the total allowable use, or what is known as a quota. The quotas may be the same for all members of the community or they may vary considerably, based on criteria such as size of the party, proximity to the resource, previous level of use, or special needs for the resource. The limits written into the early international agreements on atmospheric pollutants have mostly been freezes or percentage reductions on emissions that apply uniformly to all parties, such as the 30 percent reduction in SO_2 emissions mandated by the 1985 Sulfur Protocol and the 50 percent reduction in CFC production and consumption specified for the parties to the 1987 Montreal Protocol. By designating the same percentage reduction for all parties, these regulations have the effect of setting national quotas based on previous use of the atmosphere as a sink for the pollutants in question. Greater flexibility may be achieved by allowing quotas to be bought and sold in the form of tradeable permits to pollute or by permitting two or more users to pool their quotas and comply with them jointly.

A third type of regulation specifies *operational rules,* such as the type of equipment that can be used in exploiting the resources of a commons. For example, rules on the minimum size of mesh in fishing nets have been adopted to allow younger specimens to grow to maturity and reproduce. Air pollution can be reduced significantly by requiring use of certain technologies, such as catalytic converters in the exhaust systems of automobiles or flue gas desulfurization equipment in the smokestacks of power plants. Reductions in air pollution may also be achieved by imposing rules on the sulfur content of fuels that are burned in power plants. While such operational rules are frequently key provisions of national environmental laws, there has been considerable resistance to including them in international agreements on air pollution, except in vague wording such as "the best available technology that is economically feasible," which appears in the 1979 LRTAP Convention.

Economic disincentives based on the "polluter pays" principle are a fourth way of regulating use of a commons, which allows the polluter to decide on an emission level based on his willingness and capacity to pay taxes or fines. The residents of the English village might be required to pay a tax on the cattle they own above a certain number, which could be set high enough to deter further additions of cattle to the pasture. National governments use taxes to discourage certain types of air pollution, such as fees on the sulfur or carbon content of fuels or on the volume of smokestack emissions. States have not been inclined, however, to conclude agreements that would impose international taxes on their pollutants or require all of them to enact national sulfur or carbon taxes.

Rules of liability can also be a form of economic disincentive if polluters anticipate they will be compelled to compensate the victims of their emissions for the damages they suffer. In international customary law a state may demand compensation for harms to its people or environment caused by pollutants originating in other states, but the accused state often has the legal prerogative of declining binding third-party adjudication. The Trail Smelter case between the United States and Canada is one of the few instances of a state, namely Canada, agreeing to binding arbitration to determine whether and how much it should pay compensation to foreign victims of pollution originating within its borders, but the amount was only $78,000.[34] The concept of liability offers little recourse for those harmed by pollution that cannot be linked exclusively to a specific source, as has been the case with acid deposition, ozone depletion, and greenhouse warming.

Thus, to this point most international efforts to regulate air pollution have simply dealt with deciding *how much* states should be allowed to pollute. These amounts, as contained in international agreements, have been expressed not in absolute amounts of pollution but either as a freeze at existing levels or a certain percentage reduction that is to be achieved by a specified date by ratifying states. In negotiations on atmospheric treaties, most states have insisted on retaining the right to choose the strategies they would use to comply with the prescribed limits on their emissions, taking into account their unique circumstances. They have experimented with a wide variety of national regulatory instruments, such as equipment requirements, rules on the sulfur content of fuels, carbon taxes, and tradeable emission permits.

EVALUATING REGIMES ALTERNATIVES

Regimes for managing the use of commons may be designed to achieve a variety of goals. From an environmental standpoint, the most critical question is whether the regime will be successful in conserving the resource domain. In other words, will it prevent a tragedy of the commons? Two economic questions may also be important considerations. Will the regime allow for the greatest possible sustainable use of the resource domain? And will the regime encourage the most efficient use of economic and environmental resources in the exploitation and conservation of commons? Then there is the issue of equity. Will the rules for exploiting the common resources be fair to previous and potential future users? Finally, there is the practical matter of feasibility. How likely is it that the management scheme could be put in place and effectively implemented?

Environmental Values

Most regimes that manage commons use are set up largely to further environmental objectives, in particular preventing the depletion or degradation of their resources. In the case of the atmosphere the primary environmental goal is to avoid changes or contamination that adversely affect human health or are damaging or disruptive to the natural environment. The principal environmental objective of the Nuclear Test Ban Treaty was to reduce the exposure of people to health-threatening radioactive contaminants. The framework agreements of the other regimes also set forth ambitious environmental goals. The parties to the 1979 LRTAP Convention are expected to ensure that activities taking place within their boundaries do not cause environmental damage in other countries. Ratifiers of the 1985 Vienna Convention on the ozone layer have a general obligation to refrain from activities that are likely to cause ozone loss. The FCCC of 1992 establishes the goal of stabilizing greenhouse gas emissions at levels that would "prevent dangerous anthropogenic interference with the climate system."

Maximum Sustainable Uses

While a total ban on the uses of a commons may be the surest way of achieving environmental objectives, it may arbitrarily deny would-be users access to resources they have depended upon and that could be profitably exploited on a sustainable basis. Closing the pasture in the English village to grazing would preserve the grass cover but deny the villagers an essential source of sustenance or income. Likewise, the atmosphere has been an essential sink for pollutants from the processes of industrialization that have elevated the living standards of much of the world's population; and peoples of Third World countries are adamant that they will not agree to forgo the polluting activities that would fulfill their ambitions for economic development.

If appropriately set, limits and disincentives can be flexible ways of allowing the greatest level of sustainable use of commons. International fishery commissions have set total allowable catches on the basis of scientifically determined "maximum sustainable yields." The LRTAP regime has adopted a similar concept called the "critical load" to designate the amount of deposition of air pollutants that can be permitted without serious environmental consequences. While most countries would have to reduce emissions of SO_2 significantly if acidic deposition is not to exceed the critical load, several countries could be permitted to increase emissions without causing serious environmental damage elsewhere. Atmospheric levels of ozone-depleting pollutants had already reached such high levels by the 1990s that an abrupt phasing out of further production of them was necessary to minimize what were already unacceptable losses of stratospheric ozone. GHG emissions are currently at a much higher level than can be permitted if atmospheric concentrations are to be stabilized at an already elevated level and additional global warming is to be avoided.

Economic Efficiency

Resistance has been growing in recent years to environmental regulations that ignore the economic costs of compliance. Criticism is directed toward rules that mandate *how* emissions must be reduced, such as by requiring the installation of costly emission abatement technologies, because such rules do not permit polluters to seek out less expensive ways of achieving specific environmental objectives. Limits on emissions or pollution taxes are generally preferred on economic grounds because they allow polluters greater flexibility. Existing international agreements on air pollutants generally leave it to the ratifying states to decide upon the strategy they will use to meet their responsibilities to limit emissions.

Mandating the same percentage reduction of pollution emissions for all countries, which is the most common type of international control, may not be the most cost-effective way of achieving environmental goals. In the interests of greater economic efficiency, the plan for the Revised Sulfur Protocol of the LRTAP regime tailored specific emission reduction targets for each country based not only on what that country would have to do to close gaps between actual deposition and critical loads beyond its borders, but also on what could be accomplished at a relatively low cost. The option of "joint implementation" being experimented with in the climate change regime allows the technically advanced countries to comply with their obligations to reduce pollution by assisting less developed countries to take the initial steps toward controlling emissions. The cost of reducing pollution emissions by a given amount is usually much higher in the industrial countries. A system of tradeable permits, which have been implemented within countries but not yet internationally, can also achieve cost efficiencies by concentrating the emission reductions where they can be achieved least expensively.

Equity

Equity is an especially important consideration issue in the negotiation of international agreements because states that are not satisfied with the fairness of a proposed treaty will be reluctant to become signatories and ratifiers and be bound to its provisions. Thus, France and China refused to accept the Test Ban Treaty on grounds that it was unfair to deny them testing options that the United States, the Soviet Union, and the United Kingdom had previously used to develop their nuclear arsenals.

Equity does not necessarily imply equality, nor is equal treatment always equitable. States that have unilaterally enacted measures that have already substantially reduced or limited certain air pollutants may question whether they should be expected to achieve the same future percentage reductions as states that have done much less, if anything, to reduce their emissions. One way to acknowledge previous reductions is to push back the base year from which the percentages will be calculated, as was done in the 1985 Sulfur Protocol by designating 1980 as the base year for figuring pollution emissions.

States that historically have had relatively low emissions of air pollutants may also challenge the fairness of treaties or protocols mandating uniform percentage reductions for all countries. Should Japan, for example, which has long been much more frugal in its use of fossil fuels, be expected to reduce its CO_2 by the same percentage as the United States, even though in 1990 the average Japanese was responsible for less than half the amount of CO_2 emissions as the average American? Developing countries take the argument one step further by arguing that fairness dictates that they should be entitled to increase their release of air pollutants if necessary to implement their development plans, even while the industrialized counties are expected to achieve reductions in their much higher levels of pollution. This principle is acknowledged in the 1992 FCCC, in which developing countries are not expected to constrain their GHG emissions, and it is even conceded that they may need to increase their emissions as they develop. These issues of equity might be rephrased in terms of how a finite quantity of permissible pollution should be divided among the peoples of the world. Do all people have equal rights to pollute the atmosphere? If so, states might be allocated pollution permits based on their population sizes. If not, on what grounds should some people be permitted to pollute more than others? Should a greater share be allocated to those who became dependent on a high level of pollution long before environmental threats such as ozone deple-tion and climate change became known? Alternatively, do the highly developed countries that have already used up the lion's share of the atmosphere's capacity to absorb pollutants such as CFCs and CO_2 bear a special responsibility to compensate the less developed countries that might be more seriously affected by the problems that these pollutants have created?

The Question of Feasibility

Regardless of whatever desirable qualities a prospective scheme may have for managing a commons, the plan is hardly worth con-sideration unless it is feasible, meaning that it has a chance of being successfully instituted. The fluid physical quality of the atmosphere rules out the option of dividing it into sections assigned to states for their exclusive use. The range of possibilities is also constrained by what is politically possible, given that international regulations are not legislatively imposed but are the product of negotiations that are normally a slow and cumbersome process, especially when they involve large numbers of countries with divergent interests. Further-more, the sovereign states participating in international negotiations have the prerogative of refusing to be bound by the rules agreed to by others. These realities of the negotiation process in part explain why the regulations of the atmospheric regimes have been largely limited to relatively simple types of rules, such as bans or reduc-tions based on previous levels of air pollution.

Agreement on strong, effective rules is unlikely unless there are plausible ways of monitoring compliance. Efforts to reach agreement on a comprehensive nuclear test ban were repeatedly frustrated by uncertainties about whether underground test explosions could be detected. The Test Ban Treaty could be concluded because nuclear tests in the atmosphere, outer space, or oceans would be difficult to conceal. Bans are generally less complicated to monitor than limits because any instance of a prohibited activity can be assumed to be a violation. Assessing compliance with limits usually requires a more elaborate system of collecting information, either a self-reporting procedure that is sufficiently transparent to permit outside scrutiny or an international monitoring network, such as LRTAP's EMEP, which has provided figures on emissions of air pollutants that are generally accepted as being valid.

It is unlikely that any regime will score highly on all of these goals in addition to being feasible. For example, a regime that is successful in achieving environmental goals will in most cases not allow for maximum sustainable use. An equitable regime may necessitate compromises in economic efficiency. The test ban regime was highly successful in achieving the environmental goal of reducing the flow of radioactive pollutants into the environment, but the regime was less successful in the attainment of other potential goals, such as fairness to countries that had not yet tested nuclear weapons, although this did prove to be feasible. With refinements such as the "critical loads" approach, the LRTAP regime has achieved a greater balance between environmental and economic goals. The ozone depletion regime has been heavily oriented toward environmental goals, but equity issues had to be addressed to induce participation from key Third World countries. Developers of the climate change regime face the difficult challenge of devising international measures that will minimize global warming while satisfying Third World expectations of equity and being economically and politically feasible for the industrialized countries to implement.

CONCLUSIONS

In certain respects the atmosphere does not fit the classic mold of a commons as exemplified by the village pasture in Hardin's parable. Rather than being a typical resource domain from which things are physically taken and consumed, such as fish in the oceans, the atmosphere is primarily useful as a medium for disposing of pollutants. Nevertheless, the atmosphere has the essential properties that distinguish commons. As a resource domain it is used by multiple actors for their individual benefit. It is finite in its capacity to absorb pollutants without serious environmental damage, and the pollution that one country introduces into the atmosphere ultimately reduces the amount of pollution that others can discharge without triggering harmful environmental effects.

The atmosphere is not properly classified as common property because at any given time much of the air that comprises it resides within national airspaces. Thus, states would appear to have legal claims to jurisdiction over the air currently in the airspaces above their territories. Because air masses are constantly moving and defy containment in large quantities, it would be impossible for states to exercise exclusive control over any significant part of the atmosphere. Therefore, the atmosphere is by its nature a common resource; recent international agreements refer to it as the "common concern of mankind."

International regulatory regimes offer the only realistic possibility for limiting the amount of air pollution of either the transport-and-deposit type or the atmospheric change type. But even under the best of circumstances, it is a cumbersome process to get large numbers of sovereign states with widely divergent interests to agree on any type of rules, including simple limits on air pollution. The task would be difficult enough if conservation of the common resource were the only objective, but other considerations need to be taken into account, including maximizing use of the resource, achieving economic efficiency, and satisfying issues of equity.

Thus far the regulations contained in international agreements on air pollution have been largely limited to prohibitions, freezes, or percentage reductions, although in some agreements states have been expected to adopt the best economically feasible technologies available for abating pollution. The ban on testing nuclear weapons in the atmosphere has largely eliminated the radiation problem it was designed to address. The Vienna Convention and the Montreal Protocol as revised should, if complied with, soon begin restoring the ozone layer. Deeper reductions in emissions of pollutants are needed to reverse acidification due to transboundary pollution. Effective abatement of the acidification and climate change problems may require a greater assortment of international regulatory mechanisms than has been used previously in managing use of the atmosphere.

Chapter 9

THE PURSUIT OF ENVIRONMENTAL SECURITY

Most human aspirations are oriented toward achieving either development or security. *Development* implies an improvement over existing circumstances so that people realize more of their productive, social, and other human capacities. *Security* is the assurance people have that they will continue to enjoy those things that are most important to their survival and well-being, such as physical health, food and other necessities of life, economic sustenance, and freedom from violence.[1] People seek to further their development and security operating either as individuals or through groups ranging from families or local communities to nation-states or even global institutions, such as the United Nations.

The natural environment is a critical factor in pursuing both development and security. Human societies have developed by exploiting the bounteous natural resources of the planet that they inhabit—its soil, forests, minerals, fossil fuels, water, climate, and varied life forms. Concurrently, human beings have been awed by the forces of nature that threaten their well-being if not survival, such as extreme cold, earthquakes, tidal waves, volcanic eruptions, floods, droughts, tropical storms, pestilence, and diseases. Until the most recent moments in the long sweep of human existence, natural threats fell exclusively into the category of "acts of god." In recent decades, however, humanity itself has become a force in altering the natural environment in ways that could seriously jeopardize its fortunes.

While the concept security has been used in many contexts, the terminology national security has been used almost exclusively in the realm of geopolitics, in particular the protection of states from military threats emanating from antagonistic states or from other hostile actors, such as revolutionary or terrorist groups. Even with the ending of the Cold War, many security specialists still hold to the traditional view that use of the term *security* should be limited to threats in the military sphere. It is becoming increasingly apparent that human societies face a broader range of dangers, including economic and environmental threats, some of which are of comparable if not greater magnitude. Accordingly, rather than reserving the terms security and national security—with which people strongly identify and toward which they are willing to commit large amounts of resources—for the realm of military threats, it is appropriate to expand their use to the protection of human societies from other compelling types of dangers.

Air pollution has for centuries been a bane to human health in local areas, as was readily apparent from London's legendary "killer smogs." It continues to be a serious threat to health especially in the burgeoning cities of the developing world and the heavily industrialized regions of the former Soviet bloc. Radioactive fallout from atmospheric nuclear tests or accidents at nuclear power plants poses a long-term peril to those who receive substantial doses. Acidic precipitation has been linked to widespread damage to forests in Europe and North America, which are critical to the economies of numerous countries. These dangers pale by comparison, however, to the potentially catastrophic global consequences of increased exposure to ultraviolet radiation resulting from a thinning of the ozone layer and of significant world climate changes.

Environmental dangers raise challenges that are quite different from those of a military nature. Military threats normally emanate from the malevolent actions of enemies, whereas environmental ones are typically the consequence of routine, economic activities of friend and foe alike, and even of one's own nation. The quest for military security is often looked upon as a competition among states aimed at achieving and sustaining a strategic advantage in weaponry and preparedness, while environmental security is viewed as primarily a cooperative imperative. Furthermore, military security is usually thought of as being almost exclusively the province of sovereign states, and indeed is oriented toward their preservation as political units. By contrast, environmental security is directed more toward human health and well-being and thus is appropriately pursued at any level, from the local to the global, although the focus here will be on states.

This chapter compares the choices states can make as they seek military and environmental types of security. Despite the differences in the challenges they face in these realms, there are parallels between the strategies available for pursuing security in each of them. States can opt to use either preventive or defensive approaches. Moreover, they may decide to strive for security on their own or in cooperation with other states. Countries have been inclined to pursue military security through a defensive, self-help strategy, which has led to costly arms races that have heightened rather than reduced their insecurities. Will they display the same tendencies in seeking to enhance their environmental security? Or will they work together on a preventive approach that could lead to a more favorable and less costly outcome?

THE ENVIRONMENT AS A SECURITY ISSUE

The term security became a focus of national affairs toward the end of World War II when it was proposed as a more flexible alternative to the word *defense*. The principal peace-keeping organ of the United Nations was named the Security Council. In the United States the National Security Act of 1947 established the National Security Council to address a broader range of threats to the country's welfare than was implied by the "national defense."[2] Despite the greater apparent flexibility of the concept security, its predominant use has been in the context of geopolitical and military affairs. Little attention has been given to other major types of threats to national security, even though they may be comparable in the magnitude of their implications.

Harold and Margaret Sprout, professors at Princeton University, were pioneers during the 1960s in exploring the impacts that ecological factors such as climate, natural resources, and demographic trends had for the international political system.[3] In the early 1970s Richard Falk's *This Endangered Planet* and the highly influential, and controversial, report to the Club of Rome entitled *The Limits to Growth* drew attention to the threats to the world community that were implicit in trends in population, resources use, and pollution.[4] Since then numerous scholars, political leaders, and even military figures have suggested that the important threats to national security were not exclusively military. An interesting example of the latter is Gen. Maxwell Taylor, the former commander of United States forces in Vietnam, who wrote in 1964 that "I for one am fully convinced that the most formidable threats to this nation are in the non-military field."[5] The call for redefining the term security to acknowledge these emergent nonmilitary types of threats has been repeatedly made in the academic literature,[6] with gradually increasing use of the concepts environmental security and ecological security.[7] Arthur Westing proposed the concept "comprehensive security," with the environment being one of the principal dimensions, along with military, economic, and social/humanitarian security, any one of which he contended could not be achieved independently of the others.[8]

The environment and security have also been linked in international political and diplomatic circles, in particular the United Nations. One of the chapters in the report of the Brundtland Commission entitled *Our Common Future* is devoted to the relationship between the environment, security, and peace.[9] However, it was the Soviet leadership, in the aftermath of the Chernobyl disaster, that became the most active proponent of environmental security in the late 1980s. The Soviet Union along with its eastern European allies offered a resolution entitled "International Ecological Security" at the 1987 session of the General Assembly. The next year Mikhail Gorbachev and Eduard Shevardnadze attended the General Assembly session and proposed "an international regime of ecological security" and a program for its implementation. At neither session, however, did the Soviet resolutions on this subject receive widespread support from other United Nations members.[10]

There is considerable confusion about the concept environmental security because the link between environment and security has been viewed in two fundamentally different ways. One interpretation points to how environmental degradation and heightened competition for scarce natural resources can provoke conflicts and hostilities that may lead to violence and warfare. The Middle East is often cited as being an area ripe for environmental conflict as demand increases from Syria, Israel, Jordan, and West Bank Palestinians for the limited water supplies of the Nile and Jordan River systems and underground aquifers of the region.[11] Likewise, Egyptian leaders have warned that an interruption in the flow of the precious waters of the Nile River by its upstream neighbors could provoke an armed intervention.[12] Rapid population growth and resulting environmental strains may lead to acute conflict and violence within states that could threaten the stability of their governments.[13] This perspective on environment and security can be absorbed by the more traditional conceptions of national security, in that it simply recognizes another set of circumstances that increases the risk of armed conflict posing a threat to states.

The second interpretation, and the one that is featured in this chapter, explores the ways in which human-induced environmental changes significantly jeopardize human welfare. Thus, the terminology environmental security is not limited to situations in which the environmental factors contribute to political tensions and hostilities that could lead to military conflict. For example, the loss of stratospheric ozone poses a substantial threat to human health from increased exposure to UV-B radiation and thus is an important cause of environmental insecurity even though it is difficult to imagine how ozone loss might lead to violent conflict. Likewise, even though the natural resources of Canada and Norway have been seriously damaged by air pollutants originating in the United States and the United Kingdom, respectively, it is inconceivable that either of the victimized countries would revert to military means to try to correct the situation.

This notion of environmental security has not been without detractors. It has been criticized by traditional security specialists who warn that the concept security will lose its clarity and meaning if broadened to encompass nonmilitary dimensions, such as the environment, which involve fundamentally different types of threats and response strategies. Alternatively, some within the environmental community have also expressed reservations about linking the environment to security out of concern that the values and principles often associated with security, such as nationalism, competitiveness, hostility, and secrecy, would be inappropriately transferred to the pursuit of environmental objectives.[14] The specter of the environment becoming a new mission for armed forces in a post–Cold War era is alarming to American environmentalists, especially in view of the traditional wanton disregard for the environment in military preparations and engagements.

Nevertheless, there are compelling reasons for cultivating both an environmental dimension to security and at the same time a security dimension to the environment. Threats to the welfare of human communities are not exclusively of a military nature, and thus it distorts the meaning of security to define the concept in such artificially narrow terms. Conceiving of national security almost exclusively in military and geopolitical terms discourages consideration of other major types of threats to human welfare and an assessment of the relative risks that are inherent in each. Nor is much thought given to the ways in which the single-minded pursuit of military security can jeopardize the attainment of other types of security, as was so clearly the case during the heyday of atmospheric testing of nuclear bombs, despite the risks that nuclear fallout posed to human health. Security is inherently a multifaceted human aspiration with a variety of types of threats posing different types of challenges. Coining the phrase "environmental security" has prompted an extensive reexamination of the essence of security and enriched the debate on national goals.[15]

Likewise, there are both conceptual and practical reasons for considering responses to environmental problems from a security perspective. For the most part, environmentalism is concerned with maintaining, or in effect securing, the essential qualities of the existing natural environment, including the atmosphere, that are so critical to human beings and all other species. The security perspective encourages an anticipatory type of response that looks at contingencies and risks. From a practical standpoint, the term security adds considerable importance and urgency to environmental concerns because it strikes a responsive chord among publics. The power of the concept security is evident from the nearly $1 trillion spent annually by nations on armed forces and the vast sums individuals pay to insure their lives, health, homes, cars, and other possessions.[16] Thus, the environment may become a more salient issue on the public agenda if it is looked upon as a matter of national and individual security.

Will the quest for environmental security succumb to the nationalistic tendencies that have been so pervasive in the military realm? Such a development is by no means inevitable because the threats are very different. Furthermore, what one country does to enhance its environmental security usually will not arouse concern in other countries in the ways that its new weaponry will, even when undertaken solely for deterrent or defensive purposes. Alternatively, it should not be assumed that common environmental threats such as ozone depletion and climate change will necessarily lead countries to work together to address them. This question of whether states can be expected to strive for environmental security on their own or cooperatively with the world community will be explored later in the context of the four major atmospheric problems discussed in this book.

ATMOSPHERIC THREATS TO ENVIRONMENTAL SECURITY

To understand more fully the nature of security, it is first necessary to reflect on what it means to be insecure. Insecurities of any type arise when there is the combination of a threat and a vulnerability. A *threat* is present when happenings or developments are possible that have the potential for causing serious harm to people were they to take place. A *vulnerability* is present when people are susceptible to being adversely affected by threatening events or developments if and when they occur.[17] A state is militarily insecure when there is a threat of being attacked by another state, and it is vulnerable in the sense of not having the armed forces and weaponry needed to ward off the attack.

Naturally occurring fluctuations in weather and long-term changes in climate have always been sources of human insecurities. Intense storms such as typhoons and tornadoes have taken a heavy toll on human life and property, droughts have led to widespread hunger and starvation, and climate changes occurring over decades and centuries have undermined the viability of civilizations. The El Niño effect of 1982–83 caused loses of $4 billion in Bolivia, Chile, Ecuador, and Peru, or about 10 percent of their combined GNP.[18] Human beings have tried with some success to reduce their vulnerability to such occurrences, for example by creating reservoirs and irrigation systems to provide water for agriculture during extended dry spells or by constructing levies to protect cities and farmland along flood-prone rivers. But even the most technologically advanced societies can be disrupted by violent or extreme weather, as was evident from the devastation wreaked on south Florida by Hurricane Andrew in 1992, where losses were estimated to be $25 billion. A spate of weather-related disasters during the 1990s, including the unusually active hurricane season of 1995, has raised concern among American insurers about the viability of their industry in an era of human-induced climate change.[19]

Human beings are adding to their environmental insecurities by altering the chemical mix of the atmosphere. Some of these insecurities take the form of threats to human health. The testing of nuclear weapons in the atmosphere exposed the world's population to greater doses of radiation, which increased the danger that people would develop certain types of cancers. Industrial air pollutants cause or aggravate a variety of medical conditions such as lung disease and heart stress, which may be reflected in the reduced life expectancies of people living in areas with heavily contaminated air. Increased exposure to UV radiation due to a thinning of the ozone layer increases the risks of skin cancer and a weakened human immune system. As climate zones move with global warming, infectious diseases such as malaria, lymphatic filariases, schistosomiasis, onchocerciasis (river blindness), African sleeping sickness, dengue fever, and encephalitis are likely to spread to new regions, including the temperate areas, and afflict additional populations.[20]

More formidable threats from human-induced atmospheric changes arise from their impacts on the environment, especially in the cases of transboundary air pollution and global warming. The world's forests are especially vulnerable to atmospheric changes. Acidification appears to be a major factor in the widespread damage that has been observed in the forests of central Europe and the Scandinavian countries, and to a lesser extent those of eastern North America. A study by the Austrian-based International Institute for Advanced Systems Analysis (IIASA) estimates that acid rain will cost Europe 118 million cubic meters of wood, valued at more than $20 billion, every year for the next century unless further commitments are made to reduce emissions of acid-forming pollutants.[21] Changing climate zones, forest fires, and insect infestations associated with global warming pose an even more pervasive threat to the world's forests, but there is still considerable uncertainty about how specific types of forests in various regions of the world will be affected. Climate change could have an especially devastating effect on the vast belt of boreal forests comprised of cool-weather conifers, which runs across the northern latitudes of Russia, the Nordic countries, and North America.[22]

Atmospheric changes also have considerable potential for limiting food production, while world population continues to increase by nearly one hundred million people a year. Both acid precipitation and ultraviolet radiation have been shown to have adverse effects on food crops, but climate change seems to be the greatest threat to agriculture. Even relatively minor alterations in rainfall patterns could jeopardize the viability of farming operations in arid and semiarid regions. Reduced river flows could force a major reduction in irrigation. Agricultural pests may spread to new areas as climates become warmer. Longer growing seasons may be a boon to agriculture in some higher latitude regions but will be of little consolation to the countries where production declines substantially, jeopardizing the food security of their populations as well as their agricultural exports.[23]

Fisheries, which are already under considerable stress from over-harvesting but yet provide 16 percent of the animal protein in the world's diet, may decline further as phytoplankton succumb to increased doses of UV-B radiation, especially in the southern oceans near Antarctica where ozone loss has been the most severe.[24] Changes in ocean currents and the disruption of coastal wetlands and estuaries due to climate change and sea level rises may also seriously affect offshore fisheries. Acidification has killed off fish in numerous freshwater lakes in the Nordic countries and eastern North America, resulting in a significant loss of recreational opportunities.

Sea level rises due to global warming pose perhaps the most conspicuous threats to the environmental security of much of the world's population. A one-meter rise in sea levels would put five million square kilometers of land at risk, which is only 3 percent of the world's land but comprises one third of global cropland and is home to one billion people.[25] The small island nations are especially threatened, as was pointed out by the United Nations delegate from the Seychelles, who warned that "the [small island states] are doomed to ecological, social, and economic catastrophe within the foreseeable future. Some will even disappear. And if this happens they will take with them cultures, identities, and values that are irreplaceable."[26]

Low-lying areas are key parts of numerous continental countries, such as Bangladesh, Egypt, China, Gambia, Indonesia, Mozambique, Pakistan, Senegal, Surinam, and Thailand.[27] Among the major coastal cities likely to be affected by rising seas are Calcutta, Bombay, Shanghai, Rio de Janeiro, Buenos Aires, Jakarta, Karachi, Dacca, Manila, and Bangkok.[28] In Egypt, by one calculation, a one-meter rise in sea levels would displace 7.5 million people in a region of the Nile delta that encompasses 12 to 15 percent of the country's arable land and accounts for 14 percent of its gross domestic product (GDP). For Bangladesh a similar rise would threaten 5.5 million people and inundate 7 percent of the country's cropland, which accounts for 5 percent of its GNP.[29] Bangladesh is also susceptible to tropical storms, such as the cyclone in April 1991 that killed upwards of 125,000 people, destroyed hundreds of settlements, and devastated large areas of farmland. The incidence and intensity of such tropical storms are expected to increase if oceans become warmer as average air temperatures rise.[30]

These are only a few of the environmental threats associated with atmospheric changes that have been anticipated thus far. With time other threats, some of which may be far more ominous for humanity, will undoubtedly arise. More surprises of the magnitude of the Antarctic ozone hole are likely as scientists enhance their knowledge of the functioning of the Earth system, as critical thresholds are surpassed, as time-lagged impacts become manifest, as positive feedback loops accelerate the rate of change, and as interrelationships among environmental trends beget unanticipated consequences. Climate change is also likely to have social ramifications, such as civil unrest and migrations of people from impacted areas, which will also pose threats to the security of numerous societies. By one estimate, rising sea levels and storm surges could displace one hundred million people by 2050. This multitude of additional environmental refugees, desperately searching for places to live, would impose immense burdens on the increasingly overcrowded countries of the Third World.[31]

STRATEGIES FOR ENHANCING ENVIRONMENTAL SECURITY

Security can be enhanced by addressing either threats or vulnerabilities. The first approach of *reducing threats* is preventive in the sense of lessening the probability that a damaging event will occur, ideally to zero, or of limiting the magnitude of the threat it imposes. The threat of nuclear war could, for example, be eliminated through the total elimination of nuclear weapons by all nations accompanied by safeguards that would prevent the production of new ones. Likewise, discontinuing the testing of nuclear explosives in the atmosphere prevented additional human exposure to radioactive fallout from such tests. In the case of climate change, it is unrealistic to expect to prevent global warming completely, but steps can be taken that could contain the amount of warming that occurs within a given future time frame and thus lessen the harmful effects that would follow.

The alternative is a defense-oriented approach of *reducing vulnerabilities*. Security is strengthened by taking steps to avoid or lessen the impact on individuals or societies from potentially harmful events that do materialize. Vaccination programs have provided a defense for the human body against infectious diseases. Centuries ago thick walls were built around cities to protect the inhabitants from marauding armies; and in modern times bomb shelters and antimissile systems were constructed in hopes of providing people protection in the event of a nuclear attack on their cities. Defensive, or adaptive, approaches are the only options for security against natural threats over which humans have no control, such as earthquakes and volcanic eruptions. Damage to human communities can be lessened by constructing quake-resistant structures in areas prone to seismic activity or by keeping people from settling in the vicinity of potentially live volcanoes. Defensive action can also be taken against environmental threats caused by human activities. For example, sea walls can be built around coastal cities to protect them from rising ocean levels due to climate change.

Strategies for pursuing security can also be distinguished on the basis of whether they are carried out unilaterally or collectively. The *unilateral* approach is based on self-reliance in the sense that an actor marshals its own resources to increase its sense of security. An individual, for example, might assemble a diverse portfolio of investments to ensure future financial security or purchase a firearm to protect his household from intruders. Nations build up their armed forces to deter foreign attackers or repulse invasions if they do take place. In the environmental realm, states have on their own restricted trade in toxic chemicals that could endanger the health of their citizens.

The *collective* approach assumes an interdependence among actors in the sense that their behaviors can increase or reduce the insecurities of each other. They can agree to reduce or minimize the ways in which they pose threats to one another or cooperate on reducing their vulnerabilities. Workers join labor unions to increase their sense of job security. Nations form military alliances or global collective security arrangements that treat an attack against one as an attack against all in order to have a stronger defense that will discourage potential aggressors. Likewise, states enter into international agreements designed to limit many forms of environmental degradation resulting from human activities within their jurisdictions.

The possible combinations of approaches for reducing threats or vulnerabilities and for acting unilaterally or collectively are presented in Table 9.1. These combinations define four basic strategies for enhancing security: self- prevention, collective prevention, self-defense, and collective defense. Let us briefly consider each of these strategies in both the military and environmental contexts.<Place Table 9.1 here>

Table 9.1. General Strategies for Enhancing Security

	Unilateral	Collective
Reduce Threat	I (self-prevention)	II (collective prevention)
Reduce Vulnerability	III (self-defense)	IV (collective defense)

Self-Prevention

Self-prevention, or strategy I, consists of efforts by an actor operating on its own to reduce or eliminate a threat. An actor that is a significant cause of the threat may achieve a substantial measure of security by altering its own behaviors that give rise to threatening circumstances. If the actor's insecurities are attributable to other actors, it may be possible to take steps to diminish the threats that they pose. Such steps could be in the form of a forcible intervention or coercive tactics designed to influence the behavior of those that are posing a threat. Other parties could be approached in a noncoercive way designed to induce them to mitigate the threats that they pose. The original actor may begin the process by implementing threat-reducing actions of its own that invite reciprocation by others.

These options can be readily identified in the realm of military security. A government might try to address the concerns of frustrated ethic minorities to lessen the likelihood of civil war. A state could attempt to reduce, if not eliminate, the threat posed by another state by launching a preemptive attack against the latter's key military installations or arms production facilities. For example, Israel executed a surprise attack in 1981 to destroy Iraq's Osirak nuclear reactor in the belief that it was being used to produce fissionable materials for a nuclear bomb. An entirely different approach to self- prevention of threats would have a state unilaterally reduce nonessential defensive armaments as a gesture designed to induce other countries to reciprocate by cutting back on weapons they have that pose a threat to the first state. This latter strategy of unilateral initiatives has had its proponents, including Robert Osgood, who referred to it as Graduated Reciprocation in Tension-Reduction

(GRIT). Such an approach, however, is generally viewed as being too risky to be a realistic approach for enhancing military security.[32]

States can also adopt a strategy of self-prevention in the pursuit of environmental security. Numerous nations have adopted laws on water and air pollution from domestic sources that might jeopardize the health of their own citizens and in some instances those of other countries. It is conceivable, albeit highly unusual, for a state to intervene directly in another state to deal forcefully with a serious environmental threat originating within the latter's jurisdiction, such as an upstream dam project or a malfunctioning nuclear power plant. States may unilaterally adopt trade sanctions designed to discourage what are considered to be environmentally irresponsible practices elsewhere. For example, the United States decided on its own to ban imports of tuna caught using fishing practices that also kill large numbers of dolphins, a law that was contested by Mexico on grounds that it was a violation of the trade rules of the General Agreement on Tariffs and Trade (GATT). There are also numerous examples of states engaging in the environmental equivalent of GRIT, as they have unilaterally set goals to reduce emissions of SO_2, NO_x, or CO_2 in hopes of spurring other countries to make comparable commitments.

Collective Prevention

Collective prevention, or strategy II, involves a group of actors cooperating to address insecurities they have in common, including the threats they pose for one another. Collective prevention normally entails the negotiation of agreements that spell out what each party is expected to do to alleviate its contributions to the insecurities of the others. Collective prevention assumes confidence among the parties that all will follow through on their commitments. Confidence in the others is usually based on mutual trust or safeguards written into the agreements, such as monitoring procedures and sanctions for violations.

In the military realm reciprocal arms reduction is the predominant form of collective prevention, or what was referred to as "common security" in the report of the Palme Commission and "mutual security" by others.[33] The basic premise of the approach is that nations will feel more secure if they agree to reciprocate by eliminating, reducing, or not acquiring the conventional and nuclear armaments that are threatening one another. This type of logic underlies the Nuclear Non-Proliferation Treaty of 1968, which commits the now more than one hundred ratifying countries that did not already have nuclear weapons to abstain from acquiring them in the future, and those that did to reduce and eventually eliminate their nuclear arsenals.[34] Likewise, in the SALT I agreement of 1972 the United States and the Soviet Union agreed to limit the numbers of land-based and submarine-based missile launchers available for delivering nuclear weapons as well as to constrain deployment of antiballistic missile systems (ABMs), in order that neither country would lose confidence in its capacity to deter a nuclear attack by the other.[35]

Collective prevention has been practiced more widely in environmental than in military realms, as is apparent from the 152 multilateral environmental treaties that have been concluded up through 1990.[36] The Nuclear Test Ban Treaty of 1963 committed the United States, the Soviet Union, and the United Kingdom to stop the flow of radioactive contaminants from atmospheric nuclear testing, so as not to jeopardize human health further throughout much of the world. Other major treaties were designed to limit the threats to human health and the environment resulting from acid deposition and the thinning of the ozone layer. In all these cases a strategy of collective prevention was dictated by the reality that no country could reduce these threats effectively by acting on its own, nor could much, if anything, be done to lessen vulnerability to them significantly.

Self-Defense

Self-defense, or strategy III, presumes that actors will do what they can on their own to limit the harmful effects of threatening developments should they materialize. Vulnerabilities might be minimized through a protective scheme that insulates an actor or a population from threatening forces, or it could entail cultivating a capacity to adapt to undesired developments.

Providing for the defense of their populations has traditionally been one of the principal functions of national governments, and it is usually accomplished by attempting to have armed forces strong enough to discourage or repulse attacks from other hostile states or insurgent groups. Military security may also be enhanced by stockpiling strategic minerals and other critical resources needed to sustain a war effort, as well as food and other necessities that would make it possible for a population to survive an extended disruption of supply. While nations can do much to strengthen their defenses against conventional military attacks, even the superpowers could not reduce significantly their vulnerability to nuclear weapons delivered by ballistic missile systems.

Perimeter defenses are usually not options for defending against atmospheric threats, although one example is to build dikes as protection against rising seas. It may be more feasible to lessen some of the damage or hardships that result from them, such as by spreading lime on lakes to counteract the effects of acid deposition. People can be encouraged to reduce their exposure to the sun, especially when stratospheric ozone levels are abnormally low. Heat- and drought-resistent crops might be developed that would be more adaptable to anticipated climate changes. Governments can discourage further development on low-lying areas to limit the number of people that would be displaced by the rising sea levels or be killed by the higher storm surges that are likely to accompany global warming.

Collective Defense

While individual actors are often relatively powerless to protect themselves, they may find greater security in numbers. Thus, the fourth strategy of collective defense entails a group of actors cooperating to limit their vulnerabilities. For example, within communities police forces are established to provide all residents personal security against criminals who may commit violent acts against them or steal their property. Insurance plans enhance security by spreading risks among a larger community, as those most affected by a calamitous development can draw upon the resources the community has pooled to provide relief.

Nations have used a variety of arrangements to provide for collective defense against military threats, including alliances such as NATO and the Warsaw Pact, through which a certain group of countries commits its members to combine their military forces to confront an attack against one or more of them by a common enemy. Another example is the community-wide arrangement, known as "collective security," which is written into the Charter of the United Nations. It commits all member states to come to the defense of any one of them that is subjected to attack from any other state, even if the attacker is a party to the arrangement.

While collective defense is generally less adaptable to the enhancement of environmental security, there are some situations in which it has been practiced. A 1971 agreement negotiated in the International Maritime Organization (IMO) requires tanker operators to contribute to a fund to compensate victims of major oil spills resulting from tanker accidents.[37] In the aftermath of the Chernobyl disaster of 1986, members of the International Atomic Energy Agency (IAEA) adopted a treaty that provides for prompt international assistance in the event of nuclear accidents or radiological emergencies.[38] The 1992 Framework Convention on Climate Change provides for special assistance to the countries that are most seriously affected by greenhouse warming and the other environmental changes it triggers.

CHOOSING A SECURITY STRATEGY

While all four of the strategies for enhancing security that were outlined in the previous section are adaptable to certain situations, two of them—collective prevention (strategy II) and self-defense (strategy III)—have tended to be the principal choices for addressing both military and environmental threats. Before returning to these strategies, let us briefly consider some of the limitations of the other two possibilities—self-prevention (strategy I) and collective defense (strategy IV)—which have discouraged reliance on them.

Turning first to the military context, self-prevention by means of preemptive strikes is normally a possibility only for the strongest states with technologically advanced weaponry, and even then it can be a highly risky undertaking. Unilateral arms reductions may have the unintended effect of significantly increasing a state's vulnerability if potential aggressors do not reciprocate by making comparable reductions. States are usually leery of collective defense arrangements because they lack confidence that other countries will follow through on their commitments to come to the assistance of other states subject to aggression, especially if it means becoming involved in a costly war in which they have nothing else at stake. A key reason why the British and French decided to test nuclear bombs was their skepticism about the reliability of the American nuclear shield. Could the United States be counted on to use its nuclear weapons in the defense of England and France if the probable Soviet response would be a retaliatory attack against American cities? The collective security arrangement of the United Nations is notoriously unreliable, although it was invoked in a decisive and successful way when Iraq invaded Kuwait in 1991.

Self-prevention and collective defense also have limited potential for coping with environmental insecurities. Either the United States or the Soviet Union could have significantly lessened the radioactive fallout distributed around the world by unilaterally discontinuing its atmospheric tests, but neither was willing to take such a step for fear it would give the other a critical advantage in the development of nuclear weaponry. With the other atmospheric-related insecurities, most countries are responsible for such small proportions of the global total of the implicated pollutants that whatever they do on their own will have little effect on mitigating the threats. The smaller European countries that unilaterally reduced their emissions of SO_2 during the 1980s realized their actions would have little impact on the problem, but they hoped that their examples would prod other countries to do likewise.

Collective defense is used even less often in the environmental realm. States usually have little incentive to assist other countries to cope with damaging environmental changes unless they anticipate international reverberations, such as an increased flow of environmental refugees entering into their territories. Likewise, risk-sharing arrangements are of little value in dealing with problems such as ozone depletion and global warming, which will have significant adverse consequences for most if not all countries. Even if differential impacts are possible, broad-based participation in risk sharing is unlikely unless it is highly unpredictable which states will be the most seriously affected. This condition is clearly not the case with problems such as sea level rises due to climate change.

When it has come down to a decision between the two remaining strategies for pursuing military security, states have almost always opted for self-defense over collective prevention. Thus, in the interests of security they have devoted huge amounts of their national resources to building up their armed forces in order to maintain a balance of power with the countries perceived to threaten them. Unfortunately, the weapons systems that one country acquires to shore up its defenses often have had the unintended effect of arousing the fears of potential adversaries, who react by augmenting their military capabilities. This reaction rekindles the anxieties of the first state, which concludes that its security requires further additions to its armaments, thus starting the cycle again. Not only is such a self-perpetuating action-reaction cycle expensive for the countries locked in an arms race, but it is counterproductive in exacerbating their insecurities. The more states that threaten one other spend to secure themselves, the less secure they become. This paradox, known as the "security dilemma," was especially prevalent in the nuclear arms race between the Cold War superpowers.[39]

The alternative of collective prevention would have states agree among themselves not to build up the armaments that threaten one another. They would save substantial resources that could be devoted to other national priorities, and as security analyst Richard Smoke suggests, "an unarmed or a largely unarmed world would be a far more secure place than the quite dangerous one in which we actually live."[40] Ironically, states have persisted in the expensive and counterproductive strategy of self-defense, while passing up the alternative of collective defense, which appears to have compelling advantages.

States have a similar choice of strategies for addressing environmental insecurities, including those caused by air pollutants. They can elect collective prevention by negotiating international agreements that commit the parties to control activities under their jurisdictions that are responsible for threatening environmental changes. The alternative is the strategy of self-defense, in which states do little if anything to mitigate the environmental threats and invest their resources into trying to adapt to whatever environmental developments take place. As with military security, collective prevention clearly appears to be the wiser of the two alternatives, especially over the long run as environmental problems become increasingly severe and the costs of adapting rise rapidly along with the growing possibility of major surprises on the order of the Antarctic ozone hole. Will this logic prevail and collective prevention become the predominant strategy for pursuing environmental security? Or will states again lapse into the counterproductive tendencies oriented toward self-defense that have predominated in the quest for military security?

The Prisoner's Dilemma Game

Game theory has offered numerous insights into the strategic decisions that nations make. The game of Prisoner's Dilemma has been frequently used to explain social impediments to what could be mutually beneficial cooperation among pairs of actors.[41] At the international level the Prisoner's Dilemma game has been used to analyze the tendency of countries to be drawn into arms races, which have much less desirable outcomes for both parties than might be achieved by reciprocally limiting if not eliminating their threatening armaments.[42]

The game draws its name from a scenario in which two prisoners are suspected of being accomplices in a serious crime, but neither can be convicted unless testified against by the other. In return for turning state's evidence against the other, the prosecutor promises each prisoner a shorter sentence in the event the other testifies against him, or his freedom if the other does not testify. If neither prisoner testifies against the other, both stand to be convicted of a lesser crime that would carry a significantly shorter sentence than they would have been given if both testified against each other.

The potential outcomes of the Prisoner's Dilemma game are summarized in Table 9.2. The two numbers in each quadrant are the rank ordering of the preferences for prisoners A and B, respectively, with "1" being the most desirable outcome and "4" the least preferred. The best outcome for each prisoner occurs if he testifies against the other while the other does not testify against him (quadrant III for actor A). The most severe outcome results from failing to testify while being testified against by the other (quadrant II for actor A). The refusal by both to testify against the other results in the second-best outcome for both (quadrant I for both actors). Both testifying against each other results in the third-best outcome for both (quadrant IV for both). Paradoxically, when weighing the two options in isolation from one other, each prisoner may note that testifying against the other leads to a more favorable outcome than remaining silent, regardless of what the other does. When both act on what seems to be their self-interest, they end up with their third preference (quadrant IV), whereas if they both remained silent they would achieve their second preference (quadrant I).

A pair of mutually threatening states is faced with a similar choice in deciding whether to seek security by pursuing disarmament or by building up armaments. Each state would be most secure if it continued to arm while the other disarmed, least secure if it disarmed while the

Table 9.2. Ranked Outcomes in the Prisoner's Dilemma Game

		Actor B	
		Remain Silent (Disarm)	Testify (Arm)
Actor A	Remain Silent (Disarm)	(I) 2,2	(II) 4,1
	Testify (Arm)	(III) 1,4	(IV) 3,3

other continued to arm. Moreover, both states would be more secure and save substantial resources if they jointly disarmed, as opposed to continuing a costly and dangerous arms race. However, each sees a risk in being vulnerable to a better-armed opponent and thus feels compelled to pursue a costly and dangerous arms race.

How can the prisoners or nations shift the outcome of their relationship from quadrant IV to the more desirable quadrant I? The solution rests on reaching an agreement that reciprocally commits each to reciprocate in ways that diminish the insecurity of the other. Each party must trust the other to follow through on its commitment and not to yield to the temptation to gain a strategic advantage by not complying. Lack of trust has been a significant obstacle to the negotiation of arms agreements because of the suspicions and hostility that exist between countries that are engaged in a competitive arms race. When trust is lacking, it is important that the parties have ways of verifying in a timely way that others are complying with the agreement.

The Case of Nuclear Testing

Sorting through the options of states in the case of nuclear testing is complicated by the fact that it involves potentially serious threats to both military and environmental security. For most of the era between the Second World War and the signing of the Nuclear Test Ban Treaty in 1963, military security was the overriding consideration for the small group of countries that was testing nuclear explosives in the atmosphere. The behaviors of the United States and the Soviet Union conformed closely to the Prisoner's Dilemma game. Fearful that their military security would be compromised by falling behind the other, both superpowers invested heavily in nuclear weaponry and conducted hundreds of nuclear tests in the atmosphere, even though they probably would have been more secure both militarily and environmentally had they avoided a nuclear arms race by reaching an agreement along the lines of the discredited Baruch Plan.

Environmental considerations became increasingly salient once atmospheric tests became less critical to the further development of nuclear arsenals, after the United States began conducting some of its tests underground in the late 1950s. The governments of the nuclear powers had to consider the possibility that the health of their people was being threatened by radioactive fallout coming not only from the atmospheric tests of the other nuclear powers, but perhaps even more so by their own tests. Aside from conducting their atmospheric tests in remote areas within their borders, such as Nevada, Kazakhstan, Novaya Zemlya, and Xinjiang Province, or at distant sites in the Pacific, there was little the testing countries could do to protect their citizens from the radioactivity being transported long distances through the atmosphere.

Table 9.3 suggests the preferred outcomes of two nuclear powers facing a decision on whether to continue testing nuclear weapons in the atmosphere or to conduct all future tests underground. The first choice for both would be for both nuclear powers to conduct their future tests exclusively underground (quadrant I). The least desirable outcome would be a continuation of atmospheric testing by all nuclear powers, which would substantially increase the presence of radioactive substances in the environment throughout the world (quadrant IV). The two outcomes in which one country continues atmospheric tests have intermediate ranks in that some atmospheric fallout would continue to enter the atmosphere. Unlike the Prisoner's Dilemma game, however, the nation that ceases tests while the other continues is not placed in an especially vulnerable position vis- à-vis the other, since it can continue to pursue its security using underground tests. Furthermore, either nuclear power could presumably detect violations of a test ban and respond with a resumption of its own atmospheric testing program.

Thus, both countries would seem to achieve a more desirable outcome by testing exclusively underground, regardless of whether the other country does likewise. Nevertheless, neither superpower was ready to give up unilaterally the option of atmospheric testing out of concern that aboveground tests still had significant technical advantages that could be exploited by the other. They were willing, however, to forgo atmospheric tests jointly under the terms of the Nuclear Test Ban Treaty of 1963.

The Case of Transboundary Air Pollution

For the countries of Europe and North America the threat of acidification comes from air pollutants such as SO_2 and NO_x originating either from within or outside of their boundaries. States have adopted numerous strategies for diminishing the threats caused by pollution sources within their borders. One early strategy used widely in the industrial countries was to build tall stacks at power plants and other industrial sites, which would release pollutants high enough that air currents would disperse and deposit them over a much larger area. To the extent that the pollutants drift beyond the originating state's border, the costs asso-

Table 9.3.   Ranked Outcomes in the Nuclear Testing Case

		Nuclear State B	
		Test only Underground	Test in Atmosphere
Nuclear State A	Test only Underground	(I) 1,1	(II) 3,2
	Test in Atmosphere	(III) 2,3	(IV) 4,4

ciated with the pollution are effectively externalized and the state achieves a greater measure of environmental security at the expense of others. Other policies aim at internalizing the cost of pollution, such as by restricting the sulfur content of fuels or by requiring the installation of pollution-abatement technologies, examples being catalytic converters on motorized vehicles or smokestack scrubbers at large point sources of pollution.

The situation with transboundary pollution diverges from the Prisoner's Dilemma game in that the environmental threats that states pose to one another are typically not symmetrical because of the prevailing direction of wind currents. Heavy polluting upwind states present a substantial threat to the environments of downwind neighbors, which in return contribute little if anything to acidification occurring in the upwind state. The downwind states have little leverage to exert over their upwind neighbors and thus must resort to various forms of persuasion, such as appeals, complaints, protests, and the "mobilization of shame" to try to get them to stem the flow of transboundary air pollutants. In doing so, they may invoke principles of international customary law, such as good neighborliness and the responsibility of states to ensure that activities taking place within their jurisdictions do not cause damage beyond their borders. Upwind states usually resist such entreaties from downwind states, unless it becomes clear that their polluting activities are having serious consequences for their own people and the environment as well.

The rank order of preferred outcomes for upwind and downwind states for transboundary pollution is summarized in Table 9.4. The upwind state is largely unaffected by what, if anything, its down-

Table 9.4. Ranked Outcomes in the Transboundary Pollution Case

		Downwind State	
		Reduce Emissions	Not Reduce Emissions
Upwind State	Reduce Emissions	(I) 3,2	(II) 3,1
	Not Reduce Emissions	(III) 1,4	(IV) 1,3

wind neighbors do to limit air pollution. Thus, for the upwind state the dominant consideration may be avoiding the substantial costs of reducing emissions, which would primarily benefit its downwind neighbors. Downwind states obviously have a stake in receiving less air pollution from other states, but they too may see little advantage in reducing their emissions for the benefit of others. Thus, both upwind and downwind states may conclude that cutting back on pollutants would not be a rational course of action and accordingly end up in quadrant IV, which is more advantageous for the upwind country. However, the ordering of preferences may be reversed for either of the states if they come to realize that their pollutants are causing serious environmental damage within their borders.

The Case of Depletion of the Ozone Layer

The successes over the past decade in negotiating strong international agreements on phasing out CFCs and most other substances known to be depleting the ozone layer seem to run counter to the logic of the Prisoner's Dilemma game. One reason why most states that produce or use these substances were willing to agree to the prohibitions is the lack of any way to reduce significantly their vulnerabilities to UV-B radiation. While humans can be encouraged to reduce their exposure to harmful solar radiation, such as by minimizing the time they spend in the midday sun or by applying sunscreen or wearing sunglasses, there is no way to protect plant and animal species that cannot tolerate increased dosages of UV-B radiation. Alternatively, developing substitutes for ozone-depleting substances has proven to be a feasible, affordable,

Table 9.5. Ranked Outcomes in the Ozone Depletion Case

		Other States	
		Ban CFC's	Use Sunscreen
State A	Ban CFC's	(I) 1,1	(II) 3,2
	Use Sunscreen	(III) 2,3	(IV) 4,4

and profitable way of reducing ozone loss, thereby reducing the threats to human health and the environment generally.

The ozone depletion situation also lacks the inherent asymmetries between the states that emit pollutants and those that are affected by them, which characterize the problem of transboundary, acid-forming pollutants. Because the pollutants that threaten the stratospheric ozone layer intermingle and are distributed globally, all countries are victimized by their own emissions and those of other countries. The countries most responsible for the global ozone loses, such as the United States, can significantly reduce the threat of increased UV-B radiation to other states and themselves by phasing out the implicated substances. The environmental security of all states is enhanced when they collectively agree to stem the flow of these pollutants into the atmosphere.

The ordering of preferred outcomes for the case of ozone depletion, as summarized in Table 9.5, parallels that of the atmospheric testing case. Given the potential severity of the consequences of increased exposure to UV-B radiation and the impossibility of an effective defense or adaptation, the overriding consideration for all states is to avoid a quadrant IV outcome. Conversely, a quadrant I outcome will be preferred by most states because it would do the most to reduce the threat to which they are all highly vulnerable. Furthermore, there is relatively little to gain from adopting a defensive strategy while others are taking steps to prevent or minimize the threat (quadrant III for state A), except for potential commercial advantages from the production and use of the chemicals causing the problem. The incentive for doing this, as well as for avoiding a quadrant II outcome, is diminished by the trade restrictions on the controlled substances that were written into the Montreal Protocol and its revisions.

The Case of Climate Change

The response of nations to climate change has a greater potential for following the pattern of the Prisoner's Dilemma game than do the cases of the other three types of air pollution. While climate change parallels the ozone depletion problem in its global scope, skepticism continues in many circles about whether substantial global warming will actually take place and, if it does, have the dire consequences for the environment that have been forecast in numerous reports, such as those of the IPCC. Yale economist William Nordhaus has calculated that costs to the United States resulting from the amount of global warming associated with a doubling of CO_2 in the atmosphere would amount to only about one-quarter of 1 percent national income.[43] Some would even question whether a warmer climate would on balance be undesirable, especially in colder countries that might benefit from a longer growing season and ice-free shipping channels.[44]

The climate change case also differs in the widespread belief in some countries that it will be possible, and perhaps even much less costly, to adapt to climate changes as they occur. Adaptive strategies could range from greater investments in air conditioning (that might be offset by fewer needs for heating), development of heat- and drought-resistant crops, and building dams to impound scarcer water resources. A response to rising sea levels might include relocating people from low-lying areas and the construction of dikes and seawalls to protect coastal cities. An adaptive approach might also include strengthening the capacity of governmental institutions to anticipate and prepare for changes and freeing up markets in ways that would encourage prompt and adaptive responses to changing circumstances.[45]

The adaptive strategy may also be attractive to states because the benefits of their expenditures would be largely internalized within their borders. For example, the advantages of a seawall go exclusively to the citizens of their own nation, whereas the payoffs from a preventive strategy of reducing GHG emissions, in particular stability of climate, are shared with the world community in the form of a global public good.[46] The preventive strategy may make sense from the self-interested perspective of a state, but only if it is convinced that most other states responsible for the global change problem will reciprocate by reducing their GHG emissions, and thus do their share to maintain a collective good all can enjoy.

The basic options in the climate change case are set forth in Table

Table 9.6. Ranked Outcomes in Climate Change Case

| | | Other States | |
		Reduce CO_2	Build Seawalls
State A	Reduce CO_2	(I) 2,2	(II) 4,1
	Build Seawalls	(III) 1,4	(IV) 3,3

9.6. State A may conclude that its interests are best served by a quadrant III outcome. All other states would reduce their emissions of GHGs, thereby lessening the threat of climate change. In the meantime, state A would invest heavily in lessening its vulnerability to whatever changes do take place, such as by building seawalls. Thus, state A acts as a "free rider" as it enjoys a public good created by other states.[47] Conversely, quadrant II would be the worst possible result for state A, which would occur if other states concentrated almost exclusively on adaptive measures, while it channeled its limited resources into reducing GHG emissions. Thus, while state A takes steps to reduce its contributions to the threat of climate change for itself and other countries, it leaves itself vulnerable to the greenhouse warming resulting from the failure of other countries to reduce their GHG emissions. Among the intermediate preferences, most states would presumably be better off if all states acted to reduce the threat of global warming than if they all acted on their own to minimize their vulnerabilities.

The stage is thus set for a game of Prisoner's Dilemma. In assessing its interests each state may conclude that a defensive strategy will have a more desirable outcome regardless of what other states do. For some states, especially those that are heavy emitters of CO_2 and sanguine about their ability to adapt, a quadrant IV outcome may not appear to be significantly less desirable than a quadrant I result. Furthermore, an investment in achieving a quadrant I outcome might be discouraged by the daunting challenge of negotiating the type of international agreement that would be needed to stem climate change. Even if such an agreement were concluded, its effectiveness might be severely undermined by major noncompliers. Thus, investing available resources in collective prevention of climate change may appear to some states to be a riskier venture than focusing their efforts on unilaterally adapting to whatever changes take place.

Perceptions of national interest on the part of the dominant emitters of GHG could change if they become more persuaded of the seriousness of their vulnerabilities to climate change and the costliness of adaptive strategies. Nordhaus's estimate of costs of global warming for the United States has been challenged as being too low with the suggestion that a more realistic estimate would be 1 percent of national income— even as high as 6 percent in the long run.[48] Revised calculations of the economic and societal costs of reducing GHG emissions could also prompt a greater willingness to cooperate on minimizing global warming. The general assumption has been that achieving even modest reductions in GHG emissions would be very costly in both expenditures and jobs, but others argue that early projections in the trillions of dollars are badly overinflated and that the many benefits of reducing use of fossil fuels may even outweigh the costs.[49]

Conclusions

The case for broadening traditional conceptions of security to include environmental and other nonmilitary threats to the welfare of human communities has been made by numerous scholars and policy makers for more than twenty years. Over the past decade the demise of the Cold War, the disaster at the Chernobyl nuclear power plant, and the emergence of the "global change" threats of ozone depletion and greenhouse warming have added momentum to efforts to add another dimension to discussions of human security. However, skepticism about the concept of environmental security persists both among the more conventional national security analysts, who are concerned that the term security will lose clarity if defined more broadly, and environmentalists, who are apprehensive that linking the environment to security runs the risk of infusing an inappropriate nationalistic bias into efforts to address ecological problems that are inherently international if not global.

These reservations aside, this chapter has pointed out how parallels exist between the options available for pursuing military and environmental security. In both contexts states have a choice between a preventive approach aimed at reducing threats and a defensive effort designed to lessen vulnerabilities. They also have the options of trying to enhance their security in unilateral or collective ways. All too often states have pursued military security through self-defense, which has led to arms races that have only added to the insecurities of the states involved, rather than working collectively to limit the weapons that pose threats to one another. This counterproductive tendency is often explained in terms of a rational choice model illustrated by the game of Prisoner's Dilemma.

There is the danger that states will pursue environmental security in much the same way they have tried to enhance their military security—by employing a strategy of self-defense. Such an approach would not be directed toward avoiding or lessening environmental threats, but rather toward adapting to whatever environmental changes take place. This is not what happened in the cases of nuclear testing and the depletion of the ozone layer, and to some extent in the LRTAP case, largely because states could do little to deal with their vulnerabilities. Instead, international agreements were struck that were designed to lessen these environmental threats. In the case of climate change, however, there is the distinct possibility that some key states, the United States in particular, will opt for self-defense in the belief that adapting to a warmer climate may be both less costly and less risky than implementing an international commitment to reduce substantially their emissions of GHGs.

Chapter 10

CONCLUSIONS

The atmosphere is a single, undifferentiated mass of gases that circulates around the Earth, providing a habitat that has been conducive to the emergence and evolution of a myriad of life forms, and eventually to the human species. Living organisms, by absorbing gases from the atmosphere that are essential to their existence while releasing others back into the atmosphere, have been the primary agents in transforming the atmosphere over billions of years into the balance of gases that has prevailed for the past six hundred million years.

During the past two centuries human activities, especially industrial processes dependent upon the burning of fossil fuels, have been altering the chemistry of the atmosphere at an ever quickening pace. Humans have not only added to concentrations of such naturally occurring gases as sulfur and nitrogen oxides, carbon dioxide, and methane, they have also introduced substances not originally part of the atmospheric mix, such as CFCs, halons, and radioactive cesium-137 and strontium-90. Moreover, land-use practices have significantly diminished the world's forest cover, which along with the oceans are the major natural absorbers of CO_2 from the atmosphere. While the current global amounts of anthropogenic air pollutants seem enormous—for example, more than twenty-three billion metric tons of CO_2 are emitted per year—they have only added to concentrations of a group of trace gases, which together comprise less than 1 percent of the volume of gases of the atmosphere. Nevertheless, what may at first glance appear to be minor and insignificant changes in the chemical composition of the atmosphere can have major consequences for humans and the larger natural environment.

The human assault on the atmosphere is also a consequence of the failure of states and the international community to regulate and manage their use of a global commons, which is leading to a "tragedy of the atmosphere," to paraphrase the title of Garrett Hardin's famous essay. Such environmental tragedies can be expected when multiple actors are permitted to derive unlimited private gains from exploiting a domain having finite resources. The atmosphere has traditionally been an open-access resource that humans could use as a convenient and economically cost-free sink for many of their pollutants, which explains why it has been overused and misused as a resource for disposing of pollutants.

The international community has taken up several specific environmental problems caused by anthropogenic pollutants and, in the process, created distinct regimes targeted at the atmospheric testing of nuclear weapons, acid rain, depletion of the ozone layer, and climate change. Each regime is the product of a different diplomatic track that approached a specific environmental problem largely independently of efforts to address the other atmospheric problems.

REFLECTIONS ON EXISTING ATMOSPHERIC REGIMES

The four regimes that were described in earlier chapters in this book have had widely varying degrees of success in addressing and actually mitigating the problems they focus on. The nuclear testing regime defined by the Nuclear Test Ban Treaty of 1963 is a notable open-and-closed success story in bringing an end to a health-threatening activity. The Montreal Protocol of 1987, as amended in London, Copenhagen, and Vienna has already dramatically reduced the flow of CFCs and other ozone-depleting substances into the atmosphere. The LRTAP regime based on the Geneva Convention of 1979 and subsequent protocols on sulfur, nitrogen, and VOCs has thus far only slowed the rate of acidification in the larger European region. Finally, the nascent climate change regime based on the framework convention adopted at the Earth Summit of 1992 does very little to ameliorate global warming, a problem of potentially immense importance for the future habitability of the planet. It merely establishes institutional mechanisms that can be used to negotiate future limits on greenhouse gas (GHG) emissions. What can be learned from comparing the evolution of these four atmospheric regimes?

Awareness of Atmospheric Problems

There are two critical stages in the recognition of international environmental policy problems. The first is the initial awareness of a potentially serious problem, which stimulates international scientific cooperation and in some cases a weakly worded framework treaty. The second is the reaching of a critical threshold of concern among publics and policy makers, which prompts serious national and international efforts to mitigate the problem, including binding limits on polluting activities. The latter stage is often triggered by a precipitating event, shock, or crisis that arouses sharply heightened anxiety about the problem.[1]

The four major atmospheric problems came to light in quite different ways. In the case of transboundary air pollution, the disappearance of freshwater aquatic life in Scandinavia was the first indication of a problem, which before long was linked to acidification of the environment. The mysterious rise in acidity was later discovered to be caused by deposition of air pollutants, which in turn were traced to distant sources. The act of setting off aboveground explosions and the agonies of radiation sickness suffered by the Japanese survivors of the Hiroshima and Nagasaki blasts initially provoked concern about the potential consequences of radiation from the atmospheric testing of nuclear bombs. By contrast, the first major wave of awareness of threats to the ozone layer was touched off by the yet unproven Molina/Rowland hypothesis on what ultimately happens to CFC molecules once they reach the stratosphere. Likewise, scientific theories about the potential impacts of increased concentrations of CO_2 in the atmosphere first drew attention to the possibility of human-induced climate change long before there was any actual evidence that it was occurring.

Precipitating developments that later added to the momentum for negotiations can be identified in all the cases. Pressure for the Test Ban Treaty was revived by the large number and size of the explosions detonated in 1961 and 1962, which caused a significant rise in presence of radioactive substances around the world, and by anxieties about the dangerous state of East-West relations that were raised by the Cuban Missile Crisis of 1962. At the time, however, there was still considerable scientific uncertainty about the health effects of relatively low levels of exposure to radiation resulting from globally dispersed fallout, in part because the medical conditions this might cause do not appear for decades.

Observed environmental changes intensified concern about the other three problems, even though there was significant scientific uncertainty about whether these changes could be attributed to human causes. A critical threshold of public concern about LRTAP was reached in the early 1980s when *waldsterben*, or forest death, spread at an alarming rate through the forests of central Europe. The phenomenon appeared to be related to increasingly acidic conditions, although at the time scientists were cautious about drawing conclusions about the specific causes. The startling revelations of the Antarctic ozone hole in 1985 rekindled the sense of urgency about the precarious state of the stratospheric ozone layer and thus became a catalyst for the negotiations that led to the pathbreaking Montreal Protocol, even before scientists had conclusively linked the phenomenon to human pollutants. A series of the warmest years of the century along with a spate of regional aberrations in weather lent credibility in the public mind to the warnings about the enhanced greenhouse effect, even though atmospheric scientists counseled against drawing such a conclusion. Nevertheless, by the late 1980s climate change was on the agendas of several summit meetings and a number of ministerial meetings were convened to discuss what to do about it, which led to the beginning of formal negotiations in 1991.

International Scientific Cooperation

The creation and maturing of the atmospheric regimes cannot be understood without reference to the evolution of scientific knowledge about the atmosphere and the bevy of international scientific projects undertaken in recent years.[2] The role of science is especially important in identifying and understanding atmospheric problems and in framing policy issues because the atmosphere is a highly complex and dynamic component of the Earth system. Moreover, subtle changes in the atmosphere's chemical composition, which can be detected only by sophisticated scientific instruments, may have immense consequences for the way in which the atmosphere moderates the flow of energy to and from the Earth, with profound implications for species and ecosystems. Finally, the atmosphere must be studied holistically both in a geographical sense, which requires global monitoring and research programs, and from a comprehensive perspective that takes into account the interactions between the atmosphere and the other components of the Earth system, including the oceans, landmasses, and biosphere.

International scientific cooperation on the atmosphere has undertaken three basic types of tasks: *monitoring* the state of the atmosphere, *research* aimed at understanding atmospheric processes, and *assessment* that summarizes the state of scientific knowledge about the atmosphere to inform policy makers. Scientists from a variety of disciplines, operating either on their own or as part of larger projects, have undertaken these tasks in regard to atmospheric problems. Major projects have been organized both nationally and internationally, and by governmental institutions and nongovernmental scientific academies.

Monitoring programs keep track of the state of the atmosphere on a continuing basis in order to detect its natural vicissitudes as well as changes that are human induced. Weather and climate have been systematically monitored since the nineteenth century, and in recent decades by the World Meteorological Organization (WMO) through its World Weather Watch. The EMEP network, which has been an integral component of the LRTAP regime, has developed scientifically sophisticated ways of tracking the flow of acid-forming pollutants and the levels of acidic deposition throughout the European region. Some EMEP stations are part of WMO's Background Air Pollution Monitoring Network (BAPMoN), which gathers data on the chemical composition of the atmosphere, including levels of CO_2 and various other pollutants. The condition of the ozone layer has been observed by WMO's Global Ozone Observing System (GO_3OS). WMO has recently integrated several of its monitoring programs, including BAPMoN and GO_3OS, into the Global Atmospheric Watch (GAW) to provide an early warning of significant changes in the state and composition of the atmosphere.

Many international research projects have been undertaken to understand why the atmospheric processes occur as they do, knowledge that is useful for enhancing weather forecasts and anticipating the consequences of human activities. Among the larger questions that have been addressed are the causes of long-term climate changes, including the glacial eras, and the puzzling shorter-term El Niño episodes. The first major international efforts to understand the atmosphere better were undertaken in conjunction with the International Polar Years of 1882–83 and 1932–33 and the International Geophysical Year of 1957–58. The Global Atmospheric Research Programme (GARP) of 1968–81 and the follow-up World Climate Research Programme (WCRP) are highly successful projects that have focused more exclusively on atmospheric research. The International Geosphere-Biosphere Programme (IGBP) is a major effort of the international scientific community begun in 1986 to understand how the atmosphere interacts with the other components of the Earth system, including basic changes triggered by the planet's human population.

International scientific assessments are undertaken not to increase knowledge of the environment but to consolidate existing scientific knowledge and present it in a way that can be understood by policy makers and is relevant to international negotiations. The assessments cover not only atmospheric changes but also the impacts of them that have bearings on human communities. Some explore policy options that might be undertaken to mitigate atmospheric problems. The United Nations Scientific Committee on the Effects of Atomic Radiation (UNSCEAR) has performed an assessment role pertaining to ionizing radiation in the environment since the 1950s. International efforts to prevent depletion of the ozone layer were spurred by the WMO-UNEP assessment report of 1986, the report of the Ozone Trends Panel of 1988, and more recent synthesis reports of expert panels. Key assessments of scientific knowledge on climate change were made by scientists meeting in Villach in 1980 and 1985 and more recently on a continuing basis by the Intergovernmental Panel on Climate Change (IPCC). Combined meetings of scientists and ministers, notable examples of which are the World Climate Conferences in 1979 and 1990 and the Stockholm Acidification Conference in 1982, have been vehicles for informing policy makers.

The combination of these three types of scientific activities has been integral to the creation and development of the LRTAP, ozone layer, and climate change regimes. The assessments have been especially instrumental in bringing the weight of scientific evidence to bear on the international policy processes through which the atmospheric problems are addressed. They have summarized the matters on which scientists are largely in agreement while identifying where uncertainties remain. In doing so the assessments have not only alerted policy makers to the need for international cooperation to address the looming atmospheric problems but also framed the issues for them. The perceived objectivity, and thus impact, of the assessments has been enhanced by engaging scientists from numerous countries, including developing ones.

The International Politics of Regime Creation

The international talks and negotiations on atmospheric problems have typically seen the emergence of several groupings of states. One is an *advocacy coalition,* whose members are sometimes known as "pushers," that proposes strong international measures to control air pollutants. These proposals are resisted by a *blocking coalition* of what are sometimes called "laggard" states, or "draggers."[3] The pushers are usually the countries most victimized by the pollutants of other countries, while the resisters are commonly the chief perpetrators of the problem, who have a major stake, usually an economic one, in continuing their polluting activities. The pushers typically contend that the evidence of atmospheric threats is sufficiently compelling to warrant a precautionary approach that includes controls on pollutants; the laggards make a practice of clinging to scientific uncertainties as a rationale for delaying corrective actions that may be costly for them.

Such coalitions emerged in the talks on all four of the atmospheric regimes. The few nuclear powers conducting atmospheric tests were at odds with most other countries, especially those of the Pacific Basin where many of the tests were being conducted. As downwind victims of transboundary pollution, the Nordic countries and Canada became the earliest and strongest advocates of internationally mandated reductions on sulfur and nitrogen oxides, while the United Kingdom and the United States, being upwind states that were leading emitters of the pollutants, were the most notable laggards. In the case of climate change, the most dedicated advocates of reducing emissions of GHGs have been the countries most seriously threatened by rising seas and tropical storms, in particular the small island countries; while the major consumers and producers of fossil fuels, such as the United States, the Soviet Union, China, and Saudi Arabia, have put up the strongest resistance. Talks on preserving the ozone layer brought out a somewhat different configuration of supporters and resisters. The United States was the leading advocate of phasing out the use of CFCs in the late 1970s, when it adopted national laws banning nonessential uses of CFCs, and in the mid 1980s as talks were held that led to the adoption of the 1987 Montreal Protocol. Until 1987 the principal resistance to international controls on CFCs came from the European Community (EC), where there was concern that American firms had a competitive advantage in the development of substitute chemicals.

The nations advocating strong international action to address atmospheric problems have employed a variety of strategies to persuade other countries to join their causes. They have met separately to hone their cases in caucusing groups, such as the 30 Percent Club in preparation for negotiations on the Sulfur Protocol, the Toronto Group in negotiations on the Vienna Convention on the ozone layer, and the Alliance of Small Island States (AOSIS) in preparation for talks on international responses to climate change. Some of the more committed advocates of strong international action have made unilateral commitments to reduce pollutants in order to set examples for other countries. Various forms of persuasion have also been used, including the targeting of information—some would say propaganda—at the publics of key laggard states, as has been done by Sweden and Canada. In most instances, however, the resisters relent only when it becomes apparent that they too have an important stake in addressing the problem, as the British did on LRTAP when widespread damage to their forests was reported.

Developing countries did not become seriously engaged in negotiations on atmospheric regimes until the late 1980s, and then only in the ones addressing ozone depletion and climate change. While some Third World leaders, such as Nehru, had expressed concern in the mid 1950s about dark-skinned peoples being the principal victims of radioactive fallout, their countries had little impact on the negotiations on the Test Ban Treaty, which were dominated by the United States and the Soviet Union. Subsequently, many developing countries have declared their support for the treaty by ratifying it. The LRTAP regime is regional in scope, with negotiations limited to the European and North American members of the Economic Commission for Europe (ECE).

The industrialized countries have made a concerted effort to involve the developing countries in negotiations on the ozone depletion problem. This was done, however, only after major Third World countries with plans to increase greatly their consumption of CFCs—most notably China and India—declined to become parties to the Montreal Protocol, even though it granted them a ten-year grace period in complying with reductions in the controlled substances. Numerous developing countries later accepted the London and Copenhagen Amendments, which committed the developed countries to provide the technical and economic assistance the developing countries would need to adopt substitutes for CFCs and other controlled chemicals.

At about the same time the developing countries were drawn into talks that drafted the Framework Convention on Climate Change (FCCC) of 1992. In addressing the climate change problem, however, conflicts between North and South will be more difficult to resolve. Substantial increases in consumption of readily available fossil fuels, in particular coal, are central to plans of many developing countries to industrialize. Moreover, the equity issue looms large because the developed countries have over the past few decades helped themselves to the lion's share of the capacity of the atmosphere to absorb anthropogenic GHGs without triggering substantial climate change. The industrial countries were willing to acknowledge the primary responsibility for causing the green-house problem and to concede that they should be the ones to take the first steps to address it. It remains to be seen, however, whether the de-veloped countries will be willing to make substantial enough conces-sions to induce the major developing countries to restrain their consumption of fossil fuels.

The eastern European countries and the former Soviet Union and its successor states have constituted another key group of participants in the development of the atmospheric regimes. The Soviet Union was, of course, one of the countries primarily responsible for fallout from atmospheric nuclear testing. Furthermore, the countries of the region have been among the heaviest per capita emitters of industrial air pol-lutants, such as SO_2 and CO_2, because of their grossly inefficient use of natural resources and the antiquated technologies of their heavy indus-tries. In international negotiations the former communist countries have usually staked out a middle ground between advocacy and resistance. Their reluctance to make commitments to reduce pollution over the long run seems to be based largely on uncertainties about their economies, which have been severely depressed during the early 1990s, and the extent to which they will have access to modern technologies.

International Agreements on Atmospheric Pollution

Three of the four atmospheric regimes initially came into being as results of framework conventions, the exception being the nuclear test-ing regime, which consists of a single treaty banning aboveground tests that were raising health concerns. The LRTAP and ozone layer regimes have been further developed by supplementary protocols, which also appears to be the plan for the climate change regime. The convention-protocol approach to addressing international environmental problems has been criticized for its tendency to lapse into a drawn-out process that postpones coming to terms with a problem.[4] The approach does, however, make it possible to create institutional mechanisms that support continuing efforts to address a complex environmental problem, even while significant scientific uncertainties remain and key states are not ready to make substantive commitments. Further steps can then be taken to strengthen the regime if and when scientific evidence heightens public concern about the problem and a broad-based agreement is reached on the concrete steps that should be taken to address it. The ozone layer regime is a prototype of how the framework-protocol approach can be used effectively to address a major environmental problem in a timely way, while the LRTAP regime illustrates how the process can become protracted, especially in the absence of startling revelations that stimulate prompt action, such as the Antarctic ozone hole. The 1995 Conference of the Parties to the 1992 FCCC was disappointing to many for its failure to adopt a protocol setting up a timetable for reductions of GHGs.

The three framework agreements that established environmental regimes—the Geneva LRTAP Convention (1979), the Vienna Convention for the Protection of the Ozone Layer (1985), and the Rio Framework Convention on Climate Change (1992)—have much in common. All three acknowledge the potential seriousness of the problem at issue; call for cooperation in scientific monitoring, research, and assessment; and provide institutional mechanisms for the parties to meet periodically to consider further measures to address the problem. They also call upon the parties to make good faith efforts to begin addressing the problems. The LRTAP Convention, for example, suggests that the parties should "endeavor to limit, and as far as possible, gradually reduce and prevent air pollution" and use the "best available technology that is economically feasible." The Vienna Convention calls for "appropriate measures" to prevent human interference with the ozone layer. The FCCC goes a step further in setting a goal, but not a binding obligation, for developed countries of stabilizing their GHG emissions at 1990 levels by 2000.

Negotiated protocols that supplement framework conventions have been the vehicles for getting states to commit to limiting their emissions of the air pollutants contributing to international atmospheric problems. The LRTAP and ozone layer regimes mandate that the parties to the protocol freeze or reduce their emissions by a certain percentage by a specified year. The parties are free to decide on what domestic measures they will apply to bring them into compliance. These across-the-board freezes or percentage reductions are more of a concession to practicality and efficiency than equity because they have the effect of allocating future rights to pollute to states on the basis of historical levels of emissions, rather than on the premise that human beings have an equal right to use the atmosphere as a sink for pollutants. The practice of specifying the same percentage reductions for all states fell into disfavor in negotiations on the Revised Sulfur Protocol for the LRTAP regime, as states were asked to achieve different emission targets based on the extent to which their pollutants contributed to excessive acidic deposition in other countries.

Impacts of the Atmospheric Regimes

With the exception of the nascent climate change regime, the atmospheric regimes have had measurable positive effects in mitigating the problems that they were created to address. The amount of nuclear testing in the atmosphere declined sharply after the United States and the Soviet Union ceased aboveground tests to comply with the Nuclear Test Ban Treaty in 1963, which was reflected in a return of radioactivity in the environment almost back to natural residual levels. Sulfur emissions in Europe had dropped by more than one-third from 1980 levels by the early 1990s. The 1990s have also seen a rapid phasing out of the production of CFCs and other ozone-depleting substances controlled by the Montreal Protocol, prompting optimistic forecasts that the stratospheric ozone layer may be stabilized by the turn of the century and then begin a recovery to preexisting levels.

The treaties and protocols that set forth the terms of international cooperation on limiting pollution and preserving the atmosphere have been widely accepted, as indicated by a relatively high number of ratifications from eligible states. There have been exceptions, however, most notably the refusal of France and China to become parties to the Test Ban Treaty and of the United States and the United Kingdom to agree to the 1985 Sulfur Protocol. For the most part, the countries that ratified the agreements have succeeded in reducing their emissions of pollutants to the levels expected of them, in particular those on SO_2, CFCs, and halons. The freeze on NO_x emissions has been somewhat more difficult to achieve, and little has been reported yet on whether the parties have made much progress to reduce their emissions of VOCs by 30 percent by 1999.

Are the international regimes primarily responsible for the apparent changes in the behavior of states that are mitigating three of the four major atmospheric problems? In the absence of the Test Ban Treaty, the United States and the Soviet Union most likely would have continued testing nuclear weapons in the atmosphere. It is less clear whether the treaty and its acceptance by a large number of states were factors in the later decisions of France and China to cease their atmospheric testing programs. In the case of the ozone layer regime, the United States and several other countries acted unilaterally in the 1970s to ban nonessential uses of CFCs, but they were unwilling to take further steps to address the problem without assurances that other states would reciprocate, which only a negotiated treaty could provide.

The impact of the LRTAP regime on the behavior of the parties is more difficult to gauge. Many of the parties to the 1985 Sulfur Protocol were not only well on their way to achieving 30 percent reductions in sulfur emissions by the time the protocol was negotiated, but they also made unilateral commitments to reduce their emissions considerably further than required by the protocol. Furthermore, the reductions achieved by the eastern European countries were due more to their severe economic decline than concerted efforts to comply with the protocol. Reductions in SO_2 emissions in the European part of the former Soviet Union are also explained by changes in energy policy dictated by the availability of resources. Nevertheless, it is quite clear that the LRTAP regime, with its numerous international bodies, has developed a remarkable base of scientific knowledge on the problem of acidification. The regime has kept the countries of the European region focused on the task of negotiating increasingly strict limits on the pollutants responsible for the problem.

THE SPECIAL CASE OF CLIMATE CHANGE

Climate change stands out as the one major atmospheric problem for which there are no existing international agreements that oblige the parties to limit the polluting activities responsible for the problem. Can the relatively undeveloped state of the climate change regime be attributed to the late start in recognizing and taking up the problem and in concluding the initial framework agreement? Is it only a matter of time before the FCCC is supplemented by a progression of protocols and amendments that effectively limit the human-induced global warming?

It would be comforting to conclude that the climate change regime is progressing along the course of the LRTAP and ozone layer regimes in being based on the framework convention/protocol approach to regime creation and development. In all three cases groups of industrial countries pushed hard in the early negotiations for an initial agreement containing binding national limits on the implicated pollutants. However, in the face of strong opposition from blocking coalitions, the advocates settled for relatively weak framework conventions containing vaguely worded admonitions for the parties to take appropriate preventive actions. As with the other two framework conventions, the FCCC provided an institutional mechanism for the parties to meet periodically to take additional steps by adopting protocols or amendments. More than five years passed from the adoption of the LRTAP framework convention to the first protocol limiting emissions of acid-forming air pollutants. Agreement on the landmark Montreal Protocol mandating a cutback on ozone-depleting substances came just two years after the signing of the Vienna Convention of 1985.

Progress on the climate change regime has already fallen significantly behind the pace of the ozone layer regime, given that the first supplemental protocol containing mandatory limits on GHG emissions will not be concluded until 1997 at the earliest, five years after the signing of the framework convention at the Earth Summit. An earlier protocol on GHGs might have been expected for several reasons. First, by the time negotiations began on the FCCC in 1991, the international scientific assessment process was well advanced through the deliberations of the IPCC. Second, the subject of international rules that would freeze if not reduce GHG emissions had been discussed extensively in numerous ministerial and summit meetings since 1988. Moreover, negotiators could build on experiences gained in negotiating the Montreal Protocol and the London Amendments. Third, by 1990 the blocking coalition of major industrial states had dwindled to one country—the United States. Most of the other industrial countries had made unilateral commitments to freeze or reduce GHG emissions by 2000 or 2005. Finally, a protocol with specific national limits on GHG emissions would not have been as big a step as it was with the other framework agreements in that the FCCC provides that quantitative goal for the developed countries of freezing their emissions at 1990 levels by the year 2000.

Thus, the failure of the 1995 Berlin Conference of the Parties to take more decisive steps to address climate change was disappointing. It was not surprising, however, in view of other developments since the Earth

Summit that do not bode well for the rapid evolution of the climate change regime. Public concern about greenhouse warming seems to have declined since the late 1980s, as has media coverage, although there are some signs that the latter may be picking up in 1995–96.[5] GHG emissions have continued to rise in most of the developed countries, and few of them seem to be on track to bring their GHG emissions back to 1990 levels by the year 2000. The Clinton administration at first signaled that it would be more in harmony with other developed countries on limiting GHG emissions, but at the Berlin conference the United States persisted in its opposition to immediate international controls. It is encouraging, however, that a core group of eight industrial countries is committed to the Toronto goal of a 20 percent reduction in CO_2 emissions by 2005. Globally, CO_2 emissions have resumed an upward course after leveling off for several years due to the economic slowdown in eastern Europe and the former Soviet Union.[6]

Climate change poses an especially formidable challenge for the world community in view of the IPCC's estimate that global CO_2 emissions would have to be reduced by at least 60 percent to stabilize atmospheric concentrations at the current level of about 360 ppm. Even if such an abrupt cutback could be achieved, atmospheric concentrations of CO_2 would be nearly 30 percent higher than preindustrial levels of 280 ppm and far greater than any that have occurred over the past 160,000 years. The most radical proposal offered thus far, which came from the small island nations, would only cut CO_2 emissions by 20 percent from 1990 levels, thus allowing concentrations in the atmosphere to continue rising at only a slightly diminished rate. Even this rather modest proposal was soundly rejected by a number of the industrialized countries. Thus, humanity continues on a course that is likely to result in substantial warming, with little prospect that decisive action will be taken to mitigate the problem in the way in which the ozone depletion problem is being addressed.

Climate change will be a much more difficult problem to confront than the threat of ozone depletion because CO_2 and some of the other GHGs are generated by activities that are fundamental to modern societies, in particular those of the energy, manufacturing, transportation, and agriculture sectors. The response to the ozone depletion problem benefited from the promise of developing affordable substitutes for CFCs and the other implicated substances with relatively little economic and social disruption. Furthermore, the substitutes would be produced largely by the same chemical companies that manufactured the banned substances and presumably with a higher profit margin, which seems to explain the American industry's support for international controls at key stages in the creation of the ozone layer regime. Energy conservation and non-fossil-fuel sources of energy could substantially reduce CO_2 emissions on a global basis in the next decade or two, but probably not by the amounts necessary to stabilize atmospheric concentrations without running into insurmountable technical and economic obstacles, as well as strong political resistance from powerful industrial groups that produce and use fossil fuels and consumers who would have to alter their lifestyles drastically.

The United States has almost on its own thwarted efforts of the other industrial countries since the late 1980s to agree to binding international limits on GHG emissions. The cooperation of the United States is critical not only because it is the largest emitter of GHGs but also because numerous other countries, including large developing ones such as China and India, will be loath to make sacrifices until Americans curb their profligate use of fossil fuels. The analysis of environmental security and the Prisoner's Dilemma game offer an interest-based explanation of the underlying reasons for the obstinacy of the United States. American policy makers have a choice between international cooperation to reduce the threat of global climate change and unilaterally taking steps to reduce the nation's vulnerabilities to whatever changes may occur. Opting for the former, preventive alternatives would entail major costs to further a public good in the form of a stable climate that would be shared with the world community. Whether that public good comes into being depends upon the uncertain prospect that most of the other nations responsible for the rise in GHG concentrations would take similar steps. The alternative of defensive adaptation, which is widely believed to be viable in the United States, seems less costly and more certain because the benefits go more exclusively to its own citizens and do not depend on the cooperation of other states. The American posture is likely to change only when Americans come to the realization, as they did on depletion of the ozone layer, that adaptation is not a viable strategy for securing themselves against the prospect of catastrophic global warming.

Issues of international equity will probably also prove difficult to resolve in attempting to limit climate change. The industrial countries have already unwittingly helped themselves to most of the atmosphere's capacity to absorb GHGs without triggering climate change. If the 40 percent of the 1990 level of global emissions of CO_2—which by IPCC calculations could be allowed if atmospheric concentrations are to be stabilized—were divided equally, each human inhabitant of the planet could be allocated 1.7 mt of emissions. To comply with such a quota, the people of the OECD countries would have to reduce their CO_2 emissions by 86 percent, Americans by 91 percent. Such draconian reductions are clearly not feasible even over several decades. Moreover, if population continues to grow at projected rates, reaching 8.5 billion by 2025, allowable per capita emissions will decline to 1.0 mt.[7] It seems highly unlikely that the industrial countries will be willing to offer the developing countries enough inducements to get them to accept a level of CO_2 emissions low enough to balance off the excesses of the developed world.

Thus, a scenario is unfolding on climate change that has all the trappings of a tragedy of the atmosphere, which poses a profound threat to environmental security. The potentially devastating implications of global warming are well established scientifically and understood throughout the world, but seemingly they are not taken seriously as the peoples of both developed and developing countries pursue modern, energy-intensive lifestyles. Unfortunately, the time has passed when the world community could have adopted a purely preventive and anticipatory approach to climate change. In the coming decades more and more resources will have to be put into adapting to the effects of the climate changes to which humanity is already committed, while additional steps are taken to moderate the amount of climate change that takes place. Unfortunately, the international stalemate on limiting GHG emissions is unlikely to be broken unless there is a shock that has the magnitude of the Antarctic ozone hole, which gave a strong impetus to strengthening the ozone layer regime. Such an event could, however, evoke a defensive response in which nations scurry to do whatever they can to adapt to the disruptive changes that appear inevitable.

TOWARD A LAW OF THE ATMOSPHERE?

The international community has addressed the problems of regulating use of several of the global commons in holistic ways. The oceans are governed by a comprehensive Law of the Sea that has evolved over centuries, first as international customary law before taking a negotiated form in the Convention on the Law of the Sea, which was adopted in 1982 but did not come into force until 1994. The Antarctic Treaty of 1959 provides the governing framework for the ice-bound continent, and additional agreements have been negotiated by the Antarctic Treaty Consultative Parties (ATCP), a group of countries with interests in the region that meets every two years. The Outer Space Treaty of 1967 provides a framework for rules on activities in outer space and celestial bodies, while the UN Committee on the Peaceful Uses of Outer Space (COPUOS) is a forum for international policy making on emergent issues pertaining to that vast domain beyond national airspaces.

Despite the atmosphere's physical indivisibility and dynamic movement, there is no overarching international law, either in customary or treaty form, that addresses such fundamental issues as jurisdiction over the atmosphere and rights to use it as a medium for disposing of gaseous or particulate wastes. Furthermore, no international institution is specifically charged with the development and implementation of international policy on the atmosphere, although the principal mission of the World Meteorological Organization (WMO) is to coordinate monitoring and research on the state of the atmosphere. Nor has there been a major United Nations conference that has looked at the problems of the atmosphere in a comprehensive manner. The nongovernmental Changing Atmosphere Conference hosted by Canada in 1988 was one of the few international gatherings to take an integrated perspective on problems and policies issues pertaining to the atmosphere. A follow-up meeting of legal and policy experts, also held in Toronto, in February 1989 advanced the idea of a law of the atmosphere treaty, but to little effect.[8]

Curiously, the word atmosphere rarely enters into the lexicon of international law. The full title of the Nuclear Test Ban Treaty of 1963 does list the atmosphere as one of the three places, along with outer space and underwater, where the testing of nuclear explosives is prohibited. The Vienna Convention and the Montreal Protocol and its revisions refer to the ozone layer but make no explicit reference to the larger atmosphere of which it is a part. Likewise, the focus of the FCCC is clearly about the adverse effects to the Earth's climate that are the "common concern of humankind," not the state of the atmosphere generally, although reference is made to "atmospheric" concentrations of greenhouse gases.

One explanation for this lack of attention to the atmosphere is the tendency for international law to be developed for spatial domains that are beyond the jurisdiction of states, such as the high seas, outer space, and Antarctica, although in the latter case several states persist in claiming parts of the continent. Even the Law of the Sea is not as much about the waters of the oceans as it is about the spatial areas that the seas occupy, including the seabed and the airspace above the seas. In some respects, air is to the atmosphere as water is to the oceans. Thus, it is more common for the space through which the substances move to become the subject of legal regimes than the substances themselves. Accordingly, airspace and outer space have become the subjects of legal regimes, while the atmosphere has not. Whatever resources are found within these spatial domains at any given time—whether living such as fish or inanimate such as air, water, or minerals—are generally considered to belong to the state that has jurisdiction over that space. Efforts to manage these resources internationally, even those that flow or move through multiple national or international spaces, soon confront the principle of sovereignty of states over resources within their recognized jurisdictions, which has been affirmed in numerous contexts.

Nations have been generally willing to address specific atmospheric problems as they have arisen. The test ban and LRTAP regimes build upon the principle that states should not allow activities to take place within their jurisdictions that cause damage to other states. The regimes for the ozone layer and climate change seem to imply an extension of this basic principle of state responsibility, namely that states have a responsibility to limit activities within their jurisdictions that could alter the atmosphere in ways that would be catastrophic to human societies as well as to the environment.

The ad hoc, problem-specific approach to regulating pollution and protecting the atmosphere has proven to be quite flexible and adaptable in responding to the problems of atmospheric testing, LRTAP, and ozone depletion. It remains to be seen what will be done to minimize climate change. While some of the agreements that have been reached thus far in the form of conventions and protocols could be considered strong responses to the problems they address, there is little in them that suggests the emergence of a law of the atmosphere because they all ignore the critical issue of who has jurisdiction over the atmosphere. The suggestion in the FCCC that the global climate is a "common concern" of humanity may be a first step toward defining a legal status for the atmosphere, albeit a weak one.

A case could be made that the time has come for a concerted international effort to negotiate a basic law of the atmosphere via a process similar to the most recent United Nations Conference on the Law of the Sea held between 1974 and 1982. The underlying rationale for such an undertaking would be that the atmosphere is a critical global resource, which is indivisible and thus cannot be preserved effectively by states acting on their own. States may be asked to waive any exclusive claims they might make to the ever changing portions of the atmosphere that rise within their airspaces at any given time, and the atmosphere as a whole might be designated the "common heritage of mankind." All use of the atmosphere as a sink for pollutants that will be dispersed internationally or globally might then be made subject to international controls. Such a change would constitute a revolutionary change that many states, in particular those most responsible for atmospheric pollutants, would be loath to accept.

It is important to reflect upon the experience of the international community in establishing regimes for some of the other global commons before embarking on a major venture to frame a comparable law of the atmosphere. The Convention on the Law of the Sea that was adopted in 1982, but did not come into force until 1994, was the culmination of an effort to codify ocean law that can be traced back at least as far as 1950 and included three international law-making conferences, the third of which was held intermittently over eight years. Furthermore, the treaty drafters could draw upon an extensive body of customary law that had evolved over centuries. It should also be borne in mind that agreement on the law of the sea was possible in large part because it legitimized earlier unilateral claims of coastal states to larger portions of resource-rich ocean spaces that had previously been in the international domain, which is not an appropriate model for atmospheric law. In the case of Antarctica and outer space, the cornerstone treaties were agreed upon with considerably more ease, but at a time when there was relatively little use of these realms and thus no danger of depleting or seriously degrading resources. Furthermore, the initial treaties on Antarctica and outer space bear little resemblance to the comprehensive 1982 Convention on the Law of the Sea in that they are essentially framework agreements that were not designed to resolve the most contentious issues pertaining to jurisdiction and use of the regions in question.

Launching a major venture during the last years of the twentieth century to formulate a comprehensive global law of the atmosphere comparable to the 1982 Convention on the Law of the Sea would appear to be an ill-advised use of the limited diplomatic resources of the international community. Decades would probably pass before such a document could be crafted that would have widespread acceptance. States will be cautious about subscribing to principles that are broadly applicable to the use of the atmosphere as a sink for pollutants out of concern that they may infringe on activities considered integral to their economies, such as the generation of power from fossil fuels. Moreover, given the great differences in historical and current levels of generating air pollution, it will be difficult to forge a broad-based consensus on how to regulate future emissions in ways that the industrialized countries will accept and the developing countries regard as equitable. In the meantime what momentum has been achieved in addressing specific problems that need immediate attention, such as acid rain, ozone depletion, and climate change, could easily be lost as diplomatic energies are diverted from them to talks on a law of the atmosphere. Furthermore, efforts to conclude additional agreements that address these specific problems may also be delayed as debate proceeds on more generally applicable tenets of international atmospheric law.

The more compelling priority for the next decade is to continue and indeed to accelerate development of the more narrowly focused international regimes that address the specific atmospheric problems. The European and North American members of the LRTAP regime must significantly tighten their already quite elaborate international rules on emissions of sulfur and nitrogen oxides and VOCs in order to bring acidic deposition down to levels that will not further disrupt the natural environments of their countries. Other regions, such as the Far East, have only begun to address their increasingly serious problems of transboundary pollution. The task of preserving the ozone layer will not be finished until agreement is reached on a schedule for all countries to phase out completely the remaining ozone-destroying substances, in particular methyl bromide and HCFCs, and sufficient technical and economic assistance is committed to developing countries to enable them to adopt substitutes for the controlled substances. By far the biggest challenge for the coming years, however, will be to forge an international strategy that will cut deeply into the flows of CO_2 and other GHGs into the atmosphere, thereby containing the amount of global warming and other environmental changes that pose such a serious threat to human security.

As efforts proceed to address these specific problems, however, it is important to recall the picture from space in which the atmosphere is a narrow blue arc between the surface of the Earth and the blackness of outer space. The international scientific community has done much to illuminate the properties and dynamics of the atmosphere and its integral relationship with the other components of the Earth system—the oceans, land masses, and the biosphere. As these scientific efforts continue, it is up to the world's policy makers, with support from their publics, to act in a timely and decisive way to preserve the essential properties of the atmosphere to secure the future of humanity and the other species that inhabit the planet.

APPENDIX
INTERNATIONAL AGREEMENTS

KEY TO SOURCES:

AJIL—*American Journal of International Law.*

ILM—*International Legal Documents.*

LNTS—*League of Nations Treaty Series.*

TIAS—**US** *Treaties and Other International Agreements.*

UNTS—*United Nations Treaty Series.*

Adjustments and Amendments to the Montreal Protocol on Substances that Deplete the Ozone Layer (London, June 29, 1990), 30 ILM 541 (1991).

Adjustments and Amendments to the Montreal Protocol on Substances that Deplete the Ozone Layer (Copenhagen, 1992), 32 ILM 874 (1993).

Adjustments and Amendments to the Montreal Protocol on Substances that Deplete the Ozone Layer (Vienna, 1995).

Agreement between the Government of the United States of America and the Government of Canada on Air Quality (Ottawa, March 13, 1991).

Agreement Governing the Activities of States on the Moon and Other Celestial Bodies (New York, December 5, 1979), A/RES/34/68.

Air Quality Limit Values and Guide Values for Sulphur Dioxide and Suspended Particulates (EEC, July 15, 1980), Air Quality Directive, No. 80/779.

Conference Statement: Second World Climate Conference (Geneva, November 7, 1990); text in *Climate Change: Science, Impacts, and Policy: Proceedings of the Second World Climate Conference,* edited by J. Jäger and H. L. Ferguson, 497–503. Cambridge: Cambridge University Press, 1991.

Convention for the Protection of the Ozone Layer (Vienna, March 22, 1985), 26 ILM 1529 (1987).

Convention for the Regulation of Aerial Navigation (Paris, 1919), 11 LNTS 173 (1922).

Convention on Assistance in the Case of a Nuclear Accident or Radiological Emergency (Vienna, September 26, 1986), 25 ILM 1377 (1986).

Convention on Civil Aviation (Chicago, 1944), 15 UNTS 295.

Convention on Early Notification of a Nuclear Accident or Radiological Emergency (Vienna, October 26, 1986), 25 ILM 1370 (1986).

Convention on Long-Range Transboundary Air Pollution (Geneva, November 13, 1979), 18 ILM 1442 (1979).

Convention on the Prohibition of Military or Any Other Hostile Uses of Environmental Modification (ENMOD) (May 18, 1977), 16 ILM 88 (1977).

Decision of the Trail Smelter Arbitral Tribunal (March 11, 1941), 35 AJIL 684 (1941).

Declaration by the Ministerial Conference on Atmospheric Pollution and Climate Change (Noordwijk, November 7, 1989), A/C.2/44/5, Annex.

Declaration of the Hague (March 11, 1988), 28 ILM 1308 (1989).

Declaration on the Human Environment of the United Nations Conference on the Human Environment (Stockholm, June 16, 1972), 11 ILM 1416 (1972).

Declaration on the Protection of the Ozone Layer (Helsinki, May 2, 1989), 28 ILM 1335 (1989).

Economic Declaration, Paris Economic Summit (July 16, 1989), 28 ILM 1292 (1989).

Final Act: Declaration of Principles Guiding Relationships between Participating States (Helsinki, August 1, 1975), 70 AJIL 417 (1976).

Framework Convention on Climate Change (New York, May 9, 1992), 31 ILM 849 (1992).

Great Lakes Water Quality Agreement (Ottawa, April 15, 1972) 11 ILM 694 (1972).

Great Lakes Water Quality Agreement (Ottawa, November 22, 1978) TIAS 9257.

International Fund for Compensation for Oil Pollution Damage (London, December 18, 1971), 11 ILM 284 (1972).

Memorandum of Intent Concerning Transboundary Air Pollution: Canada–United States of America (Washington, D.C., August 5, 1980), 20 ILM 690 (1981).

Ministerial Declaration: Second World Climate Conference (Geneva, November 7, 1989), A/45/696/Add.1, Annex III.

Protocol Concerning the Control of Emissions of Nitrogen Oxide or Their Transboundary Fluxes (Sofia, October 31, 1988), 28 ILM 214 (1989).

Protocol Concerning the Control of Emissions of Volatile Organic Compounds or Their Transboundary Fluxes (Geneva, November 18, 1991), 31 ILM 212 (1992).

Protocol on Reduction of Sulphur Emissions or their Transboundary Fluxes (Helsinki, July 8, 1985), 27 ILM 707 (1988).

Protocol on Substances that Deplete the Ozone Layer (Montreal, September 16, 1987), 26 ILM 1529 (1987).

Protocol on the Further Reduction of Sulphur Emissions (Oslo, June 14,1994), 33 ILM 1542 (1994).

Treaty Banning Nuclear Weapons Tests in the Atmosphere, in Outer Space and Under Water (Moscow, August 15, 1963), 2 ILM 889 (1963).

Treaty on the Limitation of Anti-Ballistic Missile System (Moscow, May 26, 1972), 11 ILM 784 (1982).

Treaty on the Non-Proliferation of Nuclear Weapons (Washington, London, and Moscow, July 1, 1968), 7 ILM 811 (1968).

Treaty Relating to Boundary Waters and Questions Arising Along the Boundary Between the United States and Canada (Washington, January 11, 1909), 4AJIL 239 (1920 Supp.)

United Nations Convention on the Law of the Sea (Montego Bay, December 10, 1982), 21 ILM 1261 (1982).

NOTES

CHAPTER 1:
THE ATMOSPHERE AND GLOBAL PUBLIC POLICY

1. Lind, "The Earth-Home We See from Space," 3.

2. Decision of the Trail Smelter Arbital Tribunal, 684.

3. Kiss and Shelton, *International Environmental Law,* 122–26.

4. Treaty Banning Nuclear Weapons Tests in the Atmosphere, in Outer Space and Under Water.

5. Declaration on the Human Environment . . ., Article 21.

6. Final Act: Declaration of Principles Guiding Relationships between Participating States.

7. Convention on Long-Range Transboundary Air Pollution.

8. Protocol on Reduction of Sulphur Emissions or Their Transboundary Fluxes.

9. Protocol Concerning the Control of Emissions of Nitrogen Oxide or Their Transboundary Fluxes; Protocol Concerning the Control of Volatile Organic Compounds or Their Transboundary Fluxes.

10. Protocol on the Further Reduction of Sulphur Emissions.

11. See Park, *Chernobyl: The Long Shadow.*

12. Convention on Early Notification of a Nuclear Accident.

13. Convention on Assistance in the Case of a Nuclear Accident or Radiological Emergency.

14. Convention for the Protection of the Ozone Layer.

15. Protocol on Substances that Deplete the Ozone Layer.

16. Adjustments and Amendments to the Montreal Protocol on Substances that Deplete the Ozone Layer (London, 1990).

17. Adjustments and Amendments to the Montreal Protocol on Substances that Deplete the Ozone Layer (Copenhagen, 1992).

18. Benedick, *Ozone Diplomacy,* 199–211.

19. See Advisory Committee on Weather Control, "Importance of Weather and Its Modification."

20. See Taubenfeld and Taubenfeld, "Some International Implications of Weather Modification Techniques"; Weiss, "International Liability for Weather Modification."

21. Convention on the Prohibition of Military or Any Other Hostile Use of Environmental Modification.

22. See Juda, "Negotiating a Treaty on Environmental Modification Warfare."

23. Framework Convention on Climate Change.

24. G. Hardin, "The Tragedy of the Commons."

25. See Ostrom, *Governing the Commons.*

26. See Young, *International Governance.*

CHAPTER 2:
A PRIMER ON THE ATMOSPHERE AND POLLUTION

1. Moran and Morgan, *Meteorology,* 14–15.

2. Ibid.

3. International Geosphere-Biosphere Programme, *Global Change,* 7.

4. Barry and Chorley, *Atmosphere, Weather and Climate,* 1.

5. Anthes, *Meteorology,* 4.

6. Moran and Morgan, *Meteorology,* 15–16.

7. Anthes, *Meteorology,* 7–9.

8. Young, *Sowing the Wind,* 18.

9. A wavelength is the distance between the crests of waves, or alternatively the troughs, of electromagnetic radiation. Wavelengths are usually expressed in nanometers, which are a billionth of a meter. Wavelengths are inversely related to wave frequency, which is the number of waves that pass a particular point within a specified time, such as a second. Intensity of radiation is an inverse function of its wavelength and a direct function of its frequency. See Moran and Morgan, *Meteorology,* 31.

10. Lydolph, *The Climate of the Earth,* 16.

11. Makhijani and Gurney, *Mending the Ozone Hole,* 50–51.

12. See Anthes, *Meteorology,* 50–54.

13. Graedel and Crutzen, *Atmospheric Change,* 42–43.

14. See Makhijani and Gurney, *Mending the Ozone Hole,* 8–12.

15. Barry and Chorley, *Atmosphere, Weather and Climate,* 2.

16. Moran and Morgan, *Meteorology,* 43.

17. Albritton, "Our Ozone Shield."

18. Graedel and Crutzen, *Atmospheric Change,* 45.

19. Fisher, *Fire and Ice,* 18–20.

20. Ehrlich and Ehrlich, *Healing the Planet,* 21.

21. Chiras, *Environmental Science,* 43–44.

22. Wagner, *Environment and Man*, 16–17.

23. Anthes, *Meteorology*, 96–100.

24. The term *El Niño*, Spanish for "Christ Child," was first used by coastal fishermen to refer to warm coastal currents that appeared some years around Christmas, in which fish were much less abundant than in the colder currents of other years. The term *Southern Oscillation* refers to the seesawing of high and low pressure between the eastern and western Pacific. El Niños occur when air pressure is relatively low in the eastern Pacific and high in the west (see Moran and Morgan, *Meteorology*, 234–38).

25. See Wallace and Vogel, "El Niño and Climate Prediction."

26. Gore, *Earth in the Balance*, 56–57.

27. IPCC, *Climate Change 1994*, 12.

28. McGovern, "The Economics of Extinction in Norse Greenland."

29. Keller, *Environmental Geology*, 496.

30. Moran and Morgan, *Meteorology*, 17–18.

31. Bridgman, *Global Air Pollution*, 1.

32. Brimblecombe, *The Big Smoke*, 5–16.

33. Quoted in ibid., 47–48.

34. Quoted in Park, *Acid Rain*, 10.

35. Elsom, *Atmospheric Pollution*.

36. UNEP, *Environmental Data Report*, 14–15.

37. See Thompson, "East Europe's Dark Dawn"; Feshback and Friendly, *Ecocide in the USSR*.

38. See Barrie, "Arctic Air Pollution."

39. Park, *Acid Rain*, 34.

40. Ibid., 40–48.

41. The range of pH scale is 0 to 14, with 7 being a neutral value indicating that a substance is neither alkaline nor acidic. The higher the value the greater the alkalinity; the lower the value the greater the acidity. Because the pH scale is logarithmic, a reduction of 1.0 in pH value indicates an acidity level that is ten times greater; a reduction of 2.0 indicates an acidity level that is 100 times greater. See Park, *Acid Rain*, 23–25.

42. Ibid., 25–26.

43. Ibid., 26–32.

44. MacKenzie and El-Ashry, *Ill Winds*, 6.

45. Schütt and Cowling, "Waldsterben, a General Decline of Forests in Central Europe."

46. Swedish NGO Secretariat on Acid Rain, "Forest Damage in Europe."

47. Park, *Acid Rain*, 69–90.

48. Prinz, "Causes of Forest Death in Europe."

49. UNEP, *Environmental Effects Panel Report*.

50. Elsom, *Atmospheric Pollution*, 45–46.

51. See Makhijani and Gurney, *Mending the Ozone Hole,* 93–114.

52. Bridgman, *Global Air Pollution,* 52–54.

53. Albritton, "Our Ozone Shield."

54. NOAA et al., *Scientific Assessment of Ozone Depletion,* 10–11.

55. Kerr and McElroy, "Evidence of Large Upward Trends of Ultraviolet-B Radiation Linked to Ozone Depletion"; NOAA et al., *Scientific Assessment of Ozone Depletion,* 14.

56. UNEP, *Environmental Effects Panel Report.*

57. Makhijani and Gurney, *Mending the Ozone Hole,* 56–75.

58. See ibid., 76–77.

59. Smith et al., "Ozone Depletion."

60. Blaustein et al., "UV Repair and Resistance to Solar UV-B in Amphibian Eggs."

61. Anthes, *The Atmosphere,* 46–52.

62. IPCC, *Climate Change 1994,* 12–13, 44.

63. Barnola et al., "Vostok Ice Core Provides 160,000-year Record of Atmospheric CO2."

64. World Resources Institute, *World Resources 1992–93,* 12.

65. World Resources Institute, *World Resources 1994–95,* 205.

66. See Brown et al., *Vital Signs 1995,* 64–65.

67. Houghton et al, *Climate Change 1995,* 4–5.

68. IPCC, *Climate Change 1992,* 5.

69. Houghton et al, *Climate Change 1995,* 6.

70. Mitchell and Ericksen, "Effects of Climate Change on Weather-Related Disasters," 141.

71. Oeschger and Mintzer, "Lessons from the Ice Cores," 63.

72. IPCC, *Climate Change 1992,* 6, 19.

73. See Rosenzweig and Parry, "Potential Impact of Climate Change on World Food Supply."

74. IPCC, *The IPCC Assessment of Knowledge Relevant. . . .*

75. Warrick and Rahman, "Future Sea Level Rise," 100.

76. Edgerton, *The Rising Tide.*

77. Leggett, "Global Warming."

78. Elsom, *Atmospheric Pollution,* 108–9.

79. UNSCEAR, *Ionizing Radiation: Levels and Effects,* 3.

80. UNSCEAR, *Ionizing Radiation: Sources and Biological Effects,* 19.

81. Ibid., 212.

82. Ibid., 212; Eisenbud, *Environmental Radioactivity,* 277–79.

83. Ibid., 313–14; IPPNW and IEER, *Radioactive Heaven and Earth,* 15–16.

84. Park, *Acid Rain,* 80.

85. UNSCEAR, *Ionizing Radiation: Sources and Biological Effects,* 8.

86. Eisenbud, *Environmental Radioactivity,* 9–29.

87. May, *The Greenpeace Book of the Nuclear Age,* 33–35; Chiras, *Environmental Science,* 276–77.

88. IPPNW/IEER, *Radioactive Heaven and Earth,* 42.

CHAPTER 3:
INTERNATIONAL SCIENTIFIC COOPERATION

1. Davies, *Forty Years of Progress and Achievement,* 139–50.

2. Cain, "Carbon Dioxide and the Climate."

3. Davies, *Forty Years of Progress and Achievement,* 1.

4. Anthes et al., *The Atmosphere,* 4–6.

5. Ibid., 11.

6. Davies, *Forty Years of Progress and Achievement,* 1–2.

7. Ibid., 1–9.

8. Ibid., 11–16.

9. UNGA Resolution 1721(XVI).

10. Crump, *Dictionary of Environment and Development,* 112.

11. WMO, *The WMO Achievement,* 13–20.

12. Davies, *Forty Years of Progress and Achievement,* 39–44; Boldirev, "Modern Data and Applications," 158–59.

13. Ibid., 33–38.

14. WMO, *The WMO Achievement,* 8.

15. Atwood, "The International Geophysical Year."

16. Atwood, "The International Geophysical Year in Retrospective."

17. UNGA Resolution 1802(XVII).

18. Malone, "Reflections on the Human Prospect," 7–14.

19. Davies, *Forty Years of Progress and Achievement,* 70–84.

20. Thomas Malone, personal correspondence.

21. Kathren, *Radioactivity in the Environment.*

22. Ibid., 5–6.

23. Ibid., 14–17.

24. UNSCEAR, *Report to the United Nations General Assembly,* 2.

25. Ibid.

26. Ibid., 1.

27. Eisenbud, *Environmental Radioactivity,* 7.

28. Scheinman, *The International Atomic Energy Agency and World Nuclear Order.*

29. IPPNW and IEER, *Radioactive Heaven and Earth,* 161.

30. UNSCEAR, *Sources, Effects and Risks of Ionizing Radiation.*

31. Eisenbud, *Environmental Radioactivity,* 2.

32. IPPNW and IEER, *Radioactive Heaven and Earth.*

33. Cowling, "Acid Precipitation in Historical Perspective," 112A.

34. Brodin and Kuylenstierna, "Acidification and Critical Loads in Nordic Countries," 332–33.

35. Cowling, "Acid Precipitation in Historical Perspective," 112A–113A.

36. Park, *Acid Rain*, 158.

37. See Cowling, "Acid Rain in Historical Perspective."

38. OECD, *The OECD Program on Long-Range Transport of Air Pollutants*.

39. Andersson, "A European Monitoring System"; *Acid News*, December 1992, 10–12.

40. Barrie, "Arctic Air Pollution"; Soroos, "The Odyssey of Arctic Haze."

41. Levy, "European Acid Rain," 88.

42. Ibid.

43. See Roberts, "Learning from an Acid Rain Program."

44. de Koning and Köhler, "Monitoring Global Air Pollution"; Köhler, "WMO's Activities on Background Atmospheric Pollution and Integrated Monitoring and Research."

45. UNEP, *Environmental Data Report*, 12.

46. Boldirev, "Modern Data and Applications," 158.

47. Crutzen, "The Influence of Nitrogen Oxides on the Atmospheric Ozone Content."

48. Johnston, "Reduction of Stratospheric Ozone by Nitrogen Oxide Catalysts from Supersonic Transport Exhaust."

49. CIAP, *Report on Findings;* see also Dotto and Schiff, *The Ozone War*, 69–89.

50. Stolarski and Cicerone, "Stratospheric Chlorine."53.

51. Lovelock, "Atmospheric Fluorine Compounds as Indicators of Air Movement."

52. Molina and Rowland, "Stratospheric Sink for Chlorofluoromethanes."

53. Davies, *Forty Years of Progress and Achievement*, 189.

54. WMO et al., *Atmospheric Ozone 1985*.

55. Farman et al., "Large Losses of Total Ozone in Antarctica Reveal Seasonal CLOx/NOx Interaction."

56. Roan, *Ozone Crisis*, 132.

57. Ibid., 158–77.

58. Ibid., 212–18.

59. Watson, et al., "Ozone Trends Panel Executive Summary."

60. Parson, "Protecting the Ozone Layer," 47.

61. Summarized in Rowlands, *The Politics of Global Atmospheric Change*, 59–61; see also *Christian Science Monitor*, May 12, 1995, 3.

62. Kellogg, "Mankind's Impact on Climate," 115.

63. Arrhenius, "On the Influence of Carbonic Acid in the Air upon the Temperature."

64. Callendar, "The Artificial Production of CO2 and Its Influence on Temperature."

65. Revelle and Suess, "Carbon Dioxide Exchange between the Atmosphere and the Ocean . . .," 19.

66. Boldirev, "Modern Data and Applications," 158.

67. Davies, *Forty Years of Progress and Achievement*, 83.

68. Schneider, *The Genesis Strategy.*

69. Gribbin, *What's Wrong with the Weather?*

70. See Rowlands, *The Politics of Global Atmospheric Change*, 69–70.

71. White, "Climate at the Millennium," 31.

72. Davies, *Forty Years of Progress and Achievement*, 101.

73. Bierly, "The World Climate Program."

74. Davies, *Forty Years of Progress and Achievement*, 105.

75. UNEP/WMO/ICSU, *An Assessment of the Role of Carbon Dioxide and of Other Greenhouse Gases in Climate Variations and Associated Impact.*

76. IPCC, *Climate Change.*

77. *Chemical & Engineering News*, November 19, 1990, 4.

78. Aldhous, "Dissent Hits Climate Accord."

79. IPCC, *Climate Change 1992*, 5.

80. Houghton et al, *Climate Change 1995*, 4–5.

81. Obasi, "The Atmosphere: Global Commons to Protect," 7.

82. CLIVAR Scientific Steering Group, *CLIVAR: A Study of Climate Variability and Predictability*, 1–2.

83. Davies, *Forty Years of Progress and Achievement*, 95.

84. *Global Change Newsletter*, March 1992, 8–9; December 1995, 17.

85. Price, "Global Change," 20.

86. Menon, "Second World Climate Conference."

87. IGBP, *Global Change.*

88. Stern et al., *Global Environmental Change.*

89. Jacobson and Price, *A Framework for Research on the Human Dimensions of Global Environmental Change.*

CHAPTER 4: THE NUCLEAR TESTING REGIME

1. Craig and Jungerman, *Nuclear Arms Race*, 9–10.

2. Ball, *Justice Downwind*, 10.

3. National Academy of Sciences, *Nuclear Arms Control*, 191–92.

4. Norris and Arkin, "Known Nuclear Tests Worldwide, 1945–1995," 63.

5. Ibid.

6. Ball, *Justice Downwind*, 84–101.

7. Peterson, *Troubled Lands*, 202–6.

8. Lewis and Xue, *China Builds the Bomb*, 170–77.

9. IPPNW and IEER, *Radioactive Heaven and Earth*, 124.

10. Burrows et al., *French Nuclear Testing, 1960–1988.*
11. Divine, *Blowing on the Wind,* 787.
12. Freedman, *The Evolution of Nuclear Strategy.*
13. See Holloway, *The Soviet Union and the Arms Race.*
14. Ibid.
15. Malone, *The British Nuclear Deterrent,* 45–74; Laird, *France, the Soviet Union, and the Nuclear Weapons Issue,* 67–73.
16. Pierre, *Nuclear Politics,* 2–3.
17. Lewis and Xue, *China Builds the Bomb,* 229.
18. Halperin and Perkins, *Communist China and Arms Control,* 63–66.
19. Craig and Jungerman, *Nuclear Arms Race,* 25.
20. Norihisa, "Fallout and the Japanese."
21. Lapp, *The Voyage of the Lucky Dragon.*
22. Divine, *Blowing on the Wind,* 21.
23. Jack, "The Asian-African Conference"; Divine, *Blowing on the Wind,* 61.
24. Ibid., 27–28.
25. Ibid., 113–42.
26. Ball, *Justice Downwind,* 39–40.
27. Jacobson and Stein, *Diplomats, Scientists, and Politicians,* 24–25.
28. Divine, *Blowing on the Wind,* 160.
29. Holifield, "Congressional Hearings on Radioactive Fall-out."
30. Divine, *Blowing on the Wind,* 211–12.
31. Ibid., 12–13.
32. Titus, *Bombs in the Backyard,* 87.
33. Ibid.
34. Ibid., 171–85.
35. Bennett, *International Organizations,* 208–10.
36. Seaborg, *Kennedy, Khrushchev, and the Test Ban,* 235–53.
37. Ibid., 4.
38. Ibid., 5–7.
39. Jacobson and Stein, *Diplomats, Scientists, and Politicians,* 14–18.
40. Divine, *Blowing on the Wind,* 221.
41. National Academy of Sciences, *Nuclear Arms Control,* 188.
42. Norris and Arkin, "Known Nuclear Tests Worldwide, 1945–1993," 63.
43. Seaborg, *Kennedy, Khrushchev, and the Test Ban,* 16.
44. Jacobson and Stein, *Diplomats, Scientists, and Politicians,* 159–62.
45. National Academy of Sciences, *Nuclear Arms Control,* 189–90.
46. Ibid., 190.
47. Ibid., 191–92.
48. Ibid.
49. Ibid., 190–95.
50. Norris and Arkin, "Known Nuclear Tests Worldwide, 1945–1993," 63.

51. Seaborg, *Kennedy, Khrushchev, and the Test Ban*, 286–87.

52. D'Amato, "Legal Aspects of the French Nuclear Tests," 66–67.

53. Firth, *Nuclear Playground*, 97–100.

54. *U.S. News and World Report*, August 6, 1973, 30.

55. French Ministry of Foreign Affairs, *White Paper on French Nuclear Tests*.

56. Sweeney et al., *Cases and Materials on the International Legal System*, 277–78.

57. Firth, *Nuclear Playground*, 100–102.

58. Sweeny et al., *Cases and Materials on the International Legal System*, 278.

59. Firth, *Nuclear Playground*, 83–93.

60. *Christian Science Monitor*, August 11, 1995, 1, 9.

61. Halperin and Perkins, *Communist China and Arms Control*, 98–172.

62. Cited in Darnay, *Statistical Record of the Environment*, 35–36.

63. McBride, *The Test Ban Treaty*, 76–111.

64. See Sweeney et al., *Cases and Materials on the International Legal System*, 274–78.

65. D'Amato, "Legal Aspects of the French Nuclear Tests."

CHAPTER 5:
THE TRANSBOUNDARY AIR POLLUTION REGIME

1. Matsuura, "China's Air Pollution and Japan's Response to It."

2. Mylona, *Trends of Sulfur Dioxide Emissions. . . .*

3. Alcamo, et al., *The RAINS Model of Acidification*, 39.

4. Mylona, *Trends of Sulfur Dioxide Emissions. . . .*

5. Peterson, *Troubled Lands*, 42.

6. McCormick, *Acid Earth*, 15.

7. Swedish NGO Secretariat on Acid Rain, "The 100 Worst Emitters."

8. McCormick, *Acid Earth*, 15.

9. Ibid., 15, 154–55.

10. Newbury, "Acid Rain," 308.

11. McCormick, *Acid Earth*, 14.

12. Carroll, "The Acid Rain Issue in Canadian-American Relations," 142.

13. Park, *Acid Rain*, 169–74.

14. Ibid., 11.

15. Ibid., 241.

16. McCormick, *Acid Earth*, 30.

17. Ibid., 107.

18. Ibid., 160.

19. Shaw, "Acid-Rain Negotiations in North America and Europe," 98.

20. Carroll, "The Acid Rain Issue in Canadian-American Relations," 142–43.

21. McMahon, "Balancing the Interests."

22. McCormick, *Acid Earth.*

23. Kriz, "Dunning the Midwest."

24. Jancar, "Eastern Europe and the Former Soviet Union" and "The Environmental Attractor in the Former USSR."

25. OECD, *Programme on Long Range Transport of Air Pollutants.*

26. Bolin et al., *Sweden's Case Study for the United Nations Conference on the Human Environment.*

27. Final Act, Basket 2.

28. Chossudovsky, *East-West Diplomacy for the Environment in the United Nations,* 88–100.

29. Jackson, "A Tenth Anniversary Review of the ECE Convention on Long-Range Transboundary Air Pollution," 221–22.

30. Convention on Long-Range Transboundary Air Pollution.

31. See Rosencranz, "The Problem of Transboundary Pollution."

32. Hileman, "The 1982 Stockholm Conference on Acidification of the Environment."

33. Ibid.

34. Park, *Acid Rain,* 169–71.

35. Ibid., 172; McCormick, *Acid Earth,* 79–80.

36. McCormick, *Acid Earth,* 80–81.

37. Park, *Acid Rain,* 179–80.

38. Protocol on Reduction of Sulfur Emissions or their Transboundary Fluxes.

39. Ibid., 181–82.

40. Levy, "European Acid Rain," 92.

41. Ibid., 118.

42. *Acid News,* June 1993, 8.

43. Levy, "European Acid Rain," 95.

44. Boehmer-Christiansen, "Curbing Auto Emissions in Europe," 34–36.

45. Protocol Concerning the Control of Emissions of Nitrogen Oxide or Their Transboundary Fluxes.

46. Levy, "European Acid Rain," 94–99.

47. Ibid., 99.

48. Protocol Concerning the Control of Emissions of Volatile Organic Compounds or Their Transboundary Fluxes.

49. *Acid News,* December 1991, 1–3.

50. Levy, "International Co-operation to Combat Acid Rain," 61.

51. Protocol on the Further Reduction of Sulphur Emissions.

52. Protocol Concerning the Control of Emissions of Nitrogen Oxides or Their Transboundary Fluxes.

53. Downing et al., *Calculation and Mapping of Critical Loads in Europe.*

54. Hettelingh et al., "The Critical Load Concept for the Control of Acidification."

55. *Acid News,* February 1994, 11–13.

56. See Alcamo et al., *The RAINS Model of Acidification.*

57. *Acid News,* February 1993, 2.

58. See Levy, "International Co-operation to Combat Acid Rain," 61–64.

59. *Acid News,* October 1994, 10–11.

60. *Acid News,* February 1994, 11–13.

61. *Acid News,* April 1994, 2.

62. Treaty Relating to Boundary Waters. . . .

63. Great Lakes Water Quality Agreements, 1972, 1978. See also Wetstone and Rosencranz, *Acid Rain in Europe and North America,* 124.

64. Cowling, "Acid Precipitation in Historical Perspective," 118a.

65. McCormick, *Acid Earth,* 147–54.

66. Golich and Young, "Resolution of the United States—Canadian Conflict over Acid Rain Controls," 81–86.

67. *Acid News,* October 1994, 10–11.

68. *Acid News,* June 1994, 5; *Acid News,* April 1994, 3.

69. Aton Eliassen, personal interview, Oslo, May 1, 1993.

70. *Acid News,* February 1994, 11.

71. *Acid News,* December 1993, 16.

72. *Acid News,* February 1993, 2.

73. Mylona, *Trends of Sulfur Dioxide Emissions.*

74. Kotov and Nikitina, "Russia and International Environmental Cooperation," 22–23.

75. Castberg, "Common Problem—Different Priorities," 25.

76. *Acid News,* October 1994, 11.

77. Gun Lövblad, personal interview, Göteborg, April 29, 1993.

78. Persson, personal interview, Stockholm, April 28, 1993.

79. Shaw, "Acid-Rain Negotiations in North America and Europe," 95–99.

CHAPTER 6: THE OZONE LAYER REGIME

1. Cagin and Dray, *Between Earth and Sky,* 56–69.

2. Cogan, *Stones in a Glass House,* 12–15.

3. Shea, "Protecting the Ozone Layer," 85–86.

4. Ibid., 87.

5. Benedick, *Ozone Diplomacy,* 121–22.

6. Ibid., 130.

7. Shea, "Protecting the Ozone Layer," 87.

8. Gladwin et al., "A Global View of CFC Sources and Policies to Reduce Emissions," 66.

9. Maxwell and Weiner, "Green Consciousness or Dollar Diplomacy?," 26.

10. Shea, "Protecting the Ozone Layer," 87.

11. Munasinghe and King, *Issues and Options in Implementing the Montreal Protocol in Developing Countries,* 9.

12. Shea, "Protecting the Ozone Layer," 86–87.

13. Haas, "Stratospheric Ozone," 165.

14. Cogan, *Stones in a Glass House,* 21.

15. Benedick, *Ozone Diplomacy,* 27.

16. Roan, *Ozone Crisis,* 49–50.

17. Benedick, *Ozone Diplomacy,* 24.

18. Ibid., 24–25; see also Stoel et al., *Fluorocarbon Regulation.*

19. Air Quality Limit Values. . . .

20. Jachtenfuchs, "The European Community and the Protection of the Ozone Layer."

21. Morrisette, "The Evolution of Policy Responses to Stratospheric Ozone Depletion," 806.

22. Ibid., 805–6.

23. Miller and Mintzer, *The Sky Is the Limit,* 3; Roan, *Ozone Crisis,* 73–76.

24. National Research Council, *Halocarbons* (1976).

25. National Research Council, *Stratospheric Ozone Depletion by Halocarbons* (1979) and *Causes and Effects of Stratospheric Ozone Reduction* (1982).

26. National Research Council, *Causes and Effects of Stratospheric Ozone Reduction* (1984).

27. Prather, "Reductions in Ozone at High Concentrations of Stratospheric Halogens," 1984.

28. WMO, *Atmospheric Ozone 1985.*

29. Petsonk, "The Role the United Nations Environment Programme," 365–65.

30. Benedick, *Ozone Diplomacy,* 40–41.

31. Sand, "Protecting the Ozone Layer," 40.

32. Ibid., 41.

33. Rowlands, *The Politics of Global Atmospheric Change,* 105–6.

34. Sand, "Protecting the Ozone Layer," 41.

35. Convention for the Protection of the Ozone Layer.

36. Ibid., Article 2.2.b.

37. See Litfin, *Ozone Discourses,* 86–92.

38. Ibid., 96–102.

39. Benedick, *Ozone Diplomacy,* 51–67.

40. Litfin, *Ozone Discourses,* 102–3.

41. Mintzer and Miller, "Stratospheric Ozone Depletion," 87–88.

42. Parson, "Protecting the Ozone Layer," 41.

43. Jachtenfuchs, "The European Community and the Protection of the Ozone Layer," 262–67; Maxwell and Weiner, "Green Consciousness or Dollar Diplomacy?," 30–31.

44. Benedick, *Ozone Diplomacy*, 94–97.

45. Protocol on Substances that Deplete the Ozone Layer.

46. Benedick, *Ozone Diplomacy*, 78.

47. Ibid., 80–81.

48. Ibid., 93.

49. Ibid., 117.

50. Rowlands, *The Politics of Global Atmospheric Change*, 115.

51. Haas, "Stratospheric Ozone," 160.

52. Watson et al., "Ozone Trends Panel Executive Summary."

53. See Burke, "The Year of the Greens."

54. Benedick, *Ozone Diplomacy*, 114.

55. Parson, "Protecting the Ozone Layer," 46.

56. Maxwell and Weiner, "Green Consciousness or Dollar Diplomacy?," 32–36.

57. UNEP, *Synthesis Report*.

58. Benedick, *Ozone Diplomacy*, 124–26.

59. Adjustments and Amendments to the Montreal Protocol on Substances that Deplete the Ozone Layer (London, 1990).

60. Ibid., 121–22.

61. Ibid, 131.

62. See Wood, "The Multilateral Fund for the Implementation of the Montreal Protocol."

63. Benedick, *Ozone Diplomacy*, 196.

64. Adjustments and Amendments to the Montreal Protocol on Substances that Deplete the Ozone Layer (Copenhagen, 1992).

65. Rowlands, "The Fourth Meeting of the Parties to the Montreal Protocol," 27–28.

66. Parson and Greene, "The Complex Chemistry of the International Ozone Agreements," 36.

67. *Wall Street Journal,* January 16, 1996, 2.

68. Press Release, United Nations Environment Programme, Vienna, December 7, 1995. See also *New Scientist*, December 16, 1995, 7.

69. Haas, "Stratospheric Ozone," 174.

70. Parson and Greene, "The Complex Chemistry of the International Ozone Agreements," 37.

71. Chemical Manufacturers Association, *Chemical Economics Handbook,* 543.70001C.

72. Parson, "Protecting the Ozone Layer," 55–56.

73. Parson and Greene, "The Complex Chemistry of the International Ozone Agreements," 36–37.

74. Chemical Manufacturers Association, *Chemical Economics Handbook,* 543.7000D&F.

75. *Chemical & Engineering News,* January 3, 1994, 9.

76. *Christian Science Monitor,* October 23, 1995, 3.

77. *Chemical and Engineering News,* April 24, 1994, 8.

78. Metchis, "Protecting the Ozone Layer," 20.

79. *Our Planet,* no. 2, 1995, 25–28.

80. Parson and Greene, "The Complex Chemistry of the International Ozone Agreements," 55–60.

81. Rowlands, "The Fourth Meeting of the Parties to the Montreal Protocol," 29.

82. Parson and Greene, "The Complex Chemistry of the International Ozone Agreements," 38–41.

83. *Chemical & Engineering News,* September 11, 1994, 5.

84. Rowlands, "The Fourth Meeting of the Parties to the Montreal Protocol," 30.

CHAPTER 7: THE CLIMATE CHANGE REGIME

1. Houghton, *Global Warming,* 28–39.

2. Engelman, *Stabilizing the Atmosphere* and "Imagining a Stabilized Atmosphere."

3. Keeling, "Global Historical CO_2 Emissions," 503.

4. Calculated from Marland et al., "Global, Regional, and National CO_2 Emissions," 508.

5. Brown et al., *Vital Signs 1994,* 68.

6. Calculated from Marland et al., "Global, Regional, and National CO_2 Emissions," 509; World Resources Institute, *World Resources 1996–97,* 330.

7. Houghton, *Global Warming,* 29.

8. World Resources Institute, *World Resources 1994–95,* 200.

9. IPCC, *Policy Makers Summary of the Scientific Assessment of Climate Change,* 8.

10. Subak, "Assessing Emissions," 59.

11. IPCC, *Climate Change,* xxxiii.

12. Ibid.

13. Flavin and Lenssen, *Power Surge,* 25.

14. Calculated from figures in World Resources Institute, *World Resources 1994–95,* 364–65.

15. See Hammond et al., "Calculating National Accountability for Climate Change."

16. World Resources Institute, *World Resources 1994–95,* 362–63.

17. Paterson and Grubb, "The International Politcs of Climate Change," 298–99.

18. For example, Cooper, "What Might Man-Induced Climate Change

Mean?" If human beings were disrupting climatic patterns, then presumably they could also act to minimize the amount of undesired change that would take place.

19. Davies, *Forty Years of Progress and Achievement,* 101–2.

20. See Turco et al., "Nuclear Winter"; Sagan, "Nuclear War and Climate Change."

21. UNEP/WMO/ICSU, *An Assessment of the Role of Carbon Dioxide.*

22. Cavander and Jäger, "The History of Germany's Response to Climate Change," 11.

23. Kowalock, "Research Lessons from Acid Rain," 36.

24. Bush and Dukakis, "Promises to Keep."

25. Hansen, "The Greenhouse Effect."

26. Weart, "From the Nuclear Frying Pan into the Global Fire," 27.

27. Kowalock, "Research Lessons from Acid Rain," 36.

28. Harvey, "Tracking Urban CO2 Emissions in Toronto."

29. Bodansky, "The United Nations Framework Convention on Climate Change," 466.

30. See, for example, Balling, *The Heated Debate;* Singer, "Warming Theories Need Warning Label."

31. *New York Times,* June 10, 1992, 8.

32. Soroos and Nikitina, "The World Meteorological Organization as a Purveyer of Global Public Goods."

33. World Conference on the Changing Atmosphere, *Conference Statement.*

34. "The Hague Declaration on the Environment," UNEP Global Change Fact Sheet No. 217.

35. Declaration of the Hague.

36. Declaration by the Ministerial Conference on Atmospheric Pollution and Climate Change.

37. *Science News,* December 16, 1989, 394–95, 397.

38. "The Bergen Conference and Its Proposals for Addressing Climate Change." UNEP Climate Change Fact Sheet No. 220.

39. *Christian Science Monitoring,* April 20, 1990, 7.

40. *Christian Science Monitoring,* November 9, 1990.

41. Conference Statement, 497.

42. IEA/OECD, *Climate Change Policy Initiatives.*

43. Ibid.

44. *Acid News,* December 1991, 7–9.

45. IEA/OECD, *Climate Change Policy Initiatives,* 16–17, 26–27; Skjærseth, "The Climate Change Policy of the EC," 31.

46. IEA/OECD, *Climate Change Policy Initiatives,* 24–25.

47. Bergesen and Sydnes, "Protection of the Global Climate . . .," 41.

48. Zaelke and Cameron, "Global Warming and Climate Change," 282.

49. Ramakrishna, "Third World Countries in the Policy Response to Global Climate Change," 427–28.

50. "The Tata Conference on Global Warming and Climate Change," UNEP Climate Change Fact Sheet No. 223.

51. Ibid., 425–27.

52. UNEP, "Regional Climate Conferences in Africa, Asia, and Latin America."

53. "Conferences Addressing the Special Concerns of Developing Countries," UNEP Climate Change Factsheet No. 222.

54. See Eleri, "Africa's Decline and Greenhouse Politics."

55. *Our Planet,* No. 1 (1994): 4–5.

56. UNGA Resolution 212(XLV)

57. Bodansky, "The United Nations Framework Convention on Climate Change," 474.

58. Ibid., 492–517; Borione and Ripert, "Exercising Common but Differentiated Responsibility," 82–88.

59. Bergesen and Sydnes, "Protection of the Global Climate . . .," 39–41.

60. Bodansky, "The United Nations Framework Convention on Climate Change," 495–96; see also Nitze, "A Failure of Presidential Leadership."

61. See Gray and Rivkin, "A 'No Regrets' Environmental Policy."

62. Wirth and Lashof, "Beyond Vienna and Montreal," 514.

63. Paterson and Grubb, "The International Politics of Climate Change," 299.

64. Bodansky, "The United Nations Framework Convention on Climate Change," 498.

65. Ibid., 502–3.

66. Rowlands, "The Climate Change Negotiations," 148.

67. IEA/OECD, *Climate Change Policy Initiatives: 1994 Update,* 175–80.

68. Flavin and Tunali, "Getting Warmer," 12.

69. *National Journal,* July 18, 1993, 2028–32.

70. Victor and Salt, "From Rio to Berlin," 10–14.

71. Rowlands, "The Climate Change Negotiations," 150.

72. Flavin and Tunali, "Getting Warmer."

73. Flavin, "Facing Up to the Risks of Climate Change," 32.

74. Rowlands, "The Climate Change Negotiations," 153–57.

75. Flavin, "Facing Up to the Risks of Climate Change," 31.

76. Climate Action Network Global, "The 1995 Berlin Climate Summit."

77. Flavin and Tunali, "Getting Warmer," 16–18.

78. Flavin, "Facing Up to the Risks of Climate Change," 30.

79. See Carpenter et al., "Summary of the First Conference of the Parties. . . ."

80. Paterson and Grubb, "The International Politics of Climate Change," 299.

CHAPTER 8:
THE ATMOSPHERE AS A GLOBAL COMMONS

1. Quoted in Ostrom, *Governing the Commons*, 2.
2. Lloyd, *Two Lectures on the Checks to Population*.
3. See Weber, "Protecting Oceanic Fisheries and Jobs."
4. G. Hardin, *Living within Limits*.
5. Ostrom, *Governing the Commons*.
6. See Soroos, "The Commons in the Sky."
7. Ostrom, *Managing the Commons*, 30.
8. Oakerson, "Analyzing the Commons," 42.
9. Ibid., 44–45.
10. Ostrom, *Managing the Commons*, 30.
11. Olson, *The Logic of Collective Action*.
12. R. Hardin, *Collective Action*, 17.
13. Oakerson, "Analyzing the Commons," 44.
14. See Buck, "No Tragedy of the Commons."
15. Bromley, *Environment and Economy*, 29.
16. While the term *res communis* literally means "common property," in the international sphere it has evolved to refer to that which is unowned and nonappropriable, but which all are available for all to use, as under the doctrine of the "freedom on the seas." Accordingly, while domains designated the "common heritage of mankind," such as the seabed and moon, are considered the common property of humanity (see next paragraph), the term *res communis* is generally not used to describe them (Kiss, "The Common Heritage of Mankind," 430.
17. Ibid., 423–24.
18. See Luard, *The Control of the Sea-bed*, 83–96.
19. Declaration of Principles Governing the Seabed and Subsoil Thereof, GA. Res. 2749 (XXV); Convention on the Law of the Sea.
20. Agreement Governing the Activities of the States on the Moon and other Celestial Bodies.
21. See Kiss, "The Common Heritage of Mankind."
22. Birnie and Boyle, *International Law and the Environment*, 120–21.
23. Lay and Taubenfeld, *The Law Relating to Activities of Man in Space*, 36–37; Nayar, "Regimes, Power, and International Aviation," 146–47.
24. Jönsson, "Sphere of Flying," 276–81.
25. See Christol, *The Modern International Law of Outer Space*, 435–546.
26. See Vicuña, "State Responsibility, Liability, and Remedial Measures."
27. Samuels, "International Control of Weather Modification Activities."
28. Taubenfeld, "International Environmental Law."
29. Birnie and Boyle, *International Law and the Environment*, 390.

30. Utton, "International Water Quality Law."

31. Boyle, "International Law and Protection of the Global Atmosphere," 8–9.

32. Ibid., 11.

33. Soroos, "The Tragedy of the Commons in Global Perspective"; see also Mirovitskaya and Soroos, "Socialism and the Tragedy of the Commons."

34. See Sweeny et al., *Cases and Materials on the International Legal System,* 268.

Chapter 9: The Pursuit of Environmental Security

1. Soroos, "Environmental Security," 20.

2. Romm, *Defining National Security,* 3.

3. Sprout and Sprout, *Foundations of International Politics.*

4. Meadows et al., *The Limits to Growth.*

5. Taylor, "The Legitimate Claims of National Security," 592.

6. For example, Brown, *Redefining National Security;* Ullman, "Redefining Security"; Mathews, "Redefining Security."

7. For example, Mische, "Ecological Security and the Need to Reconceptualize Sovereignty"; Timoshenko, "Ecological Security"; Broadus and Vartanov, *The Oceans and Environmental Security;* DeBardeleben and Hannigan, *Environmental Security and Quality after Communism;* Dabelko and Dabelko, "Environmental Security."

8. Westing, "The Environmental Component of Comprehensive Security."

9. UN Commission on Environment and Development, *Our Common Future,* 290–307.

10. Schrijver, "International Organization for Environmental Security"; Timoshenko, "Ecological Security," 423–24.

11. Gleick, "Water and Conflict in the Middle East."

12. Myers, "Environment and Security," 28–32.

13. Gurr, "On the Political Consequences of Scarcity and Economic Decline"; Homer-Dixon, "Environmental Changes as Causes of Acute Conflict" and "Environmental Scarcities and Violent Conflict."

14. For example, Deudney, "Environment and Security"; Brock, "Security Through Defending the Environment"; Dalby, "Security, Modernity, Ecology."

15. Soroos, "Global Change, Environmental Security, and the Prisoner's Dilemma," 320.

16. Brown et al., *Vital Signs, 1992,* 84–85.

17. Buzan, *People, States, and Fear,* 73.

18. Mitchell and Ericksen, "Effects of Climate Change on Weather-Related Disasters," 10.

19. See Flavin, "Storm Warning."

20. UNEP, *Environmental Effects Panel Report,* 34–35; see also Stone, "If the Mercury Soars, So May Health Hazards."

21. Cited in *New Scientist,* August 11, 1990, 17.

22. *Acid News,* April 1995, 14–15

23. Parry and Swaminathan, "Effects of Climate Change on Food Production."

24. *Christian Science Monitor,* December 29, 1993, 11–14.

25. Jacobson, "Holding Back the Sea," 79.

26. *New York Times,* February 17, 1992, A3.

27. Jacobson, "Holding Back the Sea," 89.

28. Mitchell and Ericksen, "Effects of Climate Change on Weather-Related Disasters," 145.

29. Broadus, "Possible Impacts of, and Adjustments to, Sea Level Rise."

30. See Mitchell and Ericksen, "Effects of Climate Change on Weather-Related Disasters."

31. Myers, "Environmental Refugees in a Globally Warmed World."

32. Osgood, *An Alternative to War or Surrender.*

33. Independent Commission on Disarmament and Security Issues, *Common Security;* Smoke, *National Security and the Nuclear Dilemma.*

34. Treaty on the Non-Proliferation of Nuclear Weapons.

35. Treaty on the Limitation of Anti-Ballistic Missile Systems.

36. UNEP, *Register of International Treaties . . .;* Haas and Sundgren, "Evolving International Environmental Law," 405.

37. International Fund for Compensation for Oil Pollution Damage.

38. Convention on Assistance in the Case of a Nuclear Accident or Radiological Emergency.

39. Jervis, "Cooperation under the Security Dilemma."

40. Smoke, *National Security and the Nuclear Dilemma,* 133.

41. For example, Rapoport and Chummah, *Prisoner's Dilemma;* Axelrod, *The Evolution of Cooperation.*

42. Brams, *Superpower Games.*

43. Nordhaus, "Economic Approaches to Greenhouse Warming," 44; see also Cooper, "United States Policy Toward the Global Environment."

44. For example, Singer, "Benefits of Global Warming."

45. Committee on Science, Engineering, and Public Policy, *Policy Implications of Greenhouse Warming,* 501–14.

46. Stone, *The Gnat is Older than Man,* 161.

47. Beckerman, "Global Warming and International Action," 283.

48. Cline, *The Economics of Global Warming.*

49. See Rowlands, *The Politics of Global Atmospheric Change,* 132–42.

CHAPTER 10: CONCLUSIONS

1. Young, "The Politics of International Regime Formation," 371–72.

2. On the role of science and regime formation see Andresen and Østreng, *International Resource Management*; E. Haas, *When Knowledge is Power*; P. Haas, *Saving the Mediterranean*; and Litfin, *Ozone Discourses*.

3. See Sprinz and Vaahtoranta, "The Interest Based Explanation of International Environmental Policy."

4. Susskind, *Environmental Diplomacy*, 30–37.

5. For example, the January 22, 1996, issue of *Newsweek* carried a cover story entitled "The Hot Zone: Blizzards, Floods & Hurricanes: Blame Global Warming."

6. Climate Action Network Global, "The 1995 Berlin Summit."

7. Calculated from figures in Engelman, "Imagining a Stabilized Atmosphere."

8. "The Toronto and Ottawa Conferences and the 'Law of the Atmosphere,'" UNEP Climate Change Fact Sheet 215, 1993.

BIBLIOGRAPHY

Advisory Committee on Weather Control. "Importance of Weather and Its Modification." *Bulletin of American Meteorological Society* 39 (1957): 483–597.

Albritton, Dan. "Our Ozone Shield." *Reports to the Nation on Our Changing Planet*
2 (1992).

Alcamo, Joseph, Roderick Shaw, and Leen Hordijk, eds. *The RAINS Model of
Acidification: Science and Strategies in Europe.* Dordrecht: Kluwer Academic
Publishers, 1990.

Aldhous, Peter. "Dissent Hits Climate Accord." *Nature* 348 (1990): 188.

Andersson, Catharina. "A European Monitoring System." *Acid Magazine* 8 (1989):
4.

Andresen, Steinar, and Willie Østreng, eds. *International Resource Management:
The Role of Science and Politics.* London: Belhaven Press, 1989.

Anthes, Richard A. *Meteorology.* 6th ed. New York: Macmillan, 1992.

Anthes, Richard A., Hans A. Panofsky, John J. Cahir, and Albert Rango. *The Atmosphere.* Columbus, Ohio: Merrill, 1975.

Arrhenius, Svante A. "On the Influence of Carbonic Acid in the Air upon the
Temperature." *Philosophical Magazine and Journal of Science* 41 (1896): 237–76.

Atwood, Wallace W. Jr. "The International Geophysical Year: A Twentieth-century
Achievement in International Cooperation." *Department of State Bulletin* 35
(1956): 880–86.

Atwood, Wallace W. Jr. "The International Geophysical Year in Retrospective."
Department of State Bulletin 40 (1959): 682–89.

Axelrod, Robert. *The Evolution of Cooperation.* New York: Basic Books, 1985.

Ball, Howard. *Justice Downwind: America's Atomic Testing Program in the 1950s.*
New York: Oxford University Press, 1986.

Balling, Robert C. Jr. *The Heated Debate: Greenhouse Predictions Versus Climate Reality.* San Francisco: Pacific Research Institute for Public Policy, 1992.

Barnola, J. M., D. Raynaud, Y. S. Korotkevich, and C. Lorius. "Vostok Ice Core
Provides 160,000-year Record of Atmospheric CO_2." *Nature* 329 (1987): 408–
14.

Barrie, Leonard A. "Arctic Air Pollution: An Overview of Current Knowledge."
Atmospheric Environment 20 (1986): 643–66.

Barry, Roger G., and Richard J. Chorley. *Atmosphere, Weather and Climate.* 5th ed. New York: Methuen, 1987.

Beckerman, Wilfred. "Global Warming and International Action: An Economic Perspective." In *The International Politics of the Environment,* edited by Andrew Hurrell and Benedict Kingsbury, 253–89. New York: Oxford University Press, 1993.

Benedick, Richard E. *Ozone Diplomacy: New Directions in Safeguarding the Planet.* Cambridge, Mass.: Harvard University Press, 1991.

Bennett, A. LeRoy. *International Organizations: Principles and Issues.* 3rd ed. Englewood Cliffs, N.J.: Prentice-Hall, 1984.

Bergesen, Helge Ole, and Anne Kristin Sydnes. "Protection of the Global Climate—Ecological Utopia or Just a Long Way to Go." In *Green Globe Yearbook 1992,* 37–47. London: Oxford University Press, 1992.

Bierly, Eugene W. "The World Climate Program: Collaboration and Communication on a Global Scale." *Annuals of the American Academy of Political and Social Sciences* 495 (1988): 106–16.

Birnie, Patricia W., and Alan E. Boyle. *International Law and the Environment.* New York: Oxford University Press, 1992.

Blaustein, A., P. Hoffman, D. G. Hokit, J. Kiesecker, S. Walls, and J. Hayes. "UV Repair and Resistance to Solar UV-B in Amphibian Eggs: A Link to Population Decline." *Proceedings of the National Academy of Sciences* 91 (1994): 1791–95.

Bodansky, Daniel. "The United Nations Framework Convention on Climate Change: A Commentary." *Yale Journal of International Law* 18 (1993): 451–558.

Boehmer-Christiansen, Sonja A. "Curbing Auto Emissions in Europe." *Environment* 32 (July/August 1990): 16–20, 34–39.

Boldirev, Victor G. "Modern Data and Applications: World Climate Data Programme, World Climate Applications Programme." In *Climate Change: Science, Impacts, and Policy: Proceedings of the Second World Climate Conference,* edited by J. Jager and H. L. Ferguson, 157–61. Cambridge: Cambridge University Press, 1991.

Bolin, Bert et al. *Sweden's Case Study for the United Nations Conference on the Human Environment: Air Pollution Across National Boundaries.* Stockholm: Norstadt & Sons, 1972.

Borione, Delphine, and Jean Ripert. "Exercising Common but Differentiated Responsibility." In *Negotiating Climate Change: The Inside Story of the Rio Convention,* edited by Irving M. Mintzer and J. Amber Leonard, 77–96. Cambridge: Cambridge University Press, 1994.

Boyle, Alan E. "International Law and Protection of the Global Atmosphere: Concepts, Categories and Principles." In *International Law and Global Climate Change,* edited by Robin Churchill and David Freestone, 7–20. London: Graham & Troutman, 1991.

Bibliography

Brams, Steven J. *Superpower Games: Applying Game Theory to Superpower Conflict.* New Haven: Yale University Press, 1985.

Bridgman, Howard. *Global Air Pollution: Problems for the 1990s.* London: Belhaven Press, 1990.

Brimblecombe, Peter. *The Big Smoke: A History of Air Pollution in London since Medieval Times.* London: Methuen, 1987.

Broadus, James M. "Possible Impacts of, and Adjustments to, Sea Level Rise: The Cases of Bangladesh and Egypt." In *Climate and Sea Level Change: Observations, Projections and Implications,* edited by R. A. Warrick, E. M. Barrow, and T. M. L. Wigley, 263–75. Cambridge: Cambridge University Press, 1993.

Broadus, James M., and Raphael V. Vartanov, eds. *The Oceans and Environmental Security: Shared U.S. and Russian Perspectives.* Washington, D.C.: Island Press, 1994.

Brock, Lothar. "Security Through Defending the Environment: An Illusion?" In *New Agendas for Peace Research: Conflict and Security Reexamined,* edited by Elise Boulding, 79–102. Boulder, Colo.: Lynne Rienner, 1992.

Brodin, Yngve-W, and Johan C. I. Kuylenstierna. "Acidification and Critical Loads in Nordic Countries: A Background." *Ambio* 21 (1992): 332–38.

Bromley, Daniel W. *Environment and Economy: Property Rights and Public Policy.* Cambridge, Mass.: Basil Blackwell, 1991.

Brown, Lester. *Redefining National Security.* Worldwatch Paper No. 14. Washington, D.C.: Worldwatch Institute, 1977.

Brown, Lester, Christopher Flavin, and Hal Kane. *Vital Signs 1992: The Trends That Are Shaping Our Future.* New York: Norton, 1992.

Brown, Lester, Hal Kane, and David M. Roodman. *Vital Signs 1994: The Trends That Are Shaping Our Future.* New York: Norton, 1994.

Brown, Lester R., Nicholas Lenssen, and Hal Kane. *Vital Signs 1995: The Trends That Are Shaping Our Future.* New York: Norton, 1995.

Buck, Susan. "No Tragedy of the Commons." *Environmental Ethics* 7 (1985): 49–61.

Burke, Tom. "The Year of the Greens." *Environment* 31 (November 1989): 18–20, 41–44.

Burrows, Andrew S., Robert S. Norris, William M. Arkin, and Thomas B. Cochran. *French Nuclear Testing, 1960–1988.* New York: National Resources Defense Council, 1989.

Bush, George, and Michael Dukakis. "Promises to Keep: Ladies and Gentlemen, a Few Words on the Environment from the Next President of the United States." *Sierra* (November/December 1988): 62–65, 116.

Buzan, Barry. *People, States, and Fear: The National Security Problem in International Relations.* Chapel Hill: University of North Carolina Press, 1983.

Cagin, Seth, and Philip Dray. *Between Earth and Sky: How CFCs Changed Our World and Endangered the Ozone Layer.* New York: Pantheon Books, 1993.

Cain, Melinda L. "Carbon Dioxide and the Climate: Monitoring and a Search for Understanding." In *Environmental Protection: The International Dimension,* edited by David Kay and Harold Jacobson, 75–99. Totowa, N.J.: Allanheld, Osmun & Co., 1983.

Calendar, G. S. "The Artificial Production of CO_2 and Its Influence on Temperature." *Quarterly Journal of the Royal Meteorological Society* 64 (1938): 223–37.

Carpenter, Chad, Pamela Chasek, and Steve Wise. "Summary of the First Conference of the Parties for the Framework Convention on Climate Change." *Earth Negotiations Bulletin* 12 (April 10, 1995).

Carroll, John E. "The Acid Rain Issue in Canadian-American Relations: A Commentary." In *International Environmental Diplomacy: The Management and Resolution of Transfrontier Environmental Problems,* edited by John E. Carroll, 141–46. New York: Cambridge University Press, 1988.

Castberg, Rune. "Common Problem—Different Priorities: Nordic-Russian Environmental Cooperation and the Nikel Works on the Kola Peninsula." *International Challenges* 3 (1993): 23–33.

Cavander, Jeannine, and Jill Jäger. "The History of Germany's Response to Climate Change." *International Environmental Affairs* 5 (1993): 3–18.

Chemical Manufacturers Association. *Chemical Economics Handbook.* Menlow Park, Calif.: SRI International, February 1994.

Chiras, Daniel D. *Environmental Science: Action for a Sustainable Future.* 4th ed. Redwood City, Calif.: Benjamin/Cummings, 1994.

Chossudovsky, Evgeny. *East-West Diplomacy for the Environment in the United Nations.* New York: United Nations Institute for Training and Research, 1988.

Christol, Carl Q. *The Modern International Law of Outer Space.* New York: Pergamon Press, 1982.

Climate Impact Assessment Program (CIAP). *Report on Findings. The Effects of Stratospheric Pollution by Aircraft.* Washington, D.C.: Department of Transportation, 1974.

CLIVAR Scientific Steering Group. *CLIVAR: A Study of Climate Variability and Predictability. Science Plan.* WMO/TD No. 690, August 1995.

Cline, William R. *The Economics of Global Warming.* Washington, D.C.: Institute for International Economics, 1992.

Cogan, Douglas G. *Stones in a Glass House: CFCs and Ozone Depletion.* Washington, D.C.: Investor Responsibility Research Center, 1988.

Committee on Science, Engineering, and Public Policy. *Policy Implications of Greenhouse Warming: Mitigation, Adaptation, and the Science Base.* Washington, D.C.: National Academy Press, 1992.

Cooper, Charles F. "What Might Man-Induced Climate Change Mean?" *Foreign Affairs* 56 (1978): 500–520.

Cooper, Richard N. "United States Policy Toward the Global Environment." In *The International Politics of the Environment,* edited by Andrew Hurrell and

Bibliography

Benedict Kingsbury, 290–312. New York: Oxford University Press, 1993.

Cowling, Ellis B. "Acid Precipitation in Historical Perspective." *Environmental Science & Technology* (1982): 110A–22A.

Craig, Paul R., and John A. Jungerman. *Nuclear Arms Race: Technology and Society.* New York: McGraw-Hill, 1986.

Critical Loads for Air Pollutants. Report of the Third International NGO Strategy Seminar on Air Pollution. Göteborg, Sweden, April 10–11, 1992.

Crump, Andy. *Dictionary of Environment and Development: People, Places, Ideas and Organizations.* Cambridge: MIT Press, 1993.

Crutzen, Paul. "The Influence of Nitrogen Oxides on the Atmospheric Ozone Content." *Quarterly Journal of the Royal Meteorological Society* 71 (1970): 320–25.

D'Amato, Anthony A. "Legal Aspects of the French Nuclear Tests." *American Journal of International Law* 61 (1967): 66–77.

Dabelko, Geoffrey, and David D. Dabelko. "Environmental Security: Issues of Conflict and Redefinition." *WWW Report* 1 (1995): 3–13.

Dalby, Simon. "Security, Modernity, Ecology: The Dilemmas of Post Cold War Security Discourse." *Alternatives* 17 (1992): 95–134.

Darnay, Arsen J., ed. *Statistical Record of the Environment.* Detroit: Gale Research Inc., 1992.

Davies, Arthur, ed. *Forty Years of Progress and Achievement: A Historical Review of WMO.* Geneva: World Meteorological Organization, 1990.

de Koning, H. W., and A. Köhler. "Monitoring Global Air Pollution." *Environmental Science & Technology* 12 (1978): 884–89.

DeBardeleben, Joan, and John Hannigan, eds. *Environmental Security and Quality after Communism.* Boulder, Colo.: Westview Press, 1994.

Deudney, Daniel. "Environment and Security: Muddled Thinking." *Bulletin of the Atomic Scientists* 47 (1991): 22–28.

Divine, Robert A. *Blowing on the Wind: The Nuclear Test Ban Debate 1954–1960.* New York: Oxford University Press, 1978.

Dotto, Lydia, and Harold Schiff. *The Ozone War.* Garden City, N.Y.: Doubleday, 1978.

Downing, R. J., J. P. Hettelingh, and P. A. M. de Smet. *Calculations and Mapping of Critical Loads in Europe: Status Report 1993.* Bilthoven, Netherlands: RIVM-Coordination Center for Effects, 1995.

Edgerton, Lynne T. *The Rising Tide: Global Warming and World Sea Levels.* Washington, D.C.: Island Press, 1991.

Ehrlich, Paul R., and Anne H. Ehrlich. *Healing the Planet: Strategies for Resolving the Environmental Crisis.* Reading, Mass.: Addison-Wesley, 1991.

Eisenbud, Merril. *Environmental Radioactivity: From Natural, Industrial, and Military Sources.* 3d ed. Orlando, Fla.: Academic Press, 1987.

Eleri, Ewah Otu. "Africa's Decline and Greenhouse Politics." *International Environmental Affairs* 6 (1994): 133–48.

Elsom, Derek M. *Atmospheric Pollution: A Global Problem.* 2d ed. Oxford, U.K.: Blackwell, 1992.

EMEP. *Transboundary Acidifying Pollution in Europe: Calculated Fields and Budgets 1985–93.* Oslo: EMEP MSC-W Report 1/94, 1994.

Engelman, Robert. "Imagining a Stabilized Atmosphere: Population and Consumption Interactions in Greenhouse Gas Emissions." *Journal of Environment and Development* 4 (1995): 111–40.

Engelman, Robert. *Stabilizing the Atmosphere: Population, Consumption and Greenhouse Gases.* Washington, D.C.: Population Action International, 1994.

Farman, J. C., B. G. Gardiner, and J. D. Shanklin. "Large Losses of Total Ozone in Antarctica Reveal Seasonal CLO_x/NO_x Interaction." *Nature* 315 (1985): 207–10.

Feshback, Murray, and Alfred Friendly Jr. *Ecocide in the USSR: Health and Nature Under Siege.* New York: Basic Books, 1992.

Firth, Stewart. *Nuclear Playground.* Honolulu: University of Hawaii Press, 1987.

Fisher, David E. *Fire and Ice: The Greenhouse Effect, Ozone Depletion, and Nuclear Winter.* New York: Harper and Row, 1990.

Flavin, Christopher. "Facing Up to the Risks of Climate Change." In Lester Brown et al., *The State of the World—1996*, 21–39. New York: Norton, 1996.

Flavin, Christopher. *Power Surge: Guide to the Coming Energy Revolution.* New York: Norton, 1994.

Flavin, Christopher, and Nicholas Lenssen. "Storm Warnings: Climate Change Hits the Insurance Industry." *World Watch* 7 (1994): 10–20.

Flavin, Christopher, and Odil Tunali. "Getting Warmer: Looking for a Way out of the Climate Impasse." *World Watch* 8 (March/April 1995): 10–19.

Freedman, Lawrence. *The Evolution of Nuclear Strategy.* 2d ed. New York: St. Martin's Press, 1989.

French Ministry of Foreign Affairs. *White Paper on French Nuclear Tests.* Paris: Ministère des affaires éstrangères, 1973.

Gladwin, Thomas N., Judith L. Ugelow, and Ingo Walter. "A Global View of CFC Sources and Policies to Reduce Emissions." In *The Economics of Managing Chlorofluorocarbons: Stratospheric Ozone and Climate Issues,* edited by John H. Cumberland, James R. Hibbs, and Irving Hoch, 64–113. Washington, D.C.: Resources for the Future, 1982.

Gleick, Peter H. "Water and Conflict in the Middle East." *Environment* 36 (April 1994): 6–15, 35–42.

Golich, Vicki L. "Collaboration in the Commercial Aircraft Industry." *International Organization* 46 (1992): 901–34.

Golich, Vicki L., and Terry F. Young. "Resolution of the United States–Canadian Conflict over Acid Rain Controls." *Journal of Environment and Development* 2 (1993): 63–110.

Gore, Al. *Earth in the Balance: Ecology and the Human Spirit.* Boston: Houghton Mifflin, 1992.

Bibliography

Graedel, T. E., and Paul J. Crutzen. *Atmospheric Change: An Earth System Perspective.* New York: W. H. Freeman, 1993.

Gray, C. Boyden, and David B. Rivkin Jr. "A 'No Regrets' Environmental Policy." *Foreign Policy* 83 (1991): 47–65.

Gribbin, John. *What's Wrong with the Weather? The Climatic Threat of the 21st Century.* New York: Charles Scribner's Sons, 1978.

Gurr, Ted Robert. "On the Political Consequences of Scarcity and Economic Decline." *International Studies Quarterly* 29 (1995): 51–75.

Haas, Ernst B. *When Knowledge Is Power: Three Models of Change in International Organization.* Berkeley: University of California Press, 1990.

Haas, Peter M. *Saving the Mediterranean: The Politics of International Environmental Cooperation.* New York: Columbia University Press, 1990.

Haas, Peter M. "Stratospheric Ozone: Regime Formation in Stages." *Polar Politics: Creating International Environmental Regimes,* edited by Oran R. Young and Gail Osherenko, 152–85. Ithaca, N.Y.: Cornell University Press, 1993.

Haas, Peter M., with Jan Sundgren. "Evolving International Environmental Law: Changing Practices of National Sovereignty." In *Global Accord: Environmental Challenges and International Responses,* edited by Nazli Choucri, 401–30. Cambridge: MIT Press, 1993.

Halperin, Morton H., and Dwight H. Perkins. *Communist China and Arms Control.* New York: Praeger, 1965.

Hammond, Allen L., Eric Rodenburg, and William R. Moomaw. "Calculating National Accountability for Climate Change." *Environment* 33 (January/February 1991): 11–15, 33–35.

Hansen, James E. "The Greenhouse Effect: Impacts on Current Global Temperature and Regional Heatwaves." In *The Challenge of Global Warming,* edited by Dean E. Abrahamson, 35–43. Washington, D.C.: Island Press, 1989.

Hardin, Garrett. *Living within Limits: Ecology, Economics, and Population Taboos.* New York: Oxford University Press, 1993.

Hardin, Garrett. "The Tragedy of the Commons." *Science* 162 (1968): 1243–48.

Hardin, Garrett. "The Tragedy of the *Unmanaged* Commons: Population and the Disguises of Providence." In *Commons without Tragedy,* edited by Robert V. Andelson, 165–82. London: Shepheard-Walwyn, 1991.

Hardin, Russell. *Collective Action.* Baltimore: Johns Hopkins University Press, 1982.

Harvey, L. D. Danny. "Tackling Urban CO_2 Emissions in Toronto." *Environment* 35 (September 1993): 16–20, 38–44.

Hettelingh, Jean-Pierre, R. J. Downing, and P. A. M. de Smet. "The Critical Load Concept for the Control of Acidification." In *Acidification Research: Evaluation and Policy Applications,* edited by T. Schneider, 161–74. Amsterdam: Elsevier, 1992.

Hettelingh, J.-P., R. J. Downing, and P. A. M. de Smet, "Maps of Critical Sulphur Deposition, and Exceedences." In R. J. Downing, J.-P. Hettelingh, and P. A. M. de Smet, *Calculation and Mapping of Critical Loads in Europe; Status Report 1993*. Bilthoven, Netherlands: RIVM-Coordination Center for Effects, 1995.

Hileman, Bette, "The 1982 Stockholm Conference on Acidification of the Environment." *Environmental Science and Technology* 17 (1993): 15–18.

Holifield, Chet. "Congressional Hearings on Radioactive Fall-out." *Bulletin of the Atomic Scientists* 14 (1958): 52–54.

Holloway, David. *The Soviet Union and the Arms Race*. New Haven: Yale University Press, 1983.

Holloway, David. *Stalin and the Bomb: The Soviet Union and Atomic Energy 1939–1956*. New Haven: Yale University Press, 1994.

Homer-Dixon, Thomas F. "Environmental Changes as Causes of Acute Conflict." *International Security* 16 (1991): 76–116.

Homer-Dixon, Thomas F. "Environmental Scarcities and Violent Conflict: Evidence from States." *International Security* 19 (1994): 5–40.

Houghton, John T. *Global Warming: The Complete Briefing*. Oxford, U.K.: Lion Publishing, 1994.

Houghton, John T., L. G. Meira Filho, B. A. Callander, N. Harris, A. Kattenberg, and K. Maskell, eds. *Climate Change 1995*. Cambridge: Cambridge University Press, 1996.

Independent Commission on Disarmament and Security Issues (Palme Commission). *Common Security: A Blueprint for Survival*. New York: Simon and Schuster, 1982.

Intergovernmental Panel on Climate Change (IPCC). *Climate Change: The IPCC Scientific Assessment*. Cambridge: Cambridge University Press, 1990.

Intergovernmental Panel on Climate Change (IPCC). *Climate Change: The IPCC Response Strategies*. Washington, D.C.: Island Press, 1991.

Intergovernmental Panel on Climate Change (IPCC). *Climate Change 1992: The Supplementary Report to the IPCC Scientific Assessment*. Cambridge: Cambridge University Press, 1992.

Intergovernmental Panel on Climate Change (IPCC). *Climate Change 1994: Radiative Forcing of Climate Change*. Cambridge: Cambridge University Press, 1995.

Intergovernmental Panel on Climate Change (IPCC). *Policy Makers Summary of the Scientific Assessment of Climate Change*. Nairobi: IPCC, 1990.

International Energy Agency (IEA)/Organization for Economic Cooperation and Development (OECD). *Climate Change Policy Initiatives*. Paris: OECD, 1992.

International Energy Agency (IEA)/Organization for Economic Cooperation and Development (OECD). *Climate Change Policy Initiatives: 1994 Update, Volume I*. Paris: OECD, 1994.

International Geosphere-Biosphere Programme. *Global Change: Reducing Uncertainties*. Stockholm: Royal Swedish Academy of Sciences, 1992.

Bibliography

International Physicians for the Prevention of Nuclear War (IPPNW) and the
Institute for Energy and Environmental Research (IEER). *Radioactive Heaven
and Earth: The Health and Environmental Effects of Nuclear Weapons Testing In,
On, and Above the Earth.* New York: Apex Press, 1991.

Jachtenfuchs, Markus. "The European Community and the Protection of the
Ozone Layer." *Journal of Common Market Studies* 28 (1990): 261–77.

Jack, Homer. "The Asian-African Conference." *Bulletin of the Atomic Scientists* 11
(1955): 221–22.

Jackson, C. Ian. "A Tenth Anniversary Review of the ECE Convention on
Long-Range Transboundary Air Pollution." *International Environmental Affairs* 2 (1990): 217–26.

Jacobson, Harold K., and Martin F. Price. *A Framework for Research on the Human
Dimensions of Global Environmental Change.* ISSC / UNESCO Series No. 3. Paris:
International Social Science Council, 1990.

Jacobson, Harold K., and Eric Stein. *Diplomats, Scientists, and Politicians: The United
States and the Nuclear Test Ban Negotiations.* Ann Arbor: University of Michigan Press, 1966.

Jacobson, Jodi I. "Holding Back the Sea." In Lester R. Brown et al., *State of the
World 1990*, 79–97. New York: Norton, 1990.

Jancar, Barbara. "Eastern Europe and the Former Soviet Union." In *Environmental Politics in the International Arena*, edited by Sheldon Kamieniecki, 199–222.
Albany: State University of New York Press, 1993.

Jancar, Barbara. "The Environmental Attractor in the Former USSR: Ecology and Regional Change." In *The State and Social Power in Global Environmental Politics*, edited by Ronnie D. Lipschutz and Ken Conca, 158–84.
New York: Columbia University Press, 1993.

Jervis, Robert. "Cooperation under the Security Dilemma." *World Politics*
30 (1978): 167–214.

Johnston, Harold. "Reduction of Stratospheric Ozone by Nitrogen Oxide
Catalysts from Supersonic Transport Exhaust." *Science* 173 (1971): 517–
22.

Jönsson, Christer. "Sphere of Flying: The Politics of International Aviation."
International Organization 35 (1981): 273–302.

Juda, Lawrence. "Negotiating a Treaty on Environmental Modification
Warfare: The Convention on Environmental Warfare and Its Impact Upon
Arms Control Negotiations." *International Organization* 32 (1978): 975–91.

Kathren, Ronald L. *Radioactivity in the Environment: Sources, Distribution, and
Surveillance.* London: Harwood Academic Publishers, 1984.

Keeling, D. C. "Global Historical CO_2 Emissions." In *Trends '93: A Compendium
of Data on Global Change*, edited by Thomas A. Boden, Dale P. Kaiser, Robert J.
Sepanski, and Frederick W. Stoss, 501–4. Oak Ridge, Tenn.: Oak Ridge National Laboratory, 1994.

Keller, Edward A. *Environmental Geology.* Columbus, Ohio: Merrill, 1988.

Kellogg, William W. "Mankind's Impact on Climate: The Evolution of Awareness." *Climate Change* 10 (1987): 113–36.

Kerr, J. B., and C. T. McElroy. "Evidence of Large Upward Trends of Ultraviolet-B Radiation Linked to Ozone Depletion." *Science* 2662 (1993): 1032–34.

Kiss, Alexandre, "The Common Heritage of Mankind: Utopia or Reality." *International Journal* 11 (1985): 423–21.

Kiss, Alexandre, and Dinah Shelton. *International Environmental Law.* Ardsley-on-Hudson, N.Y.: Transnational Publishers, 1991.

Köhler, A. "WMO's Activities on Background Atmospheric Pollution and Integrated Monitoring and Research." *Environmental Monitoring and Assessment* 11 (1988): 253–68.

Kotov, Vladimir, and Elena Nikitina. "Russia and International Environmental Cooperation." In *Green Globe Yearbook 1995,* 17–27. New York: Oxford University Press, 1995.

Kowalock, Michael E. "Research Lessons from Acid Rain, Ozone Depletion, and Global Warming." *Environment* 35 (July–August 1993): 12–20, 35–38.

Kriz, Margaret E. "Dunning the Midwest." *National Journal* 22 (1990): 893–97.

Laird, Robin F. *France, the Soviet Union, and the Nuclear Weapons Issue.* Boulder, Colo.: Westview Press, 1985.

Lapp, Ralph E. *The Voyage of the Lucky Dragon.* New York: Harper and Row, 1958.

Lay, S. Houston, and Howard J. Taubenfeld. *The Law Relating to Activities of Man in Space.* Chicago: University of Chicago Press, 1970.

Leggett, Jeremy. "Global Warming: The Worst Case." *Bulletin of the Atomic Scientists* 48 (1992): 28–33.

Levy, Marc A. "European Acid Rain: The Power of Tote-Board Diplomacy." In *Institutions for Earth: Sources of Effective International Environmental Protection,* edited by Peter M. Haas, Robert O. Keohane, and Marc A. Levy, 75–132. Cambridge: MIT Press, 1993.

Levy, Marc A. "International Co-operation to Combat Acid Rain." In *Green Globe Yearbook 1995,* 59–67. New York: Oxford University Press, 1995.

Lewis, John Wilson, and Xue Litai. *China Builds the Bomb.* Stanford: Stanford University Press, 1988.

Lind, Don. "The Earth-Home We See from Space." *National Forum* 75 (1995): 13–15.

Litfin, Karen T. *Ozone Discourses: Science and Politics in Global Environmental Co-operation.* New York: Columbia University Press, 1994.

Lloyd, William Forster. *Two Lectures on the Checks to Population.* 1833 reprint. New York: Augustus M. Kelley, 1968.

Lovelock, James E. "Atmospheric Fluorine Compounds as Indicators of Air Movement." *Nature* 230 (1971): 379.

Luard, Evan. *The Control of the Sea-bed: A New International Issue.* London: Heinemann, 1974.

Bibliography

Lydolph, Paul E. *The Climate of the Earth.* Totowa, N.J.: Rowman & Allanheld, 1985.

MacKenzie, James J., and Mohamed T. El-Ashry. *Ill Winds: Airborne Pollution's Toll on Trees and Crops.* Washington, D.C.: World Resources Institute, 1988.

Makhijani, Arjun, and Devin R. Gurney. *Mending the Ozone Hole: Science, Technology, and Policy.* Cambridge: MIT Press, 1995.

Malone, Peter. *The British Nuclear Deterrent.* New York: St. Martin's Press, 1984.

Malone, Thomas F. "Reflections on the Human Prospect." *Annual Review of Energy and Environment* 20 (1995): 1–19.

Mannion, A. M. *Global Environmental Change: A Natural and Cultural Environmental History.* New York: John Wiley and Sons, 1991.

Marland, G., R. J. Andres, and T. A. Boden. "Global, Regional, and National CO_2 Emissions." In *Trends '93: A Compendium of Data on Global Change,* edited by Thomas A. Boden, Dale P. Kaiser, Robert J. Sepanski, and Frederick W. Stoss, 508–84. Oak Ridge, Tenn.: Oak Ridge National Laboratory, 1994.

Mathews, Jessica Tuchman. "Redefining Security." *Foreign Affairs* 68 (1989): 162–77.

Matsuura, Shigenori. "China's Air Pollution and Japan's Response to It." *International Environmental Affairs* 7 (1995): 235–48.

Maxwell, James H., and Sanford L. Weiner. "Green Consciousness or Dollar Diplomacy? The British Response to the Threat of Ozone Depletion." *International Environmental Affairs* 5 (1993): 19–41.

May, John. *The Greenpeace Book of the Nuclear Age: The Hidden History, the Human Cost.* New York: Pantheon Books, 1989.

McBride, James H. *The Test Ban Treaty: Military, Technological, and Political Implications.* Chicago: Henry Regnery Company, 1967.

McCormick, John. *Acid Earth: The Global Threat of Acid Pollution.* 2d ed. London: Earthscan Publications, 1989.

McGovern, Thomas H. "The Economics of Extinction in Norse Greenland." In *Climate and History: Studies in Past Climates and Their Impact on Man,* edited by T. M. L. Wigley, M. J. Ingram, and G. Farmer, 404–33. Cambridge: Cambridge University Press, 1981.

McMahon, Michael S. "Balancing the Interests: An Essay on the Canadian-American Acid Rain Debate." In *International Environmental Diplomacy: The Management and Resolution of Transfrontier Environmental Problems,* edited by John E. Carroll, 147–71. New York: Cambridge University Press, 1988.

Meadows, Donella, Dennis L. Meadows, Jørgen Randers, and William W. Behrens III. *The Limits to Growth: A Report for the Club of Rome's Project on the Predicament of Man.* New York: Universe Books, 1972.

Menon, M. G. K. "Second World Climate Conference: 29 October, 1990." In *Climate Change: Science, Impacts, and Policy: Proceedings of the Second World Climate Conference,* edited by J. Jager and H. L. Ferguson, 9–12. Cambridge: Cambridge University Press, 1991.

Metchis, Karen. "Protecting the Ozone Layer: Now It's Russia's Turn." *Surviving Together* 13 (1995): 19–21.

Miller, Alan S., and Irving M. Mintzer. *The Sky Is the Limit: Strategies for Protecting the Ozone Layer.* Research Report #3. Washington, D.C.: World Resources Institute, November 1986.

Mintzer, Irving M., and Alan S. Miller. "Stratospheric Ozone Depletion: Can We Save the Sky?" In *Green Globe Yearbook 1992,* 83–91. London: Oxford University Press, 1992.

Mirovitskaya, Natalia, and Marvin S. Soroos. "Socialism and the Tragedy of the Commons: Reflections on Environmental Practice in the Soviet Union and Russia." *Journal of Environment and Development* 4 (Winter 1995): 77–109.

Mische, Patricia M. "Ecological Security and the Need to Reconceptualize Sovereignty." *Alternatives* 14 (1989): 389–427.

Mitchell, James K., and Neil J. Ericksen. "Effects of Climate Change on Weather-Related Disasters." In *Confronting Climate Change: Risks, Implications and Responses,* edited by Irving Mintzer, 141–52. New York: Cambridge University Press, 1992.

Molina, Mario J., and F. Sherwood Rowland. "Stratospheric Sink for Chlorofluoromethanes: Chlorine Atom-catalyzed Destruction of Ozone." *Nature* 249 (1974): 810–12.

Moran, Joseph M., and Michael D. Morgan. *Meteorology: The Atmosphere and the Science of Weather.* 4th ed. New York: Macmillan, 1994.

Morrisette, Peter M. "The Evolution of Policy Responses to Stratospheric Ozone Depletion." *Natural Resources Journal* 29 (1989): 793–820.

Munasinghe, Mohan, and Kenneth King. *Issues and Options in Implementing the Montreal Protocol in Developing Countries.* Environment Working Paper #49. Washington, D.C.: World Bank, 1991.

Myers, Norman. "Environment and Security." *Foreign Policy* 74 (1989): 23–41.

Myers, Norman. "Environmental Refugees in a Globally Warmed World." *Bioscience* 43 (1993): 752–61.

Myers, Norman. *Ultimate Security: The Environmental Basis of Political Stability.* New York: W. W. Norton, 1993.

Mylona, Sofia. *Trends of Sulfur Dioxide Emissions, Air Concentrations and Depositions of Sulfur in Europe since 1880.* Oslo: EMEP/MSC-W Report 2/93, 1993.

National Academy of Sciences. *Nuclear Arms Control: Background and Issues.* Washington, D.C.: National Academy Press, 1985.

National Oceanic and Atmospheric Administration (NOAA), National Aeronautics and Space Administration, United Nations Environment Programme, and World Meteorological Organization. *Scientific Assessment of Ozone Depletion: 1994, Executive Summary.* Washington, D.C.: WMOP, Global Ozone Research and Monitoring Project—Report No. 37, 1994.

National Research Council. *Causes and Effects of Stratospheric Ozone Reduction: An Update.* Washington, D.C.: National Academy of Sciences, 1982.

Bibliography

National Research Council. *Causes and Effects of Stratospheric Ozone Reduction: An Update 1983*. Washington, D.C.: National Academy of Sciences, 1984.

National Research Council. *Halocarbons: Effects on Stratospheric Ozone*. Washington, D.C.: National Academy of Sciences, 1976.

National Research Council. *Stratospheric Ozone Depletion by Halocarbons: Chemistry and Transport*. Washington, D.C.: National Academy of Sciences, 1979.

Nayar, Baldev Raj. "Regimes, Power, and International Aviation." *International Organization* 49 (1995): 139–70.

Newbury, David M. "Acid Rain." *Economic Policy* 5 (October 1990): 297–346.

Nitze, William A. "A Failure of Presidential Leadership." In *Negotiating Climate Change: The Inside Story of the Rio Convention*, edited by Irving M. Mintzer and J. Amber Leonard, 187–200. Cambridge: Cambridge University Press, 1994.

Nordhaus, William D. "Economic Approaches to Greenhouse Warming." In *Global Warming: Economic Policy Responses*, edited by Rudiger Dornbusch and James M. Poterba, 33–66. Cambridge: MIT Press, 1991.

Norihisa, Okuda. "Fallout and the Japanese." *Japan Quarterly* 9 (1962): 27–32.

Norris, Robert S., and William M. Arkin. "Known Nuclear Tests Worldwide, 1945–1995." *Bulletin of the Atomic Scientists* (May/June 1996): 61–63.

Oakerson, Ronald J. "Analyzing the Commons: A Framework." In *Making Commons Work: Theory: Practice, and Policy*, edited by Daniel W. Bromley, 41–59. San Francisco: Institute for Contemporary Studies, 1992.

Obasi, G. O. P. "The Atmosphere: Global Commons to Protect." *Our Planet* 7, no.5 (1996): 5–8.

Oeschger, Hans, and Irving M. Mintzer. "Lessons from the Ice Cores: Rapid Climate Changes During the Last 160,000 Years." In *Confronting Climate Change: Risks, Implications and Responses*, edited by Irving M. Mintzer, 55–64. Cambridge: Cambridge University Press, 1992.

Olson, Mancur. *The Logic of Collection Action: Public Goods and the Theory of Groups*. New York: Schoken Books, 1965.

Organization for Economic Cooperation and Development (OECD). *The OECD Program on Long-Range Transport of Air Pollutants*. Paris: OECD, 1977.

Osgood, Charles E. *An Alternative to War or Surrender*. Champaign-Urbana: University of Illinois Press, 1962.

Ostrom, Elinor. *Governing the Commons: The Evolution of Institutions for Collective Action*. New York: Cambridge University Press, 1990.

Park, Chris C. *Acid Rain: Rhetoric and Reality*. London: Routledge, 1987.

Park, Chris C. *Chernobyl: The Long Shadow*. London: Routledge, 1989.

Parry, Martin L., and M. S. Swaminathan. "Effects of Climate Change on Food Production." In *Confronting Climate Change: Risks, Implications and Responses*, edited by Irving Mintzer, 113–25. New York: Cambridge University Press, 1992.

Parson, Edward A. "Protecting the Ozone Layer." In *Institutions for the Earth: Sources of Effective International Environmental Protection*, edited by Peter M. Haas, Robert O. Keohane, and Mark A. Levy, 27–74. Cambridge: MIT Press, 1993.

Parson, Edward A., and Owen Greene. "The Complex Chemistry of the International Ozone Agreements." *Environment* 37 (March 1995): 15–20, 35–44.

Paterson, Matthew, and Michael Grubb. "The International Politics of Climate Change." *International Affairs* 68 (1992): 293–310.

Peterson, D. J. *Troubled Lands: The Legacy of Soviet Environmental Destruction.* Boulder, Colo.: Westview Press, 1993.

Petsonk, Carol A. "The Role of the United Nations Environment Programme (UNEP) in the Development of International Environmental Law." *American University Journal of International Law and Policy* 5 (1990): 351–91.

Pierre, Andrew J. *Nuclear Politics: The British Experience with an Independent Strategic Force: 1939–1970.* London: Oxford University Press, 1972.

Prather, M. J., M. B. McElroy, and S. C. Wofsy. "Reductions in Ozone at High Concentrations of Stratospheric Halogins." *Nature* 312 (1984): 227–31.

Price, Martin F. "Global Change: Defining the Ill-defined." *Environment* 31 (1989) 18–20, 42–44.

Prinz, Bernhard. "Causes of Forest Damage in Europe." *Environment* 29 (1987): 11–14, 32–38.

Ramakrishna, Kilaparti. "Third World Countries in the Policy Response to Global Climate Change." In *Global Warming: the Greenpeace Report,* edited by Jeremy Leggett, 421–38. New York: Oxford University Press, 1990.

Rapoport, Anatol, and Albert M. Chummah. *Prisoner's Dilemma: A Study in Conflict and Cooperation.* Ann Arbor: University of Michigan Press, 1965.

Revelle, Roger, and Hans Suess. "Carbon Dioxide Exchange between the Atmosphere and the Ocean, and the Question of an Increase in Atmospheric CO_2 during the Past Decades." *Tellus* 9 (1957): 18–27.

Roan, Sharon L. *Ozone Crisis: The 15 Year Evolution of a Sudden Global Emergency.* New York: John Wiley and Sons, 1989.

Roberts, Leslie. "Learning from an Acid Rain Program." *Science* 251 (1991): 1302–5.

Romm, Joseph J. *Defining National Security: The Nonmilitary Aspects.* New York: Council on Foreign Relations Press, 1993.

Rosencranz, Armin. "The Problem of Transboundary Pollution." *Environment* 22 (June 1980): 15–20.

Rosenzweig, Cynthia, and Martin L. Parry. "Potential Impact of Climate Change on World Food Supply." *Nature* 367 (1994): 133–38.

Ross, Douglas, 1978. "The Concorde Compromise: The Politics of Decision Making." *Bulletin of the Atomic Scientists* 34 (1978): 46–53.

Rowlands, Ian H. "The Climate Change Negotiations: Berlin and Beyond." *Journal of Environment and Development* 4 (1995): 105–64.

Rowlands, Ian H. *The Politics of Global Atmospheric Change.* Manchester: Manchester University Press, 1995.

Rowlands, Ian H. "The Fourth Meeting of the Parties to the Montreal Protocol: Report and Reflection." *Environment* 35 (July/August 1993): 25–34.

Sagan, Carl. "Nuclear War and Climate Change." *Foreign Affairs* 62 (1983/84): 257–92.

Bibliography

Samuels, J. W. "International Control of Weather Modification Activities: Peril or Policy?" In *International Environmental Law,* edited by Ludwik A. Teclaff and Albert E. Utton, 199–214. New York: Praeger, 1974.

Sand, Peter H. "Protecting the Ozone Layer: The Vienna Convention is Adopted." *Environment* 27 (June 1985): 19–20, 40–43.

Scheinman, Lawrence. *The International Atomic Energy Agency and World Nuclear Order.* Washington, D.C.: Resources for the Future, 1987.

Schneider, Stephen H. *The Genesis Strategy: Climate and Global Survival.* New York: Plenum Press, 1976.

Schrijver, Nico. "International Organization for Environmental Security." *Bulletin of Peace Proposals* 20 (1989): 115–22.

Schütt, Peter, and Ellis B. Cowling. "Waldsterben, a General Decline of Forests in Central Europe: Symptoms, Development, and Possible Causes." *Plant Disease* 69 (1985): 548–58.

Seaborg, Glenn T. *Kennedy, Khrushchev, and the Test Ban.* Berkeley: University of California Press, 1981.

Shaw, Roderick W. "Acid-Rain Negotiations in North America and Europe: A Study in Contrast." In *International Environmental Negotiation,* edited by Gunnar Sjöstedt, 84–109. London: Sage, 1993.

Shea, Cynthia Pollock. "Protecting the Ozone Layer." In Lester R. Brown et al., *State of the World 1989,* 77–96. New York: W. W. Norton, 1989.

Singer, S. Fred. "Benefits of Global Warming." *Society* 29 (1992): 33–40.

Singer, S. Fred. "Warming Theories Need Warning Label." *Bulletin of the American Scientists* 48 (June 1992): 34–39.

Skjærseth, Jon Birger. "The Climate Policy of the EC: Too Hot to Handle?" *Journal of Common Market Studies* 32 (1994): 25–45.

Smith, R. C., et al. "Ozone Depletion: Ultraviolet Radiation and Phytoplankton Biology in Antarctic Waters." *Science* 255 (1992): 952–59.

Smoke, Richard. *National Security and the Nuclear Dilemma: An Introduction to the American Experience.* 2nd ed. New York: Random House, 1987.

Smoke, Richard. "A Theory of Mutual Security." In *Mutual Security: A New Approach to Soviet-American Relations,* edited by Richard Smoke and Andrei Kortunov, 59–111. New York: St. Martin's Press, 1991.

Soroos, Marvin S. *Beyond Sovereignty: The Challenge of Global Policy.* Columbia: University of South Carolina Press, 1986.

Soroos, Marvin S. "The Commons in the Sky: The Radio Spectrum and Geosynchronous Orbit as Issues in Global Policy." *International Organization* 36 (1982): 665–77.

Soroos, Marvin S. "Environmental Security: Choices for the Twenty-First Century." *National Forum* 75 (1995): 20–24.

Soroos, Marvin S. "Global Change, Environmental Security, and the Prisoner's Dilemma." *Journal of Peace Research* 31 (1994): 317–32.

Soroos, Marvin S. "The Odyssey of Arctic Haze: Toward a Global Atmospheric Regime." *Environment* 34 (1992): 6–11, 25–27.

Soroos, Marvin S. "The Tragedy of the Commons in Global Perspective." In *The Global Agenda: Issues and Perspectives,* 3rd ed., edited by Charles W. Kegley and Eugene R. Wittkopf, 422–35. New York: McGraw-Hill, 1995.

Soroos, Marvin S., and Elena Nikitina. "The World Meteorological Organization as a Purveyor of Global Public Goods." In *International Organizations and Environmental Policy,* edited by Robert Bartlett, Priya Kurian, and Madhu Malik, 69–82. Westport, Conn.: Greenwood Press, 1995.

Sprinz, Detlef, and Tapani Vaahtoranta. "The Interest Based Explanation of International Environmental Policy." *International Organization* 48 (1994): 77–106.

Sprout, Harold, and Margaret Sprout. *Foundations of International Politics.* New York: D. Van Nostrand, 1962.

Stern, Paul C., Oran R. Young, and Daniel Druckman, eds. *Global Environmental Change: Understanding the Human Dimensions.* Washington, D.C.: National Academy Press, 1992.

Stoel, Thomas B. Jr., Alan S. Miller, and Breck Milroy. *Fluorocarbon Regulation: An International Comparison.* Lexington, Mass.: Lexington Books, 1980.

Stolarski, Richard S., and Ralph J. Cicerone. "Stratospheric Chlorine: A Possible Sink for Ozone." *Canadian Journal of Chemistry* 52 (1974): 1610–15.

Stone, Christopher D. *The Gnat Is Older Than Man: Global Environment and Human Agenda.* Princeton: Princeton University Press, 1993.

Stone, Richard. "If the Mercury Soars, So May Health Hazards." *Science* 267 (1995): 957–58.

Sturges, W. T., ed. *Pollution of the Arctic Atmosphere.* London: Elsevier Science Publishers, 1991.

Subak, Susan. "Assessing Emissions: Five Approaches Compared." In *The Global Greenhouse Regime: Who Pays?,* edited by Peter Hayes and Kirk Smith, 51–69. Tokyo: United Nations University Press, 1993.

Susskind, Lawrence E. *Environmental Diplomacy: Negotiating More Effective Global Agreements.* New York: Oxford University Press, 1994.

Swedish NGO Secretariat on Acid Rain. "Forest Damage in Europe." *Environmental Factsheet* 1 (1992).

Swedish NGO Secretariat on Acid Rain. "The 100 Worst Emitters." *Environmental Factsheet* 5 (1994).

Swedish NGO Secretariat on Acid Rain. "The UN ECE Convention." *Environmental Factsheet* 3 (1993).

Sweeney, Joseph M., Covey T. Oliver, and Noyes E. Leech. *Cases and Materials on the International Legal System.* 2d ed. Mineola, N.Y.: Foundation Press, 1981.

Taubenfeld, Howard J. "International Environmental Law: Air and Outer Space." In *International Environmental Law,* edited by Ludwik A. Teclaff and Albert E. Utton, 187–98. New York: Praeger, 1974.

Bibliography

Taubenfeld, Rita F., and Howard J. Taubenfeld. "Some International Implications of Weather Modification Techniques." *International Organization* 23 (1969): 808–33.

Taylor, Maxwell D. "The Legitimate Claims of National Security." *Foreign Affairs* 52 (1974): 577–94.

Thompson, Jon. "East Europe's Dark Dawn: The Iron Curtain Rises to Reveal a Land Tarnished by Pollution." *National Geographic* 179 (June 1991): 36–69.

Timoshenko, Alexandre S. "Ecological Security: Response to Global Challenges." In *Environmental Change and International Law: New Challenges and Dimensions,* edited by Edith Brown Weiss, 413–56. Tokyo: United Nations University Press, 1992.

Titus, A. Costandina. *Bombs in the Backyard: Atomic Testing and American Politics.* Reno: University of Nevada Press, 1986.

Turco, R. P., O. B. Toon, T. P. Ackerman, J. B. Pollack, and Carl Sagan. "Nuclear Winter: Global Consequences of Multiple Nuclear Explosions." *Science* 222 (1983): 1283–92.

Ullman, Richard, "Redefining Security." *International Security* 8 (1983): 129–53.

United Nations Commission on Environment and Development. *Our Common Future.* New York: Oxford University Press, 1987.

United Nations Environment Programme (UNEP). *Environmental Data Report.* 2d ed. New York: Blackwell Reference, 1989.

United Nations Environment Programme (UNEP). *Environmental Effects Panel Report.* Nairobi: UNEP, 1989.

United Nations Environment Programme (UNEP). *Register of International Treaties and Other Agreements in the Field of the Environment.* New York: UNEP, 1991.

United Nations Environment Programme (UNEP). *Synthesis Report.* Nairobi: November 13, 1989.

United Nations Environment Programme (UNEP), World Meteorological Organization (WMO), and International Council of Scientific Unions (ICSU). *An Assessment of the Role of Carbon Dioxide and of Other Greenhouse Gases in Climate Variations and Associated Impact.* Geneva: WMO, 1985.

United Nations Scientific Committee on the Effects of Atomic Radiation (UNSCEAR). *Ionizing Radiation: Levels and Effects.* New York: United Nations, 1972.

United Nations Scientific Committee on the Effects of Atomic Radiation (UNSCEAR). *Ionizing Radiation: Sources and Biological Effects.* New York: United Nations, 1982.

United Nations Scientific Committee on the Effects of Atomic Radiation (UNSCEAR). *Report to the United Nations General Assembly.* New York: United Nations, 1958.

United Nations Scientific Committee on the Effects of Atomic Radiation (UNSCEAR). *Sources, Effects and Risks of Ionizing Radiation.* New York: United Nations, 1988.

Utton, Albert E. "International Water Quality Law." In *International Environmental Law,* edited by Ludwik A. Teclaff and Albert E. Utton, 140–53. New York: Praeger, 1974.

Victor, David G., and Julian E. Salt. "From Rio to Berlin: Managing Climate Change." *Environment* 36 (December 1994): 6–15, 25–32.

Vicuña, Francisco Orrego. "State Responsibility, Liability, and Remedial Measures Under International Law: New Criteria for Environmental Protection." In *Environmental Change and International Law: New Challenges and Dimensions,* edited by Edith Brown Weiss, 124–58. Tokyo: United Nations University Press, 1992.

Wagner, Richard H. *Environment and Man.* 3d ed. New York: W. W. Norton, 1978.

Wallace, John M., and Shawna Vogel. "El Niño and Climate Prediction." *Reports to the Nation on Our Changing Planet* 3 (1994).

Warrick, Richard A., and Atiq A. Rahman. "Future Sea Level Rise: Environmental and Socio-Political Considerations." In *Confronting Climate Change: Risks, Implications and Responses,* edited by Irving M. Mintzer, 97–112. Cambridge: Cambridge University Press, 1992.

Watson, Robert T., F. Sherwood Rowland, and John Gille. "Ozone Trends Panel Executive Summary." Washington, D.C.: NASA, 1988.

Weart, Spencer. "From the Nuclear Frying Pan into the Global Fire." *Bulletin of the Atomic Scientists* 48 (June 1992): 19–27.

Weber, Peter. "Protecting Oceanic Fisheries and Jobs." In Lester R. Brown et al., *State of the World 1995,* 21–37. New York: Norton, 1995.

Weiss, Edith Brown. "International Liability for Weather Modification." *Climate Change* 1 (1978): 267–90.

Westing, Arthur H. "The Environmental Component of Comprehensive Security." *Bulletin of Peace Proposals* 20 (1989): 129–34.

Wetstone, Gregory S., and Armin Rosencranz. *Acid Rain in Europe and North America: National Responses to an International Problem.* Washington, D.C.: Environmental Law Institute Publication, 1983.

White, Robert M. "Climate at the Millennium." *Environment* 20 (1979): 31–33.

Wirth, David A., and Daniel A. Lashof. "Beyond Vienna and Montreal: A Global Framework Convention on Greenhouse Gases." In *A Global Warming Forum: Scientific, Economic, and Legal Overview,* edited by Richard A. Geyer, 509–31. Boca Raton, Fla.: CRC Press, 1993.

Wood, Alexander. "The Multilateral Fund for the Implementation of the Montreal Protocol." *International Environmental Affairs* 5 (1993): 335–54.

World Conference on the Changing Atmosphere. *Conference Statement.* Toronto, June 27–30, 1988.

World Meteorological Organization (WMO). *The WMO Achievement: 40 Years in the Service of International Meteorology and Hydrology.* Geneva: WMO, 1990.

World Meteorological Organization (WMO) et al. *Atmospheric Ozone 1985.* 3 vols. Geneva: WMO (Global Ozone Research and Monitoring Project—Report No. 16), 1986.

World Resources Institute. *World Resources 1990–91: A Guide to the Global Environment.* New York: Oxford University Press, 1990.

World Resources Institute. *World Resources 1992–93: A Guide to the Global Environment.* New York: Oxford University Press, 1992.

World Resources Institute. *World Resources 1994–95: A Guide to the Global Environment.* New York: Oxford University Press, 1994.

World Resources Institute. *World Resources 1996–97: A Guide to the Global Environment.* New York: Oxford University Press, 1996.

Young, Louise B. *Sowing the Wind: Reflections on the Earth's Atmosphere.* New York: Prentice-Hall, 1990.

Young, Oran R. *International Governance: Protecting the Environment in a Stateless Society.* Ithaca: Cornell University Press, 1994.

Young, Oran. "The Politics of International Regime Formation: Managing Natural Resources and the Environment." *International Organization* 43 (1989): 349–76.

Young, Oran R., and Gail Osherenko, eds. *Polar Politics: Creating Environmental Regimes.* Ithaca: Cornell University Press, 1993.

Zaelke, Durwood, and James Cameron. "Global Warming and Climate Change—An Overview of the International Legal Process." *American Journal of International Law and Policy* 5 (1990): 249–90.

INDEX

acid deposition: early research on, 65–66; formation of, 38–39; impact on aquatic life, 41; impact on forests, 40–41; international monitoring of, 66–67; in North America, 68–69; pH values, 39–41, 112; public concern, 119–124; research on effects, 68; wet/dry forms, 38–39. *See also* air pollution; EMEP; LRTAP Convention; transboundary air pollution

Acidification Conference (1982), 127, 269

Adirondack Mountains, 122

aerosols, 26, 35, 37, 48

Africa, 33

air pollution: defined, 34; health effects, 36–37, 42, 242–43; history of, 2, 35–36, 112; London smogs, 36; photochemical smog, 37; types of, 2, 34–35; in urban areas, 2, 35–37, 53–54, 69; in USSR, 112–13. *See also* acid deposition; Arctic haze, carbon dioxide; nitrogen oxides; sulfur dioxide; transboundary air pollution

airspace, 218–19, 281

Alaska, 37

albedo, 50

Algeria, 89

Alliance for Responsible CFC Policy, 153, 160, 164, 173

Alliance of Small Island States (AOSIS), 196–97, 271

Antarctic ozone hole, 10, 43, 72–73, 155, 267

Antarctic Treaty, 14, 280

Appalachian Mountains, 122

Arctic Chemical Network, 68

Arctic haze, 37, 67–68

Argentina, 43

Aristotle, 58, 208

Arizona, 171

Arrhenius, Svante, 12, 74, 176

Atlantic Tropic Experiment, 63

atmosphere: as a commons, 18–19, 213–14; in carbon cycle, 31; composition of, 24–26; CO_2 concentrations, 46; convection currents, 27, 29; functions of, 1; history of, 24–25; in hydrological cycle, 30; layers, 26–28; legal status of, 219–23, 279–83; research on, 61–63; temperature of, 25–26, 33–34; thickness of, 1. *See also* air pollution; climate; ozone layer; troposphere; stratosphere; weather

Atomic Energy Agency (US), 93–95

Australia: in climate change talks, 197, 204; compliance with FCCC, 204; GHG emissions, 183; GHG goals, 193; opposition to nuclear tests, 104–105; site of nuclear tests, 88; ozone hole over, 43

DATE DUE

SEP 16 1990